CHINESE STATE ENTERPRISES

CHINESE STATE ENTERPRISES

A Regional Property Rights Analysis

DAVID GRANICK

The University of Chicago Press
Chicago and London

David Granick is professor of economics at the University of Wisconsin at Madison.

The University of Chicago Press, Chicago 60637
The University of Chicago Press, Ltd., London

© 1990 by the University of Chicago
All rights reserved. Published 1990
Printed in the United States of America

99 98 97 96 95 94 93 92 91 90   5 4 3 2 1

Library of Congress Cataloging-in-Publication Data

Granick, David.
    Chinese state enterprises : a regional property rights analysis / David Granick.
        p.   cm.
    Includes bibliographical references.
    ISBN 0-226-30588-0 (alk. paper)
    1. Government business enterprises—China—Management.   2. Central plan-
ning—China.   3. China—Economic policy—1976– .   4. Right of property—
China.   I. Title.
    HD4318.G73   1990
    338.6′2′0951—dc20
    89-20166

CONTENTS

TABLES

ACKNOWLEDGMENTS

My principal debt is to the World Bank and to the Chinese Academy of Social Sciences for granting me permission to use the raw materials of the case studies of twenty Chinese industrial organizations. I am particularly indebted to Gene Tidrick for having arranged this permission.

The research for this book has been supported by the Hoover Institution on War, Revolution and Peace; by a research grant from the Joint Committee on Chinese Studies of the American Council of Learned Societies and the Social Science Research Council, financed in part by The Ford Foundation, the Andrew W. Mellon Foundation, and the National Endowment for the Humanities; by the National Science Foundation under Grant No. SES-8520960; and by the Graduate School of the University of Wisconsin, Madison. Any opinions, findings, and conclusions or recommendations expressed in this publication are my own and do not necessarily reflect the views of the National Science Foundation or any of the other supporting organizations. Data, documentation, and computer codes for the quantitative questionnaires answered by the sample enterprises are stored at the Social Science Data and Program Library Service, 3308 Social Science Building, University of Wisconsin, Madison, Wisconsin 53706.

J. P. Holland and Jyh-Dean Hwang have been my assistants at various stages of the research, and I am indebted to them. Professor Mou Ying of Beijing University has helped me with translations. Dong Fureng and Jiang Chunze provided some additional data for use in creating a control variable for regression analysis of the quantitative enterprise data. Wu Jinglian, in his comments at a World Bank seminar, jolted my thinking in the direction of what has become the major theme of this study. My colleagues in the original study, particularly William Byrd, Dong Fureng, Chen Jiyuan, and Gene Tidrick, have been important direct influences on my thinking. Of the various people who provided me, as a neophyte, with guidance in obtaining the general background on the Chinese economy which was essential for this study, I am especially indebted to Loren Brandt, Nicholas R. Lardy, Ramon H. Myers, Barry Naughton, and Thomas G. Rawski. A number of colleagues and students have been particularly helpful in commenting upon various portions of the book; Daniel Berkowitz, Michael Carter, Jyh-Dean Hwang, Nicholas Lardy, and Warren Palmer should be specially mentioned. It goes without saying that none of those named above bears any responsibilities for my interpretations or factual errors.

1

INTRODUCTION

The thesis of this book is that China today is not simply one more centrally planned socialist economy, with its own minor variations from the general model, but rather that it is unique. Although it certainly falls within the class of centrally planned economies, its peculiar features are sufficiently prominent so as to represent a radical departure from the model as it is observed to operate in the Soviet Union or elsewhere in Eastern Europe.[1] Furthermore, these peculiarities cannot be attributed solely to China's state of economic underdevelopment.

The major departures lie elsewhere than in the changes which have been most responsible for the transformation of the national economy under Deng Xiaoping. Innovations have taken place in agriculture and in much of the rural nonagricultural economy, with its de facto privatization. They can also be found throughout the economy in the greater emphasis upon individual economic incentives. But while these modifications of the economic system are terribly important, their significance is not in their departure from the conventional central planning model. For example, Polish agriculture has always remained overwhelmingly private, yet this has not led analysts to regard Poland as deviating in an essential fashion from the traditional model. As to the stress in China since the late 1970s on individual economic incentives, if we consider this in its general aspect, rather than in its special form of approximations to private property, such stress has only brought the country closer than before to the traditional planning model. During the Cultural Revolution, China differed substantially from the other socialist countries in its relative disregard for individual incentives.

It is in the urban sector, and indeed in the socialist part of the urban economy, that we find those departures from the basic model which are truly socialist in that they do not rest upon any form of private ownership and, yet, are the most unique and interesting to the student of socialist economies. This book is concerned with the mainstay of this Chinese urban socialist sector: state-owned industrial enterprises and, primarily, those that are large or medium-sized rather than small. Here, where there has probably been the least economic change under Deng, we see the most interesting patterns.

1

Six aspects of control exercised over urban state-owned enterprises are unique to China among centrally planned socialist economies. Moreover, all six apply to China before the era of economic reforms at the end of the 1970s and in the 1980s, as well as afterwards. These areas of uniqueness are the following: (1) multiple-level supervision over these enterprises; (2) loose and easily overfulfilled production plans, which thus offer only limited guidance to the enterprise activities; (3) complementary to (2), availability of allocated items outside of the allocation system; (4) multiple prices for the same product and enterprise customer in a single region; (5) the nature of the *nomenklatura* control that exists over the appointment of directors and Communist Party secretaries within the enterprise; and (6) the allocation of labor and the determination of wages. (Nomenklatura control refers to control by the apparatus of the Communist Party over those in leadership positions of all types in the society.) The first five are explained in this study by a single hypothesis of the property rights of regional governmental bodies relative to one another and to the national government. The sixth is treated only briefly in the concluding chapter.

This monograph is based upon a set of twenty case studies carried out by the Chinese Academy of Social Sciences and the World Bank between December 1982 and the middle of 1985. I was a consultant on the project for the World Bank. Nineteen of the twenty case studies were of individual industrial enterprises; the twentieth was of a county administration in charge of a number of state enterprises. Interviewing within each organization was intensive, being carried out over a period of one week or longer and with notes averaging more than one hundred typewritten pages per case study. Although the interviews concentrated upon the period after 1981 and, generally, upon either 1982 or the period from 1983 through early 1985 (depending upon the enterprise), the annual quantitative data collected were for 1975–82. On the basis of the analysis of the quantitative data and interview notes, reinterviews were conducted in seven of the nineteen firms, lasting several days in each enterprise. The remaining organizations were all queried in writing or were reinterviewed in a brief fashion by investigators from the Chinese Academy of Social Sciences. Eleven of these enterprises responded fairly extensively. The degree of cooperation shown in the various organizations was such as to confirm what had been indicated to me explicitly: that the study had received permission and support from levels in the Chinese governmental structure which were considerably higher than that of the Chinese Academy of Social Sciences. Presumably, the formal support by the State Economic Commission of China was an active one.

The heart of the case study materials consists of qualitative data, along with unsystematic statistical materials, both sets having been collected during the interview and reinterview process. In addition, and of considerable interest in their own right, systematic and annual quantitative data for 1975–82 were collected for each enterprise prior to the beginning of interviewing there. A primary use of these quantitative data was to serve as a framework around which to construct the interviews within the specific organization.

In terms of the direct usage of the quantitative data—to provide the material for most of the statistical testing of hypotheses that will be done in this study—it should be noted that not only are the data fairly extensive, but they were collected under almost ideal conditions. The individuals who had prepared the data for each enterprise were carefully questioned in an effort to eliminate gross inconsistencies and to be certain of the definitions actually used in the presentation. While significant inconsistencies sometimes remained, the data seem much more reliable than is usually the case for questionnaires that are filled out in circumstances where little or no follow-up questioning is feasible.

In nineteen of the twenty case studies, the original interviewing was carried out by my colleagues in the Chinese Academy of Social Sciences. World Bank representatives participated along with the Chinese in seven of the reinterviews. I participated directly in one original interview (lasting one week) and in two reinterviews, as well as in the original study design, and also contributed questions for all the other reinterviews and for the written individualized sets of questions submitted to the remaining organizations.

Although it is this unique set of case studies that is the basis of the monograph, it has been supplemented through my reading about China. The dimensions of such reading are indicated by the fact that roughly one year of full-time work was devoted to it. Thus, I am in a position to attempt to place these materials not only into the context of studies of Soviet and East European enterprises, on which I have worked throughout my career, but also into the context of the available Western-language (primarily English) literature on the economy of the People's Republic of China and, indeed, on earlier economic and social developments in China.

In order to develop the thesis of the peculiarity of China within the class of centrally planned economies, comparison will be made with the Soviet Union and with various countries of Eastern Europe. In these comparisons, emphasis will be placed upon the experience of the Soviet Union since it is the only other centrally planned country whose economy approaches the size of that of China. However, it is solely for some East European countries that we have sets of enterprise case studies which resemble our Chinese data set, and I shall use these for comparative purposes where appropriate.

The dating of the case studies, and especially that of their quantitative materials, presents an obvious problem in providing information about the functioning of Chinese state industry in the period of the reforms carried out under the leadership of Deng Xiaoping in the 1980s. Although it is true that it was in December 1978 that the Central Committee of the Chinese Communist Party initiated the reform movement in the Chinese economy, the immediate impact was considerably less in the urban than in the rural areas. Agriculture was for most intents and purposes privatized in the early 1980s. With regard to the urban economy, however, it was not until October 1984 that the Central Committee took the major step of decreeing that the "socialist economy is a commodity economy based upon public ownership," with the concept of a "commodity economy" representing a further stage in the evolution of official Chinese thought. Only then was it announced that the role of national, mandatory planning in the state sector was to be reduced and that improved conditions for the working of a market economy were to be created. This step has been heralded as initiating a level of reform in the state sector that will eventually reach the dimensions of what has already occurred in the rural economy.

Implementation of the slogan of a "commodity economy" in the state sector through 1987 seems to have occurred particularly in relation to profit sharing versus taxation, to pricing, and to bonus payments. In October 1984 state enterprises in China were officially switched to the second phase of the substitution of corporate income tax for the remission of a percentage of profits to the state. In this phase the tax rate is eventually to be made independent of the economic situation of the individual enterprise. In May 1984 the State Council officially permitted prices to vary up or down by 20 percent from state-ordained prices; it was not until February 1985 that the limitation on fluctuations was eliminated. Enterprise bonus rates can now be established (at least formally) at a level chosen by the individual enterprise, with the state restricting such payments only by taxing them.[2]

However, particularly after 1985, further changes have also occurred. This is most striking in the case of the small state-owned enterprises, where conversion to cooperatives as well as leasing to individuals or small groups has gone quite far.[3] But such enterprises are outside the universe covered in our sample and, at least as of mid-1987, such conversions had not affected the medium-sized and large state enterprises of China.[4]

For this study, the shift of enterprises to the contractual responsibility system is the nearest counterpart. (In this system, enterprise top management is responsible for reaching stated objectives.) By mid-1987, half of all medium and large state industrial enterprises had gone to this system; a month or two later, the figure was reported as being three-quarters.[5] Although this system began on a pilot basis in 1983, its real growth appears to have been in 1986 and 1987. Yet contractual responsibility should be seen, in my view, as no more than a variant on the shift from profit sharing to income tax; its expansion may be a result of disillusionment with the slowness with which taxation has in reality become different from profit sharing.

There is beginning to be some separation of ownership from control.[6] Furthermore, legislation passed in 1986 represents early steps in permitting bankruptcy of state-owned enterprises, unemployment compensation for workers dismissed as a result of such bankruptcy, codification of the right of enterprises to dismiss unsatisfactory workers, and generalization of the principle that all new hirings in state enterprises be on the basis of terminable employment contracts.[7]

One may ask whether a set of case studies that refers essentially to the period prior to 1985 is of contemporary interest today. The answer to this question has several components.

First, the announced reforms are of four types. The main one consists of reforms that Chinese authorities expect to occur only gradually, e.g., changes in the system of taxes levied on state enterprises. The second type is reforms that will presumably be only formalistic for some time, such as the greater freedom given to the enterprise to set bonus rates.[8] The third type comprises those that probably amount to fairly minor changes from prior practice. The fourth type, that constitutes substantial and immediate change, is probably restricted to the new system for pricing goods produced outside of the state plan. Such reforms do not represent a sharp discontinuity with the immediate past.[9]

The second part of the answer is that the enterprises in the sample analyzed in this study were chosen, in part, on the basis that they were advanced, reform organizations. This criterion referred particularly to forms of profit sharing with the state, as well as to the early use of taxation in lieu of remission of profits. In this sense, the enterprises may be representative of the Chinese state economy some one to three years after the time period in which the firms were studied. This applies particularly to the period through about 1982.

The third part of the answer is that the years of the reform period that are covered (from 1979 on) have special advantages from an analytic standpoint in that they permit us to observe the effects of different sectoral market conditions within a given year. In particular, 1980 is a year in which consumer goods industries, and textiles specifically, boomed, while 1982 was a bad market year for textiles. In contrast, producer goods industries, and the engineering industries specifically, had precisely the reverse situation in these two years. Similarly, comparisons for the sample as a whole between behavior in the pre-reform and reform years have the advantage that market conditions in the second period were quite heterogeneous between years. Thus, the effect of reform can be isolated in a way that would be quite impossible if all reform years had enjoyed the same market conditions and if these had been different from those of the pre-reform period. Finally, when I consider such features of the reform period as differential centralization of product planning for different enterprises and its effect on the proportion of the supply needs of such enterprises that are met through physical allocations, I would be very uncomfortable in drawing conclusions if they could be applied only to a single set of market conditions.

Suppose that instead of assuming that a heterogeneous period was representative of reform conditions, I had concentrated on a more recent year such as 1985 or 1988, in which there was great overheating of the economy. Then I would not have been able to observe such marked diversity, either between sector or period. It should be noted that in all three years from 1984 to 1986 there was a considerably higher level of inflation than had been the case earlier.[10]

The fourth part of the answer lies in the uniqueness of the data source. In attempting to understand the contemporary Chinese economic scene, observers are in no position to ignore solid microeconomic data of the very recent past.

Throughout this book, I shall often write in the present tense. However, reference is intended to the period ending in 1983–85. Some scholars think of rapid change as occurring in 1986 and thereafter. Although as of early 1989 I see no substantial evidence for such a view, this work does not take a position on this question.

The Set of Case Studies

These Chinese studies have already been used as raw material for part of a symposium held in Beijing in August 1985 in which I participated; an edited version of most of the papers has now been published both in English and in Chinese (Tidrick and Chen 1987). But the authors of these papers were unable either to mine or to reflect on the data in the fashion that additional time has made possible for the current study.

This is because the papers were written under considerable time pressure, particularly since they could not be begun until after the re-interviews were completed in the spring of 1985. If this volume does not add substantially to what came out of the symposium, it will not be for lack of opportunity.

Uniqueness of the Data Source

With regard to Chinese state-owned industry and the study of the place of the industrial state enterprise in the planned guidance system of the economy, the data source is unique. There is nothing like it for the recent time period, most particularly because of the micro-economic quantitative data which make possible a comparison of the pre-reform and early reform period. Indeed, it is unique with respect to any period in the history of the People's Republic.

It is, of course, true that case studies of Chinese enterprises have been written elsewhere, both for this period and before and after.[11] Moreover, at least one previous Western volume provided generalizations on the basis of interviews held in a large number of enterprises (Richman 1969). But the data source analyzed here has the following special features:

1. The enterprises chosen, although certainly in no respect a random sample, can be treated as sufficiently representative of a particular universe with regard to the features relevant to the study. Although there was a bias toward the selection of enterprises with above-average accomplishment, the sample far from constitutes a set of uniform successes. (See the next section for a discussion of this critical point.)
2. A considerable number of respondents were involved in a set of different interviews within each enterprise, and each of these interviews was quite intensive. The substantial number of separate interviews made possible not only the exploration of a variety of topics within each enterprise, but also the cross checking of reported events and the reasons given for them.
3. The interview project was provided sufficiently high-level support within the Chinese government so that a reasonable degree of access and openness of information could be assured.
4. Longitudinal quantitative data about the enterprise were made available. These served as a guide for the interviews in the choice and pursuit of significant questions, as a check on the consistency of descriptions and explanations offered during the course of the interviews, and as a vehicle both for econo-

metric analysis and for comparison of the pre-reform and reform years.

When we compare this data source with those sources available for other socialist countries, it stands up fairly well. In particular, it is the only one with which I am familiar that combines detailed microeconomic, longitudinal, quantitative data with intensive interviews covering a fairly broad range of economic topics.[12]

However, it does have two major lacunae. The first of these is that, although efforts were made to arrange interviews concerning the individual enterprises with government bodies that directly supervised one or another of their activities, these efforts must in general be regarded as failures. It is true that such interviews were arranged for the vast bulk of the sample organizations and that they were of some use for six of the twenty enterprises. Furthermore, in two more cases they were of quality as good as the interviews in the corresponding enterprise, although this was not sufficient to permit them to make a net contribution. Nevertheless, and with some exceptions, the quality of the interviews in supervising agencies was poor. Most frequently, such interviews appear to have been conducted with the wrong person or persons, so that the requested information was simply unavailable. Thus, the attempt to analyze the enterprise's situation from different organizational perspectives was unsuccessful. This experience contrasts sharply with what was accomplished in a study of Romanian industry of the early 1970s (Granick 1976).

The second lacuna concerns career histories of enterprise managers. This subject, which has been pursued in considerable breadth and depth for a number of other socialist countries, is the only one which the Chinese members of the research team resisted exploring in detail. For an economic study such as mine (the underlying goals of which, it should be noted, were included in the original research project), the relevance of this gap is that I have little significant information as to what types of managerial behavior have been rewarded or penalized in terms of career development.

It seems probable, however, that no career histories of Chinese managers of the early 1980s would have been useful in providing a clue to this aspect of the managerial utility function. This is because career histories would probably have been dominated by the political changes that occurred in China throughout the previous decades, with managerial behavior of a purely economic type having had relatively slight influence on such histories. To the extent that this is the case, the research strategy of the Chinese team members would be fully justified.

The Representativeness of the Sample

While this set of data would be interesting even if it represented only a collection of case studies, I believe that it is much more than that. It is my claim that, in most relevant respects, it may be taken as representative of at least the larger and more successful units in the universe of Chinese large and medium-sized state-owned industrial enterprises. With regard to behavior, as opposed to accomplishment, I believe that it is even more representative of this universe as a whole. Not surprisingly, it is less representative of the broader set of all state-owned industrial enterprises, since only two of the nineteen enterprises (as well as the enterprises administered by the county organization that was studied) can be considered to even possibly fall into the category of "small."

In 1982 there were a total of 5,400 medium- and large-scale industrial enterprises in China. These constituted no more than 6 per cent of the total number of state-owned industrial enterprises, but they produced 66 per cent of the total net industrial output (measured in current prices) of all state-owned enterprises.[13] By 1986, such enterprises totalled 8,271, and 94 per cent of them were state owned.[14] (State-owned enterprises are defined to include those administered by state units down to the county level, but they do not include enterprises that were formerly administered by rural units [communes, brigades, and teams]; these latter are regarded as organs of collective ownership rather than of state ownership.)

During the first half of the 1980s, the role of large and medium state enterprises in providing the nation's gross industrial output increased slightly from 42 to 44 per cent of the total. Collectively owned enterprises increased far more sharply, from 21 to 28 per cent. Both gains were at the expense of small state enterprises, which declined from 37 to 26 per cent.[15] State-owned industrial enterprises are extremely heterogeneous in size. The subpopulation of large and medium-sized state industrial enterprises may be more interesting because of its greater homogeneity and, particularly, because the rise of collectively owned enterprises has not been at its expense, but only at that of small-scale state enterprises.

No detailed data are available as to the composition of the subpopulation of medium and large industrial enterprises prior to 1986. However, using the broad categories of "large" and "medium," one can see that there was some movement toward increased size between 1982 and 1986.[16] For 1986 there is a size distribution that can be compared with the size distribution of our sample.[17] Using employment as the measure of size, I obtained the results shown in table 1.1. Our sample is found to be heavily skewed toward the larger end of the size

Table 1.1 Size of Sample Enterprises Relative to the Subpopulation
(in percentages)

Number of Employees	Subpopulation of Medium & Large Industrial Enterprises (1986)	Sample of Enterprises (1982)
over 100,000	0.12	5.0
50,000–100,000	0.36	10.0
30,000–50,000	0.48	0.0
10,000–30,000	2.66	15.0
5,000–10,000	5.98	20.0
under 5,000	90.39	50.0

distribution of the subpopulation. Nevertheless, half of the sample enterprises are within the smallest size category.[18]

Turning to other characteristics of the sample, let us begin with its geographic coverage. The organizations studied were situated in fifteen of the provinces and province-level units (just over half) in China; such provinces were located primarily in the east and center of the country and contained 62 per cent of the Chinese population.

With regard to the size of the population centers in which the enterprises (or their headquarters) were located, 5 of the units were in cities with a population of over three million at the end of 1982, and another 4 were in cities of between one and three million. But the remaining 11 organizations were distributed in centers of under half a million, and probably 6 of these were in relatively small urban centers.

As to product concentration, 7 of the enterprises produced either consumer goods or their direct inputs; of these, 5 were textile producers, 1 produced a food product, and 1 produced a consumer durable. Five of the enterprises were in the producer-goods engineering industries, 6 were in other heavy industries, and 1 was in forestry. Enterprises of the county organization produced a mix of products.

As of the end of 1982, the hierarchical subordination of the organizations was also well diversified. Only 3 of the 20 were under the sole supervision of a national ministry, although for 5 others such supervision was shared with a regional-level organization. Seven were either under the sole supervision of a province, or such supervision was shared with that of a subprovincial government body. Five were supervised solely by a county and/or municipal government.[19]

An interesting standard of classification is that of the average earnings of the labor force of each organization as a proportion of those of all state employees in Chinese industry during the same year.[20] The number of the sample organizations falling into different categories in 1975 and in 1982 (the first and last years that are systematically covered by the enterprise statistics) are described in table 1.2.

The data of table 1.2 do not suggest that in the pre-reform year of 1975 the labor forces of our sample organizations were being given preferential treatment compared to those of state industry as a whole. However, by 1982 this was the case, although the average employee of almost one-third of the sample organizations still earned less than the average Chinese state industrial worker. But the significant change between the two years was the advance of half of those organizations which had previously been well below the Chinese average to a level corresponding roughly with the average.[21] This represented favorable treatment, it is true, but only of a limited sort. Moreover, we have no information as to whether such favorable treatment was peculiar to our sample organizations or was typical of what was simultaneously being done for large and medium-sized enterprises in general. The only relevant national data is for 1986. In that year, the average annual earnings in all large and medium-sized industry, regardless of the ownership status of the individual enterprise, was 11 per cent higher than that for state-owned industry as a whole.[22]

In addition to such earnings data, we also have information on changes in labor and capital productivity during the four reform years of 1979–82. These figures are presented in table 1.3. A comparison of the median figures for our sample enterprises with the data relating to all state-owned enterprises in China indicates that our sample enterprises are not strikingly atypical with regard to change.[23]

The difficulty with measuring the representativeness of the

Table 1.2 Average Earnings of the Labor Force of the Sample Organizations

	Number of Organizations	
Average Earnings[a]	1975	1982
145	0	1
126–32	3	2
117–22	1	2
106–12	4	3
101–4	1	6
95–99	0	1
87–94	4	5
75–84	5	0
Total	18	20

Note: One of the listings for 1975 in the table was actually taken from 1976, since the firm did not present 1975 data.

[a] As a percentage of earnings of all state employees in Chinese industry in the same year.

Table 1.3 Change in Productivity During 1979–82 in State-owned Industrial Enterprises (annual rate of change)

	Labor Productivity[a]	Capital Productivity[b]
All China	+2.3%	−0.15%
Sample enterprises		
Median	+1.5	−0.1
Mean (unweighted)	+8.3	+1.6
Mean, excluding one observation	+1.4	+0.2
Number of observations	18	17[c]

[a] Gross output in 1970 prices divided by the size of the total work force.
[b] Gross output in 1970 prices divided by the amortized value of all fixed capital (including housing owned by the enterprise) plus the value of all working capital held in inventories of any type.
[c] Four of these observations covered change during only three years of the four.
Source: All-China data are from *Statistical Yearbook of China 1985*, 224, 306, 309, 374. Stock data are taken as the average of end-year data for that year and for the previous one.

sample is that the relevant universe consists of large and medium-sized state industrial enterprises rather than of all state-owned industrial enterprises. But Chinese statistical data are for the most part limited to the larger universe. Tidrick and Chen (1987) evaluated the sample primarily against the latter universe. Given the standard that they used, it is not surprising that they found it lacking in 1982 by the criteria of absolute labor productivity, capital/labor ratio, and profitability. They write that perhaps the sample's greatest weakness in representitiveness is the absence of loss-making enterprises (13–16).[24] Indeed, this might seem particularly serious when one realizes that in 1982 some 25 per cent of all state industrial enterprises operated at a loss. However, when we look at comparable statistics for 1982 which give national data on gross losses, we see that during that year this 25.1 per cent of all state enterprises lost only 6.6 per cent of what all other state-owned industrial enterprises gained. In 1983 the comparable figures were 14.6 and 4.2 percent.[25] This would suggest that, among state-owned enterprises, the odds ratio of suffering losses has been heavily biased to the disadvantage of the smaller enterprises.[26] Some support for this view is found in the fact that, in 1986, only 7.0 per cent of all medium and large industrial enterprises suffered losses.[27]

Thus the problem of representativeness of the sample in terms of the appropriate universe—that of large and medium-sized state-owned enterprises—cannot be evaluated with the above data. Tidrick and Chen (1987, 15–16) also compare the size and profitability of seven of the sample organizations that have been categorized as "key enterprises" with that of other "key enterprises," and they find nothing unrepresentative in the results.[28] But this comparison errs in the opposite direction, as this universe is more select than the one I am considering.

Something can be said as to the degree to which the sample represents the universe with regard to winning prizes. In 1983, ten industrial enterprises in all of China received national awards for distinction in management; three of the ten were in the sample (Tidrick and Chen 1987, 16).[29] Even if one believes that large and medium state enterprises virtually monopolized the awards, which is certainly possible, nevertheless the sample enterprises clearly received far more than their fair share.

The situation appears to be the reverse, although to a much lesser degree, with regard to the 690 or so national prizes awarded in 1984 for quality control or product quality. Seven of the sample enterprises won ten of these awards; this 1.4 per cent of the total awards was the same as the sample's share of the total number of employees in all state-owned industry. However, this could be assumed to imply that they did much more poorly than did the average large or medium state enterprise because this subpopulation probably had a higher share of total awards than of total industrial employees.

Whatever biases exist in the sample presumably come principally from the criteria used in choosing its members, rather than simply from the absence of randomness. A critical criterion in the selection of most of the sample enterprises was that, as of the end of 1982, they should be outstanding in some fashion as to their type or degree of experimentation with "reform."[30] One might expect use of this criterion to have led the selectors to a biased choice of enterprises according to what they presumably believed was their "success." This is because enterprises which had been hailed by the Chinese media for their reform activities were also likely to have received other official and semiofficial tokens of success. For instance, this phenomenon might certainly have been expected to have played a direct role in awards given for management, and thus could easily explain the lack of representativeness of the sample along this dimension. The issue in question is how accurate was the judgment of the enterprises by the Chinese media. For this, in turn, would determine whether the actual success of the sample enterprises was strongly correlated with the media's belief as to their success and thus with their selection as leading "reform" enterprises. Fortunately for the issue of the representativeness of the sample, the chain of argument grows weaker at each link.

We have some information on this issue as it relates to product quality from the 1984 awards for product quality and quality control, with the awards based on enterprise results for the year after the one in which the enterprises were chosen for the sample. Here, as was pointed out above, there is if anything an inverse correlation between the choice of the enterprise for the sample and its success with respect to quality in the following year.[31] Furthermore, two of the five producer-goods engineering enterprises in the sample were concentrating their principal production entirely within families of products that were clearly obsolete by Chinese standards. There is nothing in this evidence to suggest that the sample is biased toward actual success relative to the universe of large and medium-size state-owned enterprises.

The outcome of this analysis is that I cannot say how representative the sample is of its universe. This is because I do not know enough about the universe. I do know that the sample is biased toward larger enterprises. It seems a fair guess to surmise that it is likely also to be biased toward greater than average success along most dimensions, and thus that it should yield an upper bound with regard to evaluation of the average efficiency of enterprises in the universe.[32] (Even this mild conclusion is weakly contradicted by the evidence on quality and quality control. The data on change in productivity during 1979–82 also fail to support the guess, although they do not contradict it.) On the other hand, as we shall see throughout this study, the enterprises chosen should in no way be viewed as "Potemkin villages"; their difficulties not only stand out to the reader, but also were prominent both in the eyes of the Chinese researchers and of the enterprise managers themselves.

In any case, what I am concerned with is the representativeness of the sample along the dimension of behavior rather than along other dimensions which directly reflect efficiency of production. It seems likely that a sample such as ours, with diverse representation as to geography, size of urban center, product range, hierarchical level of the supervising body, employment, and wage level, will constitute at least as representative a mix of managerial behavior as it will of efficiency as shown in table 1.3. This is because the types of behavior of concern in the study do not seem to be a direct function of any specific reforms represented in our sample.

Anonymity

This volume will only partially follow the usual academic convention of leaving unidentified the individual organizations in the sample. The observance of anonymity seems to me to be sound practice in general, in that it provides a degree of protection to managerial informants. In my various stints of enterprise interviewing in the Soviet Union and Eastern Europe, as well as in Western Europe and the United States, I have found that informants have always warmly welcomed this. In the single Chinese enterprise for which I participated in the original set of interviews, the interviewees seemed to respond to such an offer of anonymity in the fashion that I expected.

However, such anonymity has been abandoned—particularly as it relates to historical quantitative data about individual enterprises—in the various writings of my Chinese and Western colleagues in this research venture. The names of all the organizations in the sample and considerable quantitative data concerning each of them are contained in the publication from the Beijing symposium. (Tidrick and Chen 1987, 12–37). The full original (unrevised) questionnaire, together with the unrevised answers for three identified enterprises, are presented in two earlier publications.[33] Furthermore, various behavioral data have been identified with individual enterprises in all three of these publications.

This precedent would provide a basis for abandoning my usual practice, engaging instead in full disclosure. What I have done instead is to compromise. Where I have thought it useful to the reader, and not likely to have any potential for harm to individuals in the enterprises, I have given various identifying characteristics of the enterprise. I have done this, for example, in my description in chapter 2 of the nature of administrative control exercised over individual enterprises. Here, I have identified the enterprise by sector even though in many cases this would permit the diligent researcher to identify it by name. Nevertheless, my general rule is to preserve as much anonymity as is still possible. This position is based partly on the fact that I will be presenting materials for individual enterprises which have not so far been identified with them and which they might conceivably regard as sensitive. For such matters, protection of anonymity is still feasible. A second factor is that only a very few readers will be familiar with the enterprises concerned and thus will feel that they would have gained from identification. The third reason is that only in this way can I preserve my credibility with future interviewees both in China and in other countries.

Coverage of the Book and Organization

The thesis of China's uniqueness as a centrally planned socialist economy is developed in chapter 2. Some Western observers of China tend to consider *guanxi* (the importance of personal connections) as a critical peculiarity; one might also choose to emphasize the high proportion of government revenue and total investment in the state sector that never passes through the state budget. However, I do not consider any of these features to be both unique and particularly significant.

In chapter 2 I present four unique aspects of control over state-owned enterprises and provide a unified explanation for them that is based on the property rights of regional bodies relative to one another and to the national government. My hypothesis is that decentralization within the Chinese state sector takes the form of regional governments constraining central decision making via their recognized property rights, rather than it occurring through the Center granting power to lower bodies so as to best achieve the Center's own goals, whether these be efficiency or political objectives. Put another way, the hypothesis is that regional levels of government constitute more than hierarchical levels.

This chapter tests the explanation using the sample data on which level(s) of government exercise supervision over individual enterprises. In chapter 3 I analyze the sample data as to planning in terms of the property rights explanation, while doing the same in chapter 4 with respect to allocations and prices. Chapter 7 deals with the *nomenklatura* question and is the only organizational, as opposed to economic, chapter in the monograph.

In the above chapters the enterprise itself is treated as essentially an agent of its supervising authorities, rather than as an independent actor in decision making. In chapter 5 I explore and attempt to justify this approach by examining the types and extent of incentives that are applicable to the enterprise as an independent unit. Once again, sample data are used to test hypotheses.

Chapter 6 stands outside of the main thematic approach. It presents the rates of profit and of sales tax found in sample enterprises of different sectors of industry, and shows that the tax pattern in particular is a significant modification of the Soviet model. The behavioral implications of these differences are then explored, suggesting that, with respect to decisions on current production that treat capital stock as a given, profit maximization behavior in Chinese industry is made indistinguishable from output maximization. Chapter 8 is the conclusion and concentrates particularly on the implications of the distinctive property rights that are found in China.

To summarize, chapters 2, 3, 4, and 7 explore the fundamental hypothesis of the study concerning the property rights held by regional governmental bodies. Chapter 5 is linked to this hypothesis in that in it I attempt to justify the book's concentration on decision making by organs above the state-owned enterprise itself. Chapter 6 is independent of both of these unifying themes, but is integrated into the total work by the fact that it explains various aspects of behavior found in the other chapters that would otherwise appear anomalous.

The substantive materials of this book consist primarily of the sample and the Soviet data that are required for comparative purposes in the treatment of the theme of uniqueness. Thus, the study is limited to the period of 1975–84 in China. Materials related to earlier periods, and indeed heavy use of Western writings on the Chinese economy, are restricted primarily to chapter 2 in which the unifying property rights thesis is developed. No serious attention is given to attempting to explain the historical roots of the Chinese approach to property rights. Although amateurish suggestions might be offered, this task seems more appropriate to leave to China specialists.

As mentioned above, the sample data cover both the pre-reform and reform period of Chinese state-owned industry. This mix will be exploited throughout the book in order to look for both continuities and discontinuities between the two periods. The basic theses are believed to apply to the entire post-1975 period and probably to the early part of the 1970s as well. Although clearly the economic reforms have had an effect on state-owned industry, the similarities between years are as prominent as are the differences. In order to explore this, the statistical data have been grouped into the four-year periods of 1975–78 and 1979–82; these are then compared with one another. Statistical experimentation with dividing the data at a different year has supported the conventional wisdom on the dating of the beginning of the reform period; this is fortunate, as I would not wish to have to justify the break after 1978 solely by the statistical convenience of periods of equal length. No attention whatsoever is given to year-to-year differences, since this monograph is intended to be analytic rather than a piece of historical writing.

The presentation of sample data provides a difficult problem throughout the book. Where feasible, objective statistical data for the individual enterprises are combined into tables; the peculiarities of the individual enterprises appear here only in the fashion that they are grouped into categories relevant to the argument of the particular chapter. But sometimes such a treatment is impossible, and my subjective evaluation of the situation facing the individual enterprise was required prior to making a statistical grouping of the enterprises. In these cases, it is essential to discuss the organizations individually both in order to offer the reader an opportunity to appraise my evaluation and so as to provide a richness of context which defies statistical treatment. The perusal of data for twenty industrial organizations can, however, be dull for the reader. Thus, much of this discussion is placed into appendices.

Since this book is not intended as a set of case studies, there is no integrated treatment of any single enterprise. Some Sinologists might wish for data that identified enterprises according to their provinces, but this is purposely avoided. The influence of geography on the variables analyzed would be much more relevant to an historical study, rather than to one in which years are grouped together, as is done here. In any case, this book is concerned with attempting to achieve generalizations relevant to China as a whole rather than to individual regions.

A word of explanation may be appropriate here as to certain stylistic features:

1. Sources referred to in the endnotes are the original sources, even when I have been led to them by secondary sources, provided that I have checked the original. Where I have not checked the original, it is the secondary source that is cited.
2. For Soviet sources, the transliteration system used is that of the Library of Congress. The publishers of Soviet books are listed. Although this latter is unusual, the name of the publisher provides some limited information for the knowledgeable reader as to the trustworthiness of the work, just as is the case for Western publishers.
3. I have followed the old-fashioned custom of using only the male pronoun when referring to men and women, unless this leads to confusion. I beg the reader's indulgence.

The Targeted Readership

This book is written primarily for economists. I regard it as intended particularly for those interested in comparative economics in general, rather than exclusively in the economy of the People's Republic of China. I believe that it is informative as to the general set of centrally planned socialist economies and not solely as to the single national member of the set which is the focus of attention. This is one reason that, in almost every chapter, I have briefly discussed differing behavior in other centrally planned economies before turning to what has been observed in China.

Although the book is not intended to be light reading, I believe that most of it should be accessible to noneconomists. From this point of view, it is unfortunate that the very next chapter begins with a treatment couched in the language of game theory. But the noneconomist should be able to skip technical portions, here and elsewhere, without losing the thread of the argument—it is only in chapter 6 that it would be best to proceed directly to the conclusion; in addition, the appendices to chapters 5 and 8 should be skipped.

In each relevant chapter, the reader will be provided guidance as to sections that may be skipped without missing important information. The cost of such skipping will be both the sacrifice of textural richness and the inability to evaluate my interpretive summary of the data.

2
MULTIPLE PRINCIPALS IN PRINCIPAL-AGENT ANALYSIS

In searching for the fundamental source of the peculiarities of the operation of Chinese state owned industrial enterprises in comparison with those of the European countries of the Council of Mutual Economic Assistance (CMEA), I have been led to an institutional factor. This factor is the existence of property rights in the hands of regional organs of government, a phenomenon that unites the experience of China during the Cultural Revolution and under the reform regime of Deng Xiaoping. What is striking about it is the degree to which it differs from the situation with respect to property rights in each of the CMEA countries, as well as, for very different reasons, from the Yugoslav situation. This single difference among countries provides an analytic key to the explanation of what otherwise appears to be a set of anomalies in the functioning of economic institutions which condition the behavior of Chinese state enterprises.

Analytic Framework

The traditional Western analysis of the Soviet economy has been in terms of a central political leadership which runs a unified organization: USSR Incorporated. However, no level of the organization is in a position simply to provide a consistent set of instructions to lower levels. Rather, each level must attempt to motivate subordinates to act in a fashion which it desires; such motivation consists of a package of rewards and punishments which depend upon economic results.

The central leadership decides on the establishment and change of institutions; it takes policy decisions relating to macroeconomic allocation (investment versus consumption), production growth in one sector versus another, and income distribution; and finally, it chooses mechanisms believed appropriate for inciting appropriate execution of these policies. All of these choices are treated as reflections of the Center's utility function, which is being maximized under a set of constraints that represent not only physical limitations, but also expected economic reactions to the outcomes of the leaders' decisions. The relevant actors whose reactions are to be considered consist not only of workers and consumers, but also of administrative and managerial organizations such as ministries, enterprises, and shops within enterprises. Of fundamental importance here is that the expected reactions are only economic rather than political. No domestic threat to the central political leadership exists, or at least none that is taken account of in this treatment.

The above analysis is, of course, very much in the spirit of a principal-agent model. For it treats decision making with regard to economic parameters as if it were conducted by a single Center, which is itself homogeneous rather than composed of interest groups, and which thus has a single utility function (objective function).[1] Second, it considers the Center to give explicit consideration in its decisions to the expected responses of the rest of society in terms of its economic actions (purchases by consumers, work decisions by members of the labor force, output decisions by enterprise managers as these are affected by tautness of plans and by incentives generally). In this analysis, a homogeneous Center is treated as the "principal" and all others in society are considered as "agents."

Although the noneconomist need not be concerned about the matter, this type of model is a form of Stackelberg duopoly model, with an open-ended variable (V), or set of variables, used instead of quantity as the one subject to control by both principal and agent. In this principal-agent model, the principal controls V_1 and the agent V_2. The principal correctly assumes that the agent sets $V_2|V_1$. Thus the principal sets $V_1|V_2(V_1)$. In this respect, the principal acts as the Stackelberg leader (although the game is different from Stackelberg's oligopoly problem). The agent, on the other hand, assumes that the principal will remain with his current choice. For this reason, the agent sets $V_2|V_1$, acting as the Stackelberg follower.

It is only with regard to their respective conjectures as to the behavior of the other that the principal and the agent differ. This difference in their conjectures stems, of course, from the difference in their relative power. The Center, as principal, determines the institutional environment within which the agent makes its own decisions. The agent takes these conditions as given and unchallengeable, and reacts to them in terms of maximizing its own utility within their bounds.[2]

This unsophisticated model has taken buffeting from political scientists who regard major decisions in the Soviet Union as representing the results of interaction among special interest groups.[3] But such buffeting relates to decisions on policy, rather than those with respect to institutional change and to the creation of incentive mechanisms intended only to implement policy, regardless of what such policy may be. It is for this reason that the use of bureaucratic politics as a fundamental concept in policy making, and thus the rejection of the notion of a utility function of the Center, is still consistent with the principal-agent model. It is sufficient to establish such consistency that we make a somewhat weaker assumption than that of a unitary Center. It is necessary only that the Center—regardless of how its weighted objectives are arrived at or changed—attempts to maximize these objectives, and that it regards the maximization process per se as having no political effect on the future choice of weighted objectives for later periods. This latter subassumption amounts to the Center presuming that there exists one-way causation in which objectives affect the choice of means, but not vice versa.

Thus, both of the above political science models, when applied to the economy of the Soviet Union, can be interpreted as yielding a principal-agent model in the determination of institutions and incentive systems.[4]

When we turn to examining the organization of the state sector in China, one might use the same analysis and interpret the Center as constituting the sole principal. But if this were to be done, we would have to distinguish between two types of agents.

The first consists of the Chinese state-owned enterprises. These are quite similar to all of the Soviet agents (including intermediate bodies such as industrial ministries), rather than only to Soviet enterprises. The similarity rests in the nature of the constraints binding the Center in determining its own actions. These constraints consist both of physical ones and of others that stem from the expected responses of the agents.[5] But these are the only two sorts of constraints that are present. If, for example, the Center does not make decisions which would lead per worker income in enterprises to fall below a certain level, this is either because of the expected responses of agents (or of the labor force of these agents), or because of the arguments in the utility function of the Center, for none of these agents enjoy property rights.

In China, however, the analytic framework would also have to posit a second type of agent: namely, provincial, municipal, prefectural, and county government units. The actions taken by the Center in relation to these bodies face not only the above two sorts of constraints, but a third variety as well; namely, ownership rights possessed by these various organizations that are intermediate in hierarchical level between the Center and the enterprise. The Center is constrained against treating all of these agents similarly, as does the Soviet Center, by the existence of property rights held individually by the regional governments.

This analytic framework would, however, be clumsy. Instead of using it, I shall define the term "agent" to exclude organizations which enjoy property rights in their relation to any "principal." "Agents" include only intermediate bodies of such principals (central ministries, regional industrial bureaus, corporations, etc.) and state enterprises, and thus do not enjoy property rights.[6]

In saying that regional governmental units enjoy property rights vis-à-vis the national government and one another, what is meant is the following: Neither the Center nor an intermediate regional body, such as a province, in relation to lower bodies such as municipalities, simply takes those actions that maximize its own welfare function. This is despite the fact that such maximization would, of course, have to take account of the political and incentive implications of such actions and in this respect would reflect regional considerations. Instead, the maximizing government unit is constrained by specific property rights that belong to these individual lower bodies, and these rights differ among particular provinces, municipalities, etc.

This does not imply that such regional property rights are immutable. Higher bodies can, on the margin, change the rights of lower bodies, just as the American government (through the constitutional process) was able to alter the private property rights of its residents through instituting the income tax. But pushing such changes too far would be comparable to a revolution: it would involve the elimination of regional property rights.[7] The effect of changes in such specific rights on the existence of regional property rights in general can be pictured as a mathematical function that, at some vaguely defined point whose exact position is unknown to the higher bodies, either changes its slope drastically in the form of a kink or suffers a discontinuity. Higher bodies are viewed as resisting the temptation to move as far as this kink or discontinuity.

For the economist, this situation can alternatively be described in terms of game theory. Any two levels of regional authority may be pictured as playing a repeated Nash-equilibrium game with one another, with the outcome of this game representing payoffs to these two principals. What is critical, however, is that this game is imbedded in a larger Nash-equilibrium game that sets the rules of the smaller game. Higher bodies have the power to modify these rules as they see fit in the process of playing the smaller game. But if their modification goes too far, then the larger game breaks down. The existence of regional property rights can be interpreted as representing the unwillingness of the Center to risk destruction of the larger game.[8]

Given the above definition of "principals" in terms of regional bodies that enjoy property rights, what is striking in the Chinese scene is not only the existence of multiple principals, but also the fact that individual enterprises, as agents, frequently are subject to control by a number of principals.[9] This is the pattern which is picturesquely described by the Chinese as involving the presence of "too many mothers-in-law." It is not something which is observed in the Soviet Union or in other European CMEA countries.

It is well beyond the scope of this book to attempt to explain why the Chinese state-owned sector should function through multiprincipals, while the comparable sector in the Soviet Union has only a single principal. Nevertheless, it is worth mentioning that such a difference is consistent with the emphasis by many historians upon the force of historical continuity in influencing national behavior. The Russian government under the tsars was organized as a strongly centralized state. In contrast, Chinese government, both under the foreign Manchus from the seventeenth century on, as well as under the native Ming dynasty from the fourteenth to the seventeenth centuries, operated in a relatively decentralized fashion.[10] Despite the efforts of the central government, the authority of Chinese provincial governments rested to a large degree upon a local power structure. Chinese governmental decentralization was particularly striking after the middle of the nineteenth century.

There is a certain similarity between the situation in the contemporary Chinese state sector and in the Yugoslav socialist sector. In both, ownership rights are exercised by a multitude of socialist organizations. But individual Yugoslav enterprises are not responsible to more than one principal. Much more significantly, they (and their subdivisions, the Yugoslav basic organizations of associated labor) enjoy major property rights of their own, and such rights are probably an even more important factor in determining enterprise actions than are the rights of the regional bodies (the communes and republics). Because the locus of Yugoslav organizational property rights is at the enterprise (and lower) level, it is more useful to think of their decisions and interactions as being integrated through market relationships than by principal-agent relations. That is not the case within the state sector in China.

The reader should not be misled into believing that regional property rights are commonly recognized as factually existing in China. Even the prominent reformist Chinese economist, Ma Hong, who uses the term "regional ownership," is not expressing in this term the concept of property rights. What he means is, first, that individual enterprises are under the supervision of one or another governmental organ, whether ministerial or regional; and second, that such a supervisor generally serves as the focal point of communication among enterprises (so that all communication is vertical, and the supervisor is a party to all communications), rather than allow communication to be horizontal and take place directly among the enterprises (Ma Hong 1983, 132, 194). Such regional ownership differs in no significant way from "ministerial ownership" in the Soviet Union.

The existence of property rights held by different levels of government—i.e., the existence of a number of principals within the state sector—must be regarded as the most fundamental assumption of this work. It is justified partly by this chapter's discussion of the history of such property rights. But its main justification is by its use throughout this study in explaining data that come from the interviews in the sample enterprises.

This analysis is, of course, an application of property right theory to socialist economies. In the case of China, the property rights are held by regional bodies. The existence of such rights in China (in comparison with the situation in the Soviet Union), and their location (in regional bodies rather than in enterprises as in Yugoslavia) do more than affect allocation of resources. My ultimate interest in them is, as in the theory of property rights in general, in their effect on production decisions. My immediate interest, however, is restricted to their effect upon the workings of the management and planning system.

Facts To Be Explained

This section harkens back to the anomalies in state control over state-owned Chinese industrial enterprises, compared to those of other centrally planned economies, which were referred to in chapter 1. However, it deals with only four of these, ignoring questions of *nomenklatura* and of labor and wages.

Multilevel Supervision

In contrast to other socialist countries, it is very common in China for medium-sized and large state-owned enterprises to be under the authority of more than one higher body. In making the above international distinction, however, we must be careful to define appropriately the concept of "higher body."

If we consider the Soviet Union, it has always been perfectly normal for enterprises to receive financial plans (e.g., of profits) from one functional organization within their branch ministry or one of its subdivisions (*glavki*), and output plans from a second. Furthermore, since different functional organizations have prepared these respective plan indicators, it has also been common for them to be inconsistent. However, both functional bodies are under the same line administration within the ministry. The receipt of plan indicators from these different bodies can be viewed as an application of division of labor within the ministry, and inconsistency as being primarily a result of time pressures on the ministerial organs in sending out these planning indicators.[11]

This type of functional multiheadedness also, of course, exists in China. But this is not the fact to be explained. What requires explanation is that administrative bodies existing at different regional levels of state administration frequently give orders directly to the same enterprise and provide independent evaluations of the single enterprise.

This multilevel multiheadedness of supervision is sometimes recognized in Chinese parlance by the statement that the individual enterprise is under "joint supervision." But the term has no significant classificatory content, since it excludes many cases which might just as well be included. In my presentation of data regarding the sample organizations, I shall thus ignore the Chinese categorization of these enterprises and look instead at what I believe to be the reality of their relations.

Of the twenty organizations in the sample, there were problems of multilevel leadership in nine. In two of these nine, the higher level organization carried out most substantive planning tasks (such as investment and output planning and materials allocation), but the lower level one could appoint or remove the top management of the enterprise without being responsible to the higher body for the fulfillment of the planning tasks laid down.[12] In a third enterprise, a smelter, virtually all physical planning and all managerial appointments were by the relevant national ministry, but the municipal government did the financial planning and took all of the profits. A similar situation, with the provincial government replacing the municipal, applied to a fourth enterprise that produced steel. Here, the profit plan set by the province acted in reality as an aggregative output plan as well, since it could not be realized without producing more than the mandatory output plan set by the ministry. In a pump plant, the national ministry planned output and supplied half of the planned materials allocations; the province planned everything else, made managerial appointments and dismissals, and provided the other half of planned materials allocations. A sixth enterprise (a forestry and lumbering operation) was very similar to the pump plant, except that the national ministry and province also shared in allocating output. A seventh enterprise (a watch company) was municipally controlled, but it was the provincial authorities who provided the main market. Most of the predecessor organizations to a newly merged company (in petrochemicals) had been under ministerial planning for production and allocation, but were subject to municipal financial planning and municipal appointment of managers. In a ninth enterprise (in textiles), the province seems to have set the output plan, the ministry and the province provided the materials, and the municipality made many of the remaining decisions and took the profits.

A tenth enterprise (a producer of electrical equipment) also had difficulties, but these were of a transitional nature while the enterprise adjusted to coming under provincial leadership.

This left exactly half of the organizations without problems of multilevel leadership. Three of the ten were under ministerial control, five under provincial, and two under municipal or county.[13] Even here, in four of the ten cases (the textile firms), it was the level above the supervising one which made the basic decisions on output and materials allocation for the specific products to be produced by the sum total of enterprises under the competence of the provincial or municipal direct supervisor. But there was no multilevel leadership in these cases, since it was the direct supervisor who broke down both the targets and allocations to the enterprise level.[14]

It is true that, as in China, in the Soviet Union a large proportion of gross industrial production is produced by enterprises that fall under the multilevel authority of a national ministry and of a republic (the counterpart of the province in China).[15] But the limited significance of such regional administration seems typified by the situation in the Soviet coal industry. There is both a national coal ministry and a special republic-level ministry within the Ukrainian Republic. However, the Ukrainian ministry seems to have no more authority than does the industrial association for the Kuzbass region, which is directly under the national ministry rather than being under the jurisdiction of its own (the Russian) republic. For example, the Ukrainian ministry has the right to set additional tasks for output and profits for units under its administration, but these may sum to no more than 1 per cent of the plan that had been earlier approved for the Ukrainian ministry by the national ministry. It would appear that only in the case of financing construction is the Ukraine in a different position. Financing is done from the budget of the Ukrainian Republic, and thus there is need for coordination between the national coal ministry and the Council of Ministers of the Ukraine in presenting development plans for the Ukrainian coal industry. But even these proposals go for decision to the national-level State Planning Commission of the Soviet Union.[16]

Thus, while a single Soviet enterprise may (although rarely) receive instructions from more than one level of the planning hierarchy, the lower level body will be acting in this regard simply as an agent of the higher body. This is a completely different situation from that observed in half of the enterprises in our Chinese sample.

The underlying cause of the distinction between the two countries is the national difference in kind as to property rights held by regional governments. In China, as we shall see below, regional governments have had considerable rights both in theory and, even more, in practice.[17] In contrast, the ruling principle of financial funding of the different levels of government in the Soviet Union is the "unified budget." Regional authorities are provided with funds for particular needs as recognized by the Center, rather than as a function of their own ability to generate funds. It is true that Soviet authorities below the national level are permitted to keep the profits generated by enterprises under their administration. But the effect of the differential ability to earn such profits seems to be almost fully sterilized through the practice of annual reconsideration by central authorities of the amount of locally generated state budget funds to be kept by the localities. Since it is these funds that are overwhelmingly dominant as the source of local governmental funding, and thus even a small percentage change in this allocation can swamp the effect of a change in earned profits or other nonunified income, the marginal effect of an increase in the latter must be close to zero. A Hungarian author has described the budgetary arrangements as "primarily and decisively disincentive in character," although he believes that this is true more for the republics than for lower levels.[18]

Loose Production Plans

As we shall see in chapter 3 (see particularly tables 3.3 and 3.5), our sample is extraordinary by the standards of other socialist countries for the degree to which output plans are exceeded. Moreover, this overfulfillment has increased sharply in the reform years of 1979–82 compared with the 1975–78 period. There was plan fulfillment of 121 per cent or more in 23 per cent of the enterprise-years of the later period, versus 13 per cent earlier; and plan fulfillment of 111 per cent or more in 51 per cent versus 33 per cent.[19] (An enterprise-year refers to observations for enterprise i in year t.) In the Soviet Union, it seems unlikely that there would be any except aberrant cases of enterprises overfulfilling their output plans by more than 10 per cent.

If production plans are intended as the key device used to coordinate the economy, in the sense of causing industries or enterprises to engage in activities different from those they would otherwise choose, then we would expect fulfillment not to stray too far from the 100 per cent level. This is because there should be considerable overlap between the plan received by a unit and what the management would voluntarily choose to produce given its capital equipment and labor, as well as its incentives other than those linked to plan fulfillment.

Moreover, such fulfillment close to the 100 per cent level should be the case at the enterprise level rather than simply at the aggregate industry level. This is because of the variety of product mix with a low rate of user substitution that is produced within an industry, and because of the spatial problems of demand on rail transport that would be associated—whatever the national average was for fulfillment—with sharply differentiated fulfillment data at the enterprise level. Thus, the plan fulfillment data for our Chinese sample seem informative as to the limited degree to which production plans have been the means of integrating the economy, both before and after the industrial reforms.

Availability of Allocated Goods

As we shall see in chapters 3 and 4, the phenomenal feature of the Chinese allocation of intermediate products is not the number of such products which totally escape allocation, or even the degree of aggregation of the allocated items. The truly unusual aspect of the system is the extent to which a very high proportion of the total output, even of those products which are subject to national allocation, eludes incorporation into the national system of allocation. Moreover, this phenomenon antedates the reforms.

Table 2.1 is striking in demonstrating the limits of central control over allocations well before the end of the 1970s when the reforms began. The figures for 1965 are perhaps of particular interest, as this year is thought of as one of the high points of central control in China.[20] The data for 1978 are interesting in showing the degree to which regional governments acted as the agents of the Center in handling allocations, as well as acted as principals in allocating the large share of materials that escaped central control completely.

At least by the mid-1980s, it would also seem to have been common for even those production plans that were set by the Center—with at least the bulk of such output being subject to allocation by the Center—to be only partially backed by central allocations of necessary inputs. At an annual meeting of the Research Institute on the Work of China's Factory Directors, held in late 1984, it was claimed that an allocation shortage of 20 to 30 per cent of the required materials is common.[21]

These figures on allocations of intermediate products raise the

Table 2.1 Proportion of Individual Products That are Centrally Allocated (in percentages)

Product	Allocated Either to Enterprises or to Regional Governmental Bodies[a]						Allocated Directly to Enterprises
	1965	1978	1980	1982	1984	1986	1978
Coal	75	54	54	51	47	42	18
Steel	95	80	58	53	56	53	58
Lumber	63	81	82	57	58	30	63
Cement	71	36	29	25	21	16	...
Machine tools	...	35	...	...	...	...	24
Trucks	...	75	...	...	...	...	50
Nonferrous metals	...	...	64	...	...	...	...
Sulfuric acid	...	...	...	...	37	...	...

[a] Allocations to provinces, municipalities, prefectures, and counties are primarily for further allocation by these regional units to enterprises.

Sources: Christine Wong, in Perry and Wong (1985), 262, 266–67; in JEC (1986), 603; in "Between Plan and Market" (typescript, December 1986); and in a letter to the author (19 February 1987). Data for 1986 are from a communiqué of the State Statistical Bureau, *B.R.* 30, no. 9 (2 March 1987):24.

same issue as do the production data: Can a planning system integrate the economy under these circumstances, and why has such a situation been allowed to prevail, especially under pre-reform conditions?

Multiple Prices

In chapter 4, in addition to dealing with allocation of products and of intermediate inputs, I will also treat prices. Suffice it to say here that the Chinese economy appears to be unique, both among socialist and capitalist economies, in the degree to which there exists a system of perfectly legal multiple spot prices to be paid by industrial and commercial units for the same product delivered at the same physical location. This phenomenon occurs under conditions of price control and is not at all related to market conditions of discriminating monopolies.

The result is that a given state-owned firm will at any time find itself paying a range of prices, quite unrelated to quality, for most of its major inputs. Often it will likewise sell its products at different prices, partly depending upon the customer, but primarily determined by whether the particular physical unit being sold is considered to fall within the production plan of one or of another governmental supervisor or, for the highest point of the price range, whether it is outside the plan of all supervisors.

The traditional objection in centralized socialist economies to permitting this form of multiple prices is that it would reduce the informational content of financial data regarding the individual enterprise and would thus increase the difficulty in rational evaluation by supervisors of the performance of the enterprise. In addition, it would make financial comparisons between benefits and opportunity costs of investments even less meaningful than is inevitably the case in centrally planned economies that use state-fixed prices.

Although Chinese economists have recognized the force of these objections and have never to my knowledge challenged them, nevertheless the system of multiple prices has exploded in extent of use during the 1980s, precisely when financial criteria of evaluation have been given greatly increased importance. In short, the system has expanded at the very moment when its negative effects are likely to be most serious. But the multi-price system itself existed during the pre-reform period as well, just as did all of the other institutional phenomena noted earlier in this section. The widespread existence of this system in China, but not in other centrally planned socialist economies, is another fact in need of explanation.

The Property Rights Model and the Basic Hypothesis

The modelling treatment of this section is intended essentially as a mnemonic aid in the further reading of the book and, particularly, of this chapter. Its usefulness should be greatest in the discussion of the case studies treated below. The symbols are used only in the current section. But the propositions (with their numbers) are referred to later. The basic hypothesis is of considerable substantive importance for the book. It is tested in this chapter, as well as in chapters 3 and 4. Chapter 7 is also corroborative.

    We begin with a principal-agent model in which all principals and agents are organizations rather than individuals. Principals and agents are distinguished as follows:

(2.1a) Principals are distinguished from agents by the fact that the former enjoy property rights, while the latter do not. It is ownership over property rights that allows the principal to establish rules governing the reward to the agent and thus to act in a fashion analogous to the Stackelberg-leader in the game played with the agent.

(2.1b) Multiple principals exist within the state sector, and a single enterprise may have multiple principals. Aside from the central government, these include regional governments at the provincial, municipal, and county levels.

(2.1c) Agents include not only state enterprises, but also entities of principals that are intermediate between them and the enterprises; namely, central ministries, regional industrial bureaus, corporations.

    The property rights (P) of principals with which we shall be concerned consist of the following three, with P_o and P_f being of prime importance. These rights need not be explicitly recognized by any party, so long as all parties act as though they exist.

(2.2) P_o constitutes the property right to the use of the physical output produced by an agent.

        P_f constitutes the property right to the financial cash flow (including at least part of the tax revenue) produced by an agent.

        P_{hr} constitutes the property right to the utilization without payment of the human resources that constitute the work force of the agent.

Higher level government bodies, particularly the Center, are more likely to enjoy property right P_o than P_f. The opposite is true for lower level bodies such as municipalities and counties.

The instruments (I) available to principals for realizing their property rights are directions or resources given to agents. The instruments available to a given principal with regard to a specific agent are a function of the property rights that it possesses in the agent. Indeed, I_1 is no more than the primary form which P_o takes, as is I_5 for P_f. The instruments of relevance are the following:

(2.3)   *To realize P_o:*

I_1 is the set of orders allocating to specified users the physical output produced by an agent. It may be used for this purpose by any principal.

I_2 is the set of plans for total output, expressed either in natural units or in money, and plans for profits. It is used for this purpose solely by regional principals, particularly when a larger region or the Center exercises joint property rights to a given agent's physical output.

When property rights are divided between principals on the basis that it is the higher level that receives property right P_o, the lower level principal may attempt to determine the size of the residual physical output through use of its property right P_f. Constraints that restrict an enterprise's ability to sell its products outside the geographic area that constitutes the sphere of the principal's authority may assure that principal that such residual physical output will remain in its control.

I_3 is the set of physical allocations of inputs by the principal to the agent.

I_4 is supervision over the enterprise, with the authority to appoint and replace its top management, determine its bonuses, and affect its wage levels. This, particularly when used together with I_2, is useful for realizing P_o under conditions where an enterprise is relatively free to sell its products outside the geographic area.

To realize P_f (in descending order of importance):

I_2 is used as a means of determining the total gross financial revenue produced by the agent.

I_5 is the set of instructions to agents as to the proportion of amortization allowances and of profits to be paid to the principal.

I_3 is used as a means of providing physical resources needed by the agent in order for him to be able to earn the desired level of profits.

I_6 is the set of tax rebates, grants, and subsidies; sales of inputs by another agent of the same principal at a lower price than would otherwise be charged; and access to bank loans whose granting is within the authority of the principal. All of these elements of I_6 are means of redistributing the principal's financial resources to make what amounts to a further "investment" in the favored agent.

I_4 is used to exact financial funds, for example, as gifts to agents of the principal (for road building, schools, etc.).

To realize P_{hr}:

I_4 is used as a means of exacting free use of desired human resources by the principal. What is of relevance here is not so much the amount of such resources or the saving in cost, but rather the ability to obtain high-quality resources that would otherwise not be available at all. Professional and administrative talent appear to be particularly subject to such drain.[22]

In the following issue, one which noneconomist readers can ignore, let us express a principal's welfare as $W(P_o, P_f, P_{hr})$. In order to maximize this utility, it has available to it the vector of instruments $I_1 \ldots I_6$. Let us call this vector $\mathbf{V}_1$, and call the vector of responses by the agent $\mathbf{V}_2$. Where only a single principal exercises property rights over an agent, the principal's problem is that of choosing $\mathbf{V}_1$ so as to maximize $W(\cdot)$, given that the agent will choose $\mathbf{V}_2$ in the light of the principal's choice of $\mathbf{V}_1$.

The question of interest for us is the problem facing a principal when more than one principal exercises property rights over the same agent.

(2.4) Let $\mathbf{V}_{1c}$ = the vector of $I_1 \ldots I_6$ at the disposal of the Center (principal c).

Let $\mathbf{V}_{1r}$ = the vector of $I_1 \ldots I_6$ at the disposal of the regional principal (r).

U   = the union of sets.

The problem facing the regional principal is:

Choose $\mathbf{V}_{1r} | \mathbf{V}_2(\mathbf{V}_{1r} \text{ U } \mathbf{V}_{1c})$ so as to maximize $W_{1r}(\cdot)$.

This can be alternatively described as

$$\underset{\mathbf{V}_{1r}}{\text{Max}} \ W_r(y)$$

subject to:

$$y = y(\mathbf{V}_2)$$
$$\mathbf{V}_2 = \mathbf{V}_2^*[\mathbf{V}_{1r}(\mathbf{V}_{1c}), \; \mathbf{V}_{1c}(\mathbf{V}_{1r})],$$

where $\mathbf{V}_2^*$ constitutes the vector of actions taken by the agent when the agent maximizes its own utility subject to the constraints imposed upon it by the principals, and where y is the final "output" of the enterprise which contributes to the welfare of the regional principal. The value for that period of the regional principal's P_o, P_f, and P_{hr} is determined by y.

The posing of this problem raises two issues relating to separability of the property rights held by the different principals in a given agent. The first issue is that of achieving a distribution of such rights which eliminates a gaming relation between the two principals in the choice that each makes. For this, each must be able to choose its most appropriate vector of instruments without regard for the effect of this choice upon the other principal. The existence of separability of this type changes the second constraint in the maximization problem of (2.4) to

$$\mathbf{V}_2 = \mathbf{V}_2^*[\mathbf{V}_{1r}, \; \mathbf{V}_{1c}]$$

The likelihood of obtaining such separability seems negligible. For example, if different principals own property rights P_o and P_f in a given enterprise, their interests conflict and a gaming situation seems likely to arise whenever $d(P_f)/d(P_o) < 0$. This can occur because different weights attach to different products in the marketplace and in the welfare function of the principal possessing property right P_o, and because the quantities of specific outputs distributed by the principal holding property right P_o are frequently priced lower than when the same items are sold on the marketplace. Thus, analytic concern should be concentrated primarily within the gaming framework; the total output of the firm is most likely to be reduced below its potential by the gaming behavior of the principals. (In the language of transaction costs, one would say that such costs are too high to permit the principals to reach Pareto optimality through the use of side payments.) It is this result that leads to the Chinese complaint of "too many mothers-in-law."

The second issue, relevant for all readers, is that a situation may exist where only one principal possesses property rights in a given agent, but a second principal has command over some stream of input resources that are needed by (or would be very helpful to) the agent. The agent may be unable to obtain these resources on its own, either by money payments or through barter. Instead, the principal that has property rights in the agent obtains the resources by providing a stream of side payments to the second principal. The expected discounted value of this stream of side payments is the price paid for the stream of inputs.

(2.5) This stream of side payments to a principal without property rights in the given agent may be the right to exercise some of $I_1 \ldots I_6$ so as to extract these side payments itself. I_2, I_4, and I_5 are the instruments whose use is granted as such a side payment.

The reason that payment for inputs may take this form, when the value of the stream flowing from the enterprise lags that of the resource stream from the second principal, is that the enterprise may be regarded as a poor credit risk. The second principal improves the likelihood of actually receiving the promised payments by extracting the right to exercise designated instruments so long as its own flow of resources continues. The promised payment is now not a fixed sum of money or goods, but rather an equity position in the temporary flows of money and/or products from the enterprise. When payments are made in this way, we again encounter the problem of separability of rights to the outputs of the enterprise.

What distinguishes this flow of side payments from property rights is that there is no assurance of permanence of either the flow of input resources or of the flow of side payments.

(2.6) The flow of input resources and the counterflow of side payments rest upon temporary agreements between the two principals concerned. Each has the right to end the flow passing to the other.

The multiple-principals hypothesis of property rights, which is fundamental to the entire book, is the following:

(2.7) *Hypothesis:*
    1. All principals hold property rights (defined in [2.2]) in enterprises. These property rights are accompanied by the right to use instruments $I_1 \ldots I_6$ (see [2.3]).
    2. A principal other than the national government obtains property rights in a given agent in one of two ways: (a) by investment in the fixed capital of the agent; or (b) by historical tradition.

The role of investment is the consequence of the alleged Chinese doctrine that a given level of government should exercise ownership rights in an enterprise in proportion to its investment in the fixed capital of that enterprise. Historical tradition refers to the principal either already having had jurisdiction over the enterprise by the mid-1950s or, much more likely, to the fact that it was granted such jurisdiction during one of the episodes of organizational decentralization that occurred in China in 1958 and again around 1970. Historical tradition plays a minor role in our testing of the hypothesis; in only 10 per cent of the cases is it the basis for our classifying enterprises as confirming or refuting the hypothesis.

We must distinguish this hypothesis from the following alternative:

(2.8) *Alternative Hypothesis:*
    Individual regional bodies are given supervisory rights by the Center as a result of the Center's maximization of its own welfare function, unconstrained by the property rights of other bodies.

The alternative hypothesis presumably might be based on an efficiency analysis by the Center, in which the Center's unconstrained maximization is promoted through decentralization of the control function to the regional level. In this case, however, any differential treatment by the Center of various regional bodies and enterprises should be independent of past investments made by the individual regional governments. More interestingly, the alternative hypothesis might be rooted in bureaucratic politics, being based on a political analysis by the Center of what is needed to gain support from important regional groups within the Communist Party for factions within the leadership of the national level of the Party.[23]

The multiple-principal hypothesis (2.7) can, if data are sufficient, be readily identified in the sense of differentiating it from the efficiency form of the alternative hypothesis (2.8), which is a member of the set of bounded-rationality arguments. This is because the multiple-principal hypothesis predicts an absence of uniformity (if one sets aside the effect of property rights) in the treatment of the different regional bodies and enterprises, under conditions in which there is no basis in administrative efficiency for such heterogeneity.

More significantly, hypothesis (2.7) would also seem to be identifiable with respect to the political form of the alternative hypothesis (2.8). The multiple-principal hypothesis suggests continuity in the relation between the form of supervisory rights observed and the conditions that generate property rights. In contrast, the political form of the alternative hypothesis, since it is concerned with bureaucratic politics, should lead us to expect sharp discontinuities over time. This expectation applies particularly to a period such as that of 1975–82 when national coalitions, as well as relative power positions within the national Chinese Communist Party leadership, were changing substantially and frequently. It would be extraordinary if an unchanged linkage between regional supervisory rights and the conditions generating property rights should have served equally well the interests of all national and provincial coalitions that were in a position to make decisions regarding the locus of supervision at varying times and places throughout these years. Thus it is the degree of continuity of functional relation that should be used to distinguish the multiple-principal hypothesis from its coalition-politics alternative.

In short, the efficiency form of the alternative hypothesis (2.8) predicts that, at any moment in time, whatever "rights" may have been obtained by different regions, either through investment or through tradition, will not lead to any heterogeneity in the treatment by the Center of different regions; most concretely, they will not include preferential right to use instruments $I_1 \ldots I_6$ as specified in (2.7). The political form of the same hypothesis predicts that what appears as preferential treatment of individual regions will vary discontinuously over time.

In contrast to both, the hypothesis of multiple principals (2.7) predicts that the property rights acquired by the indicated methods will lead to heterogeneity between regions at any given moment in their relation to the Center, and that the pattern observed in any period (t) will change only gradually and in accord with further investments by the given regions.

(2.9)   The multiple-principals hypothesis (2.7) predicts that differential rights of regional governments to enjoy the fruits of production of individual enterprises will depend primarily upon past investments made by the respective governments and, in addition, on long-term tradition regarding the individual enterprise. Both forms of the alternative hypothesis (2.8) predict an absence of such dependence.

In this chapter (see table 2.2) I will contrast the predictions of (2.7) with that of (2.8).

Still another hypothesis, which is richer but less clearly specified, is that of Lieberthal and Oksenberg (1988). These authors view relations between different layers of government as being governed by intense bargaining. Side payments are seen as an intrinsic part of inter-governmental agreements. Such agreements are required even when the Center has full formal authority because local governments can otherwise introduce interminable delay. There are wide-ranging, complex agreements that take periods lasting months and years to negotiate. Lieberthal and Oksenberg perceive policy coherence as being attained through a "process of consensus building and consultations" (1988, chap. 4).

This hypothesis does not conflict with (2.7), but it is much less explicit with regard to the matters at issue in this chapter. The absence of conflict between the two hypotheses can perhaps best be observed in the main example involving regional governments that is presented by Lieberthal and Oksenberg. This concerns the Shanxi coal basin; here the treatment of the 1984 organizational change is quite consistent with my property rights hypothesis (2.7), although its approach is different (1988, 353–71).

The existence of streams of side payments that are not connected with property rights in the agent seriously threatens to reduce our ability to test the multi-principal hypothesis against its alternative (2.8). In the extreme, all negative evidence could be explained away as side payments. To minimize the force of this formulation, hypothesis testing in this chapter shall in general treat what might be interpreted as the existence of side payments as constituting disconfirming evidence for the hypothesis. The exception to such treatment is when there is particular reason—emanating from historical development in the particular enterprise in question—to believe that they are genuine side payments.

(2.10) For purposes of hypothesis testing in this chapter, no exercise by a principal of rights over an agent will be interpreted as constituting a flow of side payments unless these rights have been temporary in the particular enterprise concerned and can in addition be linked to a counterflow of inputs.

A further conceptual issue is postponed to the last section of this chapter. It relates to the question of whether the relation between different levels of government is fundamentally hierarchical, preventing us from treating each level as a principal.

History of Property Rights
Over State-owned Enterprises

Before examining in detail the property right situation in our sample enterprises, let us place the subject within the broader context of what is known about historical changes during the period since the founding of the People's Republic. Unfortunately, the nature of the available data forces me to lay the emphasis primarily upon the relations between the Center and the "local government," with the latter remaining undifferentiated among provinces, municipalities, prefectures, and counties. Not unexpectedly, there have been ups and downs in this history. But for most of the period, it seems certain that the situation differed markedly from that in the European socialist countries.

Although the information in this regard is much more sketchy than one would like, the situation is fortunately one in which there is no conflict among authorities.

Through 1953, no distinction was made among state owned enterprises as to whether they fell under central or local guidance. This differentiation was introduced at the time of the abolition of large administrative regions, each of which had embraced several provinces.[24] Large enterprises, as well as small ones, were placed under local guidance; as of 1957, these included 125 (15 per cent) of the 825 large industrial plants that were built or reconstructed since 1952. (Remyga 1982, 30–31). However, this was a period in which the Soviet planning model was very much in the ascendancy. and the division by governmental level of guidance did not seem to have such significance.

It is during 1958, at the beginning of the Great Leap Forward, that we see the first decentralization. By this time, the number of industrial enterprises under central guidance had increased from 2,800 in 1953 to 9,300. Now the number was cut back to something on the order of 1,300, the others being transferred to local guidance. What gave significance to this reduction was that a double-track system of planning was simultaneously introduced. Although central ministries continued to plan for their industries as a whole, including for enterprises under local guidance, these plans were now binding only as minimum targets. Provincial and lower regional authorities could set any targets they wished for the enterprises under their supervision, provided that they respected the constraints of product volumes which were to be delivered to central authorities. While our source does not spell out this implication, the new system would have had little impact if these regional authorities could not have kept the supplementary produce, including intermediate input items, for their own use. This condition became all the more important since it is claimed that the granting of the new regional authority completely destroyed national planning.[25]

Although I have seen no indication in the literature that clearly suggests that regions were also given independence in using the financial resources which they generated and which exceeded the nationally planned amounts,[26] this would not have been of particular importance during these years. It was command over goods, rather than over money, that mattered to state bodies at that time. Furthermore, the profit retention introduced in 1958 for most state enterprises did provide some additional funds which were under the de facto control of the regional authorities (Naughton 1986, 139).

Such regional control did not, however, outlast the Great Leap Forward with its emphasis upon voluntarism rather than coordination. The readjustment in 1961 is said to have restored the situation of 1953–57, both as to control of industrial enterprises by the central authorities and as to planning procedures.[27] Presumably, it similarly eliminated the rights of regions to retain the excess production of their remaining enterprises when such output exceeded the centrally planned quotas. In 1964 (thus preceding the Cultural Revolution), there was again some transfer of directional power away from the Center,[28] but there are no indications as to what, if anything, this transfer signified. As of 1965, the number of industrial enterprises under the direct control of the Center was back to the level that existed just prior to the 1958 slash. These enterprises produced 47 per cent of the output of all state-owned industrial plants.[29]

The next recorded decentralization of central authority was in 1970. But in fact it clearly occurred much earlier during the Cultural Revolution; given the chaos of the period, it would have been impossible for the central government to have avoided it. The following slogan, which is described as epitomizing the relationships of the 1970s, had originated at least by 1966: "Whoever builds and manages the enterprise has the use of its output."[30] Again, as during the Great Leap Forward, nothing was said as to the granting of property rights over finance to local bodies; but once more, this could not have been of any real significance.

The period of 1970–73 accomplished at a minimum a systematization and regularization of what had already been occurring during the second half of the 1960s, and it extended the decentralization to financial matters as well.[31] Ninety-five per cent of the centrally-supervised enterprises were shifted to local supervision in 1970 or thereabouts, and the share of the output of all state-owned plants that was produced by enterprises continuing under central supervision was reduced to 8 per cent.[32]

Between 1972 and 1976, in some core provinces of China at a minimum, it was regional governments that were at least theoretically responsible for allocating materials to industrial enterprises. The Center directly cared only for the enterprises left under its own supervision and, in principle, otherwise allocated materials and equipment to the regions in block grants rather than giving them directly to enterprises.[33] At a product level, central planning was limited—either throughout China or in particular regions, depending upon the item—to transferring surpluses from one region to another.

Regions were encouraged to build new enterprises by allowing them to both manage them and to keep their produce for local use. The share of state-planned investment that was fully financed and managed by the provinces and lower bodies rose from 14 per cent in 1969 to 27 per cent in 1974 and 1975.[34]

With regard to finance in general, the direct revenue of the Center was limited between 1971 and 1976 to customs duties and to the profits of the few enterprises still left under direct central control; the two together constituted only 16.1 per cent of total government budgetary revenue in 1971 and 13.8 per cent in 1972. As such centrally raised money declined between 1965 and 1976 from 33.0 to 12.7 per cent of total budgetary revenue, central expenditures fell from 62.2 to 46.8 per cent of all budgetary expenditures.

The central government's income came essentially from the sharing of the revenue of provincial governments. Provincial obligations to the national government were set at a stipulated amount of revenue to be paid to the Ministry of Finance, with specified expenditures in the region also being required of the province. But in 1971, for the first time, all supplemental revenue, as well as any reduction of expenses in meeting the nationally specified expenditures, could be kept by the province for its own purposes. In the years that followed in the pre-1978 period, various formulae were adopted for the sharing of above-plan revenues between local government and the Center. Throughout, the principle was followed that the regions were to gain at least a major share of any surpluses. A 1976 slogan emphasized that local governments were to have the power of spending such surpluses.[35] This financial change represented a major shift from the unified budget principle adopted earlier from the Soviet Union.

Similarly, in the 1969–71 period, a major independent source of funding was turned over to the provincial government. Amortization funds of enterprises had previously been completely centralized in the central budget. Since funds for major repairs were left at the disposal of the individual enterprises, and current repairs were met as current costs, these amortization funds were in fact available to be used for expansion and for new construction (Naughton 1986, 142–43).[36] Now those enterprises that were administered by local authorities were to pay their amortization funds to these authorities rather than into the central budget.[37] With enterprises shifting soon afterward from formal subordination to the Center, this new regulation regarding amortization funds was given bite. Thus control over the distribution of marginal output (at a regional level), over management of enterprises, over materials allocation within the constraint of meeting delivery targets to the central government, and over finance were all brought together at the provincial level. What is unclear, however, is the degree to which financial decentralization to the subprovincial level occurred during this period; in all probability, it did not occur.[38]

Despite the national government returning some enterprises to strictly central supervision in 1978 and unsuccessfully attempting to return a great many more in 1980; despite it once again laying claim to a portion of the amortization funds generated by enterprises; and despite the Center recapturing distribution powers over most of the products that had previously been decentralized to provincial or lower levels,[39] the tide continued in the direction of the relative strengthening of local governmental bodies. In 1980 there was a further decentralization to the local level of the financial property rights to those types of income that are included within the state budget; this time, it is certain that the grant of decentralized power included bodies below the provincial level.[40]

During the 1980s, it was said, the right to the revenue generated by a given enterprise was more related to supervisory tasks over the enterprise than to original investment;[41] this was to the financial disadvantage of the Center. Such a relation, to the extent that it existed, contradicts the property rights hypothesis (2.7). In our sample, we find that the monetary revenue generated by enterprises indeed sometimes goes to governmental bodies not possessing property rights as these are described in (2.7). However, this phenomenon seems to be to a considerable degree a residue from the pre-reform period when monetary income was of lesser importance; it declined in our sample during the first half of the 1980s.

Most clearly, as well as most significantly, the proportion of national nonagricultural investment which was financed entirely outside of the state budget—essentially by local authorities—continued to mount sharply.[42] Local governments below the provincial level gained, if they had not done so earlier, financial powers comparable to what the provinces had received during 1971–73.[43] Indeed, local control even moved—not nationally, but still in many sectors of industry in specific regions—into an increasingly significant functional area that previously had always been a sacrosanct sphere reserved to the Center: the field of foreign exchange. Furthermore, the 1979–83 period has been characterized as one in which individual national policies were consistently implemented in such a way as to grant more local control over resources than had been envisioned by the original policy.[44]

The conclusion that I draw from this history is that property rights by regional governments have existed continuously at least since the early 1970s, and probably from an earlier point in the Cultural Revolutionary period. However, the materials from the sample enterprises that are treated in later chapters relate only to the years after 1974; thus, the thesis that I wish to maintain in this study refers only to continuity of property rights during these later years. Both datings share the significant feature that the period of enjoyment of property rights by regional governments is divorced from connection with the timing of economic reform in China.

As the economy became increasingly monetized in the late 1970s and in the 1980s, the form taken by these rights became increasingly financial. But this is a matter of form rather than of content. The right to allocate the output of one's own enterprises belonged to regional governments throughout the period, and this right was substantively most important in the earlier years when financial property rights were weaker than they became later.

Principal-Agent Analysis Applied to
Supervision Over Enterprises

My objective in this section and in the appendix to this chapter is to use the sample data to test hypothesis (2.7) in which the particular form of supervision over a given enterprise is linked to the property rights that one or more principals exercise over this enterprise. Multilevel leadership, and the particular form of it found in the individual cases, is explained by property rights obtained in the fashion hypothesized in (2.7). The null hypothesis consists of alternative hypothesis (2.8). Results are summarized in table 2.2 below. For those enterprises under multilevel supervision (half the total number of cases), three cases strongly support the multiple-principal hypothesis (2.7) while one case strongly refutes it. For those enterprises that were under single-level supervision, all nine of the cases strongly support the hypothesis. I will discuss one enterprise that was under multilevel supervision so as to provide the reader with a flavor of the hierarchical relationships and of the nature of the qualitative evidence provided. I will also treat six of the enterprises under single-level supervision. The remaining cases are treated in the appendix.

Multilevel Supervision

As stated above, there were problems (other than transitional) of multilevel leadership in nine of the twenty organizations in our sample. The case of the smelter is one that I consider on balance to support strongly the hypothesis of (2.7), although it has one counter feature. The financing of fixed investment was done by the Center throughout the history of the enterprise, and allocation of both product and materials (with the important exception of electricity) was also always national. Yet, for the period between 1971 and 1983, direct supervision of the enterprise was transferred to the level of the municipality (after first going to provincial control for one year), and the municipality was granted control of the profits earned by the enterprise. In January 1984, the smelter was transferred back to so-called exclusive ministerial control; the enterprise's profits from then on were to go to the central government rather than to the province or to the municipality, and no financial compensation was to be paid to the municipality. Since profit sharing between government and the enterprise had by now become important, the relevant rate was similarly determined by the Center. However, the provincial government continued to determine the priority of the enterprise for receipt of electricity, a major and nonsubstitutable input for this industry;[45] provision of this item was a considerable burden for an electricity-short provincial economy.

Analyzing this enterprise's history in terms of the property rights hypothesis, the transfer of the smelter and its profits to municipal control in 1971 would not have been predicted. However, the transfer itself can be explained as part of the wave of administrative decentralization that was occurring nationally at this period. The transfer to the municipality of appointment power over most of the enterprise's Party and administrative staff probably also occurred in 1971; we know that it occurred sometime between then and the 1980s. Such transfer seems to have been a natural concomitant of the transfer of supervisory power. It is notable, however, that the enterprise's Party secretary and plant director continued to be appointed by national authorities; this is the only case in our sample enterprises where these posts were under either ministerial or Party Central Committee *nomenklatura* at the same time that direct supervision was at a lower level.

As to the transfer of control over profits, one can only say that these were of less importance prior to 1980 than they became later. (One might view these financial rewards as constituting side payments for undertaking managerial responsibility, but that would be counter to the spirit of [2.10].) In part, this lesser importance was because it was only in fits and starts, with 1980 representing a significant change, that China moved away from the system of a unified financial budget in which local governments at all levels had their total magnitude of financial expenditures incorporated into the central state budget, or at least into that of their province.[46] Moreover, throughout most of the 1970s (similar to the situation in all centrally planned socialist economies other than Hungary at that time), money by itself did not provide any organization with much command over real resources.

Much more weighty for the testing of our hypothesis is the 1984 transfer of profits back to the Center. This transfer, along with that of nominal control over the enterprise, is fully consistent with the property rights hypothesis. Once the resource of money had become important (allowing for time lag), its flow was made consistent with both organizational control over other resources and original investment. The most interesting aspect was that there was no financial compensation to the municipality; the municipal receipt of enterprise profits during 1971–83 appears to have been treated as having constituted a gift which was not to be continued indefinitely.

What was left unexplored in the interviews is the supply of electricity to the smelter by the provincial government. This is a resource with a high opportunity cost to the province, and the provincial authorities have not hesitated to make life difficult for another centrally administered plant that is an even heavier user of electricity. There is no indication of any extraction of resources from the smelter by the provincial government in exchange for the favorable distribution of electricity. Conceivably, municipal financial control over the enterprise was the quid pro quo until 1984 for favorable electricity supply by the province; we do not know what happened to the smelter's conditions of electricity supply after the transfer of authority.

Choice of Sole Supervisor

The six enterprises treated below are all viewed as strongly supporting hypothesis (2.7).

Of the ten enterprises subject only to single-level supervision, three are strictly under national administration. None of these three have any particular connections with another level of government, and all were developed solely with investment funds from the national government. It is true that in one case (auto), 20 per cent of the profits not retained by the enterprise go to the province rather than to the central government, and that in the other two cases the province or municipality receives some of the enterprise's amortization fund.[47] But these appear to be nothing more than side payments (or gifts) from the national government to the local authority, a means of buying good will. No power over the enterprise or over the distribution of its products has accompanied these gifts.

At the same time, the province and municipality do not appear to make any investment of resources in these enterprises. The only case mentioned of provincial allocations going to one of these enterprises is for cement to the oil field; but, in compensation, the central government has been providing investment funds for the provincial cement factories.

Indeed, the case of the automobile enterprise lends some further support to the property rights hypothesis. The enterprise had been nominally under the leadership of the province until late 1981, at which point it was transferred to the Ministry of Machine-building. It is said always to have been under the effective control of the national ministry, and the 1981 shift of nominal leadership was probably to a large extent only a change in the recipient of profits.[48] The fact that this change could be made, with a mere 20 per cent of profits being left to the province, is presumably a reflection of the level of government that had been providing the resources for the enterprise.

Two of the ten organizations are at the other extreme: under the administration of a county or a small municipality. In neither case is there an indication that higher levels of government shared in control, benefits, or the granting of resources. The one exception, which is significant, is with regard to the distribution of the final product and allocation of materials; some of each is done by the province and, in all likelihood, by the central government. But the interviews do not provide clear information as to the quantitative importance of such distribution and materials allocations.

This leaves five enterprises that are under provincial "leadership." One of these is a chemical fertilizer plant built by the province and opened in 1969. Although the ministry has made some investments in the plant, well over 90 per cent of total investment funds have come from the province. The plant was always under provincial leadership, with the exception of a few years during the Cultural Revolution when it was municipally led. None of the amortization fund has ever gone to either the ministry or to the municipal authorities, even during the years of municipal leadership. All planning is done by the province, and all planned allocation is carried out by the province. The central government does make one significant contribution: the allocation of something on the order of half the plant's needs for coal, and it should be noted that this is the plant's largest single purchase item. But there is no indication that the Center receives any compensation for this allocation.

Summary

In table 2.2 I summarize the data for all the organizations in our sample. Thirteen cases seem to confirm hypothesis (2.7), three refute it, and four cast no light upon it. Only in the case of two textile firms

Table 2.2 Summary of the Linkage Between Ownership and Control

		Organizations	
Characterization of the Evidence	All 20	Under Multilevel Supervision	Under Single-level Supervision
Supports hypothesis (2.7)	13	4	9
Strongly	12	3	9[a]
Weakly	1	1	0
Refutes the hypothesis	3	3	0
Strongly	1	1	0
Weakly	2	2	0
Irrelevant to the hypothesis	4	3	1
Insufficient evidence	2	1	1
Transition case	1	1	0
True irrelevance	1	1	0

[a]Three of these are textile enterprises. In this case, a higher level organization exercises control over the total textile production of the province, but not over the production of any specific enterprise.

under provincial administration, which are classified as confirming the hypothesis, is historical tradition taken as the basis for property rights.

This result strikes me as constituting reasonably strong, although certainly not overwhelming, support for the belief that the choice of the governmental level or levels which exercise control over the individual Chinese industrial organization is a reflection of the ownership rights of this level—obtained in the fashion hypothesized in (2.7)—with regard to the vector of production and finance of this enterprise.

Property Rights in General in the People's Republic of China

The purpose of this section is to place into a broader context the discussion of property rights in state-owned enterprises, where these rights are held by principals who are regional governments. Although the focus of the study as a whole is on state industrial enterprises, I hope that the explanatory hypothesis used in this relatively narrow analysis is not inconsistent with what is known about Chinese society in general. Since property rights are used to explain phenomena in the pre-reform as well as in later years, it would seem useful to examine the approach of the regime in both periods to various related matters.

The fact that regional governments gained property rights in state-owned enterprises after 1957 and that they were able to retain such rights at least since the early 1970s, must not be viewed as a phenomenon totally inconsistent with what was happening in other respects in Maoist China. Although in many ways the Chinese regime, particularly during the periods of the Great Leap Forward and the Cultural Revolution, was obsessed with egalitarianism and was a staunch enemy of the status quo, in other regards it was conservative and highly sensitive to vested interests. It is true, it seems to me, that it is primarily in the sense of preserving regional ownership rights of various sorts that the Maoist regime should be viewed as having been conservative. Even with this limitation, however, the Chinese government's attitude toward property rights provides much more continuity btween the operational ideology of the Maoist and of the present reform regime than is customarily believed.

This section can be interpreted in terms of the neo-Marxist writings of John Roemer, who interprets "exploitation" as having a broader base than Marxist surplus value.[49] It can be seen that Chinese regimes have been concerned with combating only a narrow subset of Roemer's concept of exploitation, that which is due to the relations of production. In this respect, all Chinese regimes have been traditional Marxists.

Agricultural Income

The development of producer taxes, both implicit and explicit, on agricultural products has been very different in China during both the pre-reform and reform years than has been the case in the Soviet Union. Given the institutional arrangements in both countries, farmers other than those on state farms are left with pretax income that includes what would be extracted from them as rent if they were tenants in a capitalist society.[50] Thus, if the government wishes to follow what both countries officially view as the appropriate principle for distributing earned income—to each according to his work—it faces the task of extracting differential rent.

Of course, a government might ignore the issue of differential rent and, in its efforts to achieve equity in post-tax income distribution, concentrate instead on the degree of per capita income equality. This latter goal might be fully served by mechanisms such as a graduated income tax, income transfers, and sales tax rates which differ depending upon the degree to which the product taxed is consumed by low-income or by higher income citizens.[51] But such attention to income equality, although consistent with the communist principle of income distribution according to need, bears no close relation to the socialist principle as this is perceived by either the Chinese or the Soviet governments.

In China, three mechanisms have been available for such extraction of rent by the government. The first is the traditional planned economy mechanism of subjecting farm units to obligatory quota deliveries of products at prices that are far below their opportunity cost.[52] The second is a direct land tax (a method eschewed in the Soviet Union). The third is the charging of high prices for inputs into agriculture that are used most heavily on high-quality land.

In the Soviet Union, the method of quota deliveries has been used to extract both differential and absolute rent from collective farms.[53] Prices paid for obligatory farm deliveries differ by region for the same crop, thus permitting price discrimination in a very crude and aggregative fashion against the regions with better geographic conditions. Much more significantly, since it is this second submechanism which permits fine-tuning, quotas set for individual collective farms have differed as a function of their calculated fertility and other natural advantages.[54] Individual farms with better conditions could have a higher proportion of their expected produce taken as quota deliveries at low prices, thus causing the average price paid by the state for a given product to be determined on a farm-by-farm basis. Note that, within a given region, the price paid for the marginal product is uniform. Even farms which fail to produce for market anything above their quota deliveries still provide consumption in kind for their members; the distribution of such goods to members can be viewed as constituting the receipt by all farms of a uniform notional price for their marginal output.[55]

While the Chinese government has abstained from utilizing the Soviet device of paying different regional prices for quota deliveries (Lardy 1983, 58), it has enjoyed an additional mechanism (land tax) to that employed in the Soviet Union. Yet the evidence is clear that changes over time in the pretax differential rent received both by individual villages (previously called communes) and by smaller units have been left untouched by the Chinese government. To show this, land tax and quota deliveries must be analyzed separately.[56] Both have shown a sharp secular decline as a proportion of agricultural output.

The total land tax levied nationally on agriculture and paid, or at least expressed, in tons of food grain, remained much the same in absolute terms during 1951–57. With the tax expressed in monetary units (for lack of data in grain), there is no indication of any particular change during 1958–59, and there is a fairly sharp reduction by 1977. Data for tax expressed in tonnage of food grain shows that the 1978 (pre-reform) levy was only 68 per cent of the 1952 level; in 1979, it fell to 56 per cent (Lardy 1983, 52, 105).[57] By 1984 it was estimated to have risen back only to the level of the 1950s.[58] Meanwhile, grain output had grown by 86 per cent between 1952 and 1978, and by 148 per cent between 1952 and 1984. Total gross agricultural output value had grown by 130 and 294 per cent between these respective dates.[59] Thus the total land tax receipts showed no net rise at all between the 1950s and the middle of 1984, although the output of the land had more than tripled.

During the 1950s when the tax system was established, the land tax was a progressive one. Prior to 1958, the rates in general were progressive with respect to individual peasant households. In 1958 progressive rates between provinces were established. The rates correlated positively with normal per capita grain output, and the top provincial rate was 141 per cent of the lowest provincial rate (Lardy 1978, 126–27).

At this early point in the P.R.C.'s history, the land tax may well have done a pretty good job of absorbing differential rent.[60] But thereafter it performed this function ever more poorly. Between 1952 and 1978, the land tax fell from 18 to 4 per cent of total budgetary revenue.[61] Moreover, by 1981 it was expected to be changed to a proportional tax between provinces.[62] Finally, aside from its sharply decreasing importance if measured as a proportion of agricultural output (a phenomenon which is well documented), there also seems to have been a failure during the 1960s and 1970s to adjust the taxes levied on individual regions despite the fact that their agricultural and population growth varied widely (Lardy 1983, 187).[63]

Quota deliveries of agricultural crops were introduced in 1953. Between 1954 and 1957, quota deliveries of grain declined by one-fourth.[64] A comparison of 1957 and 1978 permits estimates of change in the tonnage of national quota deliveries of grain ranging between −3 per cent and +17 per cent,[65] while grain output increased by 56 per cent during this period. Between 1978 and 1981, it seems likely that quota deliveries actually fell by at least one quarter,[66] although grain production increased by another 7 per cent.

Finally, let us add together the total agricultural land tax (expressed in grain, but levied on all crops) and the quota deliveries of food grain, taking the total as a proportion of the grain output of the year. It should be noted that the ratios are overstatements of the appropriate proportions, since the land tax should really be expressed as a proportion of total agricultural output. Furthermore, the decline in these ratios is understated, since grain fell as a proportion of total agricultural output.[67] Thus the two points made in table 2.3—the low ratio by the 1970s and the sharp secular decline after 1957—is stronger than indicated therein.

The third method available for extracting differential rent is

Table 2.3 Land Tax Plus Quota Deliveries of Grain
(as a percentage of grain output)

Year	Ratio
1957	24.6
1978	11.4–13.8
1981	8.2

Note: Calculations include the conversion rate used in Lardy (1983, 35) to convert tax and quota tonnage into output tonnage.
Sources: Lardy (1983, 35, 52, 105); Eckstein (1977, 68, 323); and see notes 57–61 and 64–66 to this chapter.

through the state charging high prices for industrial inputs into agriculture. This method would be successful to the degree that, on a per acre basis and regardless of the relative prices of these industrial inputs to output,

$$d(\text{value of industrial inputs})/d(\text{quality of land}) \cong d(\text{value of outputs})/d(\text{quality of land}).$$

Lardy argues that the price of such inputs in China, relative to the price of the agricultural products themselves, is high by the standards of other less developed Asian countries (1983, 112–19). But I know of no reason to believe that the relative prices of such inputs are so high and the usage of these inputs is so distributed as to fulfill the requirements of the above equality.

Moreover, if one considers the net state revenue generated by such industrial inputs into agriculture in comparison with that received from other industrial producer goods, revenue ratios are not particularly high on products going to agriculture. Indeed, data from the 1980s for profit plus sales tax, when considered either as a proportion of fixed capital or of output, show that these revenue ratios have been relatively low.[68]

Thus I reject the assertion that this method of extracting rent is clearly relevant to the Chinese economy.

Of course, an important reason for the low ratios of average tax plus quota deliveries compared with gross output is that the total Chinese population is heavily agricultural, and thus most agricultural output is consumed by its own producers. But this third-world character of the Chinese economy does not explain why the marginal rate of land tax and quota deliveries on superior compared to inferior land should be close to zero. It is this which indicates the strong property rights that have existed in agricultural land, certainly in the 1970s and probably during both the Great Leap Forward and the Cultural Revolution, even if such rights have been lodged in the locality rather than in the individual family.

The estimates of Gini coefficients for measuring income inequality within the rural population of China are consistent with the above notion that property rights were lodged in the locality. It has been estimated that the Gini coefficient for the rural population fell from 0.32 in 1934 to 0.23 in 1952, following land reform but prior to collectivization. At that point, there had been no efforts to promote regional equality. A simulation exercise on the effect of collectivization on the Gini coefficient suggests that it was minimal. Passing over the period of the later 1950s, when one might presume that the land tax would have had an effect in equalizing regional incomes, the Gini coefficient is estimated to have been at the same level in 1978 as it was in 1952. This, of course, represents considerable equalization of rural per capita incomes, both compared to China in 1934 and to other South Asian countries in the 1970s and 1980s, whose rural Gini coefficients are estimated to be much like the 1934 Chinese one. But the equalization is due entirely to changes in the property rights of individual families.[69]

The failure to centralize the receipt of differential rent from agricultural land had, as one might expect, a significant impact on the regional distribution of rural income. Of all relevant rural regions, the smallest was that worked by the production team. During the 1970s, this was the local work unit in agriculture and the most important unit in distributing collective income to the peasant households. In 1979 some 27 per cent of these teams distributed to their members per capita income that was less than 50 per cent of the average of such rural, collectively distributed income in China as a whole. Although we have no data on the percentage of total farm population in these "poor" teams, there is no evidence suggesting that the figure varied substantially from the 27 per cent standard. Moreover, central budget allocations for rural relief, even if fully concentrated on such teams, could not have added to their average income more than some 10 per cent of the national average of collectively distributed rural income.[70]

Furthermore, it should be noted that this income disparity between production teams existed at the end of a period when rural consumption standards had probably declined. Between 1957 and 1978, rural per capita consumption of grains and cotton cloth had fallen by 6 per cent, and that of vegetable oils by 43 per cent (Lardy 1983, 158).[71] In light of the sharp reduction during this period in the proportion of government revenue raised through the extraction of differential rent, the decline of rural consumption levels must have been fully concentrated on the micro-regions that enjoyed no environmental advantages (at least for those crops that they were obliged to produce). Property rights in land were respected in a period when one would have thought that they might have been disregarded because of macroeconomic developments.[72]

It is worth noting the strong parallel between this policy, followed by the central government during the 1960s and thereafter, and the tax policy of the last Chinese dynasty. Between the mid-eighteenth century and 1911, the nominal amount received from land tax (including surcharges) increased at only one-half the rate of inflation, despite the fact that the acreage of cultivated land grew by 40 per cent and that the population roughly doubled. Not surprisingly, land tax dropped from some 70 to 80 per cent of the central government's revenue to about one-third. During that entire period, the use of land survey procedures as a basis for taxation (which even earlier were honored mostly in the breach) was completely abandoned and replaced by direct apportionment of tax levies by region.[73] Although, of course, differential rent during this period was reflected in land prices and in rents charged to tenants—in sharp contrast to the absence of any such expression during the 1960s and 1970s—the treatment of the question by the central government was very similar under both regimes. It is as though both had equal respect for local rights over property in land.

Wage Income in Urban State Enterprises

Since the early 1950s, the labor force of state enterprises has been paid primarily on the basis of time wages which are governed by a national system of wage grades. Moreover, the range of earnings is not peculiarly low by international standards. For example, the range of eight grades, which excludes both apprentices and the entrance level of nonapprentices (Walder 1981, 29), typically used for manual workers within a given city and industry seems in the early 1980s to have been about 2.5 to 1.

However, during the 1960s and 1970s, relative grades (and thus earnings) within a given enterprise depended primarily upon seniority in employment either by the state or within the same factory before it was nationalized. This was because promotions between 1956 and 1977 were permitted only in 1963 and 1972. An entrant in 1960 would not have been eligible for his or her first promotion for twelve years. An entrant into the state manual labor force in 1955 could not have risen above grade 3 during the next twenty-one years. Thus, regardless of skill and actual work done, he or she could not have advanced into the upper half of the wage scale for manual workers. Yet a worker who had entered employment in the same plant some seven years earlier would often have received a wage twice as high. The same was true for white collar workers.[74]

The logic underlying the sharp restriction on promotions from the time of the Great Leap Forward was clear. Urban living standards were substantially above rural ones, and it was impossible, given the national environment and policies, to improve rural conditions. In the light of the fact that hirings of youths were vastly more numerous than total labor force separations in urban state employment, continuation of normal promotions after 1956 would have further accentuated urban-rural differences.[75]

But the restrictions on promotions signified the perpetuation of intergenerational income differences among state workers. Each new wave of promotion beginning with 1963 generally included manual workers at differing wage levels, so long as they had not reached a specified grade. Thus, even with the two years in which promotions were allowed, there was little closing of the intergenerational income gap.

Acceptance of this situation by the government implied recognition of the property rights in wage income of different generations of state employees. Because of the virtual cessation of promotions after 1955, different generations were being treated as entitled to very different expected lifetime earnings. Such governmental acceptance, of course, had negative incentive and morale effects which presumably were deplored. (Certainly they were publicly deplored in the late 1970s and in the 1980s.) But there is no indication that equity considerations were taken seriously in this regard.

The Existence of Regional Property Rights

The Chinese Communist Party historically, in its opposition to traditional property rights and in its attacks upon them, followed good Marxist practice in founding its position on the link between property and class. The Party was concerned with eliminating economic exploitation, and Marxists had always defined this in terms of the separation of the ownership of means of production from labor power.

It is true that the Chinese Party's position later broadened to include differential ownership of the means of production even when no exploitation was involved. Thus in rural areas, distinctions that were made between peasants (often using a rather fine system of classification) were along the dimension of personal wealth, even when the family did not rent out land or equipment and did not hire labor.[76] Nevertheless, the concept of wealth is relative, and the frame of reference for evaluating a family was the individual village, not the province or the nation.

To argue the other way, one might point to the desire of Mao Zedong during the Great Leap Forward, and again in 1974, to reintroduce the egalitarian system of providing cadres with rations of goods, rather than with money wages differentiated by cadre rank.[77] But these cadres were administrative officials who were either Party members or assimilated to that position, and Mao may not unreasonably have believed that they should set an example for the rest of the country and that more might be demanded of them than of others. His view was not too different from that taken in the Soviet Union during the 1920s: Party members, regardless of the posts they held, should not be allowed to earn more than a skilled blue collar worker. In neither country did the egalitarian position concerning Party members (and especially officials) long prevail, and in neither should it be extrapolated to reflect egalitarianism in general.

Similarly, Mao's fears of the creation of a "new class" of privileged bureaucrats and technicians was a far cry from a fear of regional disparities in income. Mao's concern was with the relations between groups of individuals, with these groups being arranged in an ordered pattern which was a counterpart of, and assimilated to, that conceived in traditional Marxist relationships where it was centered around the relation of the group to the means of production.

Lack of concern with inequality among different individuals within the same family is shown in the policy of health insurance in urban areas. Although medical expenses of state employees have been fully covered by the employing enterprise, state regulations called for only half of the expenses of other family members to be covered. Medical costs of workers in cooperative organizations have generally been only partially covered or not covered at all (except insofar as they were family members of state employees).[78] Since urban wives have had a lower participation rate in the labor force than have their husbands, and since a higher proportion of them work in cooperatives than in state enterprises, their health coverage has been poorer.[79]

One would expect that this differential financial burden on the family of care for individual family members must have led to better medical care for members employed in the state sector. Here was a significant intrafamily inequality, one which remained essentially unchanged even after the early 1950s when free medical care for state employees was introduced. As an explanation for this continued inequality, it may be noted that it is totally unrelated to class or to any other aspect of society which the Chinese government has ever recognized as a counterpart to class.[80]

The concentration upon reducing inequalities within small regions has not only an ideological explanation, but also a practical logic. It is such inequalities that are most readily observed by the economically disadvantaged, and thus it was their elimination which would be most likely to have popular appeal. Furthermore, equalization of regional inequalities during a period when national per capita income was not growing sufficiently to pay for it (and certainly this must have been true throughout the 1958–78 years) would have meant depressing the living standards of people who could not be associated with "bad classes" or exploitation.

The Question of Equal Opportunity

Equal opportunities, both of education and of careers, for individuals living in a given area, were of considerable concern to Chinese policy makers from 1966 through most of the 1970s. But there was no concern for equal opportunities across localities, and in particular for rural versus urban inhabitants. Superior opportunity for urbanites has, throughout the period dating from the Great Leap Forward, constituted a recognized property right.

The reduction in the standards of secondary education and the closing of the universities for a time, accompanied by an increasing proportion of the urban population that completed the devalued secondary education, promoted equalization of educational possibilities across social strata within urban areas. When the universities were reopened, the abolition of academic qualifications as the basis for admission maintained this equalization;[81] superior academic socialization within the family for children of intellectuals now became much less relevant than previously to their chances of admission to higher education.

At the same time, job opportunities—in terms of expected income, expected authority, and likely interest of the work—also became more equalized across social strata. If anything, youths receiving greater education had reduced career expectations; this was because of their greater likelihood of being rusticated to nonsuburban rural areas.[82]

But while in the period of the Great Leap Forward and in the years after 1966 there was considerable equalization of career opportunities within the urban population, the same could not be said for the relative opportunities of rural and urban inhabitants.[83] Such opportunities may well have become much more unequal than they had been under the Empire.[84] The enforcement of registration by locality and barriers to change of residence between them grew sharply in degree of strictness after the first half of the 1950s.[85] It is true that considerable rural immigration to the cities occurred during the second half of the 1950s, but the government felt free during the early 1960s to dismiss the rural workers in state enterprises and to compel them to return to their localities of origin. Although the student of manpower policies in socialist countries may at first be surprised at the extensive dismissals from state factories which occurred during the early years of the 1960s, all the literature I have seen indicates that such dismissals were concentrated entirely among the migrants from rural areas.[86] Urbanites seem to have had the same job rights as are observed in European socialist countries.

Place of birth, as opposed to social strata of birth, probably became more important than ever before in modern China in determining the life chances of the population. Within the rural population, place of birth determined access to the differential geographic advantages of land in the domain of one team versus another.[87] As between rural and urban populations, and one urban area versus another, place of birth was of overriding significance during the 1960s and 1970s with regard to expected lifetime living standards.

Issuing of Stock by State Enterprises

The 1980s have seen interest in, and experimentation with, different forms of ownership of public enterprise which have gone further in China than they have in any of the European socialist countries. Concern with how best to raise investment funds for state enterprises, how most effectively to supervise their operational management, and how to motivate their workers has taken the form of the "ownership" question. Apparently first seriously raised in China in 1978 by Dong Fureng, who was later to become the director of the Institute of Economics of the Chinese Academy of Social Sciences, the ownership issue has become a matter of increasingly practical concern since 1984.

In one sense, this question is an old one for centrally planned socialist countries. In all of them, it has taken the form of the proper proportions of private, collective, and state ownership of the means of production. In some, such as the German Democratic Republic, experimentation for a long time took the form of joint ownership of companies by private owners and by the state. But generally, pluralism of types of ownership was viewed as a problem of transition, albeit perhaps a long one, toward complete state ownership as the "higher form" of social ownership. There was little consideration of transforming state-owned enterprises into ones that would be more pluralistically owned.

We have seen the transformation of state enterprises occurring in the 1980s, at least in Hungary and China, with individuals or small groups "contracting" to run small state enterprises, pay a fee to the government, and keep the residual net income as profits. This is a significant variant on what has also been happening in other socialist countries; namely, the granting of permission to private entrepreneurs to create their own new small enterprises.[88] But this development can be viewed as a special case of the managerial argument that centralized state control is inappropriate for production units below a certain critical size. One can interpret the views of Lenin, the founder of the Soviet state, as representing an acceptance of this argument as long ago as 1921.

The Chinese discussion goes a good deal further. It relates, inter alia, to medium and large state enterprises. Some discussants propose handling the problem of motivating workers by allowing them to buy shares in their own enterprise and to participate in the enterprise's profits in the form of dividends. More significantly, others suggest that difficulties with supervision over the management of the enterprise be resolved through stock ownership by different public organizations, which together will form a board of directors to which the enterprise management will be responsible. In these latter proposals, the public organizations also receive dividends and exercise the same authority and responsibility that large shareholders can wield in capitalist firms. It is even argued that shares, whether owned by organizations or individuals, should represent more than entitlements to income and should constitute saleable property.

It is true that stockholding has, in practice, still not gone very far in China.[89] At the end of 1985 in Shanghai, 93 per cent of all shareholders were members of the labor force of the enterprise in which they owned stock, and they had contributed 70 per cent of the total funds raised through stock sales. As of late 1986, stock dividends had been used as a device for getting around governmental restrictions on bonuses and on increases in wages. To counteract this tendency, dividends were being limited nationally to 15 per cent per annum and, de facto, stock equity had become a form of debenture. In early 1987, Shanghai was still one of perhaps only two cities in China with a stock market, and this market had no more than four listed companies with trading frequently (usually?) suspended.[90] As of mid-1987, a Chinese research group concluded that shareholders in Chinese enterprises bear no risk; capital and interest are guaranteed, and dividend and extradividend rates are fixed in advance.[91]

Nevertheless, an openness is being displayed in China with regard to different forms of ownership that had not been seen anywhere else in the world of centrally planned socialist states until at least 1988. The existence of stock markets, although no more than symbolic, is only the most extreme form of this openness. It is the most recent example of the Chinese Communist Party's acceptance of property ownership over the means of production, at least so long as it can be argued that such ownership is divorced from issues of class exploitation.

Hierarchy Among Principals

A conceptual issue still to be faced in this chapter is that of how we should view the relationship between different levels of government. Is it one of hierarchy? Is it a relationship between equals?

If we wished to analyze hierarchical relations within a single organization (e.g., an American corporation), the natural model to use would be that of principal-agent, with each hierarchical level of management except the first being the agent of the top level, and with the top level setting the rules and incentive schemes intended to lead to the maximization of its own objectives. If the organization were highly decentralized, the top level might set such rules and incentives only for the second level, allowing it in turn to set them for the third, etc. In this instance, we could view each level as being the agent of the next higher level, and simultaneously constituting the principal for the one immediately below. The third case is the mixed one, where the top level decentralizes decision making in certain matters but keeps central command over all hierarchical levels with regard to others. In this case, certainly the most prevalent in large organizations, we have a situation in which each managerial body below the second level acts as the agent of multiple principals. It would seem at first sight that this is the same model that we have been using for the analysis of Chinese state industry.

Such a view of the issue would, however, be mistaken. Within a single organization, such as a corporation, no hierarchical level holds property rights which act as constraints on its relationships with higher levels.[92] With regard to Chinese state industry, the hypothesis that has been maintained in this chapter is that such property rights belong to different regional levels of government and that they are fundamental to the operation of industry. Thus Chinese state industry should not be considered as constituting a single organization, and regional levels of government should not be treated as hierarchical levels.

This standpoint need not be taken as implying that the various regional levels of Chinese government are on a par with one another.

That would be clearly erroneous. The relation is not one of equals; overriding instructions can be laid down by the central government, and probably each intermediate level exercises considerable authority over levels lower down. But this is a phenomenon to which we are also accustomed in societies based on private property; governments there enjoy and exercise powers of eminent domain. Furthermore, if one accepts, as applied to capitalist economies, the view that "the power to tax is the power to destroy," and if one considers the judiciary system as a part of government, then private property rights in a country such as the United States exist only at the discretion of government. Owners of private property are not equals with government: yet this fact does not imply that their relations with government should be treated as those existing between agent and principal.[93]

Self-restraint by higher regional bodies of government in China (promoted, of course, through considerations of domestic politics as well as of principle) is fundamental for the continuation of property rights in the hands of lower bodies. In one interpretation of my model, such self-restraint is exercised to prevent the larger Nash-equilibrium game from breaking down. The point, however, is that such self-restraint now has a history dating uninterruptedly from at least the early 1970s and probably from about 1966, and that it has continued even with major changes in government.[94] The nature of property rights held by regional governmental bodies in China may change drastically in the future; but, given the degree of security that these rights have enjoyed in the recent past and currently continue to enjoy, this is irrelevant for the analysis of their existing status.

Implicit in my hypothesis in this chapter—that state enterprises are agents with multiple principals—is the assumption that the enterprises have no property rights of their own. While their actions may be motivated by considerations of wages, bonuses, and other forms of income, enterprises should not be viewed as maximizers of their own wealth. This assumption is contrary to the desires of some (but not all) Chinese reformers.[95] Some Western analysts proceed as though they believe that this assumption no longer holds.[96] This chapter has not presented any evidence justifying the assumption. This question will, instead, be left to chapter 5 in which there will be a full treatment of incentives at the enterprise level.

On the basis of this assumption, we have seen in this chapter the mustering of evidence related to multilevel supervision that attempts to support the hypothesis. In chapters 3 and 4 I present other types of evidence. (See, particularly, tables 3.8, 3.10, and 4.2.) Analysis of the implications of the hypothesis for the functioning of the Chinese economy is postponed to chapter 8.

Appendix: Case Studies of
Supervisory Authority Over Enterprises

Multilevel Supervision

The first of the nine enterprises that were under multilevel supervision was analyzed above. The remaining eight are treated here.

The machine tool factory is a case which conflicts sharply with the multiple-principals hypothesis (2.7). Here, the plant has been directly supervised either by the province or by lower governmental bodies, and the enterprise's profits have gone to these bodies since about the time that state enterprises were divided into "centrally led" and "other" in 1953. Yet it was the Center which seems to have financed virtually all of the net investment in the enterprise; certainly this was the case during the period for which we have data (1975–82). In exchange for such ownership by the Center, the Center has historically kept part of the enterprise's production for central distribution (allocating materials needed to produce these centrally distributed products), with the province distributing the remainder of planned output. This division of the enterprise's product was probably important through 1979, but ceased to be afterward as the distribution problem for the enterprise's products became that of finding customers to absorb capacity production.

The conflict over authority in the multilevel supervisory relationship does not, however, involve the Center in any significant fashion; rather, it occurs between two local governments: the municipality and the county. Aside from the product distribution and materials allocation reserved to the Center and to the province, both of which had become relatively unimportant by the 1980s, the municipality has all relevant planning and control functions except for one. Appointment and dismissal of the Party and administrative leadership is in the hands of the county.

The stake of the county in the fortunes of the machine tool factory seems minimal. It is true that this is the largest plant in the county, and that the county receives an annual plan of industrial output and sets the output plan for the enterprise in terms of its fair share of the county plan.[97] Yet the county officials declare that the county suffers no particular penalties if it fails to fulfill its countywide industrial output plan. In fact, this statement has not really been tested, since this plan was fulfilled even in a year when the machine tool plant failed to meet the target given by the county. The enterprise as such is not formally evaluated in terms of its fulfillment of the output plan established by the county, but rather against the standard of the physical output plan decreed by the municipality. Nevertheless, the top managers of the plant are personally quite dependent upon the county.

Their dependence upon the county leadership was shown in a year when the plant's work was described by the municipality as quite satisfactory, but when it was nevertheless condemned by the county and an official reprimand went into the Party record of the director. We do not know the effect of this reprimand, but we do know that the director was dismissed some three and a half years later. The director, as a resident of the town which was the county seat, presumably had no right to move to any larger urban area. His personal fate was more likely in the long run to be under the control of the county than of the municipality.

How to explain the split authority between the county and municipality? The Chinese researchers on the project offer an historical explanation: the official authority over the enterprise has changed frequently from province to municipality to prefecture to county. Individual supervisory functions have been lost in the shuffle.[98] What is relevant from the point of view of the hypothesis is that neither the municipality nor the county has any ownership claim on the enterprise, although both provide some important inputs.[99] With neither having such a claim, the hypothesis offers no prediction as to the division of authority between the two.

The cement factory is another enterprise in which there is a sharp separation between control over product distribution and allocation of materials (which are in the hands of a national ministry) and control over Party and administrative appointments (which is in the hands of the province). In this case, however, financial control and the award of profits were combined with power over appointments. Indeed, this is the only one of the twenty organizations in our sample that fits what has sometimes been described in the English-language literature as the classic form of control over large-scale enterprises that existed after the transfer at the beginning of the 1970s of almost all the ministerial enterprises.[100] In accord with the "classical schema," the enterprise had been transferred from ministerial to provincial control in 1969. I classify this case as weakly conflicting with the hypothesis.

Despite the fact that the province was the recipient both of profits and amortization funds from the cement factory, with the central government receiving none of these, net fixed investment all came from the central government. Even a major expansion decided upon in 1982 was to have at least two-thirds of its financing provided by the national government. The two-thirds figure was suggested by the national authorities, but the provincial authorities insisted upon 100 per cent central financing. In mid-1984, the expansion was still delayed by the failure of the two parties to agree on this critical point.

Thus the property rights hypothesis offers no explanation of the division of authority observed in this enterprise. The case resembles precisely that of the smelter during 1971–83. The parallel suggests that it is not impossible that ownership will eventually triumph as in the smelter case, and that the residual supervisory functions will be transferred to central authorities. It is for this reason that the case is categorized as only weakly conflicting with the hypothesis.

The steel plant bears some similarity to the cement factory, in that profits go to the province (being shared by it with the municipality as its agent), but all investments and the bulk of materials supplied are at the charge of the Center, while output allocation is by the ministry.[101] The transfer of the enterprise from central to provincial leadership also occurred in the same year, 1969. But the key difference between the two enterprises is that power over Party and administrative appointments in the steel plant is held at the national level; thus, there was no substantial de facto division of central managerial control in the steel enterprise, even though the provincial leadership was described as "primary." I classify this case as weakly confirming the hypothesis.

The province's right to the financial returns earned by the enterprise seems to be a pure gift, made by the Center at a time when finance was much less important than allocations.[102] No managerial powers accompanied this gift.[103] We do not know whether the Center ever tried to take back these funds. We are told that the national government returned some enterprises to strictly central supervision in 1978 and attempted to return a great many more in 1980, but that political obstacles prevented it from carrying through the latter move.

The pump enterprise was under the joint supervision of the province and of a central ministry, which planned output and quality and which received monthly reports as to the fulfillment of these plans. The ministry has also in the past provided the bulk of the enterprise's fixed investment, and still supplies half of the planned allocations of materials, the province allocating the rest.[104] The province does virtually all other planning, receives the enterprise's profits, and makes Party and managerial appointments. It also provided some fixed investments to the enterprise in all but one year during the 1975–82 period. Substantial fixed investment in the enterprise was approved by the Center for the first half of the 1980s, but half of it was in the form of a bank loan for which the province would have been required to be the guarantor and, during at least two years, the province failed to approve the investment because of its doubts about the ability of the enterprise to pay off the loan.

The situation of the pump enterprise appears to be fully consistent with the ownership hypothesis. I classify it as providing strong support. Both the Center and the province invest significant resources and reap benefits, both exercise control. It is noteworthy that in the 1980s, with planning of output losing much of its significance for the product range of the enterprise, the ministry entered as a participant in the sphere of new importance: financial planning. It is the ministry, not the province, which determines the terms of profit sharing between the enterprise and the province. Here we have genuinely joint multilevel investment, benefits, and control.

The forestry and lumbering enterprise is very similar to the pump plant with regard to ownership and is classified similarly. Essentially all of the production of the enterprise is allocated; the national ministry takes some 85 per cent of the main product (timber), while the province has the right to distribute the rest of the timber and, apparently, all of the byproducts. Each governmental level allocates some of the necessary intermediate inputs. The national ministry is responsible for output planning and for investment decisions, while the province receives all of the profits and appoints the Party and administrative leaders. During the period of 1975–82 (the only years for which we have data), the Center and the province both made investments; the province's investments were 32 per cent of those of the Center.[105]

This situation of mixed control was the outcome of a history of two decentralizations and recentralizations. The forestry and lumbering enterprise began as centrally supervised in 1953, when the division of state enterprises between central and local supervision was first made. It was decentralized to the provincial level in 1958 (the first great national decentralization of enterprises), recentralized sometime during the first half of the 1960s, and then once again decentralized to the provincial level in 1970 (in the second national wave of decentralization). At this time, apparently all control over planning was put into provincial hands. Only in 1975–76 was the current supervisory pattern developed.

Another enterprise with multilevel leadership was a watch and clock factory which was officially under the sole supervision of its municipality. All of the planning instructions, appointments of Party and administrative leaders, and financial supervision came from this level. Nevertheless, provincial authorities entered directly into supervision through marketing and financial arrangements.

Some 70 per cent of the total sales of the enterprise in 1983, and a higher proportion earlier, were to a provincially controlled Commerce Department which wholesaled the production throughout the province. Since markets represented the key constraint on the growth of this enterprise, control over such a high proportion of market access represented a significant form of provincial control. With regard to finance, the provincial financial bureau had the authority to waive collection of sales tax for a period of one or more years on certain types of watches, and similarly to waive certain taxes so as to release funds for the repayment of bank loans.[106]

For this enterprise, however, there seems to be no special need to explain the role of the province. With regard to marketing, provincial control was only that of a traditional monopsony purchaser whose position had been eroded over time but not eliminated. The same power would have existed in a purely private capitalist economy.[107] As to finance, the tax revenues of the province itself are substantially involved, and it is for this reason that the decision is taken above the level of the municipality.

Thus, in this instance of multilevel supervision, there is really nothing that requires explanation. I classify this case as irrelevant to the hypothesis.

The next organization with multilevel leadership consisted of an amalgamation of petrochemical plants which had occurred in 1981. The amalgamation was an effort to resolve the problem of split supervision over a complex of plants that were closely integrated vertically; however, the split supervision of concern was not multilevel, but rather consisted of supervision being carried out by different central ministries.

Nevertheless, multilevel supervision prior to the merger did exist for five of the six plants concerned. Three of these had as their "leading body" a single municipality and two had the province. Presumably, supervision by the leading body consisted of the usual financial form and, possibly, of the appointment of Party and administrative leadership. No information is available as to the sharing of profits. One source says that profits on most products went solely to the central ministries, while another talks of profit receipts both by province and municipality; it seems probable that all three participated, but that the lion's share went to the Center. Supervision by central ministries (only one ministry being involved for any given plant) was not restricted to the combination of output planning and allocation of both products and materials. Unlike any other case in our sample, it was also of a day-by-day operational nature. Nothing is known of the financial sources of investment funds, nor of the dates when the plants came under their respective leading bodies.

After the merger, the company was first placed under the supervision of the province, but after a year it was transferred to supervision by a national corporation of the industry. Some 70 to 80 per cent of the profits were to go to national authorities, with the remainder going to the province. (The municipality's share was expropriated in the merger process; one would guess that financial compensation in some form was provided by the province.)

Here is an enterprise about which too little is known to tell whether it provides support or contradiction to the ownership hypothesis. But in either case, not much is involved. Control and benefits were always primarily in the hands of central authorities, and the merger further consolidated this situation. Although the merger was caused entirely by an effort to eliminate the presence of different supervising bodies in coordinating a production process which ideally should be fairly well integrated, all of the interview respondents treated the problem as one that was restricted to the difficulty of relations among the central ministries themselves.

The last of the multilevel enterprises is a textile plant producing cloth made both of chemical fiber and of a local sort of hemp (ramie), but not of cotton. Presumably because it is not a producer either of cotton yarn or of cotton cloth, and because it is heavily dependent for its raw material on a product grown within the province, it may be unique among the five textile enterprises in our sample. It is the only one for which physical quotas of materials allocations and product distribution for the bulk of its products are apparently not included in the product and materials aggregates given by central authorities to the province. I classify this case as providing very weak refutation of the hypothesis.

The province plans the enterprise's output in physical terms and provides most of the allocated materials. The municipality does the financial planning, determines enterprise bonuses, sets the output plan as expressed in value terms, seems to make the Party and administrative appointments, and receives the profits. The province and municipality both receive part of the amortization allowance set aside by the enterprise. Here we have genuinely split authority although, curiously, it is not one about which any complaints were made in the interviews.

The known organizational history of the plant begins a decade after its opening in 1966. Between 1975 and 1980, the enterprise was under joint provincial and municipal subordination. At that time, all the plan indicators for the enterprise were provided by the province, but we have no information as to the handling of profits. The municipality determined bonus payments in the years when this was relevant

(1978–80). It would seem that neither the province nor the municipality made any significant investments at least from 1975 onward.

In 1981 the enterprise was transferred, as part of what was said to be a broader administrative decentralization at that time,[108] to what is described as sole leadership by the municipality. The meaning of this change is, however, uncertain.[109] Profits clearly came to be planned by the municipality. Output in value terms also seems to have begun only then to be planned by the city. But the latter must be considered irrelevant, since the output-value plan is not given to the enterprise until the end of the year, at a time when it cannot have any effect. This plan was said to be established in terms of what is required to meet the municipality's total plan of industrial output, although the logic of this escapes me in view of the timing.

Between 1980 and 1985, the municipality was expected to pay a certain quota of profit revenue annually to the province, and was permitted to keep 60 per cent of all above-quota revenue. In fact, however, the municipality does not seem to have earned its base quota in any year after 1980, and thus presumably was excused from such payments. In practice, therefore, the municipality would seem not to have been affected financially by any increase in its share of the enterprise's profits after the enterprise was transferred to its "sole administration."

So far as one can tell from the interview notes, there was seriously divided authority over the enterprise only after 1980; until then, the province appeared to call the shots. Thereafter, one would have thought that there would have been problems. But as I mentioned, no complaints as to the multiheaded leadership were made.

To the degree that multilevel leadership became significant in the 1980s, and this is unclear from the record, it would appear to be completely unconnected with ownership and instead to be linked to a general ideological policy in the province. There is no reason to believe that there was any change in the benefits going to different levels of government.

Choice of Sole Supervisor

The four provincial enterprises not treated in the text of chapter 2 are all producers of textiles. Two of them predate the liberation period, and neither the province nor the central government seems to have made substantial investments in them. In both of these enterprises, all planning is done by the provincial authorities. Such planning is constrained by national output plans and materials allocations provided to the province by the central government in aggregative fashion for the province's entire textile industry. Only in one case do we have a report of the Ministry of Textiles making a decision related directly to one of these plants; this concerned a major expansion for the 1980s, which was to be financed by bank loan and which the enterprise (but not the province) was very reluctant to accept.

Of the other two textile enterprises, one was built sometime between 1949 and the mid-1960s, but there is no information as to the level of government which financed its construction. We have investment data for this enterprise for the 1975–82 period. During these years, there was investment by the province but none by the central government. This plant, like one of the first two, is an unintegrated mill producing grey yarn and cloth, with no finishing or dyeing facilities; it is integrated with the next stage of production through provincial planning. The second enterprise is the result of a 1978 merger of about eighteen different textile mills, primarily involved in weaving, but continuing through later stages of production. Yet it is not integrated, having no spinning capacity and appearing to contain only about half of the finishing capacity needed to process its cloth. No information is available as to the sources of investment for its constituent mills. There is no reason, however, to believe that any appreciable amount came from the Center. All supervision is carried out by the provincial authorities.

In summary, it seems fair to categorize all except the last of the four textile enterprises operating under single-level supervision as supporting hypothesis (2.7) concerning the link between ownership and control, and thus having multilevel supervision being a result of the existence of multiple principals for an individual enterprise. (For the last of these enterprises, we simply do not have sufficient information to view it as supporting or refuting the hypothesis.) On the other hand, in all of the four textile plants under the leadership of a province, it is the Center which controls product allocation and the allocation of the principal materials, although in aggregative form at the provincial level rather than at the enterprise level.

One might choose to describe this situation as representing "ownership" by the Ministry of Textiles. However, I think that such a view of ownership would be mistaken. Cotton textiles were subject to national consumer rationing until 1984, and the bulk of them of course went to rural inhabitants. Such rationing of final product implied the allocation of the raw cotton. Since pure cotton cloth in 1983 still constituted 61 per cent of total cloth production,[110] it was to have been expected that national control should have been extended to include chemical fibers and mixed cotton-chemical fiber cloth.

Not surprisingly, textile production was concentrated in urban areas; indeed, such concentration was furthered by the continuation after 1978 of the prohibition of the right of all rural enterprises to engage in textile production.[111] Three of the four provinces that supervised the textile plants in our sample constituted primarily urban areas (they were the administrative units of Beijing, Shanghai, and Tianjin), and they thus must have produced primarily for sale in other provinces and for exports.[112] Thus, planned central distribution of the textile products of at least these provinces and the accompanying allocation of the necessary materials represent nothing more than the decision to have planned (rather than market-determined) production and distribution of these items.

Furthermore, such "ownership" by the Center gave it no financial rights. Considering this financial aspect, as well as the uniqueness of this industry within our sample, I prefer not to treat the Ministry of Textile's position as constituting ownership.

3

PLANNING AS COORDINATION

In chapter 2 I tested the multiple-principals hypothesis (2.7) by examining whether differential patterns of supervision over individual state-owned enterprises are correlated with property rights of principals that were obtained either through investment or by tradition. In order to conduct this test, the entire known history of the sample enterprises was scrutinized.

In this chapter, I examine the annual plans set for the sample enterprises and the levels of plan fulfillment obtained. To the degree that plans are established for purposes of national coordination of the outputs and inputs of different sectors (the null hypothesis of this chapter), one would expect that the nature of the planning targets established should be independent of the property rights held by particular principals. Instead, the analysis here will show that the nature of the plans set, and particularly the degree of ambitiousness of the plan targets, is a function of the pattern of property rights exercised by different governmental bodies in the individual enterprises.

The above paragraph describes the contribution of this chapter to the integrative theme of property rights. But I will go beyond this to discuss planning more broadly, concentrating on the differences between Chinese and Soviet–East European planning for the state sector. This treatment is related to the underlying thesis of the book as to the uniqueness of China as a socialist planned society.

The level at which an output or allocation plan is set in a socialist planned society can serve two quite distinct functions. The first is that of coordination of the inputs and outputs of different production units of the economy, replacing the marketplace wholly or partially in this function. The second function is that of incentive, attempting to motivate the personnel of the unit to improve their efficiency as measured in terms of all inputs other than labor effort.[1] This chapter will deal only with the coordination function of planning; discussion of the motivational function will be postponed to chapter 5.

Writing in the period before marketization reforms began, Dwight Perkins observed that "In China, (formal) plans are the principal means of controlling current enterprise operations. There is really no alternative. No market forces exist to govern the direction of factory production."[2] I will show how Perkins' first sentence should be modified and nuanced, even with regard to the medium-sized and large state-owned enterprises, not only for the period since reforms began but also for the second half of the 1970s.

The Macroeconomic Setting

In inquiring as to the extent to which planning serves to coordinate the national economy, a first question that may be posed is the degree of product coverage and detail that is imbedded in the plans. Unfortunately, these two matters cannot be disentangled since the information that we have for China relates only to the total number of allocated products. This number is affected both by the coverage of central allocation (e.g., whether steel plate is centrally allocated at all) and by the degree of detail treated in the allocation process (e.g., if steel plate is allocated, whether it is all allocated together or whether there is separate allocation of different size classifications of steel plate).

When we consider planning from the standpoint of coordination, we see that production planning and allocation of the products to other users (including organizations selling to final consumers) are mirror images, at least theoretically.[3] Thus either set of data constitutes a satisfactory information source. For China, and for the Soviet Union as a standard of comparison, we have data as to the number of separate items that are centrally allocated. These are shown in table 3.1.

It can be seen from table 3.1 that the number of items allocated centrally are of one to two different orders of magnitude in the two countries. This has been the case throughout the history of the people's Republic of China.[4] The most relevant figures are those for all allocations taken together, and here the available China/USSR proportions range between 1 per cent in 1973 and 4 per cent at the end of the 1960s. Even when possible ameliorative factors are taken into account, there is no change in this picture.[5]

The second question is restricted to those individual items which are centrally allocated in whole or in part; for each of these individually, what is the proportion of their national output which was allocated by the Center? Here, as well, we have a difference in kind between China and the Soviet Union. In the Soviet Union, as in the other East European centrally planned economies, there is virtually 100 per cent coverage. In China, throughout at least the years between 1965 and 1986, a large proportion of such major intermediate products as coal, lumber, and cement has escaped the central allocation process (see table 2.1).

Table 3.1 Number of Products Allocated Centrally in China and
the Soviet Union

Years	By Other Than Producing Ministries		By Producing Ministries		Central Bodies Combined	
	China	USSR	China	USSR	China	USSR
1950	8		0		8	
1952	55		0		55	
1953	112		115		227	
1957	231		301		532	
1959	67		218		285	
1965	370	20,438	222		592	
1966	326	21,655	253	0	579	21,655
1968		14,498		1,814		16,312
1972	49		168		217	
1973	50	8,426	567	40,000+	617	48,426+
1978	53		636		689	
1979	210		581		791	
1982	256		581		837	
1983		9,200				
1985	23					

Notes: For China, the first column consists of allocations by the Central Planning
Commission, with the cooperation of the State Material Supply Bureau. For the
USSR, it consists of allocations made separately by the two comparable bodies. Some
additional intermediate years are available from the sources for China, but they add
nothing to the picture given above.

Central allocations include those which are made directly by central bodies to individual enterprises, and those that are made to intermediate bodies which, in turn,
allocate further down.

Sources: China data are from Naughton (1986, 128); Tang Zongkun, "Supply and Marketing," in Tidrick and Chen (1987), 229; and Wu Jinglian and Zhao Renwei, "The
Dual Pricing System in China's Industry," *J.C.E.* 11, no. 3 (September 1987): 312. The
first two (secondary) sources for China refer to different original sources which cover
slightly different years, but overlap for the vast majority of them. Identical figures are
quoted in both sources for the overlapping years. (However, these data cannot be
reconciled with those for a related series given by Christine Wong, in Perry and Wong
[1985], 259; Wong shows figures very similar to the China totals in the sources used in
the table for all pre-1978 years except for 1958, but her figures for 1978–81 are only 8
to 30 percent of the table's totals.)

USSR data for 1966 and 1968 are from Ivanov, Lokshin, and Demichev (1969,
338–40); for 1965 and 1973 they are from Kurotchenko (1975, 82); and for 1983 they
are from Ukrainskii and Kiperman (1984, 89, 92) (these later data are either for 1983
or for a year close to it). K. Kiss ("Domestic Integration of the Soviet Economy," Hungarian Scientific Council for World Economy, *Trends in World Economy*, no. 56 [1987],
43) estimates Soviet allocations by central bodies combined as being some 100,000
during the first half of the 1980s; I would, however, treat this figure with great
caution.

Putting together the answers to the above two questions, it is clear that national planning in China has never played the same sort of coordinating role that it has and does in the Soviet Union. Of course, this does not imply that the forces replacing central planning in this coordination function have necessarily been those of the market. To a considerable degree, particularly in the later pre-reform era, the Chinese economy was "cellular" ("composed of a myriad of small discrete units," each of which is highly autarkic), to use the expression of Audrey Donnithorne.[6] Nevertheless, the marketplace is and has been important.

On the basis of a fairly substantial project of enterprise interviews conducted back in 1966, a Canadian scholar reported that at that time the managements of many of the enterprises were allowed independently to determine 5 to 30 per cent of their planned outputs (Richman 1969, 474). A Chinese study of 429 enterprises (241 of which were large or medium-sized) in 1984 indicated that 24 per cent of the sample used market channels to meet over 40 per cent of their raw material requirements, and 49 per cent of the sample directly marketed 40 per cent of their products.[7] Thus the market is currently important as a coordinator, and the same seems to have been true earlier, at least during the years of 1961–65.

A similarity between China and the Soviet Union has been the relative unimportance of multiyear plans as a device for providing macroeconomic coordination.[8] In China, political stability was insufficient (except for the 1952–57 planning period) to have allowed five-year plans to be used successfully prior to the 1980s; during these later years, central control over the key variable of investment was insufficient. Five year plans seem never, even in theory, to have been brought down to the level of the individual enterprise.[9] In the Soviet Union, they were supposed to be set at the enterprise level for the 1928–33 plan period, but were not in practice. The next effort was postponed to the 1970–74 plan, and since then the five-year plans have always applied in theory to the enterprise. Soviet discussions in print, however, would suggest that they have never become truly operational. Both in China and in the Soviet Union, annual plans are the operational ones and provide whatever coordination is supplied by the planning mechanism.

Plan Fulfillment by the Individual Enterprise

The Soviet Enterprise

A proper picture of plan fulfillment by the typical Soviet enterprise must be put together from various sources. The resulting description seems to be reliable, but has serious problems of completeness with regard to one feature that is key for comparisons with China. The aspect neglected in the Soviet data is that of the level of fulfillment of the annual plan as initially approved, as opposed to the fulfillment of the figure that was still officially designated as of the end of the planning year.

First, and highly important, all available data relate performance to the annual plan, as it existed at the very end of the planning period. The Soviet author who has been most concerned with the issue of the difference between the initial plan and the final one has asserted that Soviet ministries themselves do not keep records as to the fulfillment of the initial annual enterprise plans.[10]

When we view the subject of plan fulfillment from the perspective of coordination, there is an obvious disadvantage to the use of this end-of-period criterion: the coordination schemes at the beginning of the year must have been based upon the initial plans. On the other hand, central coordinators can scarcely be expected to have ignored throughout the year developments that occurred during the course of the period, and such developments are better reflected in the end-of-year plans (called "final" from now on) than in the initial ones.[11]

We have evidence, however, that more is involved in Soviet plan adjustment than simply the taking account of developments. If plans were modified during the course of the year solely so as to reflect changes in stochastic variables that affected the objective possibilities of the enterprise to meet the original targets, then the distribution of enterprise fulfillment of final plans would be an overlay of the normal distribution on the distribution of fulfillment of initial plans. A Soviet author, Shaikin, has been interested in testing this hypothesis. He does not have data from a random sample, but presents an analysis of about two hundred Soviet enterprises. Using a x^2 test, he is unable to reject the hypothesis that deviations of plan fulfillment for sales are distributed normally around the average of initial-plan fulfillment. But he can reject the hypothesis with regard to fulfillment of the final plan; the proportion of enterprises failing to fulfill their final plan was far less than would be predicted under the normality assumption. Moreover, although the average percentage of plan fulfillment is only about 0.8 per cent higher when judged according to the final plan rather than by the initial plan, this difference is well outside of a 99 per cent confidence interval.[12] Thus figures as to fulfillment of final plans are somewhat misleading as an indicator of coordination, but we can do little more with this problem than to state the caveat.

The best evidence that we possess for showing the dimensions of the problem, although not its solution, is a comparison of data for the USSR as a whole for 1977–79. The number of enterprises failing to fulfill their plan for the first eleven months of the year ranged between 221 and 236 per cent of the number that did not fulfill their annual plan. The Soviet author who presented these statistics explained the discrepancy primarily by changes made in the annual plan during December.[13] However, although these data display a considerable degree of plan change during a single month, they do not indicate that such changes represented other than formal recognition of a situation that national coordinators had been aware of many months earlier.

Data as to fulfillment of final output plans by ministries are available for 1966–78. These show the mean fulfillment by all industrial ministries to have ranged annually between 100.16 and 102.07 per cent, with a variance ranging between 0.75 and 1.68 per cent.[14] This means that, under the assumption of normality as to ministerial plan fulfillment, a 95 per cent confidence interval for ministerial plan fulfillment in a given year would be between 99.3 and 103.9. However, since the distribution was non-normal, at least during 1969–77, the upper end of the confidence limit is somewhat higher.[15]

Some aggregative data are available as to the proportion of industrial enterprises that fail to fulfill 100 per cent of their final plans. The annual figures (presumably for output) in all of Soviet industry during the first half of the 1950s ranged between 31 and 40 per cent.[16] This was below, but at least in the ballpark, of what might have been expected from a normal distribution around 100 per cent fulfillment. The picture in the post-Stalin years for fulfillment of final output plans has been radically different, but the figures for other important plan indicators have declined only modestly. Annual data with respect to all industrial enterprises in either the Russian Republic or the entire Soviet Union show the following percentage of enterprises that failed to fulfill their final plans:[17]

> For sales (a proxy for production): 6 to 7 per cent during 1976 and 1977;
> For labor productivity (a major determinant of bonuses in that year and for the two previous ones): 16 per cent in 1976;
> For profits (the major determinant of bonuses for "reformed" enterprises during 1966–70): 18 to 22 per cent for the average of 1966–70 and for 1975 and 1976;
> For costs (a major determinant of bonuses during these five years): 21 per cent for the 1961–65 average.

We do not have any good data as to the proportion of enterprises that produce substantially more than their planned output.

Shaikin divided his sample into two groups of about one hundred enterprises each. He found that 9.4 per cent of the enterprises in one group, and 14.5 per cent in the other exceeded their final sales plans by 6 per cent or more. (The respective figures for the initial plans were 7.1 and 26.6 per cent.) [18] But we have no idea how representative the sample is, and the high intergroup variance for fulfillment of initial plans is disturbing. No other figures are available.

On this issue, we can rely only upon the conventional wisdom among both Soviet and Western scholars that Soviet enterprises rarely overfulfill substantially those plan indicators that are important in determining the bonuses earned by the enterprise staff: the reason given is the fear of a "ratchet effect" upon the plans set by the superior body for the following periods.

East European Enterprises

In the German Democratic Republic, a somewhat higher proportion of sales plans (final version) of enterprises seem in the 1970s to have been fulfilled than was the case in the Soviet Union. A comparison of average sales plan overfulfillment (some 1.6–1.7 per cent) for all of industry, with the low percentage of firms failing to meet targets (2 to 5–10 per cent), shows that the proportion of enterprises fulfilling more than 106 per cent of their targets is unlikely to have exceeded the Soviet statistics. [19] Cost-reduction targets, however, may not show nearly such high plan fulfillment; one-third of enterprises failed to meet their plans for the first half of 1973. (But recall from the Soviet data that, since it is the annual plan that matters, we would expect final annual plans to be better fulfilled than are their six-month components.) Still, a high official in the research institute of the German State Planning Commission stated in 1970 that he believed it was safe to estimate that over 90 per cent of all industrial enterprises fulfill their annual final plan for *all* of their obligatory planned targets. We seem to have here a situation not too dissimilar from the Soviet, but better with regard to plan indicators other than that for sales (output). The only additional apparent difference, and this is uncertain, is that plan changes for enterprises have been less common in the GDR than in the USSR. [20]

Interviews in six industrial ministries in Romania, covering plan fulfillment by their enterprises during 1969 and 1970, showed the data as to final plans shown in table 3.2. [21] As can be seen from the table, the proportion of enterprises not fulfilling their plans other than for production (sales) is more like the proportion in the GDR than that in the Soviet Union. The proportion overfulfilling by a sub-

Table 3.2 Final Plan Fulfillment in Romania, 1969–70
(as a percentage of all enterprises)

Type of Final Plan	Nonfulfillment	Overfulfillment[a]
Production	5–9	27
Profitability	10	23–25
Labor productivity	12	26–27

[a]By ≥3 percent.

stantial amount may well not differ from either the East German or Soviet patterns.

However, the Romanian pattern is radically different from the East German in that it is much more likely in Romania that enterprise plans will be changed during the year. Modifications were quite common for all plan dimensions in the sample ministries. In one ministry, the planning director took the position that deviations of enterprises in either direction from 100 per cent plan fulfillment were primarily due to errors in the plan assignments which he himself had given, rather than to the operating performance of the units themselves. Thus, depending on enterprises' fulfillment of their initial plans, he altered unit plans during the planning year to the degree that his own constraints permitted.[22]

The Sample Chinese Enterprises

Questionnaire data were assembled from the various enterprises with regard to their initial annual plan, their final plan, and their actual performance along the dimensions of value of output in constant prices, of profits in current prices, and of the physical output of principal individual products. The data were for each year of the 1975–82 period. If each enterprise had provided data for each of these years during which the enterprise existed, we would have had 72 enterprise-year observations for 1975–78 and 78 for 1979–82. One of the enterprises had had many recent mergers; it was able to assemble performance data, but not plan data, for the enterprises that had been taken over. Eliminating the pertinent years, the maximum number of observations possible are reduced to 68 and 75 for the two periods. The actual number of observations are given in tables 3.3a and 3.3b, and the resulting response rate for the nineteen organizations that responded at all is shown in table 3.4.

Since value of output is measured in constant prices, an anonymous reviewer suggested that plan fulfillment might be overstated in 1981 because the base of constant prices changed in that year from

1970 constant prices to 1980 constant prices. Thus, it would be possible that the plan might be specified in the former prices, while the plan results were expressed in the latter. However, I found that testing of average fulfillment of value of output in 1980 versus 1981 shows that the 1980 figures were higher (although insignificantly) for fulfillment of both the original plan and the final plan. Fulfillment in 1981 was indeed higher than the average for 1979–82, but the difference was insignificant at even the 10 per cent level.

Only fifteen of the twenty organizations provided any information as to individual physical products, but this is perhaps not too surprising.[23] However, it is unclear why the response rate differed so much between value of output and profits. Similarly, it is not obvious why the response rate with regard to the initial plan was neither much higher nor much lower. The problem lies in the nature of the source data for the earlier years that were available to the functional

Table 3.3a Performance As a Percentage of Value-of-Output and Profit Plans (in number of observations from the sample)

Fulfillment Percentages	Value-of-Output			Profit		
	Final Plan	Initial Plan	Final Plan for Firms with Initial Plans	Final Plan	Initial Plan	Final Plan for Firms with Initial Plans
1975–78	61	39	39	43	21	21
<70	5	3	3	4	4	4
70–89	2	4	2	2	1	1
90–99	5	2	3	2	1	1
100	4	4	3	1	1	1
101–10	25	13	15	9	1	1
111–20	12	6	7	16	7	7
121–30	6	5	5	2	1	1
>130	2	2	1	7	5	5
1979–82	65	47	46	53	28	28
<70	0	1	0	0	1	0
70–89	0	1	0	1	0	0
90–99	2	2	2	1	2	1
100	6	4	6	3	1	2
101–10	24	14	16	9	7	5
111–20	18	13[a]	13	10	1	3
121–30	8	7	5	7	5	5
>130	7	5	4	22	11	12

[a] One of these observations is for an enterprise for which there were no final plan data.

Table 3.3b Performance As a Percentage of Physical Output Plans
(in number of observations from the sample)

	Combined				Main Product			
	All Observations		Common Observations Only		All Observations		Common Observations Only	
Fulfillment Percentages	Final Plan	Initial Plan	Final Plan	Initial Plan	Final Plan	Initial Plan	Final Plan	Initial Plan
1975–78	104	64	59	59	42	25	25	25
<70	9	1	0	0	5	0	0	0
70–89	7	5	5	5	2	2	2	2
90–99	10	7	6	7	5	1	3	1
100	16	8	8	8	3	1	1	1
101–10	43	27	28	25	18	11	12	11
111–20	13	8	9	8	7	4	5	4
121–30	2	3	2	1	1	1	1	1
>130	4	5	1	5	1	5	1	5
1979–82	123	86	81	81	52	34	33	33
<70	3	6	3	5	1	1	1	1
70–89	0	4	0	4	0	2	0	2
90–99	3	8	3	8	1	2	1	2
100	14	9	12	9	6	4	6	4
101–10	71	38	47	37	27	15	16	14
111–20	21	12	12	10	12	4	7	4
121–30	2	4	1	4	2	2	1	2
>130	9	5	3	4	3	4	1	4

Table 3.4 Response Rate (in percentages)

	Final Plan		Initial Plan	
Type of Plan	1975–78	1979–82	1975–78	1979–82
Value of output	94	87	60	63
Profit	66	71	32	37
Physical output (single main product)	62	69	33	45

department in the enterprise which was filling out the relevant part of the questionnaire.

My impression is that the raw material on the basis of which the questionnaires were answered consisted primarily of contemporary reports that had been filed by the enterprise with planning authorities or with statistical agencies. If this is correct, I would have to conclude that different municipalities, provinces and ministries had disparate information requirements (particularly with regard to submitting planning targets), and that these also fluctuated for the same body from one year to another. Such absence of standardization would, of course, not be surprising. An alternative explanation is that the plan data did not appear in the filed reports, but had to be searched for in the enterprise files. So long as either or both solutions explain the variation in response rate, no questions of accuracy are raised. But might the variation be partially explained by a different readiness to guess that may have existed in the various organizations? Fortunately, this latter explanation is unlikely to be a large part of the reason for the differential response rate as to the value-of-output and profit plan; while its contribution to responses for initial plans cannot be determined, reported differences between fulfillment of initial plan and final plan are at least reasonable.

Table 3.5 is the fundamental table analyzing the proportion of enterprises that fulfilled different plan indicators by varying percentages, and has been calculated from tables 3.3a and 3.3b.

Table 3.5 Performance As a Proportion of Plan
(in percentages of observations)

					Physical Output			
	Value of Output		Profit		Combined		Main Product	
Fulfillment Percentages	Final	Initial	Final	Initial	Final	Initial	Final	Initial
1975–78								
≤89	11	18	14	24	15	9	17	8
90–99	8	5	5	5	10	11	12	4
100	6	10	2	5	15	12	7	4
101–10	41	33	21	5	41	42	43	44
111–20	20	15	37	33	12	12	17	16
>120	13	18	21	28	6	12	5	24
Number of observations	61	39	43	21	104	64	42	25
1979–82								
≤89	0	4	2	4	2	12	2	9
90–99	3	4	2	7	2	9	2	6
100	9	8	6	4	11	10	12	12
101–10	37	30	17	25	58	46	48	44
111–20	28	28	19	4	17	12	27	12
>120	23	26	55	57	9	10	10	18
Number of observations	65	47	53	28	123	86	52	34

Note: Data as to the fulfillment of the final plan relate to all observations, rather than solely to those that are common to the fulfillment of the initial plan.

My prime concern will be with the level of fulfillment of final plans, both because it is only such data that can be compared with those of other centrally planned economies and because of the relative sample sizes. Furthermore, if plans should change several times during a year, I wonder whether the records really show the original plan. In at least one enterprise, original plans are sometimes given only verbally, and even written plans may be provided bit by bit. It is also possible that for some enterprises and for some indicators, the "initial plan" is not given to the enterprise until well past the middle of the planning year (we know this is the case in one enterprise with respect to value of output). Lastly, we have at least one case where the final plan was 50 per cent higher than the initial one, simply because necessary imports of raw materials had not yet been arranged by higher authorities at the time that the initial plan was established. Thus we would expect that data on fulfillment of the final plan would be more reliable, and in some cases even more meaningful, than that for fulfillment of the initial plan.

Nevertheless, it is worth beginning the analysis by comparing fulfillment of initial and final plan for those enterprise-years where both observations are available. The reader is referred to table 3.3a to compare column 2 with 3 and 5 with 6, and to table 3.3b to compare column 3 with 4 and 7 with 8.

Mean and median values, with varying treatment of outliers, are shown in table 3.6. What is striking here is the closeness of these values when the fulfillment of initial and final plans are compared,

Table 3.6 Performance As a Ratio of Plan: Means and Medians (for observations common to initial and final plan)

| | Initial Plan | | | | Final Plan | | | |
| | 1975–78 | | 1979–82 | | 1975–78 | | 1979–82 | |
Type of Plan	Mean	Me-dian	Mean	Me-dian	Mean	Me-dian	Mean	Me-dian
Value of Output	105	107	114	111	104	107	113	110
Profit	108	115	145[a]	126	107	115	149[b]	126
Physical output								
Main product	154[c]	107	111	102	107	103	106	102
2nd–4th most important								
products	101	103	100	102	102	105	105	110
All	124[d]	102	104	103	104	111	102	102

Note: If one excludes a single outlying observation, these mean values are the following: [a] 115; [b] 108; [c] 115; [d] 107.

Table 3.7 Date of the Initial Plan (in 1975–82 percentages)

Date	Value of Output	Profit	Physical Output (single main product)	All
December of the pre- vious year	33	0	13	17
January	19	17	38	24
February	17	34	16	22
March	5	15	13	10
April through August	26	34	20	26
Number of observations	58	41	45	144

particularly for the variables of value of output and of profit. It is true that when I ran a test for the significance of fulfillment figures that lumped together value of output, profit, and output of the single main product, the differences between fulfillment of the initial and the final plan were highly significant.[24] Nevertheless, it is the small-ness of the differences rather than their existence that is the element of surprise.[25]

When we look at the very high and very low categories of ful-fillment in tables 3.3a and 3.5, we see for the various measures of out-put what would be expected: the number of observations falling into these categories is lower for final plans than for initial plans. This re-sult is as expected: changes in plan should be exceptional, but con-centrated in those firms whose performance is outlying when judged by the initial plan. Curiously, the results in the case of profits are coun-terintuitive: there are no consistent differences in the treatment of outliers. This may indicate the lesser importance of profit plans than of output plans in China. It is noteworthy that virtually no changes at all in profit plans occurred in our sample during the pre-reform years when we know that such plans were not very important.[26]

The dating of receipt of the initial plan is also of interest, and this is shown in table 3.7. One may wonder, however, how reliable and how meaningful these dates are. In most cases, the dating is pre-sumably for receipt of the written plan. But some enterprises may have indicated the date at which the plan was received orally, and there might be a considerable difference between the two. Further-more, a plan may well have been known for all intents and purposes months before it was finalized. Finally, the number of reportings of dates is only 34 per cent of the possible number of observations that might have been given.

Nevertheless, we may record that only 17 per cent of the initial plans were received before the beginning of the planning year, and 26 per cent were received after the end of the first quarter. Some 3 to 5 per cent even came in the second half of the year. Plans came earliest for value of output and latest for profits. These data do not appear to indicate a situation that is particularly unusual by the standards of East European centrally planned economies.

Enterprises were also asked to provide data on plan fulfillment for individual physical outputs, placing the outputs in order of importance in the production of the enterprise. The left-hand side of table 3.3b takes an unweighted grouping of such observations for as many categories (up to a maximum of four) of such products as the individual enterprise provided. But such unweighted grouping is open to suspicion. It is possible that both the planning and the observation of plans by the enterprise are much more casual as the importance of the product diminishes. Alternatively, the enterprise might pay the greatest attention to maximizing average plan performance with regard to its major product. The first hypothesis would lead to a greater variation of plan fulfillment from 100 per cent for the minor products than for the principal product, while the second hypothesis would lead to a lower mean for plan fulfillment. Both hypotheses can be visually tested most easily by examining the percentage data relating to final plan for physical output in table 3.5; differences are not large and do not provide support for either hypothesis.

A statistical test of the difference between the mean of fulfillment for the principal product and the mean for the remaining three products combined was run separately for the pre-reform and reform years, and within each of these sets of years for the fulfillment of the initial plan and of the final plan. The test is based on the assumption that the underlying populations are distributed normally with regard to percentage of fulfillment. For fulfillment of the initial plan in the reform years, the hypothesis as to the absence of any true difference in the means of the populations can be rejected at the 4 per cent significance level. For the remaining three of the four categories, the hypothesis cannot be rejected even at the 50 per cent level. When all four categories are combined, the hypothesis is rejected at the 2 per cent level.

This testing is inconclusive, but certainly points toward the rejection of the null hypothesis that there is no difference in means for the principal product and for the remaining three. Nevertheless, what is important here is the first hypothesis as to casualness of planning and of plan fulfillment for the lesser products. It is this hypothesis that casts doubt upon the meaningfulness of figures as to plan fulfillment for the lesser products. However, the evidence is all against it.[27] Thus, from now on, I shall consider only the data for the combined physical output plans.

When planning is viewed as coordination, value of output, physical output of individual products, and profits can all be treated as alternative measures of output. The role of profits as such a measure appears to a striking degree in a number of the interviews, when enterprise representatives assert that their de facto output targets in particular years consist of their profit targets, since these can be realized only through higher output than is planned in the value-of-output indicator. In the case of Chinese enterprises, in contrast to Soviet, East German, or Romanian, these separate planning targets may be given to the enterprise by different principals with varying vested interests.

It may be thought, as an anonymous reviewer has suggested, that the higher level of plan fulfillment for value of output than for physical output targets during the reform years is a result of the inflation that was occurring in this period. This is certainly possible, despite the fact that the expression of value of output in constant prices is intended to eliminate such an effect. However, there is no independent evidence indicating such an inflationary effect on plan fulfillment. The set of physical output data includes only a portion of total physical output and also has considerably lower sample coverage than does the data for value of output. I would place more confidence in the effect of inflation on the fulfillment of the profit plan, since this is expressed in current prices. (See table 3.6 for the relevant summary figures; I recommend comparing the medians rather than the means.)

Comparing plan fulfillment of the final plan for value of output in our Chinese sample with the Soviet and East European data for sales, we see the following differences in the Chinese sample during the pre-reform years:

1. The proportion of enterprise-years with underfulfillment of plan is two to three times as high in China as it has been in the Soviet Union in the post-Stalin period.
2. The proportion of enterprise-years with major overfulfillment of plan is even higher relative to the other countries. One-third of the Chinese enterprise-years fall into a category (>10 per cent overfulfillment) which presumably is virtually a null set in the other three economies.

If we consider profit as an alternative measure of output for the Chinese enterprises and compare fulfillment of this indicator with that of the sales or production indicator in the other countries, our results are the same but in more exaggerated form on the overfulfillment side.

During the reform years, however, the Chinese sample of value of output indicates:

1. A similar proportion of enterprise underfulfillment of plan as in the other countries. In this regard, the difference between China and the other countries disappears.
2. The proportion of enterprise major overfulfillment becomes even more different from the European pattern than had been the case in China in pre-reform years. Instead of one-third of enterprise-years displaying overfulfillment of more than 10 per cent, 60 per cent of them now fall into that category.

Again, profits provide a similar picture.

The physical output measure alone acts differently. In both periods, it shows a rather similar pattern to that of value of output with regard to underfulfillment, but the proportion of substantial overfulfillment, while still large by the standards of the European socialist countries, is in both periods only about half the level shown by value of output.

The Ratchet Effect Syndrome

A phenomenon frequently noted in European centrally planned economies is that of the "ratchet effect." It is argued that planners, lacking reliable information as to the performance possibilities of an individual enterprise in year (t), lean heavily upon the actual performance of the same enterprise in $(t-1)$ in their estimation of these possibilities. Thus, the more an enterprise overfulfills its plan in $(t-1)$, the greater will be its increase in plan for (t).[28]

The significance attributed to this effect is the reaction of the enterprises (agents) to the perceived behavior by the planners (principal). Since management in the enterprises is concerned with multi-period rather than with single period maximization, it tends to restrain performance in (t) when for any reason the enterprises find themselves with the potential of substantially exceeding the plan set for (t).

Note that this reaction depends upon the agent's perception of the behavior of the principal; it does not matter whether or not this perception is correct. The hypothesis is difficult for the agent to test from its own experience because individual enterprises show little variance in above-plan performance. As to using the experience of other enterprises, testing would require the use of an instrumental variable in order to hold constant the change between $(t-1)$ and (t) in the unobserved variable of true capacity of enterprise (i), and a high correlation would be expected between the change in the value of the unobserved variable and the change in both the performance and the plan.[29] Since testing by the agent is further complicated by the fact that the plans and performance for a substantial sample of enterprises over a number of consecutive years is not public knowledge (to the agents), and since "devil" theories of causation are popular the world over, it should not surprise us that management in Soviet enterprises appears to be a firm believer in the ratchet hypothesis as to the behavior of the principal and reacts accordingly.[30]

Because, as it has been argued above, we may presume that substantial overfulfillment of plan is quite rare in the Soviet Union and in Eastern Europe, there has been little opportunity in these economies for management to observe how its planners actually react to substantial overfulfillment in $(t-1)$ when it comes to setting the plan for (t). But this is not the case in China, at least for our sample. During 1979–82, one-fourth of all enterprise-years represented more than 20 per cent overfulfillment of the final plans for value of output, one-half of such years in the case of profits, and one-tenth for physical output. There is no indication in these data that planners aimed to set plans that just matched enterprise potentialities. Yet the interviews show that a number of management respondents believe that planners operate on the ratchet principle. Moreover, the respondents indicate that either they or, more frequently, the organ immediately above the enterprise, then react by restraining performance. In view of the apparent facts as to the behavior of planners, one wonders why this perception arises. This is an anomaly we will have to try to explain.

Hypothesis As To Planning

The aggregative plan fulfillment figures in tables 3.3a, 3.3b, and 3.5 hide as much as they illuminate. They fail to distinguish between, on the one hand, those plans which are intended to coordinate production with that of other units and, on the other, those plans that do not have this objective. This applies to plans along all of the targeted dimensions, whether for value of output, profits, or physical output.

For example, the petroleum field enterprise is given the value-of-output and physical output targets by its national ministry. Since almost 100 per cent of production is centrally allocated to users, these targets of production for enterprises must be closely linked with allocations made to other bodies. If a planning/allocation system is to

function effectively, authorities might be expected to aim for an anticipated distribution of plan fulfillment which does not have a very large
variance.[31] In contrast, the value-of-output target given to the machine tool factory by its county (along with another such target, sometimes with a different value, given by the municipality) seems to have
been determined primarily by the requirements of the county and
municipality for meeting their own plans of an X per cent growth in
total industrial output in the county (municipality); the factory's target is set in accord with an objective of overall development of the
locality and has no coordination function whatsoever. In this case,
there is much less reason for planning authorities to prize low variance in plan fulfillment.

Similarly, we should distinguish between two types of output
within a single plan for a given enterprise: the portion of the plan that
is backed by allocations of materials (even if the allocation does not
provide complete coverage of needs) versus the portion that is not
supported in this fashion. Such a distinction applies to all three measures of output: physical output, value of output, and even profits.

The most common form that the distinction takes is linked to
property rights in the enterprise. Here, the plan is established by a
regional body, but it incorporates a certain amount of production that
goes to central authorities for allocated distribution, for which the
Center allocates raw materials. A second form (seen in the case of the
automotive factory and the cement plant) occurs when the plan is
given by a central body and allocation is also carried out at the central
level. In this case, what is called a "mandatory" output plan, backed
by materials allocations, may be set, and an "indicative" output target
is then added but without the provision of materials.[32] The total output plan is the sum of these two. In both of these forms of the output
plan, only a portion really represents administrative coordination of
different sectors of the economy. Yet in the tables above, the figures
that describe the degree of plan fulfillment compare this total output
plan with actual production.

A variant on the above is also linked to property rights and is
seen in the case of the cement factory. The central ministry sets the
output plan, which is routinely transmitted to the enterprise by the
province. But, at least in 1984, the province actually wished to aim for
somewhat higher output (and was prepared to provide the needed
raw materials for the addition), the difference being intended for distribution by the province itself. This objective was apparently accomplished not by increasing the production plan, but rather through
setting a profit plan which implied a higher output. The enterprise
then took the implied output as its factual output plan.

This analysis of plan fulfillment by Chinese state enterprises does not apply at all to plan fulfillment in the Soviet Union or in the East European planned economies. In these countries, all production plans are (at least in principle) fully supported by allocations of raw materials, and the products are fully allocated to other enterprises. Thus the output plans, in all their manifestations, are totally integrated into coordination functions.

The analysis leads to an obvious hypothesis about plan fulfillment in Chinese medium and large state enterprises. This is:

(3.1) *Hypothesis:*
    Fulfillment of production plans covering products to be allocated to other organizations, and for which the targets are supported by allocations of materials, should have a distribution with a much smaller variance than does the distribution of production plans which do not meet these criteria.

This hypothesis is a weaker form of the hypothesis that Chinese enterprise plans which correspond to Soviet enterprise plans should have a similar distribution of fulfillment.[33] It follows from the fact that, where production plans are the basis for balancing the supply of materials within the economy, planners wish to obtain a small variance of plan fulfillment so as to assure such balancing. Since balancing freight transport availability against needs implies that above-plan output by one enterprise is not a perfect substitute for below-plan fulfillment by another that produces an identical product, variance is measured not only at a product level but also at an enterprise level.

Analysis of Sample Data

As noted earlier, of the twenty organizations in the sample, data for fifteen are available as to annual plans and output of one or more physical product. The enterprise-years were divided into two categories:

(3.2) *Definition of Categories A and B:*
    Category A—The physical output targets are set by a body which also allocates all (or substantially all) of the output to users, and which completely or to a substantial degree supports its targets through the provision of planned quantities of inputs.
    Category B—contains the residual.

For those years for which data are available, twelve organizations are in category A and five in category B.[34]

A comparison of plan fulfillment in category A and B is presented in table 3.8. The most striking result is that, in three of the four comparisons, the proportion of enterprise-years in which fulfillment was 100 (±10) per cent was substantially higher for category A. This is consistent with hypothesis (3.1).

The ratio of category A/category B for fulfillment between 90 and 110 per cent was 136–40 per cent for the final plans of the reform period and for the initial plans of the pre-reform years, and was a

Table 3.8 Performance As a Percentage of Plan: Comparison of Categories (in percentage of observations for combined physical output plans from sample)

Fulfillment Percentages	Final Plan Categories		Initial Plan Categories	
	A (allocated)	B (non-allocated)	A	B
1975–78				
<70	12	0	0	0
70–89	6	5	15	0
90–99	13	5	23	5
100	13	25	12	30
101–10	42	35	42	20
111–20	9	20	8	20
121–30	1	5	0	0
>130	4	5	0	25
90≤X≤110	68	65	77	55
<100	31	10	38	5
111–20	9	20	8	20
>120	5	10	0	25
Number of observations	78	20	26	20
1979–82				
<70	1	6	2	13
70–89	0	3	0	10
90–99	1	3	12	8
100	12	9	10	8
101–10	63	44	58	26
111–20	15	24	12	16
121–30	1	0	4	5
>130	7	12	0	13
90≤X≤110	76	56	80	42
<100	2	12	14	31
111–20	15	24	12	16
>120	8	12	4	18
Number of observations	89	34	48	38

Table 3.9 Adjusted Data for Underfulfillment of Physical Output Plans (in percentage of observations)

Fulfillment Percentages	Final Plan Categories		Initial Plan Categories	
	A (allocated)	B (non-allocated)	A	B
1975–78				
<70	0	0	0	0
70–89	6	5	12	0
90–99	15	5	24	5

striking 190 per cent for the initial plans of the reform years. During the reform years, both very low and very high fulfillment percentages showed low ratios of A/B.

The only apparent anomaly is for the pre-reform years, in which the ratio of A/B is very high for plan underfulfillment. However, when we examine the source of underfulfillments by 10 per cent or more for category A during 1975–78, the discrepancy between the two categories is accounted for almost entirely by two enterprises. Together, these organizations account for all nine of the observations of less than 70 per cent fulfillment; all relate to 1975–77.[35] One of the two enterprises was first badly affected by the chaos of the aftermath of the Cultural Revolution, working only 150 days during 1976, and it then suffered a serious fire during 1977. The second enterprise is an automotive plant, observed during the period when it had just succeeded in getting one model of truck into production and had not yet succeeded with a second. Clearly what was involved in this case was overoptimism by the planners as to how long the running-in period would last. In both these cases, there appears to have been no plan revision when it became clear that the assumptions of the original plan were not being met.

If we eliminate the 1975–77 observations for these two enterprises, the percentage of observations given in table 3.9 describes underfulfillment of physical output plans. Thus it would appear that the apparent anomaly for hypothesis (3.1) of a high ratio of A/B for substantial underfulfillment during the pre-reform years is a result of happenstance in the sample; it should be ignored. In the light of the small sample size for the second and fourth columns in table 3.9, of results for 1979–82, and of table 3.10 (see below), I would dismiss the high A/B ratio for 90–99 per cent fulfillment. However, this still leaves us with the anomaly that, during the 1975–78 years, the ratio of A/B for underfulfillment is at best equal to 100 per cent rather than being smaller as predicted by hypothesis (3.1). Let us leave this negative result for discussion after consideration of table 3.10 below.

Table 3.10 Performance As a Percentage of Plan: Comparison of
Subcategories for Value-of-Output and Profit Plans
(in percentage of observations from the sample)

Fulfillment Percentages	Value-of-Output Plan				Profit Plan			
	Final		Initial		Final		Initial	
	A1	A2	A1	A2	A1	A2	A1	A2
1975–78								
<70	33	0	27	0	0	0	0	0
70–89	0	0	0	0	0	0	0	0
90–99	7	9	0	22	0	7	0	0
100	0	4	0	11	0	0	0	0
101–10	20	68	27	67	17	40	0	0
111–20	27	18	36	0	42	40	60	0
121–30	7	0	9	0	0	7	0	0
>130	7	0	0	0	42	7	40	100
X>110	41	18	45	0	82	54		
X<90	33	0	27	0	0	0		
Number of observations	15	22	11	9	12	15	5	1
1979–82								
<70	0	0	0	0	0	0	0	
70–89	0	0	0	0	0	0	0	
90–99	0	0	0	0	0	0	0	
100	12	11	15	11	0	7	0	
101–10	25	67	38	67	27	21	50	
111–20	38	22	31	22	13	36	0	
121–30	6	0	15	0	20	0	25	
>130	19	0	0	0	40	36	25	
X>110	63	22	46	22	73	72		
X<90	0	0	0	0	0	0		
Number of observations	16	18	13	9	15	14	8	0

Note: Subcategory A1 is the set of enterprises within category A for which the same
body sets all plans. Subcategory A2 constitutes the remainder of the category A enterprises. Both subcategories are restricted to those enterprises for which those products
planned with regard to physical output are both allocated and supported with
planned inputs.

It is worth noting that the hypothesis is supported most strikingly with regard to the initial plan during the reform period. Since
the final plan is subject to revision to reflect the reality of output during the year, it is probably the initial plan that is the more significant
as an indicator of whatever interenterprise coordination the plan is intended to exercise. Thus the hypothesis weakly predicts stronger in-

tercategory differences with respect to the initial than to the final plan, and this is what we observe.

Finally, it must be remarked that the categorization for the later years is likely to be more reliable than for the earlier ones. This is because the principle of categorization relates to individual observations rather than to enterprises, and I had to do the categorization on the basis of qualitative materials in the interviews, while these in turn concentrated primarily on the most recent years. If the categorization errors are assumed to be random, this implies not only that the true distinctions between categories are in fact greater in both periods than is indicated by the data of table 3.8, but also that the difference is more substantial in the earlier period. Thus measurement error biases the observed results against acceptance of hypothesis (3.1), and does so most for the pre-reform years for which the evidence supporting the hypothesis is weaker.

When we consider that, in the case of the Soviet Union and of East European centrally planned countries other than Hungary, category B is virtually a null set, the intracategory distinction between plan fulfillment in China and in these countries is less than was suggested by table 3.5. In the cases where output plans are truly intended to be used as devices coordinating interenterprise relations, the differences among the planned economies is not as great as we might have thought from the raw data.

One can also proceed further in the discussion of plan fulfillment for value of output and for profits. This treatment rests upon subcategorization of the data for those enterprise-years falling into category A (allocated).

(3.3) *Definition of Subcategories A1 and A2:*
Subcategory A1—The value-of-output plans and profit plans that are established by the same regional body that sets the physical output plans. (In one case the latter is a province; in all other cases it is the Center.)
Subcategory A2—All other value-of-output and profit plans within enterprise-years falling into category A. These plans are always set at a regional level below that at which the physical output plans were established.

In the case of subcategory A2, we might expect that regional authorities would sometimes have a particular desire to increase the output of major physical products of enterprises in their region. The logic is that such additions would not have to be delivered to the higher body for its own allocation purposes, but would be left for use in the region. These additions might be allocated by the regional authority; if not, this authority could still ensure its use within the region by forbidding its export to other areas.[36] Since the regional authority is not empowered to make plans as to physical products for these enterprises, it establishes value-of-output plans and/or profit plans which require greater physical output than are provided in the physical output plans established by the higher body. Fulfillment by the enterprise of these aggregative plans will often be accomplished most easily through overfulfillment of the physical output plans for the enterprise's major products. In this fashion, the regional authority satisfies its desire.

In the above instances, value-of-output and/or profit plans will be set more tautly than will plans of physical output. Thus we would expect that substantial overfulfillment of the first two types of plans will be less frequent than of that for physical output and that plan underfulfillment will be greater.

For subcategory A1 (the most centralized), in contrast, there is no reason for the plan-setting body to use value-of-output and/or profit plans for purposes of influencing physical output directly. Physical output plans are available to this body as a superior device. Thus, for this subcategory, there is no general reason why value-of-output and profit plans should be more ambitious or taut than are the physical output plans for the same set of enterprises.

This leads to a second hypothesis, based on the above argument that value-of-output and profit plans should be tauter, and thus more difficult both to fulfill and overfulfill, for subcategory A2 than for subcategory A1 enterprises.

(3.4) *Hypothesis:*

Among category A enterprises (for all of which those products planned with regard to physical output are both allocated and supported with planned inputs), underfulfillment will be less and overfulfillment greater for value-of-output and profit plans among the subcategory A1 enterprises than among those of subcategory A2. (Subcategory A1 is the set of enterprises for which the same body sets all plans.)

Table 3.10 presents the available data. Sample sizes are fairly small, and for the initial profit plan are either zero or too small to be of any use. However, comparison of subcategory A1 and A2 enterprises can usefully be done for both final plans and for the initial plan of value of output. Since there are two periods, we have available six sets of comparisons. Following the procedure used in table 3.8, attention is directed to deviations of 10 per cent or more from exact plan fulfillment.

The part of hypothesis (3.4) relating to overfulfillment seems to be fairly well supported. It is strongly backed for all cases except that of the final profit plan in 1979–82. For this last case, it is supported with regard to fulfillment of 120 per cent or more, but rebutted as to fulfillment of 110 per cent or more.

However, the portion of the hypothesis relating to underfulfillment is rejected in all six cases. Subcategory A1 is higher than subcategory A2 in two cases, and they are equal in four. Such rejection also holds even if we restate the hypothesis in a much weaker form: that subcategory A1 should have less combined underfulfillment and exact fulfillment of plan than does subcategory A2. Furthermore, not much improvement is shown if the entire sample data (as shown in table 3.5) is substituted for subcategory A2 so as to gain the advantage of a larger sample size.[37]

These results suggest that lower regional bodies have felt restrained from raising output-proxy plans compared to plans for physical output when such behavior could lead to underfulfillment. This has been the case not only during the reform years when bonuses could be affected by fulfillment figures, but also in earlier years when bonuses were virtually nonexistent. On the other hand, they felt no such restraint regarding increasing plan tautness when this would affect only the degree of overfulfillment.

Remembering the results of the test of hypothesis (3.1), it would seem that both (3.1) and (3.4) could be better stated as referring only to variance occurring through overfulfillment of plan. The proportion of observations showing serious underfulfillment does not appear to be affected by whether the enterprise-years are included in Category A or B, or in subcategory A1 or A2 within category A. This is because the enterprise-years with substantial underfulfillment have constituted almost a null set. While planners have shown themselves willing (particularly in the pre-reform period) to set plans that are underfulfilled by less than 10 per cent, they have not been willing to go beyond this in their tautness.[38]

Although such behavior by planners is perhaps credible as stated above, it makes sense only if they believed that enterprise management held satisficing target objectives with regard to level of overfulfillment. This assumption requires that they believed that enterprises did respond to plan, but that they were neither maximizers with respect to the degree of plan overfulfillment, nor agents whose satisficing target levels for overfulfillment were quite moderate.[39] It seems difficult to rationalize such a set of beliefs on the part of planners, but it is possible that the problem is due to my lack of empathy with the planners in their perception of the environment in which they work.[40]

Let us return to the issue raised much earlier in this chapter as to why we find complaints in some sample enterprises as to the existence of ratchet planning (likened to "whipping a fast ox"), despite the degree of substantial plan overfulfillment which can be seen in table 3.5.

Complaints of this type, with some comments that immediate regional superiors (when these existed) have even refused to permit the enterprise to increase output beyond plan, were concentrated in seven enterprises.[41] Six of the seven were category A enterprises, to which the Center gave physical output plans, and for which virtually all of output was allocated to users by the Center. (In the sample of twenty organizations, twelve were category A, seven were category B, and one was mixed.) The seventh was the pump enterprise described in Chapter 2, for which the central ministry also planned output and even received monthly reports as to the fulfillment of these output plans. Although the output of this pump enterprise had not been allocated by the central ministry since about 1977, one could imagine that the enterprise's regional authorities might have been afraid of a return to such allocation in the future.

Table 3.8 provided data as to the degree of overfulfillment and underfulfillment of physical output plans in all enterprises of category A (allocated outputs and inputs). The reader should note the relatively small proportion of enterprise-years for this category that fell into either of the two classifications of 111–20 or >120 per cent fulfillment. Although for enterprises in category A, or for those that might soon be returned to this category, fear of ratchet planning by the Center may seem exaggerated, it is not irrational. Substantial overfulfillment of these central output plans was not so great as to offer complete protection against future underfulfillment. Indeed, underfulfillment had been substantial during the 1975–78 period and still continued into the latter years.

Thus the apparent anomaly of fear of ratchet planning, given the enterprises in which this fear was localized, is explained by the analysis of this section.

Individual Enterprise Materials

Relevant supplementary materials are available from the interviews for eleven of the twenty enterprises in the sample. Seven enterprises, and an eighth with regard to some of its important products, fall into category A (or would have, if we had had the needed plan and performance data for the physical output of all of them); three, and a fourth with regard to its single major product, are in category B. Of those in category A, three are in subcategory A1 and five in subcategory A2.

These materials relate not only to the years 1975–82 that were covered in the tables above, but also to 1983–85 which were excluded because of the paucity of quantitative information covering these years. They provide the qualitative texture of the available planning information and constitute a useful complement to the statistical materials above. They are presented in the appendix to this chapter.

Summary

The data in tables 3.8 and 3.10, along with the supplementary statistics, force us to modify hypotheses (3.1) and (3.4). Hypothesis (3.1) must be modified to exclude underfulfillment during the pre-reform years, and (3.4) to exclude underfulfillment during both periods. It would seem most appropriate to state the joint modification as follows:

(3.5)   *Hypothesis:*

Fulfillment of production plans covering products to be allocated to other organizations, and for which the targets are supported by allocations of materials, have a statistical distribution with a smaller right-hand tail above 110 per cent fulfillment than is the case for the distribution of production plans which do not meet these criteria. Enterprises of subcategory A1, for which the same body sets all plans, have a distribution of fulfillment of value-of-output and profit plans that has a larger tail above 110 per cent fulfillment than does subcategory A2, for which value and profit plans are set by different regional bodies than those which fix the physical output plans.

No noticeable difference between either categories or subcategories is found in the portion of the distribution which represents major or minor underfulfillment of plan.

The differences between categories and subcategories in degree of overfulfillment seem to be satisfactorily interpreted in terms of the varying roles of plans within the three divisions. But the suggested explanations of equality with regard to underfulfillment are unsatisfactory.

The belief expressed by informants that ratchet planning exists is justified by the fact that such informants are primarily employees of category A enterprises, for which production plans cover products to be allocated to other organizations, and for which these plans are substantially supported by the allocation of raw materials. Such enterprises had suffered underfulfillment of plans, especially during the pre-reform period but also later. The proportion of their plans with substantial overfulfillment was not sufficiently high to offer them complete psychological protection against the danger of receiving plans that were overly ambitious. Although the belief in ratchet planning seems exaggerated, it is not irrational; the type of enterprises in which such belief is found is exactly where one would have predicted, assuming that the belief existed at all.

Turning from statistical analysis to the materials concerning individual enterprises that are presented in the appendix to this chapter, I am struck by the reasons for the shift away from central allocation of the enterprises' products during the reform years. Among the eleven enterprises treated in the appendix, six showed such a shift.[42] Of the six, declines in central allocation from the pre-reform period were related to reform as such in three.[43] However, in comparing the situation in specific years within the reform period, four had reductions in the central allocation of their output in those years when market conditions were poor, and two in years when increased amounts of materials were provided from sources other than those of central allocation.[44] Although reform policy was a significant factor, it did not dominate other considerations.

Central allocations were insufficient in most of the cases to support fully the production of items for which physical output was centrally planned. This is most striking in the case of the locomotive repair plant, where it is the mandatory plan that has been poorly supported, probably since 1977. But it occurred with regard to the mandatory plan in both the lumbering and forestry and the steel enterprises during at least 1983 and 1984 (with very sharp shortages in the first of these organizations), and was also observed to some degree in the cement mill. In the auto enterprise and the smelter, the mandatory plan whose output went to the Center seems to have been fairly fully supported, but the remainder of the plan (this is not relevant to the smelter) was not. On the other hand, planned allocations of materials by the Center or province seem to have been sufficient for the petroleum field and for the textile mill in category A2.

There are two cases of the eight in category A (the locomotive repair plant and the cement plant) where the physical plan set by the Center for total output seems to have been held below plant capacity in order to provide the enterprise with above-plan output, the exchange or sale of which would provide the materials needed to fulfill the plan. There are two additional cases (the auto enterprise and the smelter) where only the Center's mandatory plan is so constrained.[45] In a fifth case (the textile plant of category A2) informants explicitly reported that growth in the physical output plan of the province was restrained so as to provide a financial incentive to the enterprise. In sum, we have reasonably clear knowledge that such constraints apply to roughly half of the enterprises whose physical plans are established by the Center; it would not be surprising if they also applied to others.

Only in one case (that of the watch and clock producer) is there plain indication that the enterprise is indifferent, and justifiably so given the reactions of its superiors, to the fulfillment of physical output targets. Such indifference applies both to plans established by the province and by the national ministry. In one of the category B organizations (the producer of electrical equipment), despite the fact that an informant claimed that the enterprise has been influenced by physical output plans received regularly from the province, it is doubtful that the influence could have been too great. One year earlier, the same man had stated that such plans did not even exist. It is true that none of these physical output plans in the two enterprises bear any relation to government distribution of the products; nevertheless, some materials are allocated to the enterprises on the basis of these plans.

Conclusion

Property Rights

The varying patterns of Chinese planning of physical output are closely related to the concept of regional property rights that was developed in chapter 2. The enterprises of subcategory A1 are either under complete national control (3 enterprises) or complete provincial control (1 enterprise). In all four of these cases, the owning body was primarily concerned with exercising its right to distribute the final product, and it chose to ensure production by providing allocations of the bulk of required materials.

Six of the enterprises of subcategory A2 were among the enterprises described in Chapter 2 as under multilevel supervision. The remaining three were textile enterprises that were under provincial control, but subject to national allocation both of materials (partially) and of final product. However, such allocation was aggregated on a provincial level, rather than being by individual enterprise.

All of the above enterprises of category A shared the characteristic that the party exercising allocation rights over the product in turn allocated this product to users. Furthermore, at least those enterprises in subcategory A1 were provided with most of their requirements of materials. In view of these two obligations, the allocating party was concerned to see that outputs and inputs (whether these latter were of capacity or of materials) should bear some reasonable relation to one another. Thus plans of physical output were set sufficiently high so that overfulfillment was relatively restrained (by Chinese standards).

In the case of category B enterprises, there was no reason to attempt to attain accuracy in the plans of physical production. The body exercising property rights over the enterprise was neither providing an exceptionally large amount of materials at less than their opportunity costs nor disposing of the final product. The supervising body's interest in the enterprise's product was essentially financial; plans of physical output were given, but served no major purpose. This was a case of single-level property rights over the enterprise's production, with the rights being exercised in financial, rather than in physical, appropriation of the net proceeds. It differed from the proprietorship of enterprises in subcategory A1 with regard to how the single-level supervising body chose to take the return on its investment.

The lower level joint proprietors of the enterprises of subcategory A2 are frequently constrained by the property rights of the higher level as to the types of plans that they can set for their enterprises. In these cases, when they wish to have available larger amounts of the enterprise's physical products within their own geographic areas than would be received solely through allocations by the higher level body, they may promote this objective by setting enterprise profit plans as well as output plans that are expressed in renminbi rather than in physical units. If they take advantage of this opportunity, then we might expect such plans to be more ambitious than they are in the case of subcategory A1 enterprises. This expectation is borne out in the relative overfulfillment figures of the two subcategories.

International Comparison

Comparison between our sample Chinese enterprises and Soviet and East European data as to plan fulfillment of value of output and of profits shows a very high proportion of enterprise-years with plan underfulfillment in China during the pre-reform years, but a similar proportion to the European during the reform period. What is most striking in the comparison, however, is the high proportion of enterprise-years with over 110 per cent plan fulfillment: one-third in China during the pre-reform years and three-fifths in the years of the reform, versus virtually none (presumably) in the European countries.

However, sales plans in the European countries are intended to coordinate the outputs of one enterprise with the inputs of others. Chinese plans for value of output do not generally serve this function. Thus it is more appropriate to look at the Chinese production plans set by authorities that allocate much or all of this production; physical output targets, for a subset of all enterprise-years in the sample, are the appropriate measure. As pointed out earlier, low variance of plan fulfillment at an enterprise level is an appropriate objective for planners when plans are used for purposes of materials balancing at the national or regional level.[46] There is no reason for such an objective when plans are not used in this fashion.

For purposes of intercountry comparison, final plans should be used, since these are all that are available for the European countries. When we look at the realization of the final plans for physical output of category A enterprises (with allocated outputs and inputs), we get the patterns for the Chinese sample shown in table 3.11. Using the last two columns in the table (as justified earlier in the chapter), we find that the proportion of enterprise-years in which there was underfulfillment straddles the Soviet figures for sales of the mid-1970s, as well as those of the German Democratic Republic and Romania. About one-fifth of the Chinese enterprise-years showed a degree of overfulfillment which would scarcely ever be seen in any of the three European countries. If we add together the proportion of enterprise-years in the Chinese sample in which fulfillment deviated from the plan by more than 10 per cent in either direction, there was no change between the pre-reform and reform periods in the accuracy of those plans intended for coordinating purposes.

It is true that the statistical regression-to-the-mean property of an aggregate would lead us to expect that the European figures for all sales of an enterprise would show greater clustering around 100 per cent plan fulfillment than would separate figures for the same enterprises for sales of individual major product categories. In the Chinese case, we are using the more disaggregated series. There is, however, nothing that we can do about this aspect of incomparability. We have

Table 3.11 Final Physical Output Plans (combined) for Category A Enterprises (in percentages of observations from the sample)

Fulfillment Percentages	All Observations		All Excluding 2 Enterprises in 3 Years	
	1975–78	1979–82	1975–78	1979–82
<90	18	1	6	1
90–99	13	1	13	1
100	13	12	15	12
101–10	42	63	49	63
>110	14	23	16	23
Number of Observations	78	89	67	89

no aggregative measure of output for the Chinese enterprises that is limited to coordinating plans.

The difference between 22–24 per cent and a virtual zero per cent presumably goes far beyond what we might expect to be caused solely by the different degrees of aggregation. It seems safe to conclude that this difference represents a major distinction between Chinese and European output plans which are meant to serve the same function.

In compensation for this wider variance in the meeting of the Chinese than of the European coordinating targets (virtually all of it on the overfulfillment end), we can point to the greater consistency in China between the original and the final annual plans for enterprises.[47] This higher degree of consistency is certainly the case in comparison to the Soviet Union and Romania; it is hard to judge with regard to the G.D.R. This must lead to less likelihood of self-restraint in enterprise performance during the early part of the year in China than elsewhere, where such restraint would be due to fear of upward plan revision for the year as a whole.

Similarly, despite the belief among managers located in a subset of the Chinese sample enterprises that planners use the ratchet principle in setting targets, it seems virtually certain that Chinese enterprise management as a whole is much less likely than are the European socialist managers to restrain output for this reason. Chinese planners are perfectly willing to set plans at levels that can be massively overfulfilled year after year.

In sum, output planning—even for those enterprises and products for which it is used to coordinate production with the allocated inputs of others—is less accurate in China than in the Soviet Union and Eastern Europe. This is almost certainly true with regard to final plans and probably, although to a lesser degree, with regard to the initial plans. Thus there is a greater need in China to rely upon devices other than planning for the purpose of coordination. In compensation, the use of planning is less likely to have a harmful incentive effect upon managers of Chinese than of European socialist enterprises.

Appendix: Planning Materials on Individual Enterprises

Enterprises of Subcategory A1 (the most centrally administered enterprises)

As was shown in table 2.1, much of the total national production of centrally distributed intermediate products escapes the central allocation process. However, aggregative data of the sort presented there begs the question of the degree to which the nonallocated portion is produced by enterprises whose output is totally unallocated, as opposed to its production by enterprises whose products are allocated only in part. It seems safe to say that the bulk is produced by the first category. (Certainly this must be true for coal, lumber, and cement, the three products in table 2.1 for which a major share escaped allocation throughout the entire period beginning in 1965.) However, the second category is also significant and seems to have become increasingly so, although for varying reasons, in the 1980s. Our sample provides no information as to the first category, but is helpful as to the second. All of the category A enterprises are relevant here, but it is the products of those in subcategory A1 that we would expect to be most tightly controlled as it is the enterprises of this subcategory that are supervised in all aspects of their operation by the Center.

Through 1980, all trucks produced by the auto plant were centrally distributed. During 1981 and 1982, however, restraint in investment allocations from the central state budget prevented many potential customers who were eligible for truck allocations from submitting purchase orders. These potential customers faced a combination of a cash constraint and the unavailability of credit. It is particularly interesting that they did not arrange to take delivery and sell to other would-be customers who did not have allocations, kiting checks to the extent necessary. In this period, 54 per cent of total truck output was sold by the enterprise on its own to customers without allocations.

During these two years, the Center seems to have aimed at providing materials for the total output, just as it had in earlier years when it allocated all of the product.[48] But this does not seem to have been so much a policy decision as happenstance. In 1981 the enterprise's output plan was established on the basis of covering all expected production. When the market for trucks weakened, the Center's purchasing quota was halved, but nothing else was changed. In 1982 the purchasing quota of the Center (received by the State Materials Bureau, in this case) began as only 40 per cent of the planned output, but the market turned around completely after the first quarter. By the end of the year, the Center's purchasing quota appears to have covered virtually all output, and materials were supplied for the full coverage. But the enterprise's deliveries to other customers were already committed and the Center, despite strong efforts, was unable to recapture these trucks.

After 1982, sales by the enterprise on its own to customers without allocations continued on a reduced but still substantial scale; the reason for the continuation, however, was completely different from that of 1981–82. In the later years, the Center divided the enterprise's output plan into a mandatory and a guidance plan, and provided only enough materials to cover the mandatory production. The State Planning Bureau was restrained in its mandatory plan by the amount of supplies that could be provided by the State Materials Bureau. The enterprise's problem in "self-sales" was to arrange its own supply.

During 1983 the enterprise was permitted to sell on its own 10 per cent of its mandatory plan (presumably to customers without allocations). Assuming that it took full advantage of this right, its additional self-sales were only about 7 per cent of production; total self-sales constituted 17 per cent of truck production, despite the fact that the physical output plan was exactly fulfilled rather than overfulfilled. In 1984 provincial authorities were allocated increased volumes of steel and the auto enterprise traded trucks for this steel. Two months before the end of the year, the enterprise estimated that its self-sales would be 80 per cent higher in 1984 than they had been in 1983, even though it had suffered the elimination of its right to self-sales of a portion of its mandatory plan.

The 1985 plan for the enterprise was based on the assumption of a massive amount of self-sales: 31 per cent of total planned output. Although this was still less than the 1981–82 proportion, it now represented a central decision rather than a faute de mieux policy. Presumably, this decision constituted a continuation and extension of the strategy of 1984; provincial authorities were being allocated larger volumes of steel in lieu of trucks, and then were left free to decide how best to use such steel. This central procedure for the distribution of trucks could scarcely be called one of increased monetization, but it did embody increased marketization.

The petroleum field enterprise, in contrast, had virtually all of its oil and natural gas output taken by the Center. In 1983 it was left with about one-tenth of 1 per cent of its production for "easing squeaky wheels"; this was supplied to local county and commune enterprises, apparently as payments for land requisitions. This policy went back to at least 1980, when some six-tenths of 1 per cent had been left for this purpose. In addition, not only was there no movement by 1983 toward reduced central allocation, but there was even a minuscule increase in its extent.

The third enterprise, specializing in locomotive repair, is operated in the most centralized fashion of all the enterprises in our sample. Not only is it under the control of a single national ministry for all of its activities and plans, receiving for these purposes allocations that are organized by the same ministry, but it also has a single customer—the identical ministry. Nevertheless, a significant portion of its inputs for current production have had to be procured by the plant itself. For 1981–83, the annual averages were 12–16 per cent for steel products, 11–19 per cent for bearings, and 25–35 per cent for copper conductors. Such procurement was done both through barter (presumably of other allocated inputs) and through purchases at free-market prices. The puzzle is: how could the latter purchases be financed?

One might guess, although there is no confirmation, that it was done through the supervising ministry accepting somewhat higher values for work carried out than was strictly appropriate. This is suggested by the fact that fulfillment of the final plan during 1975–82 was as follows:

> For the principal physical output: 101–6 per cent, except for
>   114 per cent in one year;
> For the secondary physical output: 100–2 per cent in all years;
> For value of output: 107–8 per cent during 1975–76 and
>   117–121 per cent during 1977–82.

Provided that the plans of value of output were consistent with the plans of physical output, the increase above the norm in the actual as opposed to planned valuation of work done each year, (allowed by the ministry so as to permit the enterprise to procure the necessary materials outside of planned channels) would have made consistent these three vectors of plan fulfillment figures. If we trust the evidence regarding plan fulfillment, this enterprise's reliance on the market-place during 1981–83 for a portion of supplies is something it had done regularly since 1977.

Enterprises of Subcategory A2 (intermediary in degree of centralization)

The first enterprise is the smelter of nonferrous metals. It produces three pure (as opposed to alloy) metals. A Western source guesses that, as of 1983, it refined something on the order of one-quarter of total Chinese output of two of these metals.[49] What is fascinating is the dramatic difference in the planning of the distribution of these three products despite the fact that, in all probability, there has been no change in such distribution since at least the late 1970s.

For two of the three products, virtually all of the plant's output is centrally allocated.[50] But the third product, for which this is not the case, is the one that is most important to the smelter. Moreover, and most significantly, it is one of the two for which the plant refines a large proportion of the nation's total needs.

For this third product, the Center provides both a mandatory plan (which it supports with provision of raw materials) and a total plan. Data are available for 1978, 1979, 1982, and 1983. In all four of these years (and without trend), the mandatory plan constituted between 40 and 55 per cent of the total plan, while actual output constituted between 79 and 100 per cent of total plan. Only the mandatory plan volume was centrally allocated; the remaining half of production was disposed of by the smelter itself. However, the enterprise was apparently allowed, with one major exception, to dispose of such output only to the State Materials Bureau (i.e., to the same customer as for its mandatory-plan output).[51] The exception, which is a major one, related to processing contracts signed with suppliers of materials.

The limitation on the size of the mandatory plan that is established is described as being the amount of materials (concentrated ore, an intermediate product, and scrap) that can be supplied by the Center. The refinery has succeeded in producing double its mandatory plan largely by processing concentrated ore and scrap for localities; these customers have used the refined product as a barter good. To the extent that this correctly describes the situation, the Center's policy toward the smelter is dictated by its policy toward the localities providing the raw materials. But this is not the entire story.

During 1983 some 47 per cent of the materials supporting production that was in excess of the mandatory plan came from imports of the intermediate product; only about one-fourth of this 47 per cent was a result of the smelter "teaming up" with a customer ministry to arrange these imports. For 1984 it was expected that imports would constitute about 23 per cent of such materials. There is no information on the role of imports in earlier years, but since the Center controls them, it is striking that during 1983–84 imports were allowed to be credited to the fulfillment of the guidance plan rather than solely to that of the mandatory plan.[52] For some unknown reason, the Center chose not to support the mandatory plan with any of the imports in 1983 (although this meant reducing the mandatory plan by 25 per cent compared to its normal level), and in 1984 it chose to classify only two-thirds of total imports of materials as constituting support of the mandatory plan. At least during these two years, it would seem that the Center took control through mandatory planning of a smaller proportion of total output of this product than would have been feasible within the constraints of its incentive policy toward regions.

The steel enterprise is the second one in this subcategory. This enterprise marketed by itself, rather than through the allocation system, some 6 per cent of its total production of rolled steel in 1979, 10–12 per cent during 1980 and 1982–84, and 14 per cent in the year

1981 that was one of poor demand for steel. (The enterprise is said to have had no such self-sales rights prior to 1979; they are purely a phenomenon of the reform period.) Some of these self-sales could be of output produced within the mandatory plan, and such sales could be made to customers who did not have allocations. Thus this enterprise's mandatory plan was in fact somewhat larger than the amount of production actually allocated either by the Center or the province. Moreover, this excess does not appear to have been due to the need to give the steel enterprise some of its own product for barter purposes; at least in 1984, only 15 per cent of all self-sales were of this type.

The above figures are of particular interest because the sample steel enterprise was not one of those (such as the Beijing Capital Iron and Steel Plant) that was given the special privilege of an unusually high degree of self-marketing of planned production.

The third enterprise is the forestry and lumbering concern. Between 1979 and 1983, and without any trend, 80–96 per cent of its timber output was allocated; of this allocation, 83–87 per cent went to the Center, and the remainder was left to the province.

A breakdown of the uses of total timber production exists only for 1982 (Table 3A.1). Unfortunately, this is the year of the above four in which the lowest proportion of timber output was allocated. While we do not know why this was so, one might presume that it was due to plan overfulfillment being largest in that year. As can be seen from the table, the planned residual was roughly the same size as the provincial allocation. It was used for barter as a means of paying another state organization to build forestry roads, as a payment to localities for areas that were forested, and as payment "for tending timber." This last item presumably refers to timber turned over to cooperatives

Table 3A.1 Total Planned Timber Production for the Lumbering Enterprise, 1982

Category	Actual Uses (%)
Allocated:	
Total	86.0
By the Center	75.2
By the province	10.8
Used by the enterprise	3.4
Residual:	
Total	17.1
In the output plan	10.6
From overfulfillment	6.5

composed of family members of the enterprise's own employees, and sold by them at much higher prices than would have been permitted to the state enterprise itself.

The cement plant is the fourth enterprise of this subcategory. The central ministry issues to the plant a plan for tonnage of output and provides raw materials supporting the share of the planned output which goes to the ministry for allocation to customers. The division of total output among customers during 1981–84 is shown in table 3A.2.

Since the central ministry does not provide enough materials to support the entire plan, (even in the planned allocation as opposed to actual deliveries), but only an amount sufficient to support the allocations of cement to the ministry itself, at least some 7 to 9 per cent of output has been used for barter.[53] Planned output would have been roughly sufficient to meet these two requirements. Other purchasers have been supplied essentially out of above-plan production.[54] However, one may wonder whether the ministerial output plan has not in fact been constrained by the objective of providing this supply for regional purchasers. Although output increased by 6.6 per cent between 1981 and 1983, the plan remained stable during these years. Finally, in 1984 the plan was increased by 1.1 per cent; output grew in that same year by 2.8 per cent.

The fifth and last of the enterprises in this subcategory is one of the textile plants whose output was allocated by the Center, not directly but through product quotas set for the province which was the direct supervisor of this enterprise. Since the enterprise did not produce cotton goods, its production was not rationed to final consumers.

Table 3A.2 Output of Cement Plant by Customer (in percentages)

Customer	1981	1982	1983	1984
Central ministry for allocation	92.0	88.3	86.8	85.1
Suppliers of raw materials (exchange) and railroads[a]	6.6	8.1	7.4	9.2
Cities, counties, & local units	0.9	2.3	4.0	1.4
Province	0.0	0.0	0.0	3.0
Purchasers on open market	0.4	1.3	1.9	1.2
Output as % of plan	102.4	106.9	109.1	110.9
Central ministry plus suppliers as % of planned output	101.0	103.0	102.8	104.6

[a] However, another source in the same enterprise said that such exchange during 1981–83 varied between 10 and 14 per cent annually.

Through 1982, self-sales by the enterprise ran about 5 per cent of domestic sales. These self-sales were supplied through plan over-fulfillment, which for the mill's final product was 5 to 19 per cent during each year of 1979–82. Such overfulfillment was made possible by the fact that materials allocations, although in theory intended to support only planned output, were actually overgenerous and were sufficient to cover the unplanned production. This provision seems to have been intentional on the part of the authorities; plans are said to have been increased annually by less than capacity in order to provide an incentive to the enterprise. The incentive feature was that the enterprise was permitted higher earnings for the portion of above-plan output that it itself sold at retail. (During 1975–78, in comparison, overfulfillment had been limited to between zero and 2 per cent annually.)

The situation changed drastically in 1983 as a result of the waning of the market for the company's products. Heavy imports led to this deterioration, and the enterprise was forced to take responsibility during 1983 for 80 per cent of its domestic sales. This high proportion was reduced to 40 per cent in 1984 and to a planned 30 per cent (expected to continue in future years) in 1985. But clearly the earlier situation of national allocation of the product had disappeared.

The reason for this shift to marketization had nothing to do with reform policies as such. Even the 1983 imports should not be described as being the result of such policy, but rather as an aberration. Rather, marketization represented a reaction by central distributors to a deterioration in the marketplace. It was not so much authority as undesired responsibility that was being given to the enterprise.

Enterprises of Category B (the least centralized category)

A producer of electrical equipment was, at least by 1984, the essential source of its own value-of-output plan and perhaps of its separate physical output plans as well. It seems to have been guided in the proposals it made to higher authorities primarily by sales possibilities. The advantage to the enterprise of setting a high plan was that this would be accompanied by greater planned receipt of allocated materials; the disadvantage was that the province expected about a 10 per cent annual increase in output, and that the enterprise was motivated to make provisions for achieving this growth in the future. In fact, the enterprise's value-of-output plan in each year of 1982–84 was probably very close to actual output.

The second enterprise is the textile producer of cloth made from chemical fiber and local hemp. Through 1980 the province provided the enterprise with all of its plan indicators, and it continued to set physical output plans through at least 1981. The municipality took major responsibility for the enterprise after 1980. However, materials allocations continued to be made by the Ministry of Textiles and by the province. It was the Ministry of Textiles that approved a major expansion plan in 1982, and it was the enterprise that had to be persuaded to accept it.

The enterprise began to sell part of its production itself in 1979. This portion was 18 per cent in 1981, rose to 50 per cent in 1982 as the market for the product worsened, and increased to 78 per cent during 1983, with almost all of the remainder being exported. Here is another case of growing marketization as a result of market deterioration.

The third enterprise is the watch and clock producer which is municipally controlled. It is subject to two physical output targets: one for watches set by the national ministry and one for clocks set by the province. The enterprise managers held that they would be allowed to overfulfill either target without any higher approval (sales and plant capacity, not supply of materials, were the enterprise constraints), but that such approval would be required if underfulfillment were to be acceptable.

Nevertheless, when the clock market deteriorated in 1982, the enterprise was guided in its reaction by market conditions rather than by output plans. During this year, the enterprise had a physical output plan of 1,115,000 clocks and it received allocations of materials based on this figure. Only in mid-July (after having already reduced clock production) did it request that the plan be cut back to 600,000. No action was taken on this petition, and in September the company sought a further decrease to 520,000. In mid-December the final physical output plan for clocks was reduced to the requested 520,000, and the enterprise was able to show 104 per cent plan fulfillment for the year. There had meanwhile been no reduction in the supply of allocated materials; indeed, the company was so overstocked that it planned no purchases of such items in 1983 (although it had earlier submitted allocation requests).

For the coming year, the enterprise received a plan for 500,000 clocks. But already in January, the company was counting on manufacturing only 300,000 and was scheduling production in accord with this lower figure.

In contrast, watch production in 1982 had been 880,000 units, and the physical output plan for 1983 was set at the similar figure of 900,000. Although the enterprise encountered no difficulties whatsoever with supply and was not motivated by consideration of allocations, it requested a plan of 1 million. Municipal authorities refused, at least temporarily, to raise the planned figure above that set by the national ministry, but they agreed that 1 million or even 1.2 million production would be acceptable provided that the watches could be sold. As of January, with an annual plan of 900,000, the enterprise was giving alternative production plans to its subordinate units based on the two figures of 1 million and 1.2 million.

It was clear that annual physical output plans were viewed lightly by this enterprise and that they had no appreciable effect upon its behavior. The enterprise was totally market oriented as opposed to plan oriented. The national government, which had believed since 1981 that the national watch market was threatened with saturation, did not use the available device of setting maximum physical output of watches in order to restrict such production. Nor did it employ allocation of materials as such a tool. Instead, bank policy restricted capital-expansion loans to the industry, and the national government established minimum retail prices for watches so as to avoid "ruthless competition" among producers. With regard at least to this enterprise, these measures were highly effective. The enterprise, which in 1981 had been gearing itself to produce 3 million watches in 1985, had instead been given a target of 1.4 million. As of the fall of 1985, the enterprise was expecting to produce 1.6 million.

4

MULTIPLE PRICES AND EQUILIBRIUM PRICE

In this chapter I deal with the purchases of goods and services by Chinese industrial enterprises. While in chapter 3 I discussed the planning of outputs as a means of coordination of the economy, in this chapter I am concerned with equilibration efforts directed at the input side.

The chapter's primary contribution is to my thesis of the uniqueness of China as a socialist planned economy. Just as in chapter 3, uniqueness will be demonstrated here for the pre-reform period as well as for the reform years. But this chapter also contributes to the integrative theme of property rights. Forms of input supply used for particular enterprises differ with patterns of property rights, although considerably less than is the case for the forms of distribution of the products of these enterprises. Most significant is the evidence that enterprise attitudes toward the importance of financial considerations in obtaining inputs correlate well with the property rights held by the principal(s) of the enterprise (see table 4.2).

In the concluding chapter of this book, I discuss the efficiency of the system of multiple prices in the Chinese context. The argument there will take up once again the theme of property rights, this time as applied to the second major portion of the materials presented in this chapter.

In East European socialist economies and, more particularly, in the Soviet Union, procurement of intermediate goods has been the principal bottleneck in production. A substantial literature stemming both from these countries and from the West has developed around the problem of "materials balancing." Vertical integration within a single enterprise and even a single factory, as a means of avoiding shortages of often inexpensive but vital supplies, has been a continuing and widespread phenomenon. The results have been the widely recognized phenomena of high production costs and inferior design stemming both from the small scale of output (e.g., in the case of fasteners) and from the use of inappropriate technology (e.g., the substitution of cast metals for rolled steel).[1]

In the light of the primitive nature of the balancing of inputs

112

and outputs by the Chinese, with the Center's reliance upon an extreme degree of aggregation (see table 3.1), one might have expected that the Chinese experience with procurement would be even worse than that of the Soviet Union. This is not the case, however, for our sample. My impression of the evidence is the same as that of Gene Tidrick; namely, that "the allocation of supplies (does) not constrain Chinese industrial output in the sample enterprises."[2] Shortage, with the major exception of electricity, has not been a serious problem when judged by the standards of European socialist countries. Nor does it seem that this is so simply because a shortage of electricity has been the overriding hindrance in the industrial sector, causing all other input bottlenecks to be nonbinding. Although electricity has indeed been a bottleneck, it has not been sufficiently binding to lead to that extreme result.

Clearly, to the degree that such absence of serious shortage was general among medium and large state industrial enterprises rather than being an artifact of bias in the sample, this state of the world would have been easiest for the Center to assure if prices had been allowed to settle at a market-clearing level. Indeed, by 1984 and 1985 there existed in China an officially recognized system of multi-prices for a given product. The highest of this tier of prices appears to have been market clearing. In this very special sense, the Chinese producer goods price pattern was, by the mid-1980s, a system of equilibrium prices.

What is most striking, however, is the fact that our sample data for earlier years display the same phenomenon of absence of serious shortage. This was so despite the rather limited degree of price flexibility that existed. This chapter is concerned with: (1) why this was the case; (2) why there was movement to a very complex system, permitting the attainment of equilibrium prices at social cost (through confusing price signals, particularly for investment decisions) as well as with social benefit; and (3) how one should relate an analytic treatment of the different stages of the development of Chinese pricing to such theoretic standbys of the field of socialist economics as that of disequilibrium analysis and of János Kornai's (1980) "insatiable investment hunger" and "soft budget constraint."

The organization of this chapter is as follows: first, I provide a three-stage historic analysis of Chinese industrial procurement during the 1970s through the mid-1980s; second, I present the sample data as to behavior in all three stages; and finally, I contrast the analysis with the concept of disequilibrium and with the ideas of Kornai that were developed to explain behavior under socialist central planning.

Stage Analysis of Industrial Procurement

Pre-1979

The first stage probably existed from the early period of the Cultural Revolution in the second half of the 1960s, but it is most convincingly dated as beginning during the 1970–73 period when central power was formally and substantially devoluted to the provincial level or below (see chap. 2). We may think of it as ending simultaneously with the pre-reform regime, whose demise is conventionally dated as December 1978 with the decisions of the Central Committee of the Communist Party.

This stage is one of considerable regional autarchy; a high degree of economic self-sufficiency existed at all governmental levels from the county upward, as well as at a still lower nongovernmental level (the commune). The autarkic phenomenon is best documented in the case of agriculture, where specialization by crop was virtually prohibited.[3] It existed, however, in industry as well, even at the level of the individual commune and rural county where the development of the "five small" industries was promoted through the 1970s so as to meet local production needs.[4]

As discussed in chapter 2, not only was management of state enterprises essentially handed over to local governments around 1970, but also the share of state-planned investment that was fully financed and managed below the level of the Center doubled during the first half of the 1970s. Similarly, and of even greater significance, these local levels became responsible (somewhat less in fact than in principle, however) for supplying the needs of individual enterprises out of the locality's own resources as well as out of common block allocations to the region.

Materials procurement by state industrial enterprises during this stage seems to have occurred essentially through use of the planning mechanism, with the market playing only a minor role. But the planning mechanism that was relevant to the enterprises was not nationally organized; rather, it existed at their own local levels. Thus the economy has been described by Western analysts as being "cellular," as noted in chapter 3. Although it was required that monetary payments accompany planned exchanges between state enterprises (as is almost universally the case in socialist economies), price appears to have played no significant role. There is no indication that state enterprises faced any serious cash constraint.

Of course, exchanges of goods took place as well across the borders of individual regions. Some of these exchanges were mediated through national planning; such transfers were composed mainly of the block allocations of specific goods to individual regions, and were the grossed-up counterpart to financial net grants or levies between regions. Also significant, however, was the existence of voluntary barter between regions, a barter that was indeed accompanied by money exchanges but only in a passive sense.[5] Some of these voluntary barter arrangements presumably also had a time dimension insofar as there were exchanges of equipment for later deliveries of materials produced by means of this investment. Such barter over time can be documented at least for the second stage.[6]

Because of this barter, interregional exchange ratios were important. But the key point here is that these were barter ratios, rather than ratios of the prices of the respective goods. (Net side payments in cash by one party or the other sometimes accompanied the barter.) There was indeed an interregional market, but it was one in which the monetary expression was a mere surface manifestation. Since these were free exchanges (between regions, if not between the direct participants which were often enterprises), I would suspect that the barter exchange ratios were market clearing.[7]

In the Soviet Union, state enterprises also engage in barter, although only semilegally. Presumably, the exchange ratios are also market clearing. But these exchanges differ in two major ways from the Chinese. First, they are not organized by bodies above the level of the enterprise; in carrying out such exchanges, the Soviet enterprise is the decision maker and principal rather than a simple agent. Second, the Soviet enterprise is normally in no position to exchange its own products, but rather is limited to offering materials that it itself has been allocated. The reason for this de facto limitation is that the sales plans that bind the Soviet enterprise are too taut to permit it to leave undeclared a significant portion of its own production that would then be available for trading purposes.[8] In contrast, Chinese state enterprises definitely trade their own products as well as materials allocated to them.[9] The same would appear to have been even more true in barter between regions.[10]

In the pure case of undivided supervision, where a single locality planned the production, handled the allocation of materials, and otherwise managed all enterprises in its area, one might expect that interenterprise exchanges would be restricted to those carried out within a single locality or larger region. The plan made by that locality could fully dictate the activities of its enterprises. We find this situation represented in our sample, or at a minimum in the recollections of some of the enterprise representatives.

This arrangement broke down when enterprises within the

same geographic area were under the supervision of different levels of government. A writer from the State Capital Construction Committee used such breakdown to explain why four integrated steel mills were built within a single medium-sized city.[11]

Moreover, the pattern of complete planning to the enterprise level would not work well in the case of multilevel supervision, where different regional levels had a property claim to the output of a single enterprise. In such cases, it is not surprising to learn that barter might be engaged in by the enterprise itself. Very incomplete data show that this was significant prior to 1979 for at least two, and probably for at least three, enterprises in our sample.

The existence of the above pattern, in which money values are no more than a reflection of quantitative exchanges, does not answer the question as to why there should have existed a system of multiprices for the same product in the same region during the pre-1979 years. How can this phenomenon, which appears clearly in the sample data, be reconciled with the above analysis?

The reconciliation is possible in that the price differences seem to be almost entirely accounted for by the legal status and subordination of the producing enterprises. Brigade and commune enterprises were generally permitted to charge higher prices than were state-owned enterprises. Various sorts of cooperatives were given similar privileges. Among the state-owned enterprises, county-supervised ones could often charge more than those supervised by higher governmental levels. What was rarely seen, however, was the same enterprise charging different prices for its planned and above-plan output. (Although one case of this behavior was reported in our sample, I believe that it was an anomaly.[12])

Observed price differentials for the same product are correlated with costs of production. At least on average, those producers permitted to charge higher prices suffered from diseconomies of scale; they probably also operated under poorer natural conditions (e.g., in coal mining) and had inferior capital stock. The private marginal costs (to the enterprise) could well have been considered to be substantially above the social marginal cost to the region in which the product was used. This would have justified the use of price "subsidies" as a means of encouraging production and of redistributing income to the product's nonstate producers as well as to the county governments.[13]

This analysis presumes that the price differentials of the pre-1979 period were determined primarily according to administrative rather than market considerations. Thus it does not regard the peak prices as having been set at a market-clearing level. If this treatment is correct, the existence of a system of multiple price levels does not lead to rejection of the view that interlocality exchange constituted barter.

I have still to raise the issue of why the sample data do not show serious shortages of materials during this period, given the fact that shortages have been rampant in planned economies of other countries. There would seem to be two credible explanations, both of which amount to waiving away any generalization of such sample evidence for this period.

The first possible reason is that detailed sample procurement data for the pre-1979 period are rather scarce; the interviews present far more data with regard to the 1979–83 period than for either of the other two. Thus we may be getting information for the first period which is quite atypical as a description of the procurement problems facing medium and large state enterprises during these years.

The second imaginable explanation is that our sample data are indeed representative of such enterprises prior to 1979, but that the members of this subset of industrial organizations were generally treated by the planning authorities as having "priority." Thus they could be assured of a good procurement environment even if this were impossible to provide for the state sector as a whole, let alone for all of industry.

Such priority treatment as compared with nonstate enterprises (rural commune and brigade enterprises and collective firms of various types) could be rationalized on the ground that state enterprises represent a "higher social form" than do the latter group. This ideological explanation will not do to explain their hypothesized priority relative to small state plants, but the larger scale of the medium and large enterprises probably led them to be perceived as being more efficient processors of raw materials. Whether such scale economies were genuine, were presumed to exist, or even were regarded as constituting only a potential that was as yet unexploited does not really matter for purposes of this interpretation; any one of the three could lead to a "rational" prioritization. This explanation, of course, also applies to a comparison with nonstate enterprises, thus reinforcing the ideological interpretation presented above.

1979–83

These years appear to constitute a transitional stage in which money income and profitability became much more important to the individual regions and localities. Trade between localities, while still heavily affected by flows planned at the level of the Center and of the province, as well as through barter arrangements, was increasingly motivated by profit-seeking behavior.

Such a description, I believe, is noncontroversial. What is controversial, however, is that my analysis places all of the weight upon the region/locality as the profit maximizer and denigrates the role of the state-owned enterprise. The enterprise here is viewed simply as an agent of its principal(s). In the Chinese context (if one trusts the evidence to be discussed in chapter 5) it is only the possessors of property rights who are the actors of interest.

In agriculture, production was allowed to shift considerably during this period to more profitable activities.[14] Interprovincial marketing of domestically produced grain expanded by 1983 to five times the average level of 1976–80 and to more than seven times the level of 1978.[15] It is true that these developments were to a large degree due to profit-maximizing behavior undertaken at first by cooperative bodies (teams) and later by individual households, rather than by local governments. Nevertheless, agriculture set the psychological mood for what was occurring simultaneously at the governmental level in the provinces and localities.

Localities in general engaged in substantial investment and attempted to do so primarily in the production of those products with high ratios of profits-plus-taxes to capital investment. State investments by regions and localities seem to have been concentrated particularly on such industrial projects, rather than on the previous target of expanding those products of heavy industry needed for local self-sufficiency.[16] This applied particularly to the production of consumer goods; bicycles, watches, electric fans, cigarettes, liquor, silk cloth, and candy are examples.

Such activity was accompanied by protectionist behavior (taking the form of nonprice discrimination) both at the provincial and even at the locality level, as well as by the restriction of shipments of raw materials out of a given province. In some cases, this behavior led simply to the diversion of a portion of the national growth in output of a product (bicycles, watches) to regions that were protecting their own rapidly expanding markets. In other cases (the rise of silk factories in Sichuan and of tobacco factories in Henan), restrictions on raw material shipments may have led to partial idleness of more efficient factories elsewhere (particularly in Shanghai). In both situations, however, it was the policy decisions of local government rather than of state enterprises that were decisive, and the orientation of these local governments was to a great extent dictated by profitability considerations.

From the latter part of 1979 through 1982, the central government attempted to combat inflation by exercising investment constraint. During the three years of 1979–81, 872 of a total of 1,624 active, large-scale investment projects of the Center were postponed or abandoned rather than being completed or continued.[17] Although we have no measure of investments approved by the Center as a proportion of all fixed-asset investment in state-owned facilities, we do have a proxy for this measure: namely, the proportion of all such investment that was financed through the state budget.[18] During 1980 and 1981, budgetary fixed-capital investment declined by 16 and 25 per cent, respectively; but nonbudgetary investment (which was already one-third of the total in 1979) grew by 48 and 4 per cent, respectively, during these years. Both categories increased in 1982, but by 8 and 39 per cent, respectively.[19] Annual fulfillment of budgetary fixed-capital investment plans was kept below 120 per cent, while nonbudgetary plan fulfillment was far higher in all three years.[20] It would seem that local governments were in a position to expand investments substantially (by an annual nominal compound rate of 29 per cent during 1980–82, compared with 6 per cent during 1976–79[21]) and quite consistently during these years, regardless of the desire of the Center. It is difficult to believe that they could have done so with such success if their possession of monetary resources had not been providing them with access to real resources at the expense of the Center.

Furthermore, there has been a major increase in the extra-budgetary revenue of governments and their agencies (such as state enterprises) as a proportion of budgetary revenue: from what was estimated as being less than 10 per cent during the 1953–57 period, to some 50 percent in 1980, and then to 71 per cent in 1982.[22] (For comparison, some 29 to 35 per cent of similar revenue in the Soviet Union was extra-budgetary as expressed in the various plans for the years 1966–85.[23]) When this expansion in the share of Chinese extra-budgetary revenue is added to the growth in local governments' powers over budgetary income sources placed at their disposal, the importance of the financial resources left in local hands can be judged. One can imagine the degree of motivation that individual local governments must have had to attempt to generate more of these funds for their own purposes.

A Chinese study of twenty-three cities in 1984 showed that enterprises (collective as well as state owned) and their immediate supervisory bodies within city government created 76 per cent of the extra-budgetary revenue received by these city governments, and accounted for 89 per cent of the expenditures.[24] If these figures are at all representative, enterprise net income was not being used as a cash cow for financing conventional government expenditures of a social nature. Such income can have been used in this way only to the degree (which is fairly important) that the enterprises themselves carried out such expenditures. Nevertheless, this rapidly expanding source of funds at the disposal of local governments offered these governments real promise of such possibilities of use in the future.

The retrenchment aspects of central policy during 1980 and 1981 were critical in promoting the development of marketization during this transitional period. Markets for consumer goods and construction materials for housing boomed as a result of the expansion of peasant monetary and real income. But the markets for investment goods other than construction materials, as well as those for intermediate inputs into such goods, were seriously depressed.[25] The combination of expansion of demand by the rural private sector and by local governments did not fully offset the slashing of demand by the Center. Perhaps of equal or even greater importance than the net decline in such demand for equipment and intermediate goods was the change in the personae of the purchasers. The need that suppliers faced both to search out new customers and to change the product mix of their output to meet the desires of these clients created significant adjustment problems for such suppliers. The combination of the two effects was that in 1981 steel was not allocated at all but was instead handled as a product whose sale was simply to be negotiated between a willing seller and buyer.[26] Prior to this change, in fact as early as the second half of 1979, much investment equipment had been transferred to that status.[27]

The significance of all this is that the traditional seller's market between regions (for those sales that were solely for money and at official planned prices) disappeared for major products. Barter arrangements were no longer required in order to purchase goods; in fact, our sample data even reveal the existence of tied sales. The retrenchment policy raised money income to the status of an important desideratum for state enterprises and for the local governments who were their principals. For the individual enterprise, marketization was partially but significantly replacing the previous stage's planned distribution by the locality and province.

This development is particularly interesting in terms of the perception among many observers that retrenchment and reform policies stood in opposition to one another during these years. Reform was associated with the freeing of market prices (supposedly to make them more accurate indicators of underlying scarcities), while retrenchment was linked to price freezes. The announcement by the State Council in December of 1980 that strict price controls were to be enforced has been interpreted as a temporary victory of the old guard over reformists.[28] Chen Yun, a top economic administrator since at least the 1950s and perhaps the second senior Party figure after Deng Xiaoping, is described by some as the architect of the retrenchment. Chen is viewed as being the advocate of plan and stability in contrast to market and incentives.

Such a judgment seems fair enough as applied to consumer goods, precisely those for which nonstate producers were particularly important (and thus for which price incentives were most helpful) and where strong inflationary pressures existed. The exact reverse, however, would seem to be true as to the markets for producer goods other than construction materials. With regard to bringing price equilibrium, the reform policies making prices more flexible had much less effect than did the retrenchment policies which cut back demand. During the period through 1981, it was primarily the latter that accomplished the monetization of exchange relations between regions and enterprises.

This procurement stage lasting from late 1979 through 1982 could not, however, be more than one of transition. Monetization of the state-owned, producer sector of the economy could not continue indefinitely to rest on a combination of adjustment problems and of the limiting of demand to a level below capacity. As interregional trade developed, being expanded through profit seeking by local governments operating under monetizing conditions, new methods were required to maintain prices in their newly created equilibrium status. Without such methods, there could only have been a retreat, as monetary demand once more expanded, to the earlier omnipresence of a combination of local planning and of reliance on barter for interregional exchanges.

1984 and Thereafter

This last stage represented a radical transformation of pricing. In May 1984 the State Council explicitly distinguished between production governed by plan and that taking place outside of the plan, and it permitted prices for production outside the plan to differ by up to ±20 per cent from the planned prices. In February 1985 even this limit on price flexibility was abolished. These decisions were in the spirit of the October 1984 meeting of the Central Committee of the Communist Party which enunciated the slogan that "the socialist economy is a commodity economy based upon public ownership."[29]

The new pattern represented a substantial extension of the multi-price system for an identical product. Not only was there continuation of the different prices of the pre-1979 era, variegated according to the legal status and subordination of the producing enterprises. Now, in addition, each state-owned enterprise was to be permitted to charge prices that were sharply differentiated according to the portion of its production that was allocated and the portion that was beyond this quota. The latter price was to be determined on the open market.

This dual pricing system represented a major triumph of the reformers. Most of them viewed it as part of a transition toward universal market prices for an individual product, although they argued among themselves as to whether there should instead have been an immediate move to a market-price system rather than this transitional arrangement, as well as to whether the transition period should be lengthy or brief. Others believed in a permanent dual pricing system.[30] But all the vocal members of at least the reformist camp among Chinese economists and politicians were in agreement that the freeing-up of prices on the marginal portion of output was an improvement over the previous system.

The move from the second to the third stage is usually described in political terms.[31] Certainly this is correct in the sense that a different political decision could have meant a return to the pre-1979 omnipresence of planned allocation modified by barter. But what seems clear is that there could not have been a continuation much longer of the situation in the years from 1979 to 1983. Forces promoting increased demand for producer goods at the existing price level were too powerful. Between 1978 and 1981, total annual fixed investment in nominal prices in state-owned units had actually fallen by 0.1 per cent. The explosive annual increase of 26 per cent during 1982 was reduced in 1983 to 13 per cent. But in 1984, these investments once again increased by one-fourth.[32] Fixed prices could not equilibrate supply and demand under these conditions. The need for a political decision was dictated by economic developments.

Our limited sample data for this last stage demonstrate that the differences in production costs per unit of production were substantial depending upon whether or not the sample enterprise was able to make its purchases through planned allocations. Judging from the sample data, this is the first time that per unit costs were affected significantly by such sourcing.

Procurement Data From the Sample

Procurement data from the sample are reasonably plentiful for the second stage (1979–83), although rather scarce for both the first and third. For discussion of the experience of different enterprises during the second stage, the enterprises will be grouped into five categories. While the prior and later periods will for convenience be handled as each enterprise is discussed, the categorization has no significance for these years. Data for the pre-1979 years are available only for enterprises in the second and fourth categories.

The twenty organizations of the sample are all placed into one of five groups, with four of these ranked in order of degree of centralized management and physical planning. Seventeen of the twenty fall into one or another clear category in the ordering scheme; only three are in the final, mixed category.

(4.1) *Definition of Enterprise Categories for the Second Stage:*
First category. Under purely national supervision as treated in chapter 2, and in subcategory A1 as defined in chapter 3 with regard to physical planning. (See definitions 3.2 and 3.3. Physical output targets are set by the same body that allocates output to users and that supports these targets with planned quantities of inputs. Value-of-output and profit plans are similarly established by that body.) Three enterprises.

Second category. Under joint national and local supervision and in subcategory A2. (Same as A1 with respect to physical planning and support, but plans expressed in monetary terms are established by a different principal.) Four enterprises.

Third category. Textile firms under purely provincial supervision and in subcategory A2. Three enterprises.

Fourth category. No national supervision and in category B. (Residual from category A, which relates to the setting and support of physical output targets.) Seven enterprises.

Fifth category. Mixed degree of centralization. Three enterprises.

Degree to which Allocations Meet Input Requirements

One might hypothesize that the extent to which enterprise needs are met through the allocation system is closely correlated with the degree to which these enterprises are centrally managed, and with the extent to which their own production is allocated to others through the planning system. As we shall see, the direction of the hypothesized correlation is in accord with the facts of our sample.

Such support for the hypothesis is not surprising. What is startling, however, is the weakness of the hypothesized relation, and in particular the degree to which even the most centralized category of enterprises has had to go outside of the allocation system for major inputs. While my evidence applies particularly to the second stage, the suggestion from the data and literature is that the need to go outside increased in the following stage and had also been strong in the pre-1979 years.

The following analysis of allocations according to the category of centralization in the management of production is somewhat lengthy. Six conclusions from the data are presented in the summary at the end of the section.

The locomotive-repair enterprise provided systematic annual data for 1981–83 that shows the proportion of major materials coming to it through the allocation system. The annual range of these are as follows:

> *Current inputs:* steel products, 84–88 per cent; bearings, 81–89 per cent; and copper conductors, 65–75 per cent.
> *Construction and building maintenance materials:* timber, 89–90 per cent; and cement, 41–50 per cent.

Copper conductors constitute the current input that is least supplied through the allocation system. This item, however, does not constitute a supply problem for the enterprise. The plant produces a good deal of copper scrap and is able to obtain unallocated copper conductors in return for this scrap. Steel products and bearings, on the other hand, can only be purchased on the open market or obtained through barter; the vast bulk must be acquired in the first fashion, since the plant does not produce a tradable product.

Construction materials, especially cement, are more heavily purchased on the open market. Furthermore, by late 1984 the enterprise was paying an additional 50 per cent for the cement obtained in this fashion.

Despite the fact that these open market purchases have constituted a significant portion of total material inputs, the need to go outside of the allocation system has had a totally insignificant effect on enterprise costs. The additional costs in 1982 for the above items together represented something on the order of 1 per cent of the total materials costs for the year.

The enterprise was also extraordinarily well treated with regard to electricity, despite the fact that this critical input was under local rather than national control. No limits at all were placed on its use of electricity in the rainy season. (Presumably, hydroelectric power was important in the area.) But even in the dry season, such use was only "controlled to some extent," according to an interviewee from the municipal planning authority.

The second enterprise is the petroleum field. Lumber is described as the item in shortest supply. There are conflicting statements as to whether there was any exchange of oil and gas for timber;

even if there were, it cannot have accounted for a large proportion of needs. In 1983 only 75 per cent of cement requirements and a similar portion of coal needs were allocated. The rest was purchased at an average of some 36 per cent premium for cement, and of 50 to 100 per cent premium for coal.

Although these figures seem high, the total additional costs of going outside the allocation system for these products and for all steel items seem to have been well under 1 per cent of total materials costs in 1982–83. Thus the supply pattern seems to be quite similar to that of the first enterprise.

The third enterprise is the automotive concern, for which some aspects of the supply situation were described in the appendix to chapter 3. To reiterate, in 1984, and presumably in 1985, national policy shifted to some degree toward allocating steel to provinces in lieu of trucks, with the provinces expected to trade such steel for trucks as extensively as they wished. Naturally, the coverage of the automotive enterprise's supply needs through allocations was correspondingly reduced.

During at least 1981–83 as well, the enterprise traded its final product for required materials. Rolled steel, tin, zinc, and coal were obtained in this way in 1983, as well as timber for construction during previous years. But at least some of such barter would seem to have been nonessential to solve supply problems; rather, it was done to reduce monetary purchasing costs. Thus, although 19,000 tons of coal were received in barter during 1983, coal supply was described as not constituting a problem because of the existence of a large coal mine nearby. Barter cannot unequivocally be described as an indication of a seller's market.

The plant has also engaged in "compensation trade" for three different types of materials needed as current inputs. Such trade has involved providing interest-free loans of investment funds (cash only, not goods) to one province and to two municipalities; they, in turn, are obligated to sell, at the official allocation price, specified quantities of the materials produced with the new capacity. In the case of at least two of these items, and perhaps of all three, the enterprise chose this purchase method either to avoid having to pay prices that were 50 per cent above the allocation price or to avoid high transport costs. There is no indication that compensation trade was resolving procurement problems that could not have been handled in other ways.

This enterprise reports that it has had little difficulty in receiving the precise product mix of steel that it requires, despite the fact that its allocations are expressed in aggregative form. In this regard, the enterprise is highly unusual in our sample. More typically, enterprises report that the allocated amount of an important input is sufficient to satisfy total quantitative requirements, but that product-mix problems are serious.

On the other hand, the treatment of the supply of pig iron (needed by the enterprise for foundry work) is curious. The enterprise receives an allocation sufficient for all needs; but half the allocated amount is of unusable quality and is not even ordered by the enterprise. The shortage, however, is not made up through open market purchases which are available at an illegal 50 per cent markup. Instead, the plant trades its own scrap for pig iron. Such barter is possible—despite the fact that the plant receives a mandatory target for delivering scrap to the state—because, over a number of years when truck output perhaps doubled, the scrap target was held constant.

This treatment by the Center would seem, in substance, to be comparable to the treatment of the first enterprise in this category, which was left with copper scrap to trade for copper conductors. The difference is that, for the first enterprise, this use of scrap seems to have been the explicit method by which the Center provided a substantial portion of the conductors. In the case of the auto firm, the Center not only left it with much of the scrap it produced, but also allocated pig iron to it that was scarce (as shown by its open market price), but which was supplied by a source whose product was worthless.

Since the net effect of the two treatments was identical, a comparison of these two cases should make the observer wary in evaluating enterprise complaints that allocated goods were of poor quality or of inappropriate mix. Such deliveries may represent a deliberate decision by the allocating body, as seems to have been the case here. The auto enterprise complains, as do other plants, of poor product mix of materials generally (other than steel); but without having far more detail than is available, one cannot judge the degree to which this is no more than the sort of complaint that it also makes with regard to pig iron.

In general, materials needed for current production seem to have been readily available without any significant markups from the allocation price. Electricity, coal, and paint are described as presenting no problems.[33] Allocations or ready barter substitutes, as described above, seem to have met all needs. In contrast, however, during the first half of the 1980s these satisfied only one-third of construction and building maintenance requirements. Such needs were instead filled through 1981–82 by open market purchases at no higher costs than goods bought through allocation channels; thereafter, the cost differential began to mount.

SECOND CATEGORY

The steel enterprise is the first in this category. For it, the allocation principle, which was increasingly violated at the end of the second period and during the third, was that the physical production targets set by the Center should be fully covered by allocation of inputs. The province set profit targets that implied somewhat higher physical output; but these additional implicit targets were not to be covered by allocations.

In general, allocations were sufficient to cover current input requirements (although probably not new construction and maintenance needs) through 1981 or 1982, but thereafter the situation degenerated. Total purchases outside the allocation system constituted 3.4 per cent of all purchases in 1979 and 1980, 5.4 per cent in 1981, and 8.6 per cent in 1982. (These figures may not have included barter arrangements, but those were negligible during these years.) By 1984, aside from the above type of purchases whose significance is unknown for that year, some 14 per cent of materials were obtained through barter alone.

Allocations of scrap steel, a major input into the steel smelting production process, became insufficient after 1982 to cover planned production; by 1984 these allocations were running 30 per cent below requirements. The same situation with regard to ferro-alloys faced the enterprise in 1984; but for this second major input, allocations had been sufficient through 1983 rather than only through 1982. The need to barter steel for coke began in 1983. For other inputs, allocations appear to have held up into the third period.

This is the only enterprise in our sample for which electricity was allocated directly by the national State Planning Commission. In China as a whole, there are said to be some three hundred such enterprises. This allocation was sufficient for the production of steel as such, but some auxiliary factories of the enterprise had to be shut down periodically due to power shortages.

The lumber and forestry enterprise is the second in this category. During both the second period and the beginning of the third, allocations by the Center and the province together ran an estimated 45 to 52 per cent of total purchases of materials.[34] In 1983, 70 per cent of steel, 50 per cent of cement, 40 per cent of coal, and only 10 per cent of plate glass were supplied through such allocations.

However, a portion of the shortfall between requirements and allocations was due to the fact that this state enterprise conducted substantial additional activity through cooperatives, most of whose members were dependents of the employees in the state enterprise.

Workers in these cooperatives in 1982 constituted 87 per cent of the number employed by the enterprise itself. Since these cooperatives appear to have received no materials allocations, the enterprise provided them with a portion of its own allocations. This enterprise decision does not seem to have been taken into account in the allocations made by central and provincial bodies; thus such allocations were higher, and perhaps considerably higher, as a proportion of enterprise needs as these were evaluated by the authorities than the 50 per cent as evaluated by the enterprise itself.

The third enterprise is the cement factory. Over the years 1981–84, some 7 to 9 percent of output was used for purposes of barter for raw materials, and another 1.5 to 6 per cent was sold outside of the plan. On an annual basis, 8 per cent in 1981 and 12 to 13 per cent during 1982–84 was available for these two purposes together. Since the barter ratios were more favorable to this cement factory than were the official prices set for the items bartered (necessitating net cash payments by the factory), it seems unlikely that the enterprise had available for open market purchases any appreciable amount of supplementary bank funds left over from its free sales. Thus it seems reasonable to think of a stable 7 to 9 per cent of materials as being supplied outside of the allocation system throughout 1981–84. There is no indication of a change during the third stage of procurement compared with the second.

Nonetheless, some of the shortfall in allocations may be viewed differently by the authorities than by the enterprise. During the first quarter of 1984, half of all the cement bartered (which constituted about one-third of the usual total barter for the year) was used in exchange for coal. This is not prima facie surprising for a cement plant. However, since the factory was in an isolated area and only one-fifth of consumer needs for coal were supplied by the locality, an unknown portion of this coal was used by the plant to provide the supplementary household requirements of its workers. Thus this enterprise was in a rather similar position to the lumbering concern in that it used allocated fuel and resources for unplanned purposes.

It is particularly interesting that continuously since 1967, which was the date of the original commissioning into operation of this plant, the enterprise has been authorized to retain some of its production to use for barter. In this important regard, our informants explicitly recognize continuity over all three procurement stages.

Enterprise informants complain that electricity supply (primarily hydroelectric) is insufficient during four months each year. But it is interesting that other enterprise informants, in a different context, treat annual output as a function of equipment capacity rather than of electricity supply. This is an example of the difficulty of evaluating complaints (seen often in the national press) of electricity being a frequent bottleneck in production.

The fourth enterprise, which is in this category only for the years 1974–77 and falls into the fifth category thereafter, is the producer of pumps. During this first procurement stage (but also during the second), it received only about 45 per cent of its three principal inputs through the allocation system, yet had no difficulty in purchasing the rest without either barter or the payment of price supplements. What is critical here is that this remaining 55 per cent was not purchased by the enterprise on the open market; rather, it was supplied by provincial wholesale authorities outside of the system of either central or provincial planning. Here we have an interesting example of the same provincial authorities supplying both planned and unplanned volumes of the identical input to the same enterprise with no price differential. In this case, one may wonder as to the significance of "allocation" through provincial channels. Indeed, municipal authorities in another province, in discussing their own provisioning of their enterprises in this fashion, raised the same question.

The fifth and final enterprise of this category is a petrochemical producer. No useful information is available as to its supply situation.

THIRD CATEGORY

This category consists of three of the four textile enterprises that are directly under provincial management. Their respective provinces' output of the relevant textile products are subject to distribution by the Center, and thus each enterprise's production is kept under fairly tight provincial control. The enterprises are located in three separate provinces.

All of these enterprises have been fully supplied with direct materials inputs through the provincial allocation system. One of them (a user of cotton) reports that there have been no shortages since the 1960s. A second (a user of imported wool) had only 60 per cent of its needs met through allocations during 1984. But, this appears to have been the only year of a shortfall and, even then, domestic wool was available for purchase although it was of poorer quality and commanded a higher price. Indeed, the allocations of wool during each year of 1978–82 were sufficiently generous so as to allow an annual output level of at least 5 per cent overfulfillment of planned production, and in two years they permitted 12–14 per cent overfulfillment.

Shortages of electric power, resulting in plant stoppages, were complained of by one of the three enterprises. The same enterprise suffered from the fact that its allocated dyestuffs had to be ordered at least six months before arrival. Generally speaking, however, problems were very minor.

The situation was quite different with regard to materials for maintenance and construction. Representatives of two of the three mills commented that they received only a portion of their needs through the allocation system, while the third had problems with the allocated product mix. During late 1983, one of the enterprises suspended some building projects while awaiting deliveries of allocations of steel products, timber, and cement—it must be added that all of these inputs were available at higher prices on the open market.

The case best developed in the interview notes is that for one of the two plants poorly supplied through the allocation system with these materials needed for maintenance and construction. During 1983, only 12 per cent of its needs for steel products and about 17 per cent of those for timber were received in this way. Cement allocations were only partially enforced; shippers typically provided short-weight of 10 to 20 per cent during 1983.

But most interesting is that, for this last enterprise at least, the situation during the 1980s was no more than a continuation of past experience. Capital construction projects in 1961 and in 1975 had been supplied primarily through purchases made by the mill on the market, rather than through allocations. It is true that the needs for an expansion program in 1979–81 were provided by allocations, but this was the exception in the history of this plant.

The experience of these enterprises can be generalized by saying that current production needs were well provided through the allocation system, but that maintenance and capital construction had to be supplied heavily through the marketplace. Moreover, for at least one enterprise, this had been true during the pre-1979 stage as well as later.

FOURTH CATEGORY

Two of the members of this most decentralized category are also textile enterprises. The first of these received allocated yarn, which seems to have covered the vast bulk, but not all, of its requirements. Dyestuff allocations covered about 80 per cent of needs. As was the case for the textile firms in the third category, allocations of building materials were less complete. Nevertheless, even in the beginning of the third procurement stage, they covered two-thirds of requirements of steel, timber, and cement.

Although dyestuff allocations did not meet all the needs of this first enterprise, it is interesting that shortages during the first procurement stage were mainly due to the failure of the enterprise to order from fear of overstocking.[35] Clearly, the danger was in the overstocking of particular colors rather than of dyes in general. Nevertheless, especially for mills operating under quite decentralized conditions, it is remarkable by the standards of centrally planned economies that the enterprise-customer should have been restrained in its placing of orders. Such restraint is even more notable in that it occurred under allocation conditions and was due solely to the financial costs of carrying unnecessary materials inventories.

The second enterprise uses a locally grown type of hemp as its principal input. In general, both in China as a whole and in this province, this raw material has not been allocated, but the sample enterprise was one of two in its province that was supplied by allocation. This allocation was sufficient to meet all needs through 1983, although there seems to have been a substantial shortfall in 1984.

Chemical fibers were also received primarily through provincial allocation, albeit no guarantees of supply were given. In 1982 original allocation was only 30 per cent of the request submitted, but the remainder was purchased without either difficulties or the need for payment of higher prices. Part of chemical fiber requirements were supplied separately by the foreign trade organization located in a neighboring province. The organization provided a stated tonnage (of imported fiber) for every 100,000 meters of textiles that was exported through it by the enterprise. What is interesting is that this "market" receipt seems to have been at a lower price than that used for allocations, and this practice dates from the first procurement stage early in the 1970s.

The enterprise receives its dyestuffs by allocation and, unlike the textile enterprise in the third category, is able to place orders (at least for domestic dyes) close to the time when the materials are needed. Similarly, spare parts are allocated to the enterprise, as is coal: 80 per cent of the need for coal was allocated in 1983, but one-fifth of it turned out to be unusable.

The municipality determined electricity supply, for which there has been a local shortage, for this textile enterprise. In doing so, it shows the enterprise special consideration: when there is a shortage of electricity in the area, it is usually the aluminum factory next door that is cut off while the textile enterprise is protected. One might guess that this procedure results from the relative electric consumption per unit of product of aluminum versus textiles, with the municipality's allocation policy being dictated by an effort to maximize its output and/or profits subject to an overall electricity constraint. (The textile enterprise's profits have gone to the municipality: nothing is known as to the distribution of the profits of the aluminum plant.)

But the rationale given by the municipality to the interviewers is a different one: it mentions the importance of the textile enterprise and the fact that it would complain if it were cut off. This would suggest that "voice" may play some role in the context of at least this particular municipality.

The machine tool factory is the third enterprise in this category. The quality of the procurement data for this enterprise appears to be unusually good, particularly for comparisons of the situation in 1979 and earlier with that existing in 1982. Concerning procurement for this enterprise, the year 1979 would seem to be representative of the situation faced during the first stage of procurement, and 1982 of that met during the second stage.

During the pre-reform years of 1976–78, some 80 to 90 per cent of all materials supplies were allocated. The proportion could not have changed drastically through at least the first half of 1983.

Both in 1979 and in 1982, barter accounted for one-fifth of the total receipts of unallocated supplies. In 1979 half of the factory's barter items consisted of its own products and the other half of allocated steel. We do not know these relative proportions with regard to 1982, but we do know that the factory continued to barter away allocated steel, with only the type of steel changing in comparison to 1979.

The fact that open market purchases were four times as important as barter even in 1979 may seem surprising. But, it is accounted for by the principal products of nonallocated supply, which in both periods were coke, lumber, and coal. Prior to 1979 and in 1982, market sales of the latter two products in this province were made at prices at least one-third higher than the allocation price, regardless of whether the production was by state-owned or collectively owned bodies. Enterprises that had permission to engage in unplanned sales (apparently very unusual in China for state enterprises) were particularly attracted to free sale of their products rather than to barter arrangements. Thus the machine tool factory had little choice as to the method of obtaining unallocated supplies.

Considering individual major materials, the machine tool enterprise prior to 1979 received pig iron solely through allocations. Although the original allocation each year was only 60 percent of requirements, it was always supplemented sufficiently during the course of the year. In 1982 allocations still constituted 93 per cent; the remainder was purchased by the plant from other users, at a markup of 12 per cent to cover handling costs and freight.[36]

Rolled steel was received entirely through allocations prior to 1979, and 95 per cent was still supplied in this fashion in 1982. The principal type of steel used (a carbon structural steel) was subject to a

14 per cent markup for handling expenses and freight when purchased outside of the allocation system; such purchases were supplied by the procurement bureau of either the county or the municipality. For this type of steel, the supply situation had been even a bit easier in the pre-reform stage than it was in 1982.

Steel castings and standard brick for refractory purposes in casting were provided solely through allocations in both stages. In contrast, paint (subject only to local allocation) was primarily bought on the "marketplace" prior to 1979 and in 1982. In both stages, this "marketplace" was a municipal chemical administrative body that charged an 8 per cent markup. Since both allocation and "marketed" paint came from the same source, one might suspect that the low proportion of paint supplied through the allocation system was due to a very minor price "fiddle" on the part of the allocating body.

In contrast to all of the above items, only some 10 percent of coke requirements were allocated (this was by the province). This low proportion held before 1979 and in 1982, and in both stages part of the remainder was bought at higher prices from the same producers who supplied the allocated amounts. Such market purchases were at a markup of 14 per cent plus freight prior to 1979, and at a markup in 1982 which had been reduced to 8 per cent plus freight. Such movement toward more, rather than less, uniform pricing in the reform period is an example of the heterogeneity that exists in China and is frequently remarked on by Western observers.

Of lumber purchases, only one-third came through the allocation system pre-1979 and in 1982. In both stages, another one-third was purchased from collectives made up of youth who did a small amount of lumbering in state forests and who were dependents of regular state employees. The last one-third was purchased from furniture manufacturers who presumably had received it through allocations. This last group sold at a price that was some two-thirds above the allocation price in the pre-1979 era, and their price had risen by 1982 to a figure as high as 111 per cent above allocation price.

Coal constitutes the last major input, and its treatment is extremely interesting. The municipality allocates coal and provides this enterprise with 60 to 70 per cent of its requirements. But the same municipality provides allocations that constitute varying proportions of needs for different enterprises. The proportions for a given enterprise remain reasonably stable from year to year, but they differed between enterprises in 1982 within a range of 50 to 80–90 per cent of needs as defined by the municipality.

Such varying proportions of coverage of needs through allocation by the same body was a matter of deliberate municipal policy, while the percentage received by any individual organization seems to have been a matter primarily of historical accident. The machine tool enterprise, for example, had been transferred to the municipality's administration about 1979, and its allocation quota for coal went to the municipality along with the enterprise itself. In 1982 the municipality still provided the original allocation tonnage, supplemented only by an amount to replace fuel oil which the enterprise had previously burned but was no longer allowed to use.

The remaining portion of coal needs were supplied in 1982 by state coal enterprises from above-plan output at a 34 per cent markup. In the years before 1979, the machine tool enterprise had similarly purchased about one-third of its needs on the marketplace, paying a markup of about 30 per cent.[37]

An electrical equipment enterprise is the fourth in the category. While the description of the supply situation during the second half of 1982 and during 1984 is the most detailed and reliable part of the procurement information for this enterprise, the description given of earlier periods is richer than what we have for most other plants.

The period 1958–63 (identified at another point in the interviews as being 1960–64) is one in which no central allocations were given to this enterprise, although it is said that regional (and perhaps central) procurement agencies helped when they could. The enterprise depended primarily upon purchases in the open market. In contrast, 1964–78 is described as a period when the plant (then almost always under provincial supervision) received all of its supply through planned allocations. It was said that, when there was a shortage of such supply, it was made up primarily by the province, but the national ministry of the industry also provided some supplementary materials.

This last statement should presumably be interpreted as implying simply that there were supplements to original allocations when these supplies were either insufficient or not forthcoming from producing plants. The period 1964–78 is treated as a group of years in which neither barter nor open market purchases by the enterprise played any significant role in procurement.

In contrast, the years from 1979 through the first half of 1982 are described as ones in which materials were readily available on the market. This specifically relates to the two principal plant inputs of silicon steel (which was even purchased at discounts from the official state price) and copper wire. During the next two and a half years, however, allocations provided about three quarters of all requirements; significant maneuvering by the plant was required to obtain the rest of its needs.

During 1982 the enterprise received 56 per cent of its requirements of silicon steel through allocation. However, it should be remembered that market purchases were easy to arrange during the beginning of the year, so that allocations probably met all needs once the market tightened. During 1983 allocations constituted 81 per cent of supply; the remainder was arranged by the plant itself at a 10 per cent price supplement. In this year, however, half of the allocated silicon steel consisted of imports. Although the plant was not required to pay for these in foreign currency, it was charged a higher price than the normal one. The extra costs involved in these imports of silicon steel during 1983 constituted 4 per cent of total materials costs, amounting to some 45 per cent of what profits would have been without such higher prices.

In 1984 80 per cent of the silicon steel needs were allocated. Of the remainder, however, only 2 per cent were purchased outside of the planning system and at the official state price. The remaining 18 per cent consisted of "advances" against allocations that would be made in 1985. Such borrowings were arranged both from the provincial and from the municipal supply authorities, and also from the plant's principal supplier against planned deliveries that would be scheduled in 1985. When asked what such borrowing would do to the plant's situation in 1985, the enterprise respondents compared the situation to the borrowing by a son from his father. If things go well, the enterprise may repay; if not, it may be unnecessary to repay.

Copper wire was readily available on the market through the first half of 1983, and no wire allocations were made to the enterprise during that year. However, during the second half of 1983 the provincial authorities provided copper (presumably scrap) to the plant, which it in turn sent off to two wire drawing plants for "reconversion." It is interesting that the terms of such barter differed between the two plants: in tonnage terms, two tons of wire (including insulating material) for every ton of copper from one plant, but only one and one-third tons of wire for the same ton of copper from the other.[38] This sort of market imperfection is what one might expect to occur in a barter system. By 1984 copper wire allocations were made in the traditional form of the wire itself and were sufficient to meet needs.

This plant, as is the case for others in our sample whose supply situation was compared by informants with that of state enterprises not in the sample, has been allocated a somewhat higher proportion of its needs than is customary in its province. But the difference is not immense. In 1983 it received through allocations 80 per cent of rolled steel requirements, in contrast to 50–60 per cent for all state enterprises taken together. In 1984 the respective figures were 82 and 60 per cent. Thus, the pattern described for this enterprise may not be too distorted a picture of what was happening for other state machine-building enterprises in that province.

The county with seventeen state enterprises under its management is the fifth organization. Because of the small size of these subordinate enterprises and the low level of the government body in charge of them, we might have expected them to have supply problems that were especially severe and to be unusually dependent upon their own efforts in solving them. Indeed, during the procurement stage through 1983, allocations seem to have provided only some 20 to 30 per cent of all their supply needs.

One of these plants (producing fertilizer) engaged in compensation trade during 1982 and 1983 in order to obtain additional raw materials; this involved investing in a mine in another province. At the time of the interviews, however, this rather recent gambit had as yet been unsuccessful; the supplying province was unable to meet its planned deliveries to the national government, and thus the mine was not permitted to provide its unplanned obligation.

Electricity in late 1983 was described as a shortage item. But the effect of the shortage was primarily to reduce the workweek of these enterprises from the normal six days to five, rather than to lead to unexpected blackouts. This is the only case where we have heard of differential pricing for electricity, with a higher price being charged to a plant when it exceeded its usage quota. Perhaps this differential pricing was related to the fact that the power plant ran at least partly on imported fuel oil, and presumably more electricity could be generated at an additional financial cost.

The sixth enterprise in this category is a foodstuff producer, using primarily sugar and flour. During the years through 1978, both inputs were provided entirely through planned channels. By 1982, in contrast, only 40 per cent of the sugar was allocated. Differing prices were being charged for sugar allocated by the Center and by the province, but these differences amounted to only 1.8 per cent and thus were inconsequential. Open market purchases, on the other hand, were being paid for at a price 11 per cent above the central-allocation price. Allocated sugar seems to have been sufficient to provide the materials for all of that portion of the plant's own products which were sold at state-set prices.

The last of the enterprises is the watch and clock factory. It received the vast bulk of its supplies through the allocation system. But, as has been described in the appendix to chapter 3, these allocations were taken lightly.[39] As of early 1983, it was believed in the enterprise and by its municipal authorities that the enterprise could obtain much greater supply if it wished to do so. Both organizations held that, if market conditions were to permit the sale of one-third more watches than were called for in the production plan serving as the basis for allocations, there would be no difficulty in receiving additional planned supplies at the same price. This was despite the fact that all materials for watches were in theory nationally allocated. Indeed, it was pointed out by a representative of the municipality that it is difficult to distinguish between allocated and open market procurement for this firm; the municipal procurement bureau will supply materials without allocations if it has them available.

Despite the fact that materials for direct production were available without difficulty at allocation prices, this enterprise probably had 30 per cent higher costs of materials for watches than did Shanghai enterprises. The Shanghai advantage was explained by an enterprise informant as in all likelihood being due to plants in that city being able to obtain materials that are more precisely of the dimensions and qualities desired by the watch producer; this in turn was partly a result of the Shanghai plants being geographically closer to and in better contact with suppliers, and partly to their purchasing in larger volume. Since our sample enterprise spent 40 per cent of total production costs on materials for direct production, we are talking here of a major competitive disadvantage. Full availability of supply, even without the charging of a price markup, is only one element of the procurement problem.

As in the case of other enterprises, obtaining materials for maintenance and construction was somewhat more of a problem than when they were intended for direct production purposes. Allocations for the former purposes were insufficient for the enterprise needs. At those times when above-plan production was available from state enterprises, much could be bought at allocation prices because the firm bartered coupons entitling the bearer to purchase scarce varieties of watches which the firm produced.[40] (These coupons then became a fringe benefit to the workers of the supplying firms.) If the watch enterprise purchased nonrationed amounts from the provincial wholesale organization, then it paid a supplemental 6 per cent handling charge. However, supplemental cement was, in practice, available only from a commune factory that in 1982 charged about 40 per cent above the allocation price. Some machine tools were purchased at 25 per cent above the allocation price; this markup seems to have been unusual nationally through 1982 and was probably due to the specialty nature of such equipment needed for the watch industry.

FIFTH CATEGORY

The three enterprises in this category represent a mixed degree of centralization. Their procurement picture presents no features that are new compared to what has been already described. Since this category does not fit into the pattern of ordering enterprises by degree of centralization, it does not seem worthwhile to comment upon the enterprises in it.

SUMMARY

By and large, the three plants of the single most centralized category seem to be the best supported through allocations. In the least centralized category, the small enterprises of the county organization receive the smallest portion of their needs from allocations. But other than this, there is no systematic difference among categories.

This situation is in sharp contrast to the close linkage of national supervision with the national allocation of the final product. In the three cases of management of the enterprises by the Center alone, the products were mainly allocated and there was also the best supply support through allocations. In four and one-half of the six instances where the Center exercised joint supervision with a local body, the enterprise outputs were also mainly allocated.[41] However, allocations of materials to these enterprises were no more prominent a feature of supply than they were for the two categories of enterprises for which the Center did not exercise any managerial function.

Thus, what seems to be the traditional view of Western observers is supported by our sample insofar as centralized management and centralized allocation of the product tend to go together. But this view is rejected in that centralized management and the allocation of the inputs have only the loosest of connections. The system of national allocation of products can indeed be regarded as a specialized phenomenon restricted to a select group of major state enterprises, but the allocation of inputs cannot be treated in this way. The sample contradicts the view that central management, product allocation, and input allocation constitute a package. That is, the belief that while most of the state industrial sector is outside the realm of central planning, the portion that lies within this set receives plans for outputs and inputs that are reasonably similar to what is observed for all enterprises in other economies, such as that of the Soviet Union, that are subject to universal central physical planning. However, so far as the evidence of our sample goes, this is neither the case today nor was it during the 1970s.

The second conclusion that can be drawn is that allocations have provided much better support for inputs required for current production than for those needed to carry out maintenance and new construction. This appears to be true in all three procurement stages. Such differential support emerges very strongly from the sample data.

The third conclusion—weaker because of greater data limitations for the first and third stages than for the second—is that allocations were most important as a proportion of total supply during the first stage, played an intermediate role beginning with 1983 or 1984 as the demand for capital equipment and for inputs for producer goods turned upward and again exceeded supply, and were least significant during the second stage for which we have the most data. Their importance eased and grew again with the Chinese business cycle for capital equipment and for intermediate producer products. But what are as striking as the differences between procurement stages are the similarities.

The fourth conclusion is that barter has been a significant source of supply in all three stages. The barter of some portion of the enterprise's own production was widespread. Indeed, at least three of the plants (automotive in the first category and lumber and cement in the second) have been allowed to keep part of their planned output for purposes of such barter. In contrast, barter of allocated materials seems to have been less significant, even though some allocations (e.g., of copper in 1983 to the electrical equipment enterprise in the fourth category) were made purely for barter purposes.

The fifth conclusion is that compensation trade became fairly widespread during the 1980s, with monetary investments being undertaken by the medium and large state enterprises represented by the sample in return for promised long-term shipments of materials at the allocation price. This followed the promotion of such trade by the national government since 1982. Three of the twenty organizations of the sample made such investments, although in no case were they quantitatively important to the sample enterprises. The organizations concerned were completely variegated with regard to category of centralization: one in each of the first, fourth, and mixed categories.

The sixth conclusion is that it is sometimes difficult to distinguish between supplies that are allocated and those that are sold by the same distributing agency without allocations. This was explicitly noted in the interviews within the watch and clock enterprise in the fourth category; the problem was also observed with regard to the pump plant in the second category. This comingling of categories is probably linked to the matter of property rights for regional levels of authority; the "owner" of the enterprise has every reason to attempt to supply its supplementary needs when that is both feasible and profitable. This explanation seems to be appropriate for at least the two enterprises noted here.

Imports

The pattern usually observed in centrally planned economies is that the quantities and structure of imports are determined by central authorities, and that enterprises pay for them in domestic currency and at the same price they pay for domestic products. The domestic economy is isolated from the world economy in terms of both export and import pricing. This seems to have been the general pattern in China as well during the first procurement stage. Indeed, foreign trade has been described as having been one of the few completely centralized sectors during the years 1975–78.[42]

Thereafter, there was some shift to local control of foreign trade both by provinces and localities and by individual enterprises. Further decentralization occurred during the third stage of industrial procurement.[43] A major feature of the move from central control was the retention of foreign exchange by exporting firms and by their supervisory bodies. One Chinese author writes that, on average, 10 per cent is left to the enterprises alone.[44]

The sample shows one basic regularity and one variation with respect to the treatment of imports. Although some of the sample enterprises exported a major portion of their output, none appear to have used foreign exchange retentions to finance imports of inputs used directly in production. Instead, all such imports were paid for exclusively in Chinese currency. Foreign exchange reserves were used by the sample enterprises solely for imports of equipment, licenses, magazines, and the like, as well as for expenses of personnel sent on missions.

On the other hand, two enterprises specifically noted that they did not pay for imported materials at the domestic price. The automotive enterprise in 1984 was importing some 2 per cent of its rolled steel requirements, with the central government determining the specific types of steels that could be imported. Yet these imports were paid for at the international price, which was converted into Chinese currency at the official exchange rate. The electrical equipment enterprise in 1983 received half of its silicon steel allocation in the form of imports; it paid 35 per cent above the domestic allocation price, despite the fact that this was an allocation rather than a market transaction. No information is available for other enterprises as to the price paid for imports.[45]

Cost of Open Market Purchases

Through the second stage of procurement developments, the monetary costs of open market transactions seem to have added little to the total production costs of enterprises. In 1982, for example, they constituted only about 1 per cent of the total materials costs of the locomotive-repair enterprise in the first category.

Even in 1983, when conditions were beginning to change, supplementary materials costs were not large. They still probably constituted only about 1 per cent of the materials costs of the one textile enterprise in the third category for which we have data. But the electrical equipment enterprise spent about 4 per cent of its total materials costs on the supplementary charges incurred as a result of half of its silicon steel allocations being supplied through imports. The lumber and forestry enterprise may have also spent about 4 per cent on supplementary charges for all of its materials and fuel purchases.

The above figures are extremely crude. They represent compilations of additional costs for those open market purchases that were noted by one or another informant in an enterprise as having been significant during the particular year. They also require comparisons with what the allocation price would have been, and such comparisons are chancy because data are not available as to the detailed product mix of the purchases. Nevertheless, they represent appropriate orders of magnitude.

Thus it would appear that supplementary purchasing costs did not appreciably affect the profit and loss statements of the sample enterprises prior to 1984, when for the first time state enterprises were generally permitted to charge substantial price supplements for supplying above-plan output. Unfortunately, we have no data on the significance of such costs for our sample enterprises in 1984.

The low level of supplementary purchasing costs is relevant to the assertion made by Zhao Ziyang (prime minister at the time) that it was the larger and more centrally controlled state enterprises that paid the costs of industrial reform in the period through the spring of 1985.[46] Although Zhao did not elaborate, presumably he was referring to the fact that such enterprises engaged in fewer sales in the marketplace than did others and that, even when they did make such sales, they were in general unable to charge substantially more than allocation prices until 1984. Thus it was their profitability that suffered, while that of the smaller enterprises increased, as national market sales expanded.[47]

This claim appears to be true, at least qualitatively, for the second procurement stage. Within our sample, it was in general the more centralized enterprises that had least access to the marketplace for their products; this involved some involuntary sacrifice of sales price on their part. In contrast, only the single most centralized category of enterprises gained systematically greater access to allocated materials than did the other three categories, thus receiving the compensation of paying lower prices for their inputs.

But, of course, there was not much to the matter quantitatively. Within the sample of medium and large state enterprises, the supplementary costs of purchasing on the open market were not great. Enterprise losses in potential profits from the growing marketization of the 1979–83 period of reform did not amount to anything substantial. The growth in profitability of small enterprises (particularly, in all probability, nonstate ones) does not seem from our sample to have occurred at the substantial expense of the larger state firms.

Whether the situation changed in 1984 and thereafter is, unfortunately, a question on which my sample sheds no light.

Cost Considerations in Procurement

REJECTIONS OF ALLOCATIONS

In the Soviet Union, it is virtually unheard of for an enterprise to reject allocations of materials. Indeed, it is by no means clear that an enterprise would have the legal right to do so; contracts between enterprises are supposed to be drawn up on the basis of output programs and allocation plans that the enterprises have received from higher authorities.

In contrast, one of the enterprises in our sample had a large proportion of its output rejected for purely financial reasons during two consecutive years. Two other enterprises report rejecting allocations of materials that they needed. Given the relatively minor cost effects of entering the open market for purchases, such rejection is perhaps not too surprising in the light of product mix and quality problems.

During 1981, recipients of allocations for trucks from the automotive plant in the sample failed to exercise these allocation rights. The quantitative dimensions of such failure were sufficient to leave the plant with 50 per cent of its production to market on its own. The same was true during the first half of 1982. The problem for the recipients of allocations was not that of price and its resulting effect on the costs of production of the recipients' own products. This was described as having been an unimportant consideration in their decisions. Rather, the constraint on purchases was purely and simply a cash bind. Neither investment funds from government bodies nor loans from the bank were being made available in sufficient quantities to finance these purchases.

In one case in which sample enterprises themselves rejected allocated materials (the date is unknown, but is prior to 1983), the allocation was of steel usable for expansion of capacity. The province allocated the steel, but only on the condition that the enterprise accept additional steel of types that it did not need. The enterprise refused, and instead purchased other steel on the market and at a higher price to replace the allocation. The informant complained in the interview that this tied-allocation and its refusal raised the cost of investment above its expected level. But the Soviet counterpart enterprise would have been happy to pay for unneeded types of supplemental steel, for it could then easily have traded them for materials that it did require. It is striking that the Chinese enterprise preferred to go to the marketplace.

The second case (in a different province) was the allocation of pig iron as a current input to the automotive enterprise in the first category, as discussed above. At a time when pig iron on the open market was priced 50 per cent above the allocation price, the enterprise regularly rejected half its allocation. Although it is true that the enterprise engaged in barter rather than paying this market price, presumably its barter transactions involved the sacrifice of an equivalent potential receipt of monetary payment for the delivery of scrap.[48]

VERTICAL INTEGRATION

Some sample interviews contain unsubstantiated comments as to the existence, in Chinese state enterprises in general, of a pattern frequently observed elsewhere in which vertical integration has been developed to reduce dependence upon outside suppliers. But the sample data themselves provide no evidence for such generalizations. This lack of substantiation is in marked contrast to the data readily available in the literature with regard to Soviet enterprises.

The closest thing to support of this claim in the sample is the argument by one informant that some of the mergers and associations with other semi-independent enterprises, which were organized on a considerable scale by the clock and watch factory, were motivated by a desire to obtain a more stable source of watch components. This informant provided two specific examples of mergers that he claimed had been motivated in this way. However, from what is known about the plants concerned, one of these examples strikes me as totally incredible and the second as implausible.

More broadly, the formation of these watch associations was inspired primarily by two marketing considerations: (1) breaking down local protectionism in areas far from the enterprise's main factories, and (2) serving as a highly profitable outlet for the use of excess capacity of these factories in the production of individual components. Tax-avoidance considerations must also have played a role. There is no basis of support in the data for the claim that securing sources of supply was a significant motivating factor.

The automotive enterprise would have seemed a natural candidate for such vertical integration. About one-third of the value of its trucks consists of parts bought from independent enterprises, and 70 to 80 per cent of this one-third is provided by some eighteen factories founded at the same time as the automotive enterprise. Yet informants insist that the enterprise has never even considered establishing its own factories to produce such parts.

Similarly, this enterprise has rejected the notion of either founding or taking over through merger plants to produce raw materials. Such vertical integration was once considered with regard to a cement plant, but the proposal was rejected by the top management of the automotive enterprise on the basis that managerial resources would be spread too thin if they were to get into this business.[49] Such conscious rejection of vertical integration by this automotive enterprise is consistent with the evidence from the interviews that there was an absence of serious supply difficulties.

The case of the pump enterprise is the most interesting. This plant is directly managed by a body within the provincial administration that has some supply facilities of its own. Among these are a foundry and a heat treatment facility, which the pump enterprise uses having no parallel facilities of its own.

The foundry has a capacity sufficient to meet only half of the needs of the enterprises under the administration. In outside purchasing (all information is for years prior to 1984), the pump enterprise is forced to adopt low quality standards if it is to be able to place orders. For example, when 80 per cent of the castings supplied by the seller meet specifications, all are treated as being of satisfactory quality and must be paid for at full price. The pump enterprise is dissatisfied with this situation, but is powerless to change it. Similarly, the heat treatment facility of the administrative body is insufficient for the needs placed upon it.

Nevertheless, as of the end of 1983, no investments were being made to expand either the foundry or the heat treatment facility under the administration. Nor was the pump enterprise investing in such facilities on its own. The reason in both cases was that, at existing state prices, casting and heat treatment work were both considered to be "unprofitable."

Given the alternatives facing the enterprise and the administration, such a narrow financial view was probably self-defeating. What is intriguing, however, is the fact that the decision should have been made on narrowly financial grounds rather than in terms of production requirements. This would not have happened in the Soviet Union.

OTHER PROFITABILITY CONSIDERATIONS

Even more striking is the evidence in the interviews as to the extent to which enterprises sacrifice both current and future production for the sake of financial soundness and profitability. Out of our sample of twenty organizations, the interviews reveal cases of this occurring in seven of them; in an eighth, the supervising organization took the same stand. Since no systematic effort was made by the interviewers to find such cases, doubtless more than the recorded two-fifths of the sample gave preference to finance over output in at least some of their decisions. This result is in sharp contrast to the conventional wisdom, which in my view is correct, as to what occurs in the Soviet Union and in East European centrally planned economies. Let me discuss the eight Chinese cases in some detail.

The first instance is in textiles (a fourth category enterprise) and goes back to the pre-1978 procurement stage when the reporting enterprise was formed through the merger of a number of state-owned mills. In these years, the dyeing plants suffered frequent shortages of dyestuffs. The reason for the shortages was not penury on the part of allocating bodies or even changing requirements with regard to the mix of dyes. Rather, it was that the dyeing mills placed insufficient orders because of their fear of overstocking. For them, the danger of overstocking was that it involved tying up working capital and bearing the accompanying interest charges arising from bank borrowing.

The second instance is in the fertilizer factory (mixed category) and refers to the situation in 1983. A major gas container was defective, and the limit on the degree to which its leaks could be mended had been fairly well reached. Not only was the container believed by the relevant department manager to be a serious safety threat but, if it broke down, the production of one-fifth of the basic product of the plant would be halted for three months. The response of the factory had been to apply to the province for an outright grant to purchase a new container; as of late 1983, frequent reapplications had accomplished nothing.

In view of the perceived risk to continuity of production, it is the response of the factory that is intriguing. Management desired to eliminate the risk only if this could be done at no financial cost to the factory itself. Despite the fact that the price of a new container would have been only about 10 per cent of the profits earned in 1982, the factory did not during 1983 consider making the expenditure from its own funds. Nor did it attempt to borrow the money from the state bank, although presumably a loan would have been much easier to obtain than a grant.

One and one-half years later, the factory was finally reconciled to financing the purchase from its own retained profits. But some two to three years had elapsed since the danger had become significant, and the plant would still have to count on considerable delay before receiving the replacement container.

The third instance occurred in the smelter (mixed category), whose production of its principal product has been constrained by the lack of scrap. Particularly in view of the fact that the smelter's capacity is unbalanced, expansion of scrap usage would have been an especially convenient way to more fully use the available smelting capacity.

However, the smelter was constrained by government policy to produce only the pure metal; output of alloyed metal was to be the exclusive domain of small refiners. The price of the refined pure metal was tightly controlled by the government and was set at a level that was low relative to that of alloys. Because of this differential in prices for the respective finished products, the scrap price (uncontrolled in practice) was bid up by the alloy refiners and by the producers of processed products made from the pure metal. The resulting price of scrap was considered financially prohibitive by the large smelter in our sample. The smelter used scrap only to the degree that it was able to negotiate processing agreements with localities; it did not enter into the scrap market on its own account. Thus, its own profitability concerns dominated its desire for higher physical output.

The above three cases all refer to purely financial restrictions on the full use of existing plant capacity. The remaining five relate to such restrictions on the expansion of capacity.

Three of these cases, all in 1983, were ones in which it was the enterprise's own decision that restrained its expansion. The first was in a textile mill (third category) in which shortages of allocated steel, timber, and cement forced the suspension of several construction projects. The mill's management declared in the interview that these materials were available locally in the marketplace, but of course at higher than the allocation prices. Rather than making such purchases in order that construction could continue, the mill preferred an indefinite delay in bringing its additional capacity on line.

The second case was in the machine tool plant (fourth category). The management of this factory was eager to apply for a loan to produce a new product that promised to be highly profitable, but it was unwilling on principle to accept any bank loans to improve existing products. This attitude was motivated by the fact that, for loans for new products, regulations in effect at the time permitted repayment to be made out of total profits. Since the vast bulk of such profits would in any case have gone to the supervising municipality, little of the repayment would have come from the enterprise's own funds. In contrast, loans made for improvement of existing products had to be repaid completely from the portion of profits that were retained by the enterprise itself.

The third case was in the county organization. Here, according to the loan officer of the local branch of the People's Bank, various of the seventeen state enterprises within the organization were completely inactive in applying for loans for technical improvement of products or processes. Indeed, some had even refused loans that the bank branch had offered them.

The fourth case was also one of enterprise reluctance to expand, but it occurred in 1982 and the reluctance was overcome by pressure from above. It related to a textile enterprise (fourth category) that was under municipal authority. A major expansion project had been approved by the national Ministry of Textiles in 1982, with 77 per cent of the financing to come from short-term loans from the Construction Bank and the rest from a grant by the municipality.

The municipality was eager to take up the project, according to the enterprise, because of the creation of jobs. On the other hand, the firm refused at first to accept the loan. Interviews in the textile mill indicated that the reluctance was for financial reasons.[50] The enterprise finally acceded only on the insistence of municipal authorities.

The last case was the pump enterprise during 1982–83 (a period in which the enterprise fell into the mixed category). About December 1981, the national ministry approved a plan for short- and intermediate-term investment in the enterprise to take place during 1981–85. This involved a 1.1 million renminbi investment by the central government (with no return of the principal being required), 1 million renminbi of bank loans, and 0.1 million renminbi of investment by the enterprise. As of December 1983, the People's Bank had approved the loan, but the provincial authority was refusing to permit the enterprise to accept the package deal.

The reason for reluctance by the provincial financial department was that, as the supervising authority over the enterprise, the province received the lion's share of its profits. Since the terms of the loan called for repayment out of the total profits of the enterprise, it was the province which was ultimately liable if post-repayment total profits were reduced as a result of the loan. Thus the provincial financial department had more to lose than did the bank from an unsound loan. Unlike the bank, the financial department was unconvinced that the loan was financially sound; presumably, the greater conservatism of its financial prognosis stemmed from this greater stake in the financial outcome of the investment.

Summing up, two-fifths of all the sample enterprises gave preference to financial over production considerations in some incident that was reported in the interviews. However, it should be noted that none of these eight organizations fell within the two most centralized categories of enterprises and only one was in the third. In contrast, four of the seven that were in the least centralized category reported such events. Puzzlingly, all three of the enterprises in the category of mixed degrees of centralization also reported them. (See table 4.2 below.)

Placing to one side the mixed category, financial considerations have a substantially greater influence on enterprises operated in a decentralized fashion than on those under central guidance. If we extrapolate these sample results to the larger universe of all state-owned enterprises (including small ones), we would presume that enterprises responsible for over half of all industrial production by state firms have given priority, at least at times, to financial over physical results. Moreover, this was true well before the autumn 1984 pronouncement by the Communist Party's Central Committee that "the socialist economy is a commodity economy."

Multiple Prices and Equilibrium Analysis

We have seen that multiple prices for the same good at a given time and place have existed during all three stages of industrial procurement. This is also the case for consumer goods in other centrally planned socialist economies, particularly but not exclusively for agricultural items. But it seems to be unique to China, or virtually so, with respect to items purchased by state enterprises: capital goods and intermediate products.

However, it is only in the third stage beginning in 1984 that such multiple prices should be associated with the principle of equilibrium price. During the first two stages, multiple prices existed essentially for social and incentive reasons. In view of these limited functions, there was nothing to prevent each of these prices from being fixed by some unit of government in time-honored socialist fashion. Indeed, this is what occurred.[51] There is no cause for believing that during the first stage the highest of these multiple prices either cleared the market or was expected to do so. When there was a transformation of sellers' into buyers' markets at the beginning of the 1980s, this occurred through financial retrenchment and structural alteration of demand rather than as a result of changes in the pricing system.

In contrast, the third stage saw the introduction of freedom in pricing for the marginal output of virtually all producers. Judging from our sample, one would guess that there were no enterprises in China that did not purchase at these free prices their marginal needs for at least some inputs. Since it is a tenet of neoclassical theory that it is the effect on the margin that matters, it would not seem overstated to declare that this third stage introduced the principle of equilibrium prices. Of course, these Chinese prices constituted a very peculiar member of this class of prices.

Our interest here is in inquiring into what was and was not gained by such movement from disequilibrium to equilibrium pricing for producer goods.

Disequilibrium Analysis at a Macroeconomic Level

The theoretic treatment of price disequilibrium in centrally planned economies grows directly out of the Barro-Grossman analysis.[52] As such, it is oriented solely to macroeconomic issues. In contrast, the issues here are entirely microeconomic. Although the matters involved go under a similar name, in reality they do not even border on one another.

The significance of the Barro-Grossman treatment is that it asks about the interrelation between the consumer goods market and the labor market in a capitalist society, and treats them symmetrically. If, for whatever reason and in the short run, exchange in one or the other of these macroeconomic markets occurs at a disequilibrium point ($P\ Q$) that lies on either the supply or demand function but not on both, what will be the effect on the other function in the other macroeconomic market? When it is the labor market that is in disequilibrium, we have the Keynesian effect upon demand in the goods market. When there is price fixing in the consumer goods market, we have a comparable shift to the left of supply in the labor market. In both cases, one ends up with a multiplier effect on quantities in the goods market through the repercussion of shifts in functions in both markets.

The work of Richard Portes and his colleagues on disequilibrium in centrally planned economies is addressed to the same issue.[53] The point in question is whether the aggregate consumer goods market is in disequilibrium. Its significance is with regard to its import for the labor supply function and for whether tightening of fiscal/monetary policy is appropriate as a device for removing those disequilibria that obviously exist at a microeconomic level in the consumer goods market.

János Kornai's negative comment on the finding of Portes et al. that such aggregative disequilibrium does not exist in general—i.e., that Kornai's "shortage economy" is not a general characteristic of consumer goods markets in centrally planned economies—should be interpreted in the same fashion. Although Kornai's emphasis is microeconomic (many individual goods markets are characterized by excess demand at any moment), its significance is macroeconomic. Kornai argues that when consumers cannot satisfy their demand for one item and thus substitute another, such "forced substitution" appears in Portes' aggregate demand measure but does not really belong there (1980, 451–53, 476–79). Since some of aggregate demand is of this forced substitution type, he insists that equilibrium of aggregate supply and demand on the goods market does not have the implication either for labor supply or for fiscal/monetary policy that is given to it by Portes and his coworkers.

In contrast to the above literature, the problems involved in equilibrium versus disequilibrium in the Chinese markets for producer goods are entirely microeconomic. They are issues of efficiency of resource allocations between goods. They do not relate directly to consumer goods markets or to labor markets because disequilibria of this type in all centrally planned economies are usually rather completely sterilized and prevented from having an effect (other than through allocative efficiency within the producer goods sector) upon either of these markets. Thus the change from disequilibrium to equilibrium similarly has no such effect.

Disequilibrium Analysis at a Microeconomic Level

During the first two stages of procurement history, there were no forces working at a microeconomic level to bring about equilibrium of supply and demand for individual products. Although there were indeed multiple prices, all were set by governmental bodies. In the third stage, in contrast, the marginal output of each intermediate and capital good was sold at a free price. One would expect that this price would represent an equilibrium. But the relevant question is that of how to characterize the supply and demand functions that were being equilibrated.

Let us consider a single product sold at three different prices. Let P_1 represent the allocation price, P_2 the price set for sales by collectives and county enterprises, and P_3 the free market price. Q_1 and Q_2 represent planned and allocated production corresponding to P_1 and to P_2. **X** is the vector of all other arguments entering into either the demand or supply functions. Then, in the third procurement stage, these functions may be described as follows:

$$(4.2) \quad Q_d = f(\mathbf{X}, P_3 | Q_1, Q_2, P_1, P_2)$$
$$Q_s = g(\mathbf{X}, P_3 | Q_1, Q_2, P_1, P_2)$$

The equilibrium of $Q_d = Q_s$ bears one very important similarity to the usual price equilibrium in which each product has only a single price. Namely, since enterprises can legally barter or sell inputs that were allocated to them at less than the market price, fixed prices affect both output and input-combination decisions only to the degree that a cash (borrowing) constraint is binding. So long as an interior solution to the optimizing problem is feasible, the user will be free to allocate his funds so that the marginal value product of renminbi expenditure on each input is the same. Similarly, individual multi-product suppliers can allot their residual capacity, after producing (or purchasing on the open market) the required amount of Q_1 or Q_2 of each planned product, so that the marginal value product of each item produced is the same. These are two very important short-run efficiency conditions.

But this is the only such similarity to the usual market solution. For, in the short run, both the demand and supply functions are dependent upon *administrative decisions* that have been made as to Q_1, Q_2, P_1, and P_2.[54]

In the long run, the demand and supply functions are dependent not only upon the above administrative decisions, but also on the administrative decision as to the expansion of the total capacity of the product itself and of the capacity of items produced by the purchasers for which this product is an input. Alternatively, if it is the enterprise itself that makes the investment decision, such a decision will depend upon the enterprise management's expectation as to future administrative decisions. Assuming that we are modelling long-run demand, the decision as to expansion of the output for which this product is an input will depend upon ($[Q_{1a} - Q_{1b}]$, $[Q_{2a} - Q_{2b}]$), where a refers to future administrative decisions if the enterprise makes the investment, and b refers to the same decisions if the investment is not made. The decision will also depend upon $[P_1 - P_2]$ and $[P_1 - P_3]$, which are the per-unit costs of these expected future administrative decisions. An identical approach is used in modelling long-run supply.

The outcome of this analysis is that the "equilibrium" quantity and price is not a result simply of market conditions, but also of administrative decisions and/or expectations as to future administrative decisions. The socialist economy may be a commodity economy, but it consists of commodities whose free market prices are heavily affected by planning decisions.

Kornai's "Soft Budget Constraint"

Kornai's Treatment

János Kornai begins with three assumptions. One is general to modern societies while the second is specific to socialist, centrally planned economies. The third, which is largely implicit and seems to me to be needed to provide grounding for his argument, is primarily an informational principle viewed as applicable to all large organizations.

The general assumption is that an exogenous and insatiable investment drive exists at the level both of the enterprise and of any intermediate (noncentral) body, whether it be situated within or above the enterprise. This leads to an insatiable demand for production inputs. The demand arises from an identification by managers with their units, their resultant belief in the importance of the units' activities, and thus a desire for them to grow. In socialist economies, this drive is also likely to exist at the level of the central planners, but when it does, the effect is no more than to reinforce the more fundamental psychological drive that operates at the micro and intermediate levels.[55]

"Shortage" and "suction" economies are defined according to whether their normal state is one of excess demand or excess supply. What is significant in determining if a given economy will be one or the other is whether its micro units are subject to "hard" constraints, i.e., to a vector of budget constraints that is efficacious in limiting their effective, voluntary demand for resources. Constraints on current production, or their absence, go along with the existence or absence of constraints on investment (Kornai 1980, 201, 62–63).

Kornai's second assumption, specific to centrally planned socialist economies,[56] is that the vector of budget constraints that exists for the enterprise is "soft" rather than "hard." The enterprise is not subject to impersonal constraints imposed by the marketplace, but rather to constraints imposed by the planners. Constraints imposed by human beings are, however, always subject to negotiation. In particular, those to be imposed in the future can be influenced by the actions taken currently by the enterprise management. This seems to be the meaning of the statement that the vector exists, but that it fails to function in the way that constraints do in neoclassical theory. Soft constraints take the form of physical allocations, permission to hire labor, investment allotments, loans, etc.

It is true that Kornai's entire emphasis is upon those constraints that are financial. In fact, his use of the term "budget constraint" explicitly refers solely to a financial budget. But, aside from the important consideration that those constraints that take the form of physical allocations of inputs are treated by Kornai as being subject to negotiation rather than being impersonal, his reasoning implicitly applies to physical constraints as well. If not, in a society where enterprise behavior is unaffected by financial concerns (as Kornai assumes), there is no reason for any connection between a shortage economy and soft budget constraints. The financial budget constraint could be infinitely soft, yet hard constraints on the enterprise with regard to resource allocations might prevent the emergence of a shortage economy.[57] So far as production is concerned, the economy would be purely a natural one. Thus Kornai's assumption as to the "softness" of the budget constraint can be extended to the meaning of budget that is customary for economists in problems of maximization under constraints.[58]

The significance of this second assumption is that the enterprise is essentially unconstrained, except by tactical considerations, in its requests to superiors for additional resources.[59] If it can obtain them, virtually no opportunity cost is exacted in return (Kornai 1980, 194).

The third assumption, which I think is needed for Kornai's argument, relates to the fact that central planners receive false information from enterprises and intermediate bodies. Since an agent is evaluated by its principal in terms of plan fulfillment rather than according to external criteria, the agent is motivated to use its command over information to influence the targets set. The assumption required by Kornai is that the central planners are unable to compensate in making their decisions despite awareness of the biases in the information they receive. For this reason, combined with other institutional relations found in socialist economies, central planners are incapable of transforming the constraints on the enterprises into hard and binding ones.[60]

Kornai's Analysis and the Chinese Sample

This analysis of Kornai's does not seem to me especially applicable to our sample of Chinese state industrial enterprises during the second historical stage of industrial procurement, let alone during the third.

The reason for this, even if we assume (as I do in this section) that his other two assumptions are applicable, is the failure of Kornai's second assumption of soft financial budget constraints to apply to these state enterprises as a group.

The basis for this view is not the fact that these sample enterprises have faced a much more favorable supply situation than would have been anticipated in the shortage economy described by Kornai. One might always posit that either the sample or its entire universe of medium and large state enterprises is insulated from a shortage economy which has otherwise permeated Chinese society. Kornai indeed asserts that a socialist government is capable of diverting shortages from one sector to another. In his view, it is incapable only of eliminating them from all sectors simultaneously (1980, 552–56).

Rather, my rejection of the applicability of Kornai's approach to the Chinese sample is due to the observed frequency with which bodies below the Center made decisions that limited their own requirements for production inputs. Two-fifths of all sample enterprises were observed to be subject to financial constraints that took precedence over Kornai's posited psychological drive for expansion of current and future production. In four known cases, investment opportunities were rejected for explicitly financial reasons; in a fifth, investment was delayed for such reasons. This stands in contrast to Kornai's statement that no one has ever seen a manager of a socialist firm who would voluntarily reject an oppportunity to invest.[61] It also contrasts with the views of various Chinese economists concerning Chinese state industry as a whole.[62]

Let me attempt to explain why Kornai's approach, which is generally accepted as being descriptively accurate (whatever its analytic virtues may be) with regard to the Soviet Union and Eastern Europe, applies so poorly to the Chinese sample.

The analysis is summarized in table 4.1. My concentration is not on the enterprise at all, but rather on the unit of government that exercises property rights over the particular organization. It is the characteristics of the governmental unit, as well as the extent to which this unit's behavior is influenced by financial considerations, that determine the degree to which the financial constraints it lays down for its state enterprises will be hard or soft.

In the allocation to the enterprise of real resources (materials are the ones of interest here), all levels of government in China are themselves similarly constrained and are in a position identical with that of the national government in the Soviet Union or in Eastern Europe. A resource constraint is binding on each of these governmental units, and the unit has no choice but to function within it.[63] To the degree that the governmental unit fails to impose genuinely hard re-

Table 4.1 The Role of Government As the Potentially Constraining Body

	USSR Government	Chinese Government	
	National	National	Regional
Constraint on governmental body:			
Real resources	Limited ability to expand	Limited ability to expand	
Monetary resources	Unlimited ability to expand	Unlimited ability to expand	Limited ability to expand
Effect of constraints on the enterprises under the given unit of government:			
Real resources	No difference between regimes		
Monetary resources			
When real resources are allocated	Constraint is soft	Constraint is soft	
When markets for producer goods are available	Constraint is soft	Constraint is soft	Constraint is as hard as for real resources

source constraints on its subunits and through them on its enterprises, it will be for the identical reason in China as in the Soviet Union.

The situation is different as regards financial constraints. With respect to Eastern Europe, Kornai writes that "The central bank is . . . an endogenous element of the system which must meet the demand for money" (1980, 532). This, of course, is feasible because any national government can create money using the central bank as its instrument. Equally, there is no financial constraint that is binding on the Chinese Center; it is free to act in the same fashion as does the state in Kornai's model of the centrally planned socialist economy and to leave totally soft the financial budgetary constraints placed on its enterprises.

In contrast, the Chinese provincial, municipal, and county governments are not in this fortunate position. If the concept of the property rights of the central government means anything, then provincial and local governments will not be given free access to the money-creating powers of the Center and of its central bank. Or, to be more accurate, this prohibition must hold in periods when there exists a marketplace for producer goods in which money can be used by such regional governments and their agents to obtain natural resources. Even then, of course, the central government may follow a policy of tight or loose money, or even nullify completely its monetary controls. At least in years when the central government places restraints on lending by the banks, regional governments themselves face binding financial constraints. Whether or not they choose to impose only soft constraints upon all of their enterprises or upon a subclass of them, the regional government itself must operate within a hard constraint. For such governments, the situation with regard to resource constraints and financial constraints is identical.

This logic suggests that, during the first stage of industrial procurement (the pre-1979 period), Kornai's approach should have been fully applicable to Chinese state enterprises. The fact that part of their supplies were obtained through barter should not have affected the issue. This is because the natural products left to the enterprises for barter purposes were subject to the same aggregate real-resource constraint on the principals, regardless of whether such principals were the Center or a regional government. Since the amount of resources that individual regional governments and their agents could command from the Center or from other regions was largely independent of their financial position,[64] the property rights of the Center need not have prevented the national government from restricting itself to the imposition of only soft financial constraints on these governments.

However, monetary income became of significance to the various principals in the reform years of the second and third stages. In this situation, the property rights of the Center could be protected only through the national government reserving for itself the power to create money. Hard financial constraints must have been imposed upon the provincial and lower regional governments. Thus such regional bodies, in these two procurement stages only, were presumably in a different position from the national governments of Eastern Europe.

The effect of such constraints on regional governments is most strongly exemplified in our data by the national market for trucks in 1981; of the allocation rights for those trucks produced by the automotive plant in our sample, half were left unexercised because of a cash bind on the would-be purchasers. Similarly, there appears to have been only restrained demand for steel in the same year, as shown by the fact that it was not allocated at all, at least not in the province of one sample enterprise.

Such constraints in the early 1980s were insufficient to prevent the expansion of investment that was under the influence of regional governments, but such expansion must have been much less than would have occurred without constraints on the issuance of bank credit. Going beyond the period of our study to a year of rapid inflation such as 1988, one may presume that central controls on lending were much weaker. Yet even then, regional governments could not have helped being aware that central policy could change and that they could be held to hard constraints in paying off such loans, whether the payback was made from enterprise profits or from foregone regional tax revenue.

From the different positions of regional governments during the reform years, the following hypothesis might be set forth:

(4.3) *Hypothesis:*
   Regional governments during reform years acted differently toward those enterprises that were under their authority than they had done earlier, and differently from the way that the Center was currently treating its own enterprises. The financial budget constraints imposed upon the state enterprises under regional authorities were likely to be as hard as, although no harder than, the resource constraints.

Despite the fact that such financial budget constraints might still be fairly soft, they would be considerably harder than those imposed upon the enterprises directly under the control of the Center.[65]
   If hypothesis (4.3) holds, one might expect that the state enterprises subject to diverse authorities would themselves respond differently to opportunities to expand either current or future production. Those enterprises under the financial control of the Center could in all periods expand without risk, counting upon their financial budget constraints remaining soft. But for enterprises under regional control, such expectations would have been very rash during the second and

Table 4.2 Preference Given to Financial Over Production Considerations

Category of Centralization	Number of Cases of Preference for Finance	Number of Enterprises in Category	Financial Preference As a Percentage of Enterprises
In first stage of periodization			
All	1[a]	20	5
In second and third stages of periodization			
First and second	0	7	0
Third	1	3	33
Fourth	4[a]	7	57
Fifth	3	3	100
Of these:			
Under municipal or provincial financial authority	3[b]	3	100
Under central authority	1[b]	1	100

[a] One of these occurred in the first stage as well as in the second.
[b] One of these was under the financial authority of the Center after 1 January 1984. The case occurred both earlier and later.

third stages, although not during the first. For them, there would be a genuine danger of being "squeezed" in the future. Thus we may test expectations of different categories of enterprises.

Indeed, the hypothesis does very well in predicting the sample observations, as is shown in table 4.2. During the first stage of the industrial procurement periodization, cases that run counter to the Kornai analysis were observed in only 5 per cent (one of twenty) of all the enterprises. Similarly, in only 12 per cent (one of eight) of the enterprises that were under either the direct financial or physical planning control of the Center in the second and third stages were there such counter cases. In sharp contrast, we observe such instances during the second and third stages in 62 per cent (eight of thirteen) of those enterprises under both the financial and planning control of the provinces, municipalities, and counties. This seems like quite strong support for (4.3).

Since hypothesis (4.3) emerges directly from the property rights approach of chapter 2, such evidence favoring this hypothesis provides further support for the basic property rights approach to the Chinese sector of state industry.

5

THE INCENTIVES FACING THE ENTERPRISES

I have proceeded a considerable distance in this book without seriously considering the issue of what motivates enterprise managers in the actions that they take. My concern has been entirely with the supervising organs that are above the level of the enterprise, and I have used enterprise data primarily to test hypotheses about these organs: the principle underlying the choice of those bodies that are to supervise specific enterprises, how enterprise plans are set, how materials inputs are apportioned, and how "hard" should be the financial constraints on the activities of the enterprises. Even where I have dealt with the behavior of enterprises themselves,[1] I have given no attention to motivational matters. This chapter is intended to justify the earlier neglect by mustering the information that can be gathered from the sample as to the likely enterprise motivations.

If it were reasonable to presume that enterprises act as passive agents—i.e., that they make the same decisions as would the leaders of their supervising organs (principals) if the latter had all the information that is available at the level of the individual enterprise—then neglect of the enterprise level would be fully justified. The same would be the case if deviations from this standard of behavior were random. However, even the latter and weaker form of the presumption is extremely strong. Departures from this presumption might be thought of as possibly occurring for two reasons.

The first is that enterprises are not agents at all, but rather act as principals. This would happen if the welfare of the enterprise and its personnel depended primarily upon the results, cumulative over time, of the enterprise's actions combined with stochastic changes in the environment. Such a functional relation contrasts with dependence upon the evaluation of individual-period results by bodies outside the enterprise. The way in which I have categorized the situation of organizations that constitute principals is that they are able to accumulate wealth and act as maximizers of the present value of their wealth.

The second reason for possible departure is that, although enterprises are considered to be agents rather than principals, the incentive system to which they respond leads to systematic deviation from the desires of the principals. If this were the case but all enterprises were to act with the identical direction and degree of deviation from the wishes of their own principals, then it would still be appropriate to begin—as we have done—with the principals. Although agents would not be passive, their actions would still be a one-to-one transformation of the desires of their respective principals. It is only if enterprises are provided incentives to respond similarly to the same conditions in their nonhierarchical environment, without regard to the identity or objectives of their principal(s), that I might appropriately have ignored the interests of principals and proceeded directly to an analysis of the enterprises themselves.

An illustration of this second reason is the following: If incentives to the enterprise are linked to percentages of plan fulfillment according to any plan indices whatsoever, the identity of the principal is critical since it is the principal that makes the plan. It is worth exploring, as I have done, whether principals differ systematically as to their criteria of plan formation.[2] On the other hand, if incentives for all enterprises are linked to some absolute standards (e.g., to profitability as a percentage of capital invested), then the identity of the principal is irrelevant to the enterprise's behavior.

I will begin this chapter with consideration of incentives specific to upper managers of enterprises and will then proceed to a treatment of those incentives that are common to the entire work force of individual enterprises. The surprising result is that, in Conan Doyle's words, the dog doesn't bark. That is, enterprise managers have no pecuniary incentive to pursue interests opposed to those of their workers. Just as interesting is that the income of both groups is divorced from the degree of attainment of measurable success indicators, even to those of plan fulfillment.

The message of the chapter is that performance incentives probably do exist, but that rewards are distributed at the discretion of the supervising agencies. In distinction to the situation facing Soviet enterprises, rewards are not paid in accord with the degree to which objective criteria, established ahead of time by supervisory organs, are met.

Incentives Specific to Upper Managers

Western analysis of enterprise behavior in centrally planned socialist economies has rested primarily upon studies of the economy of the Soviet Union. Examination of the pattern of the 1930s (Granick 1954; Berliner 1957) showed that Soviet industrial enterprises exercised considerable de facto autonomy in the decisions and actions that they took. Such autonomy can be viewed as resulting from the recognition by central authorities of their inability to obtain and utilize the information required if they were efficiently to make all decisions centrally. Studies of the postwar years (Richman 1965; Berliner 1976) indicated that such autonomy has remained a permanent feature of the Soviet economy.

Given the importance of autonomy, interest naturally developed as to the question of how it was exercised. Joseph Berliner (1957) suggested an approach that was to be the dominant one thereafter: enterprise managers acted (subject, of course, to various caveats) in such a way as to maximize the monetary bonuses that they received. In my own work, I extended such maximization to the expected discounted lifetime earnings, and treated current bonus receipts and expected change in career prospects as the two determinants of such earnings.[3]

Four features of this dominant approach are critical. The first is that the central actor in the story is the director of the enterprise, taken as the representative of the enterprise's top management. The relevant decisions in the enterprise are viewed as being made by top management, rather than by any wider group within the enterprise itself. To the degree that the Communist Party secretary of the enterprise plays a significant role in such decisions—and the literature generally denigrates such a role—he is treated as being simply another member of top management whose interests coincide with those of the other members.

The second feature is that the enterprise decision makers are considered as economic men, maximizing their economic income. (In this approach, personal reputation and authority are variables that tend to move together with the economic dependent variable; thus economic income can be taken as a proxy for noneconomic desiderata as well, so long as the latter are limited to those enjoyed by the individual and his family.) Their actions are not subject to direct influence through changes in their own ideological preferences. This feature of the approach follows the neoclassical tradition in economic analysis.

The third feature, more significant for this chapter than are the first two, is that the managers' decisions are conceived as being made in their own interests rather than to promote the well being of the total labor force of the enterprise. It is true that higher bonuses for Soviet top managers can be gained only if fairly proportional bonuses are also earned by the entire group of white collar workers of the enterprise, and particularly by the professional and managerial subgroup as a whole. It is also the case that enterprise managers have a stake in protecting the earnings of the blue collar workers of the enterprise; this follows from the existence of an active labor market in the Soviet economy.[4] Nevertheless, the above approach to enterprise decision making regards the attainment of satisfactory levels of bonuses and of average earnings of the enterprise's total work force as constituting constraints upon the top management's maximization process rather than as being incorporated into the maximand itself.

The fourth feature has two components. The first consists of the assumption that, for reasons peculiar to the Soviet Union in the years since World War II, earning bonuses rather than advancing careers has been given pride of place by Soviet managers. The second is the fact that bonuses are attached solely to success in meeting standards that are subject to continuous measurement. Managerial effort to maximize performance that is so measured leads to decisions that are dysfunctional from the standpoint both of central planners and of the intermediate (ministerial) supervisors of the enterprise.

It is the special elements contained in this fourth feature that has given the approach its power. For it is this feature which leads to the implication that supervisory bodies are regularly unable to direct enterprise managers to pursue the supervisors' own desiderata.[5] The incentive system is such as to lead to systematic deviations of enterprise behavior from what is desired by higher administrative organs, and these authorities have been incapable of changing such behavior despite considerable tinkering with the incentives. Because of this implication, and only because of this, the prediction of enterprise behavior requires more than a knowledge of the objectives of central planners. It also demands the specification of a utility maximand for enterprise managers, as well as the modelling of the incentive system that serves as an intermediary between the objectives of the central planners and the utility maximand of the enterprise managers.

In this treatment, enterprise managers are agents rather than principals. Nevertheless, an analysis of their utility functions, as well as of the relation between their decisions and the maximization of these functions, is of interest. This interest arises for the traditional reason underlying most principal-agent problems: asymmetry of information between the agent and the principal.

In this section I will explore the data for various socialist countries viewed in terms of the above approach. For my purposes, I have pulled out the second and third features as assumption (5.1).

(5.1) *Assumption:*
    Enterprise behavior is determined by managers maximizing their own discounted lifetime earnings. The key components

in such earnings that are of interest here consist of managerial bonuses and the development of managerial careers.

Soviet Enterprises

Bonuses, mostly paid monthly and quarterly, constitute a very substantial portion of the earnings of managers of Soviet industrial enterprises. For all managerial and professional personnel taken together, this ratio was in the range of 12 to 19 per cent during the 1950s, fell to between 8 and 9 per cent during 1960–64, and then rose sharply and steadily to reach 24 per cent in 1970. In 1973, 1979, and 1980, it was still 20, 24, and 20 per cent, respectively. Even more significantly, the ratio in 1973 was 50 per cent or higher for one-fourth of enterprise upper managers.[6]

A question that must always be posed with regard to bonus payments in any country is the degree to which they are genuine bonuses that fluctuate in relation to performance (however evaluated), as opposed to being no more than delayed wage payments that are always awarded. Data from four different samples are available covering 1934, 1950, 1956, and 1959–64, and all show the same result: the payments are genuine bonuses. Taken together, the four samples display the existence of considerable differences between both individuals and enterprises, as well as major fluctuations for the same individual from month to month or at least from quarter to quarter. The 1934 data are the most convincing because they are based on a substantial sample. They cover all top technological managers in enterprises of heavy industry for a single sample month. Only 15 per cent of the sample received any bonus, but for those that did, it averaged 26 per cent of total monthly earnings (Granick 1972, 279–82).[7]

Soviet bonuses have always been formed by first creating a bonus pot for a given enterprise and then distributing this pot in a fashion that takes account of individual contributions. The apportionment of the pot is done within the enterprise and is based heavily on subjective factors. We know virtually nothing that is systematic about the process, although the impression gained from available Soviet writings is that the distribution is fairly egalitarian within a given category of personnel. The literature has concentrated instead upon the first stage: the creation of the bonus pot.

Throughout the period of central planning in the Soviet Union, the size of the enterprise bonus pot has depended upon enterprise performance relative to plan. It is the annual plan, rather than its monthly or quarterly divisions, that is by far the most important in determining the total pot for the year. The size of the pot can be broadly described as consisting of two linear discontinuous functions that are upper semicontinuous; the point of discontinuity has been normally, but not invariably, where the proportion of plan fulfillment is 100 per cent. There is a substantial difference in the size of the pot earned by just reaching, as compared with just failing to reach, this point of discontinuity. Plan fulfillment is defined as a weighted average of the plan fulfillment of a small number of well-specified, measurable, and continuous variables.[8]

The clarity of the meaningfulness of plan fulfillment is muddied in practice by the propensity, invariably decried by Soviet writers, of supervisory bodies to alter the plans (i.e., bonus criteria) of enterprises during the course of the year (see chap. 3). Although the occurrence of such change in the yardstick is certainly not extraordinary, it cannot be so common and so great as to render meaningless the notion that plans are to serve as a standard against which performance is judged. The evidence supporting this statement is the success both of Soviet and of Western writers in explaining malfunctions in the economy of the Soviet Union by adaptations of behavior by enterprise managements to the plan-fulfillment criteria of success.

East European Enterprises

Field studies conducted during 1970 and 1971 within industrial units of the German Democratic Republic (GDR) and of Romania (Granick 1976) demonstrated that the situations in these two countries radically differed, and that both varied sharply from the pattern in the Soviet Union and from the dominant model used for explaining enterprise behavior in centrally planned economies.

The pot available for East German bonuses, for all except top managers of enterprises, is formed in a fashion similar to that in the Soviet Union. Since the end of 1971, however, such bonuses have essentially constituted delayed wage payments; the difference that existed between the guaranteed bonus fund and the maximum enterprise fund that might be earned was in 1972 no more than approximately 3.2 per cent of total labor force earnings.[9]

In contrast, bonuses received by top managers could be high. Unlike the situation in the Soviet Union, however, the vast bulk of these were not attached to the fulfillment of planned targets for specified, measurable variables. Instead, they were granted at the discretion of the supervisory body.

This suggests that the model presented earlier should have no explanatory power for the behavior of East German enterprises (or of the next higher German organizational units, the *Kombinate*). Top management is not compelled by labor market considerations to adopt policies expected to yield maximum bonuses for the enterprise labor force; not enough money is at stake as a pot for the entire group of workers and employees for this really to matter. Nor does pursuit of their own bonus interests oblige such top managers to follow policies inconsistent with the desires of their supervisory bodies. This result follows from the discretionary power of the supervisory body in awarding top management bonuses (Granick 1976, 196–201).

The Romanian pattern varied from both the East German and the Soviet. Prior to 1970, bonuses seem to have constituted a proportion of total industrial earnings rather similar to what was observed at the end of the 1970s in Soviet industry. This system was abolished at the beginning of 1970 on the basis that it was unworkable; as described by Romanian industrial administrators in interviews, the bonus proportion was so high that in practice it had come to be treated as constituting purely delayed-payment wages. In 1970 these bonuses were incorporated into normal wages and salaries, and a fresh system was initiated.

The new system created various bonus funds, but their total was very small as a proportion of earnings. What continued unchanged, however, was the earlier arrangement for paying bonuses to top management; as in the GDR, such bonuses were not linked to any specific success indicators and were paid at the discretion of supervisory bodies. The maximum amount of such bonuses for top managers of enterprises (and of the next higher industrial units, the *centrale*) seems to have been only about 12 per cent of base salary.[10]

The Romanian system was thus similar to the East German in that it provided no monetary motivation to enterprise managers to deviate from the policies desired by their supervisory bodies. Where it differed, however, was that it provided relatively small incentives to follow such policies. Unlike the East German pattern, the fluctuating bonuses of Romanian top managers were very low by the standard of Soviet industrial managers (or of American, for that matter).[11]

Chinese Enterprises

BONUSES

Data are available on bonuses received by top management in eleven of our twenty sample organizations. For each year, the data are an average in money for the top management group as a whole. In general, bonuses of top managers were smaller as a proportion of their base earnings than was the case for the average worker in their enterprises. The first question to be posed with regard to these data is: How selective is this management circle? How "top" is top management?

The size of the upper management group for the nine of these eleven enterprises for which I have information ranged in a given organization in 1982 from 6 to 71, and constituted 0.02 to 0.58 per cent of the organization's work force. There was no substantial change in the proportion within individual enterprises over the entire period of 1975–82. Typically, this group is likely to have included both the Communist Party secretary and his deputy, and sometimes the trade union secretary, as well as those who would be regarded as holding managerial jobs when judged by more conventional criteria.[12] It is clear that we are dealing with a group that is above the hierarchical level of middle management.

Although this group's income was substantially higher than that of the average employee in the same enterprise, the ratio of total bonuses to money income was not exceptionally large.[13] Interviews conducted during the middle of 1966 in thirty-eight industrial enterprises showed that none of the enterprise directors, vice directors, or Party secretaries in these firms were eligible for bonuses, and apparently had not been for several years, despite the fact that other enterprise personnel in the majority of these enterprises were still receiving bonuses at that time (Richman 1969, 240). In the years 1970–77, only insignificant bonuses were paid to anyone.[14] In 1978 a few experimental firms began more substantial payments,[15] and in 1979 bonuses became universal in state industrial enterprises throughout China. For the five years of 1978–82, we have bonus data covering both top management and all employees for a sample of ten enterprises and thirty-seven enterprise-years.

Let us assume that the monthly money subsidies for the group of top managers were the same as those received by the average employee in the same enterprise in the same year.[16] On this basis, we can calculate the following: The proportion of bonuses to money income for top managers was less than 60 per cent of that paid to all employees in 40 per cent of the enterprise-years, was 60–80 per cent in another 35 per cent, was 81–100 per cent in 11 per cent, and was above 100 per cent in only 14 per cent of the cases.[17] Clearly, Chinese top management in state enterprises was not being singled out as a group whose incomes were to be made peculiarly sensitive to bonus awards.[18] If anything, bonus distribution was being used as a mechanism for reducing, albeit in a minor way, relative income inequalities within the enterprise.[19]

All of this strongly suggests that, to the degree that top managers of Chinese enterprises attempt to maximize their own personal bonuses, they can do this best by maximizing the total bonus pot in their enterprise. Given the enterprise's lack of control over the size of its labor force, such behavior would be indistinguishable from attempting to maximize average employee bonus for its own sake. Since our sample size is considerably larger for this latter variable than for top management bonuses, it is more convenient statistically to test the dependence of the average employee bonus, rather than that of average top management bonus, on performance indicators for the enterprise. This test will be postponed to a later point in this chapter.

Nevertheless, I have analyzed changes between contiguous years within the same enterprise both in the absolute size of top management bonus and in such bonus as a proportion of average employee bonus, in relation to six indicators of enterprise success.[20] Specifically, I examined individually those enterprise-years in which relative bonuses changed sharply. None of our six success indicators display any ability to systematically explain the variations.

This absence of relation is exemplified in two enterprise-years within a single sample enterprise. In 1981 the absolute bonuses of top management in this enterprise fell by 20 per cent, and the ratio of these bonuses to that of the average employee fell by 33 per cent. This was a year in which the only success indicators that changed were those of fulfillment of the plan targets; even these did not drop below 107–9 per cent. In the next year there was a return to the 1980 bonus situation, although all success indicators were down somewhat and fulfillment of plan was for the first time even a trifle below 100 per cent. Nor are these results explained by one-year lags, since the 1980 success indicators were all up significantly compared with 1979, while 1980 plan fulfillment figures were a solid 119–32 per cent. Initial and final plan figures were identical in all years.

One might, of course, consider temporal changes in the average base salary, rather than in bonuses, of top management, arguing that reward for performance may take this permanent form. Such reasoning is reinforced by the fact that, even as late as 1984, it could be claimed that national policy was to keep the ratio of average bonus to average base wage fixed between enterprises.[21]

Multiyear data for the variable of base salary exist for eleven enterprises; change in these figures appears erratic. These data are the most contaminated by what is, for our purposes, "noise": namely, change both in the number of people included in the top management of a given enterprise and in the personae of such managers. Thus there seems to be no point in trying to pursue explanation of change in this variable.

CAREERS

Unfortunately, we have no systematic data on the career changes of top managers in our sample. There is, however, some useful information in two different sample studies carried out during 1985 by Chinese research organizations.

Before turning to these studies, however, it is worth noting that between the end of 1981 and late 1985, the directors of at least three of our twenty sample enterprises were dismissed. Chinese informants were categorical that all of these job changes represented genuine dismissals, rather than normal retirements or transfers.

Two of these directors had headed what could be reasonably considered as among the three most entrepreneurial of the twenty enterprises.[22] Both of these men were dismissed on the formal ground of personal peccadilloes (accepting a minor bribe and having an affair with a coworker), but it is difficult to believe that either would have been dismissed for this reason alone.[23] So one may wonder from this succession of events whether a successful entrepreneurial record has been treated as a relevant basis for managerial career protection and advancement even during the reform years of the 1980s.

However, when one looks at the statistical record of these enterprises, it would seem that all three dismissals might be justified on grounds of performance. The enterprise under the first director, who was dismissed at the end of 1981, had had a fine history of profitability and output expansion through the date of his dismissal. On the other hand, the following year was to be a calamitous one, and it is possible that this was clear to his supervisory body before that year began. The director had for some years been following a policy of rapid expansion, and it is conceivable that this had led to disapproval by the time of his dismissal, when the market for his products had already soured.

The second director had also promoted rapid expansion and had used merger devices for this purpose. Profitability figures had declined sharply in 1980, remained stable for one year, and had then declined sharply once more. The output plan for 1982 was underfulfilled. While we have no further statistical data after 1982, it is possible that his dismissal in the fall of 1983 was a response to this record.

The third director's plant had seen a deterioration in profit rate in 1978, stability at this lower level during 1979–80, and then further deterioration in 1981 with no recovery in 1982. Profit as a proportion of what was originally planned at the beginning of the year ran only 57 to 67 per cent during 1981 and 1982. Although the director was at the time supported by his prime supervisory body, the county committee had in 1982 placed into his Party record an official reprimand for bad managerial work. He was dismissed in 1985.

None of these events can be taken as evidence that the dismissals resulted from poor evaluations of the work of these directors.

Nevertheless, the record of a substantial dismissal rate in our sample enterprises is not inconsistent with the view that lack of economic success can have a serious effect on a managerial career in China. Thus our sample data, although at first suggesting that economic performance is not a significant factor in career development, must on a closer look be found to be quite inconclusive in this matter.

I will now consider in some detail the two Chinese samples referred to above, which present snapshots of managerial personnel during mid to late 1985. Sample A consists of the 3,000 large and medium-sized industrial enterprises that had undergone two readjustments in the 1980s in personnel of the leadership groups, the second occurring during the first half of 1985.[24] This sample constitutes over one-third of the total number of large and medium-sized enterprises in the country, but it is the third that had most altered the personae of its leaders. Sample B includes nine hundred industrial enterprises in eighteen cities; four-fifths of the individuals studied are from state-owned enterprises, and about half of the total enterprises sampled are large or medium sized.[25] The process of selection for sample B is unknown, and nothing can be said as to its representativeness with regard to any specific population of industrial firms. However, sample B must have been chosen according to a very different criterion than that used for sample A. This is shown by the fact that, in sample B, there was not a massive proportion of managers who had been appointed to their current positions during the first half of 1985, as was presumably the case in sample A. Instead, almost half of the appointments in sample B occurred during 1984.

Sample B is described as covering "managers and professionals"; two-thirds of this sample consists of directors and deputy directors, and the other third are all Party secretaries and deputy secretaries of the enterprise or of one of its subunits. Sample A provides statistics on "managers and professionals"; an average of thirty-one per enterprise are included, and the only two categories specifically singled out for individual treatment are directors and Party secretaries of the enterprise. It seems reasonable to believe that the coverage of sample A, like that of sample B, was probably limited to line managers, although it reached considerably further down into middle management than did sample B.[26]

Table 5.1 indicates that the managerial groups concerned are fairly young. What is interesting, however, is not their age as such but rather the following facts:

A. There is consistency in the age distribution between the two samples;

Table 5.1 Age of Managers in Industrial Enterprises During the Second Half of 1985 (in percentages)

Age	All Managers & Professionals		Enterprise Directors[a]	Party Secretaries (all levels of organizations)
	Sample A	Sample B	Sample B	Sample B
≤40	20	28	23	17
41–50	63	51	56	47
>50	17	21	21	36
<36	. . .	11	7	7
>55	. . .	4	3	5

[a]The language of the original Chinese source is ambiguous as to whether these figures are restricted to the directors of the enterprises themselves, or whether directors of individual factories within multifactory enterprises are also included. The former seems more probable.

B. There is almost universal retirement from these line managerial posts by age fifty-five;[27]
C. The age distribution of factory directors is much the same as that of the total sample.

This last fact is intriguing because it suggests that a very high proportion of the enterprise directors are likely to have been chosen from among lower managers who at the time of such selection, or at most a few years earlier, were occupying a hierarchical level similar to that held contemporaneously by those executives who later became one of the many deputy directors in the enterprise. Thus, it was not seniority, with its pattern of promotion through the ranks, that brought the directors to their posts.[28]

The second set of materials to be discussed, all taken from sample B, is summarized in table 5.2 and provides data on the careers of the current enterprise directors, deputy directors, and Party secretaries. Only one-seventh of them had been appointed to their present post prior to 1981,[29] and a bare one-third had reached the hierarchical level of deputy enterprise director by that time. Yet virtually all had been promoted both to the post and level from other positions within the same enterprise.[30]

Information as to the level of education of top managers is consistent with the above results. The great bulk of managers in sample A had received a higher education: 89 per cent of enterprise directors, 81 per cent of Party secretaries, and 74 per cent of upper management as a whole. In sample B, 53 per cent of all the managers and profes-

Table 5.2 Careers of Enterprise Managers and Party Secretaries
(as a percentage of total as of mid-1985, based on year of entrance)

Period	In Current Post	At Hierarchical Level of Deputy Director or Higher	In Current Enterprise
pre-1981	13.9	37.8	
pre-1980			91.7
pre-1977	4.9	19.9	
pre-1975			81.4

Note: Data are from sample B. Statistics as to the length of time in current post are taken from the original Chinese source. The hierarchical level is not clearly specified in the source. The interpretation of it as being that of deputy director was made by Professor Mou Ying of Beijing Normal University. Alternatively, the original Chinese source can be interpreted as referring more vaguely to the level of "upper manager," as this term is treated in the data for our own sample enterprises. In the enterprises of our sample, people at this level constituted 0.02 to 0.58 per cent of the labor force.

sionals in the state-owned enterprises had also attained this educational level.[31] This is very different from the situation that existed in mid-1966, when a sample of enterprise directors averaged about nine to eleven years of education (i.e., at most one or two years of senior high school), and enterprise Party secretaries only about eight or nine years.[32]

These figures can best be evaluated when remembering that as late as 1954 in the United States, only 57 per cent of top managers in large companies had college degrees (however, the East European figures seem comparable to the Chinese).[33] Furthermore, in China, during the second half of the 1960s and the first half of the 1970s, there had been a strong bias against such "intellectuals"; not too many of them are likely to have worked as middle or upper managers (as opposed to technicians) during these years. Viewed against this background and in light of the limited proportion of the Chinese industrial labor force with a higher education,[34] one can appreciate the degree to which educational considerations currently dominate the managerial appointment process. By the mid-1980s, managerial selection in medium and large Chinese enterprises must have been based almost entirely on the level of education of those candidates who were considered to be otherwise eligible.[35]

I interpret the above career data as suggesting the following conclusions:

(a) Promotions are primarily internal. Top managers, just as other personnel, in the 1980s tended to be promoted from within their own enterprise. In sample B, at least 80 per cent of the directors,

deputy directors, and Party secretaries appointed after 1980 had previously been in the same enterprise for a minimum of four years. In
contrast, 62 per cent of a sample of directors in mid-1966 had come
directly to this post from a position outside of the enterprise.[36]

(b) The maximand of top managers is significantly affected by
the fact that their careers are quite unlikely ever to take them beyond
their current enterprise.[37] Senior managers (including Party secretaries) of enterprises are not prone to give great weight in their managerial decisions to the effect of such choices on their own promotion
outside of the enterprise.

(c) Promotion to enterprise top management during the first
half of the 1980s has not followed a steady path of progress through
middle and upper managerial ranks. Rather, the four principal criteria (aside from the role of personal relationships) must have been
Party membership and loyalty, higher education, at least minimal
work experience, and being sufficiently young to have time to make a
contribution in the new post before reaching age fifty-five.[38] It is unlikely that the evaluation standards governing promotion could have
also included an obligatory record of having headed a successful
lower unit.

(d) People who were already in top management posts in the
early 1980s were likely to have been rather fatalistic as to their chances
of keeping their positions. Age and lack of higher education were
the two most probable reasons for being pushed out; there was little
that a person could do about either. Although shifts in the political
wind within Party circles were much less substantial or consequential
than they had been in earlier decades, they were nevertheless of
significance and must have affected careers at the enterprise level
as well as in higher bodies. There seems little reason for top managers to have believed that successful efforts on their part to improve
the performance of their enterprises would make a great difference
in the chances of keeping their posts. This conclusion is quite consistent with a statement, made in the context of a discussion about
directors of enterprises, that was addressed to me in late 1985 by one
knowledgeable Chinese. The statement was to the effect that no
one in China loses his post simply because of a negative evaluation of
his work.

SUMMARY

The analysis of the role of bonuses for upper managers has been
based on the 1978–82 data of our own sample of enterprises. Examination of the role of career considerations for this group has been

based on two other samples which describe the characteristics of such managers during the second half of 1985. Both analyses lead to the same conclusion: namely, that it is unlikely that Chinese top managers have been guided in their managerial decision making by maximization of some combination of personal bonuses and of probable future career developments. At a minimum, the analyses demonstrate that the hypothesis that top managers are guided by prospects of personal bonuses is nonidentifiable when contrasted with the alternative hypothesis that they are guided by the maximization of average per capita bonuses in their own enterprise. (This latter hypothesis will be examined below.)

Thus we would seem well advised to abandon, in application to Chinese large and medium state industry, the dominant analytic approach to managerial decision making within socialist planned economies that has been developed from the experience of the Soviet Union. In this respect, we are doing no more than should be done on the basis of the Romanian experience alone.

Incentives Common to the Labor Force As a Whole

Having dropped the assumption that the appropriate maximand in determining enterprise behavior is the direct promotion of the welfare of the top managers, we now turn to an alternative assumption that the maximand is the mean welfare of the total labor force of the enterprise. Let us begin by attempting to rationalize this choice.

First, the current average total income of top managers is, by international standards, a very low multiple of that of all employees in their enterprise. Taking as the unit of measurement each enterprise-year (of both the pre-reform and reform years) for which we have data, there was roughly an equal distribution of the cases between a multiple of 150 per cent or less, 151–75 per cent, and 176–200 per cent. Only 7 per cent of the cases were above this last level.[39] This is quite a small multiple not only by Western standards, but also by those of the Soviet Union and of all of the East European countries for which we have data.[40] It also seems to constitute a low multiple compared to top earners within the health field in China, as well as representing low absolute earnings in relation to those of top Chinese hospital doctors or administrators.[41] It was not until the autumn of 1986 that there was an official call to increase the multiple.[42]

Furthermore, it should be recognized that a high, if unknown, portion of this multiple is a spurious result of the relative age distribution of top managers as compared with all employees. As in virtually all economies, top managers are considerably older on average. In

China, even more than in other countries, base wages rise with age; thus the reward for occupying a managerial post is even smaller than the raw multiples would indicate.[43] Particularly in light of the low interenterprise mobility of top managers, pursuit of their own financial self-interest would direct them to follow policies designed to promote the average money income of the personnel of their enterprise.

Second, I would guess from the Western literature that there exists a degree of esprit de corps of the total work force of the Chinese state enterprise—a building of one's life around one's work unit, and thus a sharing of a peculiar degree of solidarity among all members of the unit's staff—that is not readily matched elsewhere except in Japan.[44] Such solidarity is doubtless enhanced by the job stability of the factory's labor force. The influence of this solidarity on the choice of the maximand of top managers is likely also to be strongly reinforced by the memory, and fear of repetition, of the political history of recent decades. In those years, the chaos and reversal of traditional relationships must have caused a manager's reputation with the mass of his subordinates to have been an important element in determining his personal fate.[45]

It is true that the above forces affecting top management are counterbalanced by the virtual absence of a labor market in the state enterprises. Unlike his East European counterpart, the Chinese manager is not compelled to promote the interest of his rank-and-file workers by the threat that they will otherwise quit. I would hazard, however, that the effect of this counterbalancing effect is weak compared with the first two categories of influences.

Finally, of course, it is not sensible to hold that enterprise behavior anywhere is determined solely by decisions of top management; rank-and-file actions are also relevant. Absenteeism, waste of raw materials, low quality of output, and the like are strongly affected by whatever attitudes are pervasive in the general work force. This is particularly the case in the Chinese environment of the "iron rice bowl" (no dismissals), in which managerial disciplinary powers are weak. To the degree that we are concerned with the psychological disposition and the behavior of the rank and file of the labor force, it is reasonable to take average welfare as the appropriate maximand.

The choice of this maximand for purposes of further analysis does not imply rejection of the view that top managers may be motivated to pursue expansion or the improvement of design, quality, and production processes for their own sake. Rather, the choice serves the same purpose as does the assumption of profit maximization in the neoclassical treatment of the capitalist enterprise—it is a simplification that is believed to be useful for analytic purposes.[46]

In the remainder of this chapter I will work with assumption (5.2) rather than with assumption (5.1) which is the foundation of the dominant approach to enterprise behavior in centrally planned socialist economies.

(5.2) *Assumption:*
Enterprise behavior is determined by the maximization of the mean discounted value of the lifetime earnings of the primary families of the current work force of the enterprise.

Family earnings are introduced because, assuming that mean welfare of the work force is what is being maximized, effects of enterprise behavior on the earnings of family members not currently employed in the enterprise are highly relevant to such welfare.

Change in Welfare in Individual Enterprises

Let us assume, as has been proposed, that average welfare in the enterprise is the maximand around which the enterprise personnel would like to organize their effort. Then we should ask whether such welfare is subject to influence from what occurs in the enterprise, or whether it is determined solely by macroeconomic forces. To the degree that it is the latter, welfare in the enterprise is a maximand that is irrelevant to enterprise behavior.

Our first stab at this problem will be to see whether the relative welfare situations of the various enterprises in our sample vary over time. To the extent that there is no change, it would be reasonable to conclude that enterprise behavior has no influence.

For this purpose, let us use average annual monetary income as our proxy.[47] We have such data for all years of 1975–82 for seventeen of the twenty enterprises in our sample. Table 5.3 presents the results, converting each enterprise's figures into a proportion of that of all state employees in Chinese industry in the same year.

As can be seen in the table, there was very little relative change in average earnings within the sample during the pre-reform years. The earnings of not one of the enterprises altered during these three years by more than 11 per cent when taken as a proportion of the earnings of all state employees in Chinese industry. When ranked with respect to earnings among the group of organizations within the sample, half of the enterprises failed to change their rank by more than one level and none changed by more than three.

To allow for proper comparison with the earlier period, the reform years are represented by 1979–81 (with 1978 as the base year)

Table 5.3 Changes in Index of Average Earnings of the Total Labor Force
of the Organizations (in number of organizations)

Description	1975–78 (1)	1978–81 (2)	1978–81 (3)[a]	1975–82 (4)
Peak-year index as proportion of low-year index for a given enterprise within the period[b]:				
≤111 per cent	17	9	9	2
112–19 per cent	0	4	3	7
≥120 per cent	0	4	0	8
Maximum change of rank within the sample within the period (years need not be consecutive):				
0–1 level	9	1	1	1
2–3 levels	8	5	4	4
4–5 levels	0	3	3	2
6–8 levels	0	7	4	8
10–13 levels	0	1	0	2
Peak year index ≥120 per cent *and* change of rank ≥6	0	3	0	6
Total number of enterprises included here	17	17	12	17

Note: The index of average earnings consists of the average earnings in the individual enterprise as a percentage of those of all state employees in Chinese industry in the same year.

[a] The five excluded organizations are supervised exclusively by either a county or a municipality, not counting the three municipalities with provincial status. Two of them produce producer goods, two consumer goods, and one both types. Only one of them was located in a large urban area. See discussion in text below for full explanation of the significance of this category of organizations.

[b] When the figures are adjusted to eliminate the effect on average earnings of the change in the number of personnel in the enterprise, we are left with the following as our best approximation of the remaining differences: from 19 enterprises, 1979–82— ≤111 per cent for 2 and ≥120 percent for 5.

rather than by 1979–82. Over these three years (the same number as was available for measuring change during the pre-reform period), eight organizations saw their earnings index change by more than 11 per cent, and four of these had a change of 20 per cent or greater. Half of the enterprises changed their rank by more than five levels.[48]

Most striking of all is the summary figure for 1975–82 as a whole. During these seven years, one third of the enterprises changed their earnings index by at least 20 per cent *and* altered their rank within the sample by a minimum of six places. There was considerable volatility in relative average earnings among the firms in the sample, and this movement was heavily concentrated within the reform years.

Change within the pre-reform period is partially explained by the combination of differential bonuses, paid primarily during 1978, and by increases in basic wages in 1977–78. But all of these taken together were quite minor.[49] One sees this demonstrated most convincingly in the relative stability of nominal average earnings in state industrial enterprises in China as a whole: 1975 through 1977 showed small declines and 1978 was only 6 per cent higher than 1975 had been. Relative variations in earnings within the sample are probably due primarily to differential growth rates in enterprise work forces (with faster growth representing an increase in the number of the lowest-paid young workers) and, to a lesser degree, by differential retirements of the higher-paid older workers.

Thus the degree of volatility during 1975–78 of relative wages between enterprises can be used as a benchmark. It represents interenterprise changes that are fairly independent both of alterations in the authorities' views as to what should be provided to these specific organizations or to categories into which these enterprises fell, and of any other influence by the individual enterprise on its welfare position. Judged against this standard, the reform years are characterized by marked change.

The first approach to examining the volatility during these years is to inquire as to the degree to which change in a given enterprise's relative average earnings (earnings as a proportion of those of all Chinese state-owned industry in the given year) is explained by state variables over which the enterprise has no control. This is done for the period taken as a whole, using as the dependent variable the ratio of such earnings for a given enterprise in 1982 divided by the same enterprise's earnings in 1978 ($EARNAVCHIIND_{1982}/EARNAVCHIIND_{1978}$). (See the appendix to this chapter for the full explanation of the mnemonic terms of this paragraph.) The independent variables consist of the production sector into which the enterprise falls (consumer goods, producer goods, or mixed), the hierarchical level of its supervisory body (HIER), the size of the urban population of its locality (POP), and the average earnings of all state employees in the province where the enterprise was located (PROVST). OLS regression with the use of a constant shows that the ratio ($EARNAVCHIIND_{1982}/EARNAVCHIIND_{1978}$) was uninfluenced by whether the enterprise produced consumer or producer goods. On the other hand, the level of its supervisory agent(s) (HIER) was both significant and substantial in that it favored the five enterprises that were supervised solely by a municipality or county; these had been disadvantaged in 1978, while by 1982 they had reached or at least approached parity.[50]

This influence of the state variable of supervisory level was what led me to provide the alternative column in table 5.3 for 1978–81, in which these five enterprises are eliminated. Using this restricted sample, the difference between the pre-reform and reform years is greatly reduced.[51] Nevertheless, the difference remains substantial with respect to the proportion of firms varying in relative income by 12 to 19 per cent during the period, and with regard to change of rank. It is this column that expresses best the variation in relative average earnings that is specific to the individual enterprise, rather than including changes common to an entire category of state-owned industry.

The volatility of this reform period, together with the exclusion of the hypothesis that state variables constitute the sole important causal factors, can be interpreted as a necessary, although far from sufficient, condition for our believing that enterprise behavior could have a significant influence on enterprise welfare during these years.[52]

While EARNAVCHIIND is the principal variable used in measuring variability of earnings, creation of the alternative dependent variable EARNADJ represents an attempt to capture the negative effect on the average earnings of an enterprise which results from rapid growth in its workforce. EARNADJ is generated by starting from EARNAVCHIIND (the average earnings of the enterprise's labor force treated as an index of average earnings for all Chinese state-owned industrial enterprises in the same year). I then modify EARNAVCHIIND to get EARNGROWTH by taking account of the percentage increase during the previous two years in the average number of personnel (TOQST) in that enterprise.[53] This is done by applying the OLS-estimated regression coefficients α and β from the regression:[54]

$$\text{EARNAVCHIIND}_t - \text{EARNAVCHIIND}_{t-2} =$$
$$\alpha + \beta \, (\text{TOQST}_t / \text{TOQST}_{t-2}) + \varepsilon_t$$

to derive

$$\text{Expected value of EARNGROWTH}_{i,t} =$$
$$\text{EARNAVCHIIND}_{i,t-2} + \{\alpha + \beta(\text{TOQST}_{i,t} / \text{TOQST}_{i,t-2})\}$$

Although the variable EARNGROWTH fails to differentiate between a situation in which many workers retire in a given year and are replaced by youths, and one in which there is neither gross inflow nor gross outflow of labor, it does at least partially reflect the effect of changes in the labor force.[55]

EARNGROWTH represents the original value of average earnings two periods earlier, minus the decline in average earnings due to the increase in the labor force.[56] To eliminate the effect of the growth in labor force, I define

$$
\begin{aligned}
\text{Expected value of EARNADJ}_{i,t} &= \text{EARNAVCHIIND}_{i,t} \\
&- \text{EARNGROWTH}_{i,t} + \text{EARNAVCHIIND}_{i,t-2} \\
&= \text{EARNAVCHIIND}_{i,t} - \{\alpha + \beta(\text{TOQST}_{i,t}/\text{TOQST}_{i,t-2})\}, \\
&\text{with } \beta \leq 0
\end{aligned}
$$

Note b in table 5.3 reports the effect of using EARNADJ rather than EARNAVCHIIND as a measure of earnings. The ratio of the peak-year to the low-year index value for individual enterprises has been increased rather than reduced by this substitution.

Our confidence in this result—that the change in relative average earnings of individual enterprises has other causes than solely the decline in average earnings along with seniority as an enterprise's labor force increases—is slightly strengthened by the fact that EARNADJ as well as EARNAVCHIIND displays substantial interyear volatility for individual enterprises. For the reform years, there appears to be a considerable volatility of relative wages between enterprises that cannot be explained by systematic factors characterizing the state of the individual enterprises. It is this result that is the message of this section.

Comparison of the Sample Enterprises with All State Enterprises

Before proceeding to develop regression equations to explain differences in average earnings across enterprise-years, I will first look at the degree to which the sample enterprises are typical with respect to the values of possible explanatory variables. Particularly since the sample is not a random one, it could deviate sharply from its parent population with regard to the values of explanatory variables, while at the same time there would be relatively little variance within the sample itself. In that case, regression equations drawn from the sample data would not be informative.

As explained in chapter 1, the relevant universe is the population of all medium-sized and large state-owned industrial firms in China. Unfortunately, we have no data as to this population except for 1986. Instead, our comparison must be with the population of all state-owned industrial firms, including the very small ones. Furthermore, we have no breakdown even for this broader population in terms of sectors within industry. Finally, the available comparisons are all of financial indicators relative to capital, and the weakness of capital data will be shown in chapter 6. Nevertheless, even a very

Table 5.4 Financial Indicators of Sample Enterprises Relative to All State-owned Industrial Enterprises in China[a]

Year	Profits/ Net Capital[b]	(Profits + Tax)/ Net Capital[b]	Profits/ Undepreciated Fixed Capital in Production Facilities	(Profits + Taxes)/ Undepreciated Fixed Capital in Production Facilities
Part A (in percentages)				
1976	165	168		
1977	154	159		
1978	143	155		
1979	167	167		
1980	205	197		
1981	220	206		
1982	181	170		
Part B (index of change in relative values of Part A[c] [1976 = 100])				
1976	100	100	100	100
1977	94	95	97	97
1978	87	92	97	105
1979	101	99	100	99
1980	124	117	124	119
1981	134	122	138	127
1982	110	101	112	104

Note: Capital data are the averages of the end of the preceding and of the current year.
[a] Data are provided for an unweighted average of thirteen enterprises. An analysis of a similarly unweighted average of eighteen enterprises over the years 1979–82, the period when the percentages in part B differ most from 100, shows 1980 as the high year and 1982 as falling below 1979 in each column.
[b] Net capital is defined as the amortized value of fixed capital plus the value of all working capital held in inventories of any type.
[c] For the last two columns, the standard used is only a proxy of what is desired. Since no data are available on fixed capital in production facilities alone for all Chinese state enterprises, the denominator for the all-China data used is taken as undepreciated fixed capital of all types (including housing). The indexes with regard to change represent what would be calculated for these two columns if their part A portion had been written following the above system of calculation.

poor comparison is better than none. Table 5.4 provides such a comparison for the thirteen enterprises that supplied data for all years of 1976–82.

Part A of the table shows that the sample enterprises were, throughout all years, 40 to 120 per cent more profitable than were Chinese state-owned industrial enterprises as a whole. In 1986 the eight members of our sample for which we have such data had a ratio of profits to net capital for which the unweighted average was 147 per cent higher than the population of all state-owned industrial enterprises. For the years 1976–82, one would think that these figures are in part a reflection of the situation in the small state-owned enterprises that are not in our sample. It is likely that they also represent sectoral composition in the sample; timber is the only product produced by our sample enterprises that has been singled out in the literature as a low-priced (i.e., low profit or loss) item. Part B of the table, which shows the changes during 1977–82 in the relative values of the financial indicators, appears much more meaningful for our purposes than does part A.

On the basis of part B, it is only during the years 1980 and 1981 that our sample enterprises displayed positive financial change that was markedly different from that of all state-owned industrial enterprises. Thus these are the two years of concern with regard to representativeness. An examination of the EARNAVCHIIND data of relative employee earnings provides further perspective with regard to these years. Considering all eighteen sample enterprises for which we have data for 1978–82 as to average earnings, and taking such earnings as a proportion of those of all state-owned industrial enterprises in China, no more than nine of the enterprises reached their peak ratio during either 1980 or 1981. Indeed, three descended to their lowest ratio in one of these years. There was sufficient dispersion so that it would not be correct, as we might have feared, to describe the peak period of superiority as being sharply concentrated within these two years.

Regressions Explaining Average Earnings and Bonuses

EXPLANATORY INDEPENDENT VARIABLES

If we were to choose our explanatory variables on the basis of Chinese explanations of formal instructions as to what should affect bonus payments, the relevant variables would consist of the following:

1. Fulfillment of less than 100 per cent of the planned values of all of the following: output, profit, cost, product mix breakdown, quality, raw material usage, labor productivity, and use of working capital. It is the plan as finally established, not the original plan, that is taken as the standard. Failure to meet planned targets is supposed to reduce the bonus funds available for the total labor force, but no increases in bonuses are provided for above-plan performance.[57]

2. Profits per member of the labor force that are retained by the enterprise, rather than being passed on to the supervisory

government unit or to the state budget. This is because such profits serve to finance bonus payments.[58] One might also think that wage increases would be lower and rarer in enterprises which were in a poor financial position.

3. Success in meeting tasks for which special bonuses are awarded to the enterprise (in terms of so many renminbi per member of the labor force). These include such tasks as reduction of fuel consumption, but the winning of a special award is the most prominent ground for additional bonuses.[59]

None of the above variables are, however, directly useful to us for regression purposes. During the 1979–82 period, there were only 2 enterprise-years (out of 65 in the sample) in which there was less than 100 per cent fulfillment of the final plan for value of output; 2 (out of 53) for profits; 2 (out of 52) for the single, principal physical output; and 6 (out of 123) for all physical outputs (up to four) for which the enterprise received plans. Nor did the qualitative interviews mention plan underfulfillment of other less important plan targets. The analysis in chapter 3 indicated the reason: all plans have been set at levels that have made them very easy to overfulfill.

With respect to the second criterion, profits retained by the enterprise are not an indication of enterprise performance per se, but rather reflect a combination of this and of the supervisory body's decision as to how much of the profits should be passed on. This decision would seem to be closely related to plan fulfillment and may be better treated in that guise. Thus I have chosen to represent retained profits by a pair of independent variables: total profits earned per unit of some proxy for inputs, and total profits earned as a percentage of the final plan for profits.

The third criterion is one for which our sample contains information only on national awards. In 11 of 75 enterprise-years, we know that such an award was won; in 4, we have no information at all; and in 60, the probability is quite high that no award was obtained. We shall examine below the effect of winning a national award (using its receipt as a dummy variable) on the average earnings and bonus of the enterprise's labor force in the same year.

Procedures used in the Soviet Union for determining wages and bonuses suggest that plan fulfillment should be treated not as a criterion that distinguishes only between fulfillment and failure to fulfill plan, but rather as one in which the percentage of plan overfulfillment is also important. If we use as our criterion for the relative importance of different plans the evaluation given by Chinese managers in interviews, by far the most important enterprise plans in China consist of those for profits and for output. Both of these are treated in the regressions as continuous independent variables. (Introducing discontinuity at 100 per cent fulfillment has no statistically significant effect on the regression coefficients.[60])

If we think of profits earned as a success criterion rather than only as a source of funds for increases in labor force earnings, then profits + sales tax receipts + amortization (hereafter, called "cash flow")[61] might well be substituted as the numerator in the profits/input ratio. This is because supervisory authorities have a strong financial interest in the receipt of both sales tax and amortization funds, as well as in profits.

Finally, when we ask ourselves what mathematical function of profits would be most appropriate as a success indicator, we would want a function that deducts from total profits a charge for capital used (employing a common interest rate in all sectors, plus a differentiated risk premium), and then takes the residual as a proportion of total capital stock. We have, however, no basis for making such a deduction, nor is there any indication that Chinese authorities think in such terms. This leaves us with crude ratios as proxy candidates for the desired one. Three are available: profits/number of personnel (Profits/Personnel), profits/unamortized value of fixed capital invested in production facilities (Profits/Capital),[62] and Profits/Sales.

RESULT

The appendix to this chapter describes the control variables ("Control") used in the regressions that were run and presents the results. Here it is sufficient to point out that neither bonuses nor average earnings, nor the change between years for a given enterprise in either of them, display statistically significant dependence upon any measurable variable (except for control variables) that we have at our disposal.[63] This was the case despite the fact that, after some failures to find any significant coefficients for the variables of interest, I engaged in considerable "data mining" and tried numerous linear equation specifications. This procedure was justified on the basis that the relevant problem had turned out to be analogous to testing whether there were any fish in a pond, rather than how many of different kinds there were.

A possibility worth investigating was that the variable Profits/Personnel is significant for those firms that are under decentralized control. To test this, regressions were run separately for the seven enterprises in the fourth category of chapter 4 (in which enterprises were not subject to the physical allocation of their product combined with substantial allocation of materials in support of production, and all of their supervisors were below the national level). Regressions using Profits/Personnel and control variables showed no statistically significant results, regardless of whether the independent variable was taken as EARNAVCHIIND or BONUS. Regressions were also run using both Profits/Personnel and Profits as Percentage of Final Plan as the independent variables, with and without the most important portion of Control. This second set of regressions reduced the available observations from twenty-seven to sixteen, and nothing of interest appeared here either.[64]

This general absence of a relation between the variables of interest holds when control variables are introduced. Without the use of such variables, our sample regressions would support the belief by various observers of the Chinese economy that profits do matter for average earnings. (See eqs. [5] and [6] in table 5A.1.) In the absence of data that permit the running of regressions, observers could take account of control variables only in an informal fashion. This is extremely difficult to do.

Housing Incentives

Up to this point in my examination of incentives affecting the work force of an enterprise, I have limited myself to examining direct financial rewards. However, incentives provided in kind may also be of major significance. Such is the case particularly in centrally planned socialist economies, since various goods and services are typically not freely available in the marketplace. In China's urban areas, housing is the principal such item that may serve as an incentive.

A study of two hundred Chinese cities, which is undated but was presumably conducted during 1981 or 1982, showed that 18 per cent of rented housing, when measured in terms of floor space, was owned by individuals, 29 per cent by municipal administrations, and 54 per cent by enterprises and administrative organizations that rented only to their own labor force.[65] It should be noted that in Shanghai at least, enterprises construct housing and turn it over to the municipal authorities to run, but reserve use of the housing for their own work force.[66] Such housing would not be included in the 54 per cent figure, although its usage is identical, so that the figure understates the importance of enterprise-owned housing.

Data are available as to per capita housing space provided in seven of the cities in which our sample enterprises are located, and per household housing space in the corresponding enterprises can be

compared with these figures.[67] Using what seem to be reasonable estimates of the number of persons per household (4.0) and of living
space as a percentage of total space (60),[68] we find that the space provided by seven of the sample enterprises in 1982 was the following
proportion of the level for their own city: for two enterprises, 155–210
per cent; for three, 130–40 per cent; and for the last two, 85–95 per
cent.[69] These data provide support for the conventional wisdom concerning Chinese urban housing; namely, that the provision of housing
by the enterprise is normally quite an attractive perquisite to its
workers.[70]

Such housing investment comes from two sources: state grants
(or bank loans earmarked for capital construction projects) and profits
earned and retained by the enterprise. It is said that during the lengthy
period of 1967–76 there was almost no state investment in housing
(Perkins and Yusuf 1984, 128). In the 1980s when housing construction boomed both in rural and urban areas, it was being financed
largely from nonstate sources: it has been estimated that retained
profits financed about 60 per cent of all urban housing built in the beginning of the 1980s.[71] Although this figure seems to imply that virtually 100 per cent of enterprise-owned housing is paid for from
retained profits, our sample data include at least two cases in which a
state grant for expansion of production facilities (or, post-1981, a
loan) was accompanied by a grant (loan) for housing construction.[72]
The justification in these instances was presumably that utilization of
the added production facilities would require major growth of the labor force.

In the appendix to this chapter I explore the question of whether
the expansion of enterprise-owned housing was related either to absolute profitability of the enterprise or to its profits as a percentage of
final plan. Since an analysis of data for individual years would have
made no sense, expansion was measured between 1978 and 1982. Unfortunately, this approach reduced the total sample size to the number of enterprises for which I have housing data. Despite limiting the
number of control variables to only one or two, I found that the degrees of freedom in the regressions ranged only between 2 and 5.

There is somewhat more evidence in the case of housing than
of money income that the profit performance of the enterprise yields a
payoff to the work force. This is indeed what we would expect, since
housing construction is financed predominantly with the enterprise's
own retained profits. However, it is not the amount of profits earned
per worker that matters. Instead, it is the degree of fulfillment of the
profit plan. Presumably, this is because of the influence of such fulfillment on the amount of profits that the enterprise is allowed to retain.

Employment for Family Members

The last incentive to be investigated is that of jobs created for family members of the employees of the enterprise. There are two subdivisions of this type of incentive. The first is hiring a family member as a regular employee of the enterprise itself. This provides entrée into the privileged employment that is represented by the state-owned sector.[73] The second is employment in a cooperative enterprise that was created by the state enterprise and is dependent upon it. This is viewed as inferior, but is still desired by workers in a society with an excess supply of urban labor. It is particularly attractive for wives who are too old to be hired as a regular state worker (over twenty-three and twenty-five years of age in two large enterprises, under thirty in a third).[74] Either of these types of employment of family members may have a much greater effect on total family income than would any likely increase in wage or bonus of those workers who are already employed. This was particularly the case in 1979 and at the beginning of the 1980s.

In the appendix to this chapter, I show that there is no evidence that such employment creation is related either to the enterprise's absolute level of profitability or to its profitability as a percentage of plan.

Conclusion

Summary

This chapter began with a presentation of the case that Chinese top managers of medium and large state-owned enterprises either have not been in a position to maximize their own personal welfare through strategies affecting enterprise performance or, if they have been able to do so, this phenomenon would not be statistically identifiable in comparison with maximization of the average welfare of the employees of their enterprise. This led to the assumption that enterprises act in such a way as to maximize the expected average welfare value of all employees.

Using average money earnings as a proxy for average welfare, we saw that there was great variation in the relative position of individual sample enterprises during 1979–82, in contrast to what had occurred during the pre-reform years of 1975–78. Even when I omitted those enterprises that were solely under municipal or county supervision, the variation during 1979–81 was substantially greater than in 1975–78. It seems reasonable to hypothesize that the performance of state-owned enterprises was being evaluated by supervisory authorities during the reform years and that rewards were correlated with this evaluation. But all attempts to measure such evaluation by objective standards, whether these were profit ratios or plan fulfillment ratios, failed. Expansion of housing, in contrast, does seem to reflect use of the objective standard of the plan fulfillment ratio, but the size of the sample (seven observations) is too small to provide any confidence in this last result.

Discussion

My inability to measure evaluation by objective standards seems to be contrary to the expectations of various Western experts on the Chinese economy. Thus Barry Naughton, writing about state-owned industrial enterprises in China, declared that "A program of material incentives that rewards efficient production has been comprehensively implemented by linking bonuses and enterprise benefits to profitability."[75] In this sense, my findings represent data that are unanticipated in the field. Because the sample showed such data, I was led to look for confirmation or refutation outside the sample.

The absence of objective indicators of successful enterprise performance (which is proxied by rewards granted to the enterprise) is consistent with the results of the single Chinese study I have seen reported. This was an analysis of 429 enterprises, located in twenty-seven cities. Of the enterprises, 56 per cent were medium-sized and large state enterprises, 9 per cent were small state enterprises, and 35 per cent were collectives. During 1984–85, only 3 per cent of the total variation in per capita bonuses could be explained by differences in gross profits, as these worked their effect through the intermediate variable of profits retained by the enterprise.[76]

In the light of the "irrationalities" of regulated pricing systems as these are used in any country, it would be difficult to interpret the profitability of an individual enterprise as necessarily being reflective of its efficiency, or even to interpret a change in the first as reflective of a change in the second. Indeed, the weakness of such a connection has been a principal rationale offered by Chinese reformers in arguing for the linkage of economic reform of the control system to price reform.

To the degree that Chinese supervisory authorities at different levels have taken as fundamental the irrationality of their pricing system, it would be reasonable for them to have rejected profit results of state enterprises as the independent variable that should determine reward.[77] Indeed, we have an explicit statement with regard to the province of Anhui through 1983 that supervisors did not use the profit criterion.[78] In such rejection, Chinese authorities would not have been any different than authorities in the Soviet and East European planned economies.

It is less clear, however, why Chinese supervisors should have lacked all confidence in the plans for enterprises as appropriate standards of efficiency, for it is the supervisors themselves who have set these plans. Nevertheless, it would seem to be the case that they have felt this way. The evidence consists both of the lack of statistical relation within the sample between plan fulfillment and bonus payments, and of the customary statement of the formal principle that the level of overfulfillment should have no effect upon bonus receipts of an enterprise. Supervisory authorities, to the extent that they have evaluated enterprises at all, appear to have relied solely on subjective criteria.

At first sight, it would appear that an exception to this was the recognition through supplementary bonuses of the winners of national competitions. In four of the five cases for which we have precise data, there was indeed a bonus payoff to enterprises when they won special national awards.[79] But decisions as to the amount of the bonus award were made locally, and one might suspect that extraneous considerations may well have played a role in such decisions.[80]

One particular bonus payment observed in the sample, although unconnected with the winning of a national award, is of exceptional interest. An enterprise received a special bonus in 1981 for its accomplishments in technological development. The per capita bonus amounted to some 7.9 per cent of per capita annual earnings, and it was over and beyond the official limit on the ratio of bonuses to base wages.

This bonus was linked to the production of a special one-off (one of a kind) machine. But the customer plant did not receive a bonus, despite the fact that it was that organization that had originated the design of the machine. Moreover, since both enterprises were under the same supervisory authority, it was a single body which made the bonus decision for the two plants. The research institute (under a different supervisory body) that did the actual design work also did not receive a bonus. A final point of interest is that the bonus award to the producer was made a year before the machine was tested and deemed of acceptable quality. It is thus difficult to explain the granting of this special bonus to the supplier, except on the ground that the low base wages earned in this enterprise led its supervising organ to believe that it was appropriate to raise average earnings by whatever device could be found.

If we define an enterprise's income as current consumption of goods and services by its work force, it would seem likely that a state-owned enterprise can indeed influence its own per capita income. It does this by performing those actions which lead to a high performance evaluation by its supervising body. But there is no way, except through building housing, that the enterprise can accumulate wealth; receipt of income in future years depends essentially upon current evaluations of the enterprise in a given year. Income for the enterprise cannot be viewed as a return on wealth (except partially with respect to housing services). Thus the enterprise is not a "principal"; it is at best an "agent."

Indeed, the lack of variation in annual earnings among enterprises during the pre-reform years would suggest that that period should not be described in terms of a principal-agent game. An enterprise was neither rewarded nor punished, regardless of what it did. Since 1979, it seems likely that the principal-agent treatment is appropriate. But even as an agent, the Chinese sample enterprises have been peculiar by the standards of operation used in the Soviet Union. The Chinese enterprise could not determine its optimal strategy through knowledge of the various payoffs for specific results. The absence of objective criteria of success makes the game between the enterprise and its supervisory body appear relatively undefined in the usual sense of game theory.

A Puzzle

What remains to explain is why, under these circumstances, the management of the Chinese sample enterprises has paid as much attention to market conditions as is indicated by the informants in these enterprises. Judging from the consistent tone of the interviews, it would seem that both middle and senior enterprise managers are quite as concerned with earning profits as are their Western counterparts. Moreover, this is more the case in the sense of profit maximizing than of satisficing.

Similarly puzzling is the rather good record of the sample enterprises in improving both capital and labor productivity during the reform years (see table 1.3 and note 23 in chap. 1). The median compound annual rate of improvement in both labor productivity and capital productivity was 1.5 per cent.[81] This record, however, may be explained by the large potential for improvement that had been accumulated during the earlier "ten years of turmoil"; I have no data on this.[82] Thus my focus will be on attempting to explain the attention that our sample organizations, and presumably large and medium-sized state enterprises in general, give to market conditions.

It might be possible to try to frame an explanation in terms of institutional factors; namely, the influence of the Chinese Communist

Party or even of the trade unions. But this seems a weak approach and shall not be pursued.

Economic historians have emphasized the importance of markets in the everyday life of traditional China. Ramon Myers, referring to the entire period of the Qing dynasty (covering all of the eighteenth and nineteenth centuries), estimated that villages marketed perhaps one-fifth to one-half of their total production of crops and handicrafts. Gilbert Rozman has stressed the high ratios that existed in Qing China between the number of small, periodic markets in county-seat types of towns and the number of intermediate-size markets in cities with a population under 3,000, and of larger markets in cities with a population of 3,000 to 10,000. The Chinese ratios, which are interpreted as indicating the degree to which marketization permeated the countryside, were far higher than those in premodern England, France, Japan, or Russia. Loren Brandt has given a similar emphasis for the period between the late nineteenth century and the late 1930s.[83]

Rozman has also underscored the importance in traditional China of impersonal, contractual patterns of transactions in land, labor, and credit. Between landlord and tenant, for example, "specific obligations and responsibilities would normally be waived only when a community consensus was reached that harvest conditions did not warrant full payment of rent." He believes that China may have given a weighting to contractual arrangements that was unusually high for premodern societies.[84]

It is possible that it is the Chinese tradition of being attuned to markets that has led managers in our sample enterprises to adapt so fully and rapidly to marketization practices, at least once these were espoused by senior political authorities. Perhaps such adaptation was also due to the current market orientation of individual peasants and of members of small collective enterprises in rural and urban areas, all of whom had a substantial material stake in the successful use of markets. This latter orientation, particularly as it was accompanied by the "reform" propaganda conducted in the name of the highest authorities, may have established a milieu in which managers found it natural to act in the same fashion. Furthermore, although our data suggest that there were no rewards for this kind of market behavior, managers may have believed that there were or, more likely, that there would be such rewards in the future.

The reader may find these reasons, taken together, to be sufficient to explain the behavior of the managers in our sample enterprises. However, if this is not the case, he or she shares my viewpoint. Although it is regrettable to leave the matter in this inconclusive fashion, I am unable to push any further toward a more definitive result.

Appendix: Regressions for Incentives Common to the Labor Force As a Whole

Control Independent Variables

These collectively are called "Control," and consist of the following:

YRSEC: A set of dummy variables that distinguish between organizations producing consumer goods and those producing producer goods, and that combine this sectoral distinction with temporal distinction for each individual year of 1980–82. The year 1979 is treated without regard to sector of activity.

HIER: A set of dummy variables distinguishing among the enterprises according to whether their direct supervisory body is at the level of: (1) a county or municipality; (2) a province, either alone or together with a county or municipality; (3) a national body together with some local one; or (4) a national body alone.

POP: A set of dummy variables that describe the population size of the urban area in which the enterprise is located or headquartered. The smallest size is quite small; the second category is larger, but still ≤ 500,000 population; the third is between 1 and 3 million; and the fourth is ≥ 3 million. All population figures refer to urban population only.

PROVST: A single variable that is an index of the average wage in all state-owned enterprises in 1983 in individual provinces. Each enterprise is given the value of its province.

The above control variables were selected on the grounds of being both intuitively reasonable and of yielding (with use of a constant) a high $\bar{R}^2$ (0.454 with a Durbin-Watson of 1.599) for the reform years. (EARNAVCHIIND is the independent variable.) A variable that provides results virtually identical to PROVST is an index of collectively distributed income per capita in rural areas by province. Still another variable was tried as an alternative to both POP and PROVST; this consisted of the index, specific to the individual locality of the enterprise, that is used by the national government to adjust to local conditions the average wages paid nationally. For such government adjustment, the locality's index value is applied to the nominal base wage paid to a specific grade of worker in all state enterprises in that industry in China. Surprisingly, this alternative variable had much lower explanatory power than did POP and PROVST taken together.[85]

Regressions Explaining Average Earnings and Bonuses

Nine independent variables have been used: Profits/Personnel, Profits/Capital, Profits/Sales, "Cash Flow"/Personnel, "Cash Flow"/Capital, "Cash Flow"/Sales, Profits as Percentage of Final Plan, Output Value as Percentage of Final Plan, and whether or not a national award was won. In addition, the control variables defined above—YRSEC, HIER, POP, and PROVST—have been used. All regressions are run in OLS form with a constant.

Five dependent variables are regressed against combinations of the above independent variables. These are: average earnings of the enterprise as a percentage of the average in all Chinese state-owned industry in the same year (EARNAVCHIIND); a form of this adjusted for growth in the labor force (EARNADJ); average bonuses + subsidies paid during the year (BONUS); and changes between years in EARNAVCHIIND and in BONUS for a given enterprise. Regressions were limited to the reform years 1979–82, i.e., to those years for which the rankings of earnings of the sample enterprises were volatile. Full or partial data are available for nineteen of the twenty organizations in the sample.

Different equation specifications were not judged by their F-statistics, since even the equations that limited the independent variables to Control are highly significant by this test, and my objective was not to obtain a correct specification per se. Rather, since my concern is exclusively with the coefficients of the independent variables of interest, and since I ended up trying many different equation specifications, the concept of "significance" was restricted to t-statistics for these relevant coefficients. This is the meaning given to the term significance in the following paragraphs.

Examination of regression statistics quickly eliminated Profits/Sales and "Cash Flow"/Sales as candidates for independent variables. The remaining four ratios of profits and of "cash flow" yielded results that were fairly similar to one another, but the most significant coefficients were found using the Profits/Personnel ratio. Since this is also the one that is the most intuitively appealing (as a source of funds both for wage increases and for bonuses), further reporting will be limited to it, to the two plan fulfillment variables, and to the dummy variable for receipt of a national award. EARNADJ was eliminated as a candidate for a dependent variable on the basis that it yielded no significant results (in terms of t-statistics for individual coefficients) when regressed against any combination of independent variables.

Various lag relations were also eliminated, since they yielded no statistically significant regression coefficients. Independent variables were lagged in the three alternative forms of lag$_{-1}$, unlagged +

lag$_{-1}$, and lag$_{-1}$ + lag$_{-2}$, with dependent variables being unlagged. Dependent variables were also expressed as (Variable$_{1982}$ − Variable$_{1978}$), with the independent variables being the Σ_{1979}^{1982} variables.

Finally, the national awards variable was eliminated, yielding only a nonsignificant coefficient, regardless of whether it was used alone or in combination with others.

Turning to the unlagged form of the independent variables, no significant relation appeared for year-to-year changes in average earnings (EARNAVCHIIND$_t$ − EARNAVCHIIND$_{t-1}$). The same failure occurred when the dependent variable was taken as (BONUS$_t$ − BONUS$_{t-1}$).[86] Nor was there any significant relation when EARNAVCHIIND was regressed on any single independent variable combined with the control variables.

The only barely significant results are shown for the regression of BONUS on Profits/Personnel, and for both EARNAVCHIIND and BONUS on the combination of all three unlagged variables: Profits/Personnel, Output as Percentage of Final Plan, and Profits as Percentage of Final Plan (see table 5A.1). But even in these equation specifications, the only coefficient that is significant or close to significant at the 5 per cent level is that of Profits/Personnel.

When one takes account of autocorrelation among the observations for each enterprise individually, with the resulting overstatement of the t-ratios of the coefficients, we must conclude that no combination of independent variables is statistically significant at the 5 per cent level on a two-tail test. This is strongly reinforced by the fact that our procedure has been to "mine" the data in order to see if anything at all appears; given such mining, it would be statistically unusual to find no t-ratios above the numerical value of two.

Further evidence against the notion that the Profits/Personnel ratio has an effect on either EARNAVCHIIND or on BONUS is the following:

1. There is no statistically significant effect of Profits/Personnel on EARNAVCHIIND when the two variables of performance as a percentage of plan are excluded from the specification. Yet their coefficients are both very close to zero and not significant when combined with Profits/Personnel. When each of the plan performance variables is taken alone (aside from Control, which is always retained), the coefficients are similarly not significant.
2. Both one-year and multiyear changes in EARNAVCHIIND or BONUS for a given enterprise are statistically insignificant when regressed on the three independent variables together.
3. When independent variables are lagged in any form, the co-

efficient of Profits/Personnel is insignificant even when this
variable is combined with the two plan performance variables.

The only additional evidence supporting the view that the
Profits/Personnel ratio has an effect is twofold. The first consists of
eqs. (5) and (6) in table 5A.1, which show high statistical significance;

Table 5A.1 Regression Equations for Explaining Average Earnings and
Bonuses in a Given Enterprise-year (1979–82)

Eq. No.	Dependent Variable	Con-stant	Control	Profits/Per-sonnel	Output as % of Final Plan	Profits as % of Final Plan
1	EARNAVCHIIND	x	x	x		
2	EARNAVCHIIND	x	x	x	x	
3	EARNAVCHIIND	x	x	x		x
4	EARNAVCHIIND	x	x	x	x	x
5	EARNAVCHIIND	x		x		
6	EARNAVCHIIND	x		x	x	x
7	BONUS	x	x	x		
8	BONUS	x	x	x	x	
9	BONUS	x	x	x		x
10	BONUS	x	x	x	x	x
11	BONUS	x		x		
12	BONUS	x		x	x	x

| | Profits/Personnel | | | | Degrees of | |
	Coefficient	$\partial \log(D)/\partial \log(I)$ [a]	*t*-value	$\bar{R}^2$	Freedom	Durbin-Watson
1	0.060		0.746	.449	57	1.549
2	0.164		2.056	.493	43	1.957
3	0.087		0.964	.582	33	1.050
4	0.132	0.05	1.908	.732	26	1.707
5	0.162		2.626	.074	73	0.758
6	0.295	0.11	3.799	.222	42	0.910
7	85.6	0.13	2.143	.554	49	1.299
8	102.9		2.352	.522	42	1.455
9	7?.7		1.681	.586	33	1.451
10	97.4	0.16	2.111	.547	26	1.727
11	28.8		0.795	−.006	65	1.370
12	79.4		1.772	.007	42	1.798

[a]The column heading is only a loose description. The coefficients were not calculated
with logs, as it is believed that this would be a misspecification. Instead, they represent the partial derivative of the percentage change in the dependent variable with
respect to the percentage change in the independent one, taken at the vector point
that represents the mean value of both variables. Using D for the dependent variable,
I for the independent one, and M for the mean value, this is $(\partial D/\partial I)\,(M_I/M_D)$.

however, these regressions not only exclude the control variables but also have quite low $\bar{R}^2$. The second is for the subsample of eight enterprises for which data are available on the number of pensioners in 1982. For this subsample, eq. (1) of table 5A.1 shows a coefficient of 0.017, a change of 0.07 per cent in the average value of the dependent variable for 1 per cent change in the independent variable, a t-value of 3.640, an $\bar{R}^2$ of 0.874, 21 degrees of freedom, and a D-W statistic of 2.193. Given the fact that the coefficient is very close to zero in this subsample, the fact that it is significant should not be taken as meaningful.

Regressions Explaining Expansion of Enterprise-owned Housing

Looking at the change in space provided per household lodged by the ten enterprises for which we have such data, three showed a slight decline or stability over the entire period of 1975–82, one a 5 per cent increase, and six an increase of 12 to 18 per cent.[87] Similar statistics are available as to per capita dormitory space provided by eight enterprises: in two, there was a decline of 8 to 14 per cent over the 1975–82 period; three were stable; one had a 6 per cent increase; and the remaining two had increases of 24 to 39 per cent. These figures represent a considerable range of enterprise behavior. Although it is difficult to generalize about them, the growth (especially in household space) is sufficiently modest so that one is fairly safe in concluding from our sample data that enterprise housing construction has been used primarily to increase the proportion of the work force enjoying the fringe benefit of enterprise-owned housing, rather than to enlarge the size of this benefit for those who had already been receiving it. Doubtless this emphasis on expansion of the number of the privileged is related to the criterion used for awarding housing. In all the sample enterprises for which we have information, the main criterion was seniority within the enterprise's labor force rather than work skill or status on the job.

Data are available for seven enterprises over the period 1979–82 that allow us to test whether the increase in the proportion of the enterprise's labor force lodged in enterprise housing was responsive to the level of enterprise performance.[88] There is no point in using annual data for a dependent variable of this sort, so we are limited to a single observation per enterprise.[89] In the regression whose specification is most intuitively appealing (eq. [1] of table 5A.2), a 1 per cent change in the average ratio of profits per member of the labor force during 1979–82 led to a 0.27 per cent change in the average proportion of staff lodged in enterprise housing. Despite the fact that there were only 2 degrees of freedom in the regression, the coefficient was significant at

Table 5A.2 Regression Equations for Explaining Expansion in Enterprise-owned Housing During 1979–82

Variables	Equation					
	1	2	3	4	5	6
Dependent:						
Proportion of the work force in enterprise-owned housing in 1982 (1978 = 100)	x	x	x	x		
Independent:						
A. Average annual ratio, 1979–82						
1. Profits/Personnel	x	x	x			
2. Profits as Percentage of Final Plan	x	x		x		
B. Control						
3. Percentage of staff lodged in enterprise housing in 1978	x		x	x		
4. Growth in labor force, 1978–82	x		x	x		
C. Constant	x	x	x	x		
Dependent:						
Average space per family in enterprise-owned family housing in 1982 (1978 = 100)					x	
Independent:						
A. Average annual ratio, 1979–82						
1. Profits/Personnel					x	
2. Profits as Percentage of Final Plan					x	
B. Control						
3. Average space per family in 1978					x	
C. Constant					x	
Dependent:						
Total space available in enterprise-owned family housing in 1982 (1978 = 100)						x
Independent:						
A. Average annual ratio, 1979–82						
1. Profits/Personnel						x
2. Profits as Percentage of Final Plan						x

Table 5A.2 (Continued)

Variables	Equation					
	1	2	3	4	5	6
B. Control						
3. Percentage of staff lodged in enterprise housing in 1978						x
4. Growth in labor force, 1978–82						x
C. Constant						x
Statistics:						
Profits/Personnel						
1. Coefficient	0.700	1.023			0.569	
2. $\partial\log(D)/\partial\log(I)$[a]	0.27	0.39			0.26	
3. t-value	2.74	1.99	−0.28		2.18	0.004
Profits as Percentage of Final Plan						
1. Coefficient	0.006	0.010		0.003		0.552
2. $\partial\log(D)/\partial\log(I)$[a]	0.70	1.10		0.40		0.55
3. t-value	4.52	4.36		2.07	0.44	5.53
$\bar{R}^2$	0.95	0.76	0.61	0.84	0.39	0.96
Degrees of freedom	2	4	3	3	5	2
Durbin-Watson	1.76	2.21	2.07	2.19	1.96	2.13

[a]The column heading is only a loose description. The coefficients were not calculated with logs, as it is believed that this would be a misspecification. Instead, they represent the partial derivative of the percentage change in the dependent variable with respect to the percentage change in the independent one, taken at the vector point that represents the mean value of both variables. Using D for the dependent variable, I for the independent one, and M for the mean value, this is $(\partial D/\partial I)\ (M_I/M_D)$.

better than a 5 per cent confidence level with a two-tail test. Profits as a Percentage of Final Plan had a much larger effect and was significant at a 1 per cent confidence level; 1 per cent change led to a 0.70 per cent change in the dependent variable. The remaining two variables (used as controls) had significance levels of approximately 5 per cent with a two-tail test, and both had the correct sign (negative).[90] Note that in this case there are no time series data, and thus the issue of autocorrelation (with resultant overstatement of the t-values) does not arise.

Eq. (5) in table 5A.2 is intended to test the effect of performance on the growth of the average space per family for those households that enjoyed enterprise-owned housing. Here, however, some enterprises present their housing data in terms of total square meters, and others only in terms of "living space." In the case of two enterprises that present both sets of data, the ratio averages 60.8 per cent.[91]

It is this ratio that is used for conversion purposes in eq. (5), and it results in a 1 per cent change in the average Profits/Personnel ratio leading to a 0.26 per cent change in average space per family in 1982. The *t*-ratio here is significant at the 5 per cent confidence level in a two-tail test. No other experiment with the effect of performance on this dependent variable yielded any results of interest.

Finally, a third dependent variable was used; namely, the growth in the total space available in the enterprise for family housing. This is shown in eq. (6). Instead of this combining both our previous dependent variables into one, it simply acts as a transformation of the interpretation of eq. (1) that is provided by eqs. (3) and (4); the Profit/Personnel ratio has no statistically significant effect on this variable.

Employment for Family Members

Since our sample enterprises generally gave preference in new hirings to the children of members of the current labor force, opportunities for state employment may be represented by the percentage growth in the enterprise's labor force between 1978 and 1982.[92] Taking such growth as the dependent variable, it was regressed upon the average amount of Profits/Personnel during 1979–82, as well as upon that variable together with the average figure for Profits as Percentage of Final Plan. Regressions with 17 and 10 degrees of freedom, respectively, show no statistically significant relation.[93]

We have no time series data on employment in dependent cooperative enterprises, but figures are available for fourteen sample enterprises with regard to such employment in 1982. Taking for our dependent variable such employment as a proportion of state employment in the parent enterprise, regressions were run with the same independent variables as mentioned above. Once more, with 12 and 7 degrees of freedom, respectively, no significant relation appeared.[94]

6
ELEMENTS OF PRICE

Price formation has long been recognized as a major sore point in all centrally planned socialist economies. Since most prices are set by the state, government pricing policy dominates the establishment of relative prices. With planning being conducted primarily in terms of physical inputs and outputs, relative prices have historically played only a minor role in all such economies. This has been the case both in the allocation of capacity between different products and in making decisions about the combination of inputs to be used in the production of a given product. Such lack of influence of relative prices has been deplored for decades by both academics and administrators in these countries.

Attention to relative prices, at least for producer goods, has arisen from two concerns. One is the provision of appropriate information in a usable form to decision makers operating above the level of the individual enterprise. Economic administrators in socialist economies came to recognize that it was essential to have some common denominator in which the varying factors relevant to decisions might be expressed; decision makers were unable to grapple directly with the myriad of disperse factors relevant to issues such as investment. Price serves as such a common denominator; but clearly, to the degree that it has been out of contact with social opportunity cost, it has performed that function badly.

The second, more recent concern is with the informational and incentive prerequisites for achieving sensible results from marketplace decentralization in socialist economies. The desire by the government to achieve a significant degree of decentralization through the marketplace has been stronger in China in the 1980s than in any other of the centrally planned socialist economies except for Hungary. Yet prices of consumer and of producer goods, as well as of the factors of labor and capital, have remained essentially under administrative control. Thus it is still meaningful, even today, to think of Chinese prices as responding primarily to government policy with regard to price formation.

Such policy can be analyzed in terms of the approach taken as to how enterprise profits (including negative ones, i.e., subsidies) and sales tax, the two principal elements in the budgetary revenues of all levels of Chinese government, should be distributed between products.[1] Of course, pricing strategy can deal only with planned profits rather than with achieved profits. Nevertheless, since one would expect a high correlation between the two for a given product, one may use achieved profits as a good proxy.

This chapter, with the exception of the conclusion, should probably be skipped by readers who are noneconomists. In it I will analyze the shares of major components of product price that exist in the sample enterprises of my study, distinguishing particularly between the situation for consumer items and for other goods. I concentrate upon the share of wages in costs that include both wages and expenditures on intermediate materials and fuels, and contrast the resulting pattern with that observed both in the Soviet Union and the United States. I explain the difference between the Chinese pattern and that of the other two countries by the peculiarities of Chinese sales tax policy. The implications for the difference in pricing structure will be examined theoretically to suggest resulting incentives that exist both for Chinese enterprises and for their principals.

This chapter is related to the book's thesis as to the uniqueness of the Chinese state-owned sector within the set of centrally planned economies. Here, this has to do with the form taken by taxation, which has major implications for the share of wages in total costs. More narrowly, however, the link between this chapter and the rest of the book is with regard to the incentives that exist for Chinese regional principals. The unimportance of unit wages as a proportion of revenue per unit of output, and thus the weakness of financial incentives to economize on wage expenditures, explains some of the behavior shown by the regional principals of enterprises which would otherwise seem anomalous. It also explains why, more than in other countries, behavior by Chinese enterprises that is profit maximizing might well be misidentified by the observer as output maximizing.

Sales Tax and Profits

Both in the Soviet Union and in China, government revenue consists primarily of sales tax and of the profits of state enterprises.[2] In China these totalled 88 per cent of budgetary revenue in 1980 and, in all probability, constituted an even higher proportion of total government revenue, including nonbudgetary. In the Soviet Union in the same year, the proportion was 64 per cent of budgetary income.[3] If we compare the proportions of total government budgetary revenue coming from the sum of sales tax (almost all levied on industrial products) and from the profits of industrial state-owned enterprises alone, the figures for China and the Soviet Union were 88 and 53–55 per cent, respectively. This latter difference between countries is accounted for essentially by the fact that Soviet government revenue is more diversified, both among state enterprises of different sectors and among different taxes levied upon state and cooperative enterprises. In neither country was the sum total of taxes levied on agriculture, direct taxes on individuals, and net receipts of borrowing from the population of great significance.[4]

From the viewpoint of the governments in both countries, there is no essential difference between profits of state enterprises and sales tax levied on the sales of these enterprises. Both are paid over to governmental bodies, with the exception of profits retained by the enterprises and used for bonuses, fringe benefit expenditures, and investments; such expenditures would presumably be met from the government budget if a portion of profits was not left to the enterprises to fund them. In both countries, prices paid by purchasers are set as the sum of planned costs, planned profits, and sale tax per unit of product.

Sales Tax in Price Formation

For the Soviet Union, the process of price formation can be modelled as follows:

$$D_i = f(P_i, P_j, A_i, Y)$$
$$S_i = g(P_i, P_j, O_i, I_i)$$

where D and S are demand and supply, respectively, i and j refer to products, P is price, A is allocation to a user, Y is money income, O is an output plan of a supplier, and I is incentives attached to the production of specific goods. For consumer goods, since these are not rationed, A has a zero coefficient in the demand equation; for producer goods, on the other hand, Y has a zero coefficient.

Within this framework, the vector $\mathbf{P}$ of all prices is set so that:

(6.1) $S_i \leq \bar{D}_i \leq (1 + \alpha_i) S_i$ with probability δ_i over the expected lifetime of these prices,

where α refers to the unsatisfied notional demand at existing prices that is tolerated by the central planners, and $(1 - \delta)$ to the degree of uncertainty that is acceptable. $\bar{D}_i$ is the notional demand that would exist if enterprises did not need input allocations in order for their demand to be effective.

Proposition (6.1) is based upon the notion that central planners wish to avoid not only any excess supply of individual goods, but also permitting unsatisfied notional demand (as this would exist in the absence of allocation constraints) to exceed an identifiable level that is specific to the particular good. The permissible level of such unsatisfied notional demand (α_i) will naturally be greater for producer goods than for consumer goods, since the latter do not require allocations; between consumer goods, one would expect that α_i would generally be lower for goods that are considered necessities than for luxuries.

Since prices are set bureaucratically, it is not administratively feasible to change too many of them with any frequency. (In fact, Soviet prices for individual products have had an average lifespan of about fifteen years.) Thus the calculation of $\hat{P}_i$ must take into account the expected development of both S_i and $\tilde{D}_i$ over the period involved, being set so as to minimize some function (g) of the risk $(1 - \delta)_t$ over the time period. $\mathbf{P}_i$ is set so as to minimize

$$\int_{t=1}^{t=T} [g\,(1 - \delta_i)]_t\, dt \,|S_{i,t}, \tilde{D}_{i,t}$$

Given the complexity of the calculation involved, it is not surprising that many errors should occur. Only the most serious and egregious ones can be corrected through price changes. It is true the A_i, O_i, Y and, to a limited degree, I_i are subject to roughly annual variation through either microeconomic or macroeconomic (for Y) instruments, but central planners strongly prefer not to have their decisions on the use of such instruments forced by considerations of (6.1).

If $\mathbf{P}_i$ is thought of as the sum of costs, profits, and sales tax, then planned profits plus sales tax for product i must be determined in the light both of the projected supply and demand functions and of the projected values of their arguments other than price. Furthermore, if, for incentive reasons, central planners wish to avoid having planned profit rates vary sharply as between products i and j, with the variation being out of the control of the central planners, then they must set sales taxes that are highly differentiated by product unless a_i and/or $(1 - \delta_i)$ are extremely large.

Since consumer goods are not rationed, sales taxes are levied and, by repute, are indeed quite differentiated. I am not aware of data for the Soviet Union, but Hungary, prior to its economic reform in 1968, had in force some three thousand different rates (Granick 1976, 258). Presumably, the Soviet figure would be in the same ballpark.

On the other hand, sales taxes are in general not levied in the Soviet Union, either on intermediate goods or on capital items.[5] The reason is that, since it is intended that A_i rather than $\mathbf{P}_i$ be the binding constraint on the demand for such goods, the a_i that can be tolerated by central planners is extremely large.

In contrast to the situation in the Soviet Union, sales tax in China is in principle levied on all industrial products. Indeed, it is a tax that cascades when one product is used as an input into the production of another, although in some cases the cascading effect is eliminated. This difference in national taxation practice should be expected to have an effect on the relative shares of the purchases of intermediate products and of wages in the costs of production.

In addition, one would expect that industry must carry at least as large, and presumably a heavier, relative financial burden in China than in the Soviet Union, although the reverse is shown in table 6.1.[6] This is due to China having the larger share, in the two countries' total budgetary revenues, of the combination of sales tax and of profit remittances to government that are levied on industry. Yet China's industrial output is smaller as a proportion of national income when the total is defined to exclude profits as well as indirect tax in the two countries.[7] Thus the share of profit remittances plus sales tax in total value of industrial output (similarly defined to exclude profits and indirect tax) must be substantially higher in China than it is in the USSR.

Chinese and Soviet Data

Table 6.1 presents the basic ratios for the components of the value of output in the two countries. The Chinese figures refer to the average values during 1975–82 for the enterprises in the sample,[8] while the Soviet refer to industry as a whole in 1972. The data in this table represent the most detailed branch comparison possible, the degree of aggregation being dictated by that found in the Soviet national input-output table. For the Soviet Union, the ratios relate to the individual subbranch as a whole. For China, in those cases where more than one enterprise is contained within a single subbranch, each enterprise is given equal weight. For both countries, bonuses paid to workers and staff of enterprises are deducted from profits (in the cases where this has been their source) and are included in wages. Sales tax data for China reflect not only the legislated tax rates and the product mix produced, but also the exemptions and reductions granted to the individual sample enterprises in the relevant years.

In both countries, profit + sales tax is either siphoned off to higher bodies or, when part of the profits are left to the enterprise, used for purposes specifically approved by such bodies. Thus it is their sum, rather than the individual components, that are of prime importance. If prices were to mimic those of a competitive economy in equilibrium, one would expect their ratio to total invested capital to

Table 6.1 Chinese-Soviet Comparisons by Branch

| | Percentage of Value of Output | | | | | | | |
| | Profits | | Profits + Sales Tax | | Wages | | Amorti- zation | |
Branch of Industry	C	U	C	U	C	U	C	U
Ferrous & nonferrous metallurgy	21.3	16.8	27.6	16.8	3.3	8.8	2.8	6.0
Oil extraction	36.3	50.6	41.5	50.6	4.2	3.2	12.0	12.6
Cement	27.9	15.8	41.5	16.9	3.4	9.2	7.8	10.4
Fertilizer	5.5	16.5	8.6	16.7	6.5	10.7	8.8	8.8
Lumbering	19.8	10.6	27.8	10.7	23.8	32.4	9.0	6.4
Petrochemical	18.8	7.3	44.5	39.5	1.5	1.4	2.6	3.4
Machinery & equipment	19.7	18.6	24.1	25.0	8.1	18.1	3.5	4.1
Capital equipment only[a]	19.7	19.3	24.1	19.3	8.1	19.0	3.5	4.6
Watches[b]	14.6	25.1	43.6	32.9	9.2	22.5	4.6	3.2
Textiles	20.9	7.2	33.8	23.5	4.1	5.7	0.9	1.1
Food confections	2.5	8.4	6.8	23.2	3.0	3.3	0.6	0.5
All medium & large industrial enterprises[c]			25.7[d]		11.4[d,e]		9.4[d,e]	
All industry[c]		12.0		22.3		10.5		3.7

| | Materials & Fuels Purchased (as % of Value of Output) | | Wages (as % of Materials Purchased) | | Profits + Sales Tax (as % of Fixed Capital used in Production; original, undepreciated value) | |
	C	U	C	U	C	U
Ferrous & nonferrous metallurgy	66.7	67.6	6.3	13.1	41.1	21.0
Oil extraction	40.8	33.4	10.6	9.4	78.5	30.6
Cement	47.3	62.9	7.4	14.6	33.5	14.1
Fertilizer	66.8	62.9	9.9	17.0	7.6	14.1
Lumbering	26.8	49.0	90.2	66.2	2.0	19.6
Petrochemical	66.4	55.6	2.3	2.6	80.0	131.5
Machinery & equipment	55.8	50.8	14.77	37.2	41.3	49.6
Capital equipment only[a]	55.8	54.6	14.77	37.2	41.3	34.9
Watches[b]	37.0	39.6	17.1	56.9	83.0	86.5
Textiles	61.2	73.6	6.6	4.0	132.5	226.0
Food confections	86.4	72.9	3.6	4.5	67.1	345.0
All medium & large industrial enterprises[c]	53.5[d]		21.3[d,e]			
All industry[c]		62.5		16.9		
		60.4[f]		18.3[f]		
All state-owned industry[c]					28.7[g,h]	41.8[g,i]

Table 6.1 *(Continued)*

Notes: C = China; U = USSR.

Chinese data are constituted from the sample enterprises and are unweighted annual averages of 1975–82. The exception is the data for all medium and large industry, which refer to 1984 only. Soviet data refer entirely to 1972.

The term "profits" (except where otherwise specified), as used in this table, excludes that portion of total profits that is used for paying bonuses. The profit figure for both countries is net of losses by individual enterprises within the same branch, but there are no such losses in the Chinese sample data except for some plants within the single organization of the county administration.

Wages include bonuses paid from any source. However, they do not include social security payments made by the enterprise.

Amortization is a broader concept in Soviet than in Chinese usage, since it includes all allowances for major capital repair, although not for current repair. In Chinese usage, capital repair is financed from a different accounting item. (This makes one particularly sceptical with regard to the national figures of amortization as a proportion of value of output.)

"Materials purchased" data have a wider meaning in the case of the Soviet Union. There they refer to the sum of all materials used, paid c.i.f. For some products, an unknown portion of this represents double counting in that these materials are produced within the user enterprise. For the Chinese sample enterprises, they represent genuine purchases c.i.f. However, such data are derived by the investigator as (gross output − net output − amortization) and seem to contain the highest component of random error of all Chinese data presented in this chapter.

"Fixed capital" covers all fixed assets owned by the enterprise and used for production purposes. Housing, restaurants, clinics, etc. that belong to the enterprises are excluded.

The source from which the Soviet data are taken lists sixteen subbranches which can be matched with those eighteen Chinese enterprises that can be categorized into a single branch and for which there is information. The Chinese data for the ten branches presented in the table consist of unweighted averages of the enterprises within these branches. For consistency, the Soviet data are also averages of the relevant subbranches with these subbranches being weighted by the number of Chinese enterprises in each.

Soviet data are from Gallik, Kostinsky, and Treml (1983), table 1-A. They consist both of reconstructions of the 1972 input-output table of the USSR and of supplementary estimates for the same subbranches. The wage and amortization data are believed to be more reliable than are those for profit and sales tax. The Chinese figure for each enterprise consists of the unweighted average of that enterprise for all years that are available within the span of 1975–82. Output data are in purchasers' prices.

[a] "Capital equipment" partially excludes consumer durables from the Soviet subbranches by excluding the amount of sales taxes paid by these subbranches. There are no consumer durables produced by those Chinese enterprises included either in "machinery & equipment" or in "capital equipment"; thus the Chinese figures are identical in both rows.

[b] The Soviet data refer to the precision instruments industry. Since most of these goods are not sold to consumers, the ratio of sales tax to output in the Soviet Union is strongly understated.

[c] This includes mining, oil drilling and lifting, and electric power generation.

[d] *Statistical Yearbook of China 1986*, 279, 283–84. Data for 1984.

[e] This is an overstatement. Both amortization and wages are estimated as residuals that include other items such as auxiliary materials for amortization, and transport and social security payments for wages.

Table 6.1 *(Continued)*

[f] These are 1978 data from a Soviet source that must be relying on different underlying data (V. I. Pavlov and A. N. Spektor in *Ekonomika i organizatsiia promyshlennogo proizvodstva [EKO]*, 1981, no. 4:15–16). Wage data are stripped of the social security component given in the source by using the social security percentage for industry calculated from Gallik, Kostinsky, and Treml (1983), table 1-A. This set of data provides useful confirmation of the percentages from the primary source.

[g] These data do not make any deductions from profits for their use in paying bonuses. In the case of the Soviet Union, such a deduction would have been 8.3 per cent of total profits plus sales tax.

[h] All data are taken from *Statistical Yearbook of China*, various years. For years prior to 1980, only figures for all fixed assets taken together (rather than for production assets alone) are available as end-of-year data. This lacuna is treated by assuming that the annual change in the proportion of production assets to total fixed assets was the same during 1975–79 as was the case on average during 1980–85. The figure for 1975 requires further extrapolation because of the absence of beginning-of-year data for that year.

[i] These are national data for all state-owned, independent accounting, industrial enterprises, including those under the administration of nonindustrial departments (*Narkhoz SSSR v 1972 g.*, 60, 697–99).

be the same among all sectors within a given country. The last columns of table 6.1 present such data as to return on fixed capital used in production.[9]

The similarity between the two countries in the pattern of profit + sales tax, taken as a ratio of fixed capital, is considerable; in both nations, textiles, petrochemicals, and consumer durables cluster at the top of the range and fertilizer and logging are at or near the bottom. But other intermediate products (metallurgy and cement) yield a considerably higher return in China and, in general, interbranch differences are less in that country.[10] The Soviet category of "machinery and equipment" in table 6.1 includes the highly taxed consumer durables, but these are not produced by the Chinese sample enterprises in this category. Thus the Chinese-Soviet comparison for capital equipment should more appropriately contrast the Chinese ratio of profits + tax to fixed production capital for "machinery and equipment" of 41.3 per cent, with the Soviet ratio of 34.9 per cent for "capital equipment."

The principal reason for both the similarities and differences lies in the way that sales tax is levied. The Chinese government copies the Soviet pattern in setting the highest rates on oil products, consumer durables, and textiles. But not only does it differ sharply with regard to the rate charged on food manufactures,[11] but it differs most significantly in that it charges more equal rates than does the Soviet Union between major sectors of the economy.

Table 6.2 compares the branch data for the Soviet Union that

Table 6.2 Comparison of Three Different Sources of Soviet Proportions of Profits + Sales Tax to Output (in percentages)

Branch of Industry	1972 Input-Output	(Profits + Sales Tax)/Output	
		1972 Offical Data	1980 Official Data
Construction materials (cement)	16.9	11.4	6.6
Lumber, woodworking & paper (lumbering)	10.7	12.1	7.1
Capital equipment	19.3	13.0–16.8	12.8–16.7
Light industry (textiles)	23.5	30.7	32.9
Food industry (food confections)	23.2	36.5	49.8
All industry	22.3	24.2	25.2

Note: The subbranches included in parentheses in four of the rows represent those treated in the first column. The second and third columns refer to the branch as a whole. The branch of light industry consists essentially of the textile, clothing, and footwear subbranches.

1972 Input-Output: Described in table 6.1. In contrast to the other two columns, data used are for detailed subbranches. Where these subbranches are combined, the combination represents an average weighted by the number of Chinese enterprises in each. "Capital equipment" in this column differs from that in the other two not only because of the different weighting of subbranches, but also because of the limited number of subbranches included in this column's representation of the industry.

1972 Official Data: Data relating to output and profit by branch are taken from *Narkhoz SSSR v 1972 godu*, 166, 699. Total output in all industry in current prices is from ibid., 161. Total sales tax is taken from ibid., 699, and is distributed by branch according to the proportions given in Gallik, Kostinsky, and Treml (1983), table 1-A. However, this distribution by branch adds together all taxes paid by each subbranch, rather than weighting each subbranch by the number of Chinese enterprises contained in it. It is necessary, for purposes of comparability with column 1, to deduct profits used for bonuses from the total of profits plus tax. This calculation assumes that the proportion of total profit + tax used for bonuses was the same in each branch as in industry as a whole (8.3 per cent in 1972). Due to the bias implicit in this calculation, the differences between branches that are reported in columns 2 and 3 of the table are less than the true differences. This reinforces the conclusion that I draw from this table.

The lower figure for "capital equipment" is obtained by using the assumptions that all sales tax levied on the production of the machinery and equipment industry is restricted to consumer durables, and that the rate of profit is identical on capital equipment and on consumer durables. The higher figure applies to the machinery and equipment industry as a whole, and should be taken as a limiting upper estimate. The true figure is probably close to the lower percentage cited.

It should be noted that alcoholic beverages are included under food in this column, and that the sales tax is substantially higher on such beverages than it is on solid food.

1980 Official Data: The methodology is identical to that described above for the year 1972. Data relating to output and profit by branch, to total industrial output, and to total sales tax, are taken from *Narkhoz SSSR 1922–82*, 156, 552, 151, and 549, respectively. The proportion of total tax + profit used for bonus was 7.4 per cent.

were used in table 6.1 with an alternative breakdown for the same year as well as for a later year. This comparison is intended to give an indication of the degree of robustness of the ratios with respect to different data sources and different years. There is considerable robustness for industry as a whole, but unfortunately this is not so for individual branches. However, what is most significant is that the figures in the second and third columns of table 6.2 all vary from those of the first column for the same industrial branch in such a way as to strengthen the key conclusion drawn earlier on the basis of table 6.1; namely, that interbranch differences are less in China than in the Soviet Union.

Table 6.3 takes up the theme of sectoral comparisons in more detail and for China alone. Profits, sales tax, and cash flow as a proportion of output value are contrasted for capital goods, intermediate products, and consumer items. Cash flow (defined as sales tax, amortization allowances, and profits other than those used to pay worker bonuses) constitutes the broadest category of funds passing under the control of authorities above the enterprise level.[12] Amortization is appropriately included because other funds are available in China for current maintenance and for capital repair (Naughton 1986, 142–43).

The reader may wonder why these components of price are not compared with the total value of capital so as to yield a return on capital. The reason is that, for the sample enterprises, the data as to fixed capital, being measured in terms of original cost, bear only the vaguest relation to replacement costs. The capital equipment enterprises appear to have a higher capital/output ratio than does either the integrated steel firm or the smelter of nonferrous metals. More error than insight would be introduced by developing such ratios. However, the reader who wishes to do so can use the data in table 6.1 to make such a calculation.

The top portion of table 6.3 compares the unweighted mean values for each of these categories, while the lower part provides a test of significance as to the difference between each of these means and the grand mean for the sample as a whole. Capital equipment shows a statistically significantly below-normal set of ratios of profit plus tax and of cash flow, in contrast to intermediate products which show an above-normal cash flow. Consumer goods as a whole are not significantly different from the grand mean. It is true that, if we attempted to map these figures into a transformation measuring return on capital valued at its opportunity cost, one would presume that consumer goods would show a significantly higher ratio than would either capital equipment or intermediate nonoil products. Nevertheless, it is striking that the differences in rates of return between categories of

Table 6.3 Comparisons Between Chinese Industrial Branches
(sample data: 1975–82 mean)

Branches of Industry	Percentage of Value of Output			
	Profits	Sales Tax	Profits + Sales Tax	Cash Flow
Capital equipment	19.2	4.4	23.5	27.0
Intermediate products	21.6	7.6	29.1	35.6
Oil & oil products	27.5	7.9	35.3	42.6
All other	19.2	7.5	26.6	32.8
Consumer goods	17.4	14.0	31.4	31.4
Textiles	20.9	12.9	33.8	33.1
Consumer durables	14.6	29.0	43.6	48.2
Food products, confections	2.5	4.3	6.8	7.4

Note: As in the previous tables, profits exclude that portion used for payment of bonuses.

The number of enterprises for the first three columns were as follows: 5 (row 1); 7 (row 2) with 2 and 5, respectively, for the subcategories; and 7 (row 5), with 5, 1, and 1, respectively, for the subcategories. For columns 1–3, n [= years × enterprises] = 140.

The number of enterprises for the fourth column were: 5 (row 1); 7 (row 2), with 2 and 5, respectively for the subcategories; 6 (row 5), with 4, 1, and 1, respectively, for the subcategories. For column 4, $n = 131$.

	Significance levels of the above percentages from the grand means of the sample (z values)		
	Profits	Profits + Sales Tax	Cash Flow
Capital equipment	0.02	** −3.37	** −3.12
Intermediate products	1.78	0.24	*2.12
Nonoil products	0.02	−1.37	0.42
Consumer goods	−1.29	1.69	0.49
Textiles	1.32	**3.30	0.60

*Significant at the 5 per cent level.
**Significant at the 1 per cent level.

goods are not so great as to translate into statistically significant differences in the profit margins earned on output value.[13]

Experiments were also made to see whether modifications of sample selection would change the results. The first alternative was to take account of missing data for individual years by restricting the total sample of years for any single enterprise to those that are comparable between 1975–78 and 1979–82;[14] "comparable" was defined in terms of the number of years from the beginning of the subperiod.

Since profit rates were higher on average during the second set of years than during the first,[15] this was intended to avoid artificially pushing up the ratios for those enterprises for which data was missing. The second alternative was that of using only the subsample for the years 1979–82. This procedure was similarly intended as a response to the fact that the profit/output ratio increased over the period, as well as to the possibility that this increase might have been distinctive between sectors.

The effects of these experiments were to change the ratios of profit + tax and of cash flow for capital goods from being statistically significant at the 1 per cent level (as reported in table 6.3) to being nonsignificant at the 5 per cent level in both of the alternative measurements, and to change the ratio of profit + tax for textiles in a similar fashion. This further strengthens the case made earlier as to the weakness of Chinese intersectoral differences in the rate of return on capital.

One is always on thin ice in treating individual enterprises as representative of their subbranches. Yet this is what we have been doing. It seems desirable to make any check possible with regard to such representativeness.

For six of the enterprises, comparison can be made with profitability data published for 1979 that cover all state-owned enterprises at the county level and above. The published branch data refer to total profits (without excluding the portion used for bonuses) and take these as a ratio of the end-of-year value of total amortized capital.[16] Sample data for 1979 have been converted to the same definition. The resulting profit ratios for 1979 are as shown in table 6.4.

In watch production, the reason that the sample enterprise's output was much less profitable in 1979 than was output of the industry as a whole is presumably because the national industry was concentrated in Shanghai, where efficiency and economies of scale were

Table 6.4 Profit as Proportion of Total Amortized End-of-Year Capital Stock, 1979 (in percentages)

Subbranch	Published Branch Data	Sample Data
Watches	61.1	12.5
Petroleum (refining)	37.7	70.6[a]
Oil fields	34.1	59.6
Lumbering	4.8	12.6
Cement	4.4	23.7
Chemical fertilizer	1.4	10.9

[a]Data from 1981. This is the first year in which this organization, an amalgamation of others, existed.

considerably higher than in outlying provinces such as where our sample enterprise was located. The sample watch enterprise's rate of profitability doubled between 1979 and 1980 as its scale of production increased. The different ratios for cement may be accounted for by the fact that the sample enterprise in this sector obtained considerable economies of scale compared to the large number of very small, county-level, state plants. Other differences are not explicable in such a ready fashion.

But the fault may be with the subbranch data as well as with the sample. The source used above for subbranch profitability gives the average rate for all state-owned industry as having been 12.3 per cent in 1979, in contrast to the State Statistical Bureau's figure of 16.1 per cent.[17] Furthermore, as indicated above, data as to fixed capital seem to me to be too unreliable to permit figures concerning this measure of profitability to yield much information.

The result that the differences in profit and cash flow markups on cost are not substantial between industrial sectors is somewhat different from what seems to be the conventional wisdom among Western specialists on China. Nicholas Lardy, for example, depicts the Chinese price structure as one in which raw materials and intermediate goods have been assigned low prices so that the profits of state-owned enterprises will be concentrated in the final stages of the production process.[18] Jonathan Unger describes most of heavy industry as earning low profits relative to the consumer goods industry.[19] The sample data do not exactly contradict these statements, but they suggest that, while the statements may be true, the degree of sectoral difference is not very important.

This outcome from the sample may seem surprising in view of the virtual unanimity among Chinese writers as to the irrationality of prices and as to their failure to represent true costs. A description offered by a team from the Chinese Academy of Social Sciences provides what well may be the solution to the puzzle. The authors state that, during the 1981–85 period, prices of raw materials and energy remained too low, while prices of processed products (which presumably included intermediate products) were too high. In general, they assert, it is farm and mine products that are too cheap.[20] A second source singles out timber and mineral products as being particulary low priced.[21] A third source provides data for 1978 that shows the petroleum industry to be highly profitable (similarly to our sample); it points to agricultural equipment and particularly to coal mining as being least profitable.[22] Aside from timber and oil, all of the products of the enterprises in our sample are of processed goods other than farm machinery; thus the sample excludes most of the items described in the Chinese sources as having low prices.

Materials Purchases and Wages

The Impact of Sales Tax

The previous section has shown that the ratio of profits plus sales tax to output is much more similar between consumer goods and other products of industry in China than is the case in the Soviet Union. Here I shall model this result, adding a characterization of the process by which the costs of financing of the government, plus net investment, plus stockholder income are distributed in the American economy. (Together, these items are analogous to what is financed by industrial profits plus sales tax in China.) Our interest is in the effects of these differences on the expenditures for materials and fuels purchased by enterprises taken as a percentage of wage costs. Thus I shall assume identical technology, degree of vertical integration, and labor productivity (in real terms) across countries.

The simplest form of the model contains a single type of labor (l), which produces an intermediate good (x), an end-use product desired by the government (g), and a consumer good (c). There are no capital goods, no savings, and no income receipts by the public except in exchange for labor services. Let:

x = homogeneous intermediate good required to produce x, g, and c;
g = homogeneous good desired by the government;
c = homogeneous good desired by consumers;
l = homogeneous labor, required to produce x, g, and c;
w = wage;
p = price excluding any tax on the product;
$\tilde{p}$ = price including tax.

The economy is characterized by Leontief production isoquants. The input-output matrix can be described as follows:

$$x = a_{xx}x + a_{xg}g + a_{xc}c$$
$$l = a_{lx}x + a_{lg}g + a_{lc}c$$

The constraint on prices of consumer goods that is common to all three models is expressed by

$$w \cdot l - \text{direct tax} = \tilde{p}_c c$$

The values of x, g, c, l, and a_{ij} are identical in all three models. Throughout, w is taken as the *numéraire*, and the government must raise through taxes a total revenue of $p_g g$ ($\tilde{p}_g g$ when g is taxed), called Z hereafter.

In the China 1 model, the government raises the money needed to purchase g by levying a sales tax which bears the same ratio to gross value of output for all products (x, g, c). In the Soviet Union model, the government raises the required funds by levying a similar sales tax exclusively on c. In the United States model, there are no indirect taxes and the government raises its required funds through direct taxes on individuals.

In the Soviet Union model, the rate of sales tax $a = Z/p_c c$. In the United States model, the rate of income tax $\beta = Z/w \cdot l$. In the China 1 model, the rate of sales tax

$$\phi = Z/(p_x x + p_g g + p_c c) = (1 + \phi)\, p_g g/(p_x x + p_g g + p_c c).$$

If taxation is ignored, we can solve from the input-output matrix for zero-profit prices. Let p_x = the price of x when x is not subject to tax, and $\tilde{p}_x$ = the price including tax. The zero excess-profits condition is that

$$p_x x = a_{xx} x \cdot p_x + a_{lx} x \cdot w;$$
$$\text{thus } p_x = a_{lx} \cdot w(1 - a_{xx})^{-1}.$$

Because intermediate products (x) are not taxed in either the model of the Soviet Union or that of the United States, this equation also holds for their $\tilde{p}_x$ values once taxation is introduced. For the China 1 model, however,

$$\tilde{p}_x - a_{xx} \cdot \tilde{p}_x + a_{lx} \cdot w + \phi \cdot p_x = p_x + \phi \cdot p_x (1 - a_{xx})^{-1}.$$

Because $0 < \phi < 1$, and $(1 - a_{xx}) > 0$, $\tilde{p}_x$ in the China model $> p_x$. Since all of these three models treat w as the *numéraire*, we can conclude the following:

(6.2) Consider, in the three models, the impact of the different methods of raising government revenue on the price of intermediate goods relative to wage. This impact is identical for the Soviet Union model, with its indirect taxes on consumers, and for the United States model with direct taxes on consumers. In other words, $\tilde{p}_x/w$ is the same. In contrast, the price ratio is higher in the case of the China 1 model.

The intuition behind this difference is that the Chinese tax, in distinction to that of the United States or of the Soviet Union, is levied on intermediate as well as on other goods. Although it is true that this tax on intermediate goods cascades into the price of consumer goods and thus into wages, the tax measured in real terms that is directly levied on consumer goods has been reduced compared to the Soviet model; the tax on intermediate products makes up the difference. Using as the *numéraire* the wage rate, which is determined by the price of consumer goods, the price of intermediate goods rises. It should be noted that the spreading of the sales tax to g is irrelevant.

The China 2 model is intended for direct comparison only with the China 1 model. Its purpose is to take account of the fact that agricultural goods produced by peasants outside of the state sector are subsidized rather than subject to a positive sales tax. The China 2 model keeps the same values for x and g as in the earlier model. It also maintains the same homogeneous l, but subdivides it into labor employed in industry and in agriculture. Wages may, but need not, be the same in both sectors. The consumer good of the China 1 model is here interpreted as having been composed of two distinct items, an industrial and an agricultural consumer good which are produced in fixed proportions, with p_c constituting an index number corresponding to these proportions. In both models, the intermediate good is used in the production of x, g, and the industrial consumer good, but not of the agricultural consumer good. The only labor going into the production of the intermediate good is labor employed in industry. The China 2 model treats the industrial and agricultural consumer goods and labor of the China 1 model separately, but their quantities remain the same. Where the China 2 model uses the identical symbol as did the China 1 model (e.g., $\bar{p}_x$), subscript 2 is appended.

Thus, with respect to quantities, the China 2 model is only a more elaborated form of the China 1 model. Where they differ is with regard to the sales tax, which is not levied on agricultural consumer goods; these goods are neither taxed nor subsidized. Let:

c_i = homogeneous consumer good produced in the industrial sector;

c_a = homogeneous consumer good produced in the agricultural sector;

l_i = homogeneous labor required to produce x, g, c_i;

l_a = homogeneous labor required to produce c_a;

w_i = wage of l_i;

w_a = wage of l_a;

$c_a = f(l_a)$

$\phi_2 = Z/(p_x x + p_g g + p_{c_i} c_i)$

and the constraint on the prices of consumer goods becomes

$$w_i l_i + w_a l_a = \tilde{p}_{c_i} c_i + p_{c_a} c_a.$$

In this China 2 model, p_x has a comparable formula to what it did above in the China 1 model. Here,

$$\tilde{p}_{x_2} = [1 + p_{g_2} g_2 (p_{x_2} x_2 + p_{g_2} g_2 + p_{c_i} c_i)^{-1}] \cdot [a_{l_i x_2} \cdot w_i (1 - a_{x_2 x_2})^{-1}].$$

A comparison of $\tilde{p}_{x_2}/w_i$ in the China 2 model with $\tilde{p}_x/w$ in the China 1 model depends solely on a comparison of

$$\tilde{p}_{g_2} g_2 / (\tilde{p}_{x_2} x_2 + \tilde{p}_{g_2} g_2 + \tilde{p}_{c_i} c_i)$$

with

$$\tilde{p}_g g / (\tilde{p}_x x + \tilde{p}_g g + \tilde{p}_c c).$$

By construction, $g_2 = g$, $x_2 = x$, but $c_i < c$. The remaining issue consists of the magnitudes of the relative prices, all expressed in terms of their respective *numéraires*.

Following what was done earlier in the case of p_x, zero excess-profit conditions are used to express the six prices: $\tilde{p}g_2/w_i$, $\tilde{p}_g/w$, $\tilde{p}_{x_2}/w_i$, $\tilde{p}_x/w$, $\tilde{p}_{c_i}/w_i$, and $\tilde{p}_c/w$. Resulting equations are solved simultaneously for these prices in the China 1 and China 2 models, respectively. After some tedious algebra, we find that the $\tilde{p}_{x_2}/w_i$ of the China 2 model is almost certain to be larger than the $\tilde{p}_x/w$ of the China 1 model.[23]

This conclusion would also hold, although the increase would be less, if intermediate goods entered as inputs into agricultural consumer goods (c_a). What is required for the result is that l_a should produce only c_a, rather than also producing raw materials that enter as inputs into x.

The intuition behind this result is that now part of consumer expenditures by the industrial labor force are shielded from tax, while none of the expenditures on intermediate products are so shielded. Thus the money wage rate for industrial labor can be lower relative to the price of intermediate products and yet have the same purchasing power over consumer goods as a whole.

(6.3) The China 2 model, in which agricultural goods are not subject to sales tax, almost certainly increases the ratio found in the China 1 model of intermediate products relative to industrial wages. It thus yields a result which deviates even further from that of both the Soviet Union model and the United States model.

Up to this point, we have assumed that the real economies are unchanged in all of the models. Let us now introduce the assumption that the proportion of g (products purchased by the government) to total output may change at the expense of c, and inquire as to the effect of such a change on the ratio of prices of intermediate products and labor. It turns out that, although this would be significant for an evaluation of factors involved in the evolution over time of Chinese prices, it is largely irrelevant to a single-period, cross-country analysis. It is thus mainly a red herring, but one that is worth analyzing briefly.

Examining the formula given above for $\tilde{p}_x$ in the models for the Soviet Union and the United States, we see that g does not enter into the formula and that there is no effect. On the other hand, the ratio of g to $(x + g + c)$ enters into the formula for $\tilde{p}_x$ in the China models, raising this price as g increases. (Note that total output—$x + g + c$—is stable by assumption.)

The intuition behind this result is the following. In the Soviet Union model, a rise in g leads to an increase in sales tax levied on c. Thus the prices of consumer goods rise and the real wage falls, but there is no change either in the nominal wage or in $\tilde{p}_x$. Similarly, in the United States model, an increase in g results in an increase in direct taxes on wage earners. Post-tax wage falls, but pretax wage and $\tilde{p}_x$ are unaffected.

In contrast, an increase in g in both China models leads to an increase in sales tax on x as well as on g and c (c_i in the China 2 model). Money wage is unaffected, but $\tilde{p}_x$ rises together with $\tilde{p}_g$ and $\tilde{p}_c$ (P_{c_i}).

(6.4) A change in the proportion of goods purchased by the government relative to total production has no effect on the ratio of prices of intermediate products to nominal wages in either the Soviet Union or the United States models. However, it has a positive effect in the Chinese models.

The implication of (6.4) with regard to the ratio that is of interest to us—namely, to $[\tilde{p}_x/w]_{\text{China}}/[\tilde{p}_x/w]_{\text{US or USSR}}$—is the following:

1. The ratio is an increasing positive function of $[g/(g + c)]_{\text{China}}$.
2. The ratio is not a function of $[g/(g + c)]_{\text{US or USSR}}$.
3. The ratio is not a function of the ratio $[g/(g + c)]_{\text{China}}/[g/(g + c)]_{\text{US or USSR}}$.

Due to the last implication, I shall not pursue the issue of the $[g/(g + c)]$ ratio as a contributing factor to international differences in the $\bar{p}_x/w$ ratio.

Chinese, Soviet, and American Data

Table 6.1 above, and tables 6.5 and 6.6 below, present the empirical data as to the reciprocal of the expenditures on intermediate goods relative to labor. Table 6.5 provides the Chinese-American comparison in the greatest detail possible, selecting from the U.S. Census of Manufactures those American subbranches in which the output most closely resembles the products of the firms of the Chinese sample. Table 6.6 presents the processed figures for three-way comparisons of the countries.

There is one source of bias that cannot be removed from the statistical comparisons. Recognition of its existence, however, only reinforces the conclusions to be drawn. Since the American data are based on establishment data, transfers of intermediate products from one plant to another within the same company are treated here as purchases of materials. In the Chinese sample data, such transfers would be excluded since the information is based on the enterprise as a unit. The Soviet data go still further; some unknown portion of the registered purchases of materials represent transfers within the same establishment. Thus, compared to the Chinese data, the American ratios of $wl/p_x x$ shown in the tables are biased downward and the Soviet are biased downward even more strongly. Both biases are due to an overstatement of the volume of intermediate goods, judging by the criterion of the Chinese definition.

In table 6.5, with eighteen Chinese-American comparisons, the Chinese ratio of wages to purchases is lower in seventeen cases regardless of whether one uses the 1939 or 1977 U.S. census data. If we could eliminate the data bias, the disparities would be even larger. Although the differences between the 1939 and 1977 proportions shown in the U.S. Census of Manufactures are often so great as to fill us with trepidations about the reliability of such comparisons, the evidence of this table is overwhelming.

When it comes to finding explanations for these intercountry differences, one might think of three main potential reasons (the respective levels of economic development is not one of them[24]). The three possible reasons are:

1. The effect of distinctions in the system of taxation.
2. The degree of vertical integration present within the individual enterprise or establishment.

Table 6.5 Chinese-American Comparisons by Subbranch of Industry

	Wages as % of Materials and Fuels Purchased		
	China	U.S.	
Subbranch of Industry	1975–82	1939	1977
Integrated steel	11.3	42.9	37.8
Primary nonferrous metal (excluding aluminum)	1.3	a	8.4
Crude oil	10.6	92.4	58.1
Cement	7.4	62.1	36.1
Fertilizer	9.9	18.2	14.4
Lumbering	90.2	19.6	26.4
Petrochemicals	2.3[b]		15.9
Petroleum refining	2.3[b]	9.8	2.6
Electrical machinery	8.0	71.5	57.3
Pumps	28.2	79.8	52.3
Auto industry	12.0	61.7[c]	12.2
Locomotives, frames and parts	17.2	107.8	37.2
Machine tools, metal-forming	8.4		81.2
Watch and clock	17.1		62.6[d]
Cotton textiles (narrow)	5.0	73.3	>39.1
Weaving, woolen	6.7	28.0	48.1
Linen	9.8	55.0	40.7
Candy manufacture[e]	3.6	37.0	23.6

Chinese Data: These are from the sample, with eighteen of the twenty organizations being covered. Only in one subbranch are data for two enterprises combined. See table 6.1 for a description of the data.

United States Data: These are from the U.S. Census of Manufactures. Contract work is included as part of materials and fuels purchased, being comparable in this respect to the treatment of the Chinese data. Statistics are given by establishment, rather than by enterprise; thus transfers from one factory to another within the same company are considered as purchases, unlike the treatment in the Chinese statistics. Wages are only for personnel engaged in manufacturing activities and thus have a narrower employee coverage than do the Chinese data.

[a] Primary nonferrous smelting (excluding aluminum) was 58.1. I have no explanation for the enormous difference between the 1939 and 1977 figures.
[b] The operations of a single Chinese enterprise covered both of these industries.
[c] Automobiles and equipment.
[d] Data from 1963. Thus the American industry, like the Chinese enterprise, produced mechanical rather than electronic products in the year analyzed.
[e] This is a weak match between countries.

    3. The relative efficiency of industry in the two countries in utilizing direct labor, as opposed to utilizing materials and fuel, in the production process.[25]

As was argued in the previous subsection, explanation (1) pushes the Chinese-American ratios in the observed direction.[26]

One might expect that, if anything, the second (vertical integration) explanation would do the reverse. For, quite apart from the definitions employed, one would suppose that the American economy would be more rather than less characterized by interfirm market relations. As to the third (relative efficiency) explanation, one would expect that it also would work against the observed data. This is because there is virtually a total absence of a labor market in the state sector in China, and employment there is often expanded simply in order to create jobs. As there is much more of a market for intermediate products, one would presume that Chinese enterprises should show greater efficiency in the use of materials and fuel than in the use of labor.

Thus it would appear that the Chinese-American comparison of expenditure ratios must be completely dominated by the systems of taxation in use in the two countries.[27]

The Chinese-Soviet comparison in table 6.6 is much less sharp than is the Chinese-American comparison. Nevertheless, it is consistent with the view that differences in systems of taxation are of prime importance.

Table 6.6 Chinese–American–Soviet Comparisons by Branch of Industry

Branch of Industry	Wages as % of Materials and Fuels Purchased (as a ratio between 2 countries)	
	China/ U.S.	China/ Soviet Union
Ferrous and nonferrous metallurgy	23	48
Oil extraction	18	113
Cement	20	51
Fertilizer	69	58
Lumbering	460	136
Petrochemicals & petroleum refining	88	88
Capital equipment	40	45
Watches	28	30
Textiles	18	165
Food confections	15[a]	80

Note: China–U.S. comparisons are based upon table 6.5. In each case, the highest Chinese/U.S. ratio is selected. Grouping of subbranches from table 6.5 is done by taking an average of these highest ratios, using a weighting according to the number of sample Chinese enterprises in the subbranch. China–Soviet Union comparisons are taken from table 6.1.
[a] This is a weak match between countries.

Conclusions

Relative Efficiency in Materials Usage

The following proposition seems to be the least reliable of the conclusions to be presented. The evidence supporting it is solely that which arises from the Chinese-Soviet comparison cited immediately above. In fact, the difficulties involved in the Chinese-Soviet comparison make me so hesitant to try to squeeze out further information that I would rather label this as a suggestion rather than a conclusion.

The suggestion drawn from the comparative data is that the Soviet Union is relatively inefficient in the use of raw materials and fuel, while China is relatively inefficient in the use of labor. This suggestion, if correct, would explain why the Soviet and Chinese ratios are so much closer together than are the American and Chinese ratios.

This proposed explanation of the data is completely consistent with the relative role of markets in the two countries. The labor market is a genuine one in the industrial sector in the Soviet Union (Granick 1987, ch. 2), in sharp contrast to the situation in China. One would expect that this should permit Soviet enterprises to be more effective in obtaining the types of labor that they require. On the other hand, as seen in chapter 4, the market for intermediate products is much more lively and responsive to demand factors in China. This should have the effect of permitting Chinese enterprises to do better in purchasing the materials inputs that can be most efficiently used, rather than whatever substitutes happen to be available.

Factor-Substitution Possibilities

The low level of wages in China, relative to the price of materials and fuels, is perfectly consistent with respective factor availability. To the degree that state industrial enterprises are in a position to substitute labor for materials and fuels, this effect of the distribution of taxes would seem to promote efficiency.

Now it is true that the Chinese state-owned industrial enterprise has relatively little autonomy to engage in such a tradeoff. Nevertheless, considerable autonomy is enjoyed both by provincial governments and, of greatest importance, authorities at a lower regional level. As we shall discuss briefly in chapter 8, their willingness to pursue employment objectives is greatly furthered by the fact that the financial cost of doing so is only minor.

Output Maximization

In contrast to the favorable effect on factor proportions, decisions that are more readily institutionally feasible are negatively affected by the tax system. Cash flow (excluding bonuses paid from profits), which is the financial aggregate of greatest significance to the Chinese principals of the enterprises, appears extraordinarily high as a proportion of gross output. To the degree that the national and regional principals and their agents are motivated by financial concerns, their behavior with regard to current operations is likely to be indistinguishable from output maximization. In the tradeoff between output expansion and the minimization of current average costs, reliance on purely financial criteria may be expected to result in very little attention to costs.

Table 6.1 is the basis for comparing the Chinese sample with the Soviet branch statistics. The ratio of cash flow (profits + sales tax + amortization) to output was higher in China in seven of the ten branches.[28] Such a difference results from the following: (1) the practice followed in both countries of relying upon industrial profits and sales tax on industrial products to provide the bulk of government revenue, (2) the fact that the Chinese government pushes this principle further than does the Soviet government, and (3) the relative importance of industry in the gross national product of the two countries.

In two of the branches shown in table 6.1, the Chinese sample enterprises earned an average cash flow margin of only 7 to 17 per cent. But in all of the other eight, returns averaged 28 per cent or higher over the eight years. With earnings of this magnitude, there was little financial reason for any principal to wish its enterprises to be overly concerned with costs. Output expansion has been the name of the game.

From this, we would expect that demand for intermediate products would be quite inelastic with respect to price. If this is so, such inelastic demand should impart a strong inflationary bias to the market prices for intermediate products. This places a considerably greater strain on the Chinese system of multi-prices (in terms of its susceptibility on the margin to inflation) than would be the case if there were a lower ratio of cash flow to sales in Chinese industry.

Limited data have come to my attention on changes in such market (and thus marginal) prices for intermediate products. At fairs held in Shanghai in which intermediate products and capital goods are sold, with comparable data available for five product groups, the "high" price by mid-1985 was 106 per cent of the peak price during 1979–81 for 1 to 1.5 mm steel sheet, 134 per cent for cement, and 152–63 per cent of the previous high for 6.5 mm steel wire rod and for zinc and aluminum ingot. In 1985, four of these five products were selling for 187–205 per cent of the price charged to users in 1981 for those purchases made through the materials supply system, while wire rod was selling at 273 per cent.[29] The most comparable general price index published is that of retail prices of industrial products in rural areas; this rose only by a total of 11 per cent between 1979 and 1985.

The speed with which the marginal price of three of the five intermediate products moved upward between 1981 and 1985, combined with the high ratio of the marginal price of all five products to the lowest 1981 allocation price, seems consistent with the argument that demand is price inelastic.

Tax Structure and Monetization of the Economy

Unlike the situation in the Soviet Union, differences among major industrial sectors in the profit and sales tax markups on cost do not appear from our sample to be substantial in China. It seems fair to extend this result to the statement that profit and sales tax as a proportion of capital investment are similarly much more homogeneous between major sectors in China than in the Soviet Union. Assuming the validity of the latter statement, there is an interesting conclusion that can be drawn.

Since 1978, in regions where profit + tax rates differ substantially between individual products, regional principals have attempted to expand output of the high profit + tax products. Monetization of the economy thus caused regional protectionism in such products. The development of such protectionism against "imports" led to many complaints by Chinese commentators, but it was economically bearable because it was limited to individual products.

One might guess that the situation would have been insupportable if there had been similar large-scale favoring of industrial consumer goods as a whole. In this case, monetization of the Chinese economy might well have led to a situation in which regional governments attempted to concentrate all of their new investments into the production of industrial consumer goods and neglected both intermediate products and capital goods as far as was possible. If this had been the case, monetization of the economy would probably have foundered under its own weight; it could have proceeded only after tax reform.

In this regard, and given the existence of multiple principals, the Chinese form of sales tax has been much more hospitable to permitting monetization of the economy than would have been a sales tax of the Soviet type in pre-reform China.

Chinese Enterprise Behavior and Kornai's "Soft Budget Constraint"

We saw in chapter 4 that when financial and production considerations were perceived as being in conflict, two-thirds of those enterprises in our sample that were under the financial and physical planning control of the provinces, municipalities, or counties, gave precedence to financial considerations in at least one observed instance during the post-1978 years. In particular, such enterprises were reluctant to accept bank loans under conditions in which the financial perspectives were unattractive. Such behavior appears to be quite different from that which has been observed among state enterprises in the Soviet Union and Eastern Europe, and which has led Kornai to his "soft financial budget" formulation for these economies.

How, then, account for the clearly observed appeal of Kornai's formulation to Chinese academic economists? Why have they tended to view it as the appropriate one for describing their own economy? Let us put to one side the cynical thought that academic economists, both in China and elsewhere, may be unreliable guides as to the qualitative nature of what is currently occurring in their own countries. What remains as an explanation?

One major element is the shielding of unprofitable state enterprises from bankruptcy (although not from takeover) in China, just as in other centrally planned economies. A second is the "iron rice bowl": the virtually absolute protection of the jobs of employees in state enterprises, whatever may be the financial condition of their organization. A third is that, when one examines the behavior of state enterprises in current (as opposed to investment) activities, a characterization of these enterprises as output maximizers subject to no financial constraints is a hypothesis that appears to fit the observed facts fairly well, although not completely.

The nature of Chinese pricing of industrial products, with its high ratio of profit plus sales tax as a proportion of price, provides an alternative and completely distinct explanation to that of the soft financial budget constraint for the third element. The distribution across industrial branches of this profit + sales tax leads to wages being an insignificant portion of Chinese enterprise costs. This does not explain the existence of the second element above, but it is a factor that may be of considerable significance in the ability of the "iron rice bowl" to continue despite the existence of hard budget constraints pressing on local-level principals of state enterprises. It is only the first element (protection from bankruptcy) that is totally outside the explanatory schema presented in this chapter.

7

INTERNAL ORGANIZATION OF
THE ENTERPRISE

This brief chapter treats three topics in the internal organization of the enterprise. They were chosen because of the light cast upon them in the interviews. Of these three, it is the first that is by far the most interesting. As will be seen, the relation within the enterprise between the Communist Party organization and the managerial hierarchy have departed from the pattern established in the Soviet Union, and the differences have not been solely along the lines commonly noted. Significantly, my theme of regional property rights can fruitfully explain much of the variation here, just as I have found it to do in other areas of my analysis of state enterprises.

The other two topics are less engaging. One of these is democratic management within the enterprise; experience here has not been fundamentally different from that observed in Eastern Europe. The second is the treatment of first-line shop floor supervision. Although this is radically distinct from what I have heard of anywhere else in the world, I have no explanation to offer and can only note the surprising phenomenon.

Party Committee versus Director Control Within the Enterprise

The Soviet Experience

In the Soviet Union, control over industrial enterprises is conducted through two quite distinct channels of line authority.[1] The first is the normal state channel, running from the Council of Ministers of the USSR, through the ministry in charge of a given sector of the economy, down to the enterprise. This is the formal channel for the setting of plans, input allocations and constraints, bonus funds for the enterprise, and appointments and dismissals of top personnel. Except for a decade during the 1950s and 1960s, this channel has always been vertical. The essential chain of command is national and functions by sector rather than locality.

The second channel is that of the Communist Party. Its principle of organization has always had a different basis; namely, that of the region. Starting at the center with the Politburo and Secretariat of the Central Committee, it evolves through the republics (comparable to the Chinese provinces), the regions, and the cities. Although each of these levels has organizational subdivisions along sectoral lines, the chain of command within the Party is by regional level. The system has been compared by Jerry Hough (1969) to that of the French prefectures, where a single person (and his staff) traditionally exercised responsibility for integrating all state activities within a given geographic region.

At the level of the state enterprise, the director is responsible to and appointed by the next level in the state channel. Within enterprises of any magnitude, the position of secretary of the Party in the enterprise is a full-time post just like that of director. The Party position, however, is normally under the supervision of the local city Party committee, or even of the Party committee of a district within the city, and its occupant owes his appointment to that committee. Thus, if only for jurisdictional reasons, relations between the enterprise director and the enterprise Party secretary are always delicate. The same applies within major subunits of the enterprise, such as factories.

In 1929, quite early in Soviet experience with central planning, a formal solution to the problem was found. This was labelled "one-man control and authority." It means that both the director and the shop superintendents who are his appointees are personally responsible for all decisions made at their level in the enterprise. On the other hand, these managers should accept "useful" suggestions. If the Party committee of the enterprise or the trade union disagree with a management decision, it can appeal the matter outside the enterprise; but, during the appeal process, the decision is to be implemented. Should the manager ignore a recommendation by the Party committee that is later approved by higher authorities as correct, he will generally be considered to have acted "bureaucratically." However, if he accepts the suggestion, he does so on his own responsibility and will be held personally accountable for the results.

This formal solution to the problem did not, of course, resolve it in practice. There has been continuous search for a balance between the right and obligation of the manager to make his own decisions, and the right and obligation of the Party committee of the enterprise to evaluate these decisions and to guide the director in his decision-making process. To the degree that the Party committee is represented by its secretary, a full-time functionary of the Party, the conflict is personified. The industrial literature of the 1930s fully reflects this continuous stress; so too does a discussion in the press that occurred in 1965.[2]

Despite the permanently conflictive nature of the problem, the solution of 1929 placed higher cards into the hands of the enterprise director than into those of the secretary of the enterprise Party committee. It was the director who was empowered, indeed obligated, to make the decision. The conventional Western wisdom, which I have no reason to question, is that the post of enterprise director has been by far the more important of the two from the early 1930s until today.[3] It is only at the level of the city Party committee and higher that the Party secretaries have exercised major decision-making power.

An historical instance that supports the conventional wisdom is the experience of the 1920s and early 1930s when Party cadres, who combined political credentials and administrative experience but had little technical expertise, were sent into enterprises as directors. Often, their two immediate tasks were limited to supervision over current managers who were knowledgeable but politically suspect, and to rapid absorption of technical knowledge so that they would be capable of replacing these men in fact and not solely in name. Since their principal immediate function was that of control, one might have thought that they would have been named as enterprise Party secretaries rather than as directors. The fact that this did not happen is a good indication of the relative authority of the two posts. It was apparently believed that control could be exercised from the post of director more effectively than from that of Party secretary.

The Chinese Experience

The problem met in shaping the administration of Chinese state enterprises has been identical to the one faced by Soviet authorities: that of appropriately combining state and Party control. Although the Chinese began by implementing the Soviet solution in which the director exercises one-man control and authority, they abandoned this pattern in 1956.[4] Only after 1984 (in practice, not until 1987) did they move back to it, while continuing doctrinally to emphasize that their system was fundamentally different due to its stress on democratic management.

During a long period, beginning after 1956 and ending between 1985 and 1987, direct decision making by the Party committee of the enterprise was stressed.[5] This was intended to be collegial decision making; however, from the late 1950s until 1979–81, it in fact seems to have generally meant a continuation of one-man control and authority. What is commonly recognized as having differentiated this system from that in the Soviet Union is that the authority was the

Party secretary rather than the director of the enterprise. Under a decision of 1978, which enterprises in our sample carried out mainly during 1980–81, there was the creation of the system in which the factory director had responsibility, but it was under the leadership of the Party committee. This was a return to the name and, I would suspect, to the reality of the immediate post-1956 period; there was a division of areas of competence between the Party secretary and the director, but not between the enterprise Party committee and the director.[6]

The question of interest in this experience is why, for a thirty-year period between the mid-1950s and the mid-1980s, the Chinese could afford the luxury of placing authority elsewhere than in the hands of the enterprise director. The Chinese have continually experimented in this field, beginning and ending with what was essentially the Soviet solution. In contrast, the Soviet Union has never deviated from its 1929 decision. Certainly it is not the case that Soviet leaders have been loath to engage in organizational change; their whole record of reshuffling demonstrates the contrary.

The above question is particularly acute for the first half of the 1980s—precisely those years to which our sample data relate—when power within the enterprise was effectively divided. But it also concerns the previous twenty-five years, when the post of Party secretary of the enterprise was the seat of authority. We shall find the answer in the appointment process where, during all periods, a major distinction existed between the Chinese and the Soviet enterprises. This distinction, in turn, is a function of differential property rights in the two countries.

THE NOMENKLATURA SYSTEM[7]

Both in China and in the Soviet Union since at least the early 1930s, membership in the Communist Party has been virtually a requirement for the post of director in any medium-sized or large enterprise. In both countries, all positions of responsibility come under the jurisdiction (within the *nomenklatura*) of one or another Party body; appointment, dismissal, and election (where relevant) must be approved by the appropriate Party committee and may be initiated by it. So much for the similarity. But this leaves completely open the question of which Party body enjoys the *nomenklatura* privilege over the posts of enterprise director and of enterprise Party secretary.

In the Soviet Union, the *nomenklatura* system is organized on a regional basis. The Party committee with this privilege is always a regional one, and the level of the relevant committee (up through the national Central Committee of the Party) depends upon the importance of the post concerned. Ordinarily, the director of the enterprise appears to be within the *nomenklatura* of a higher level Party committee than is the secretary of the enterprise Party committee. For enterprises of a substantial size, the post of director is likely to be within the *nomenklatura* of the central committee of the USSR or of the relevant republic; in contrast, the Party secretary is much more prone to be in the *nomenklatura* of the Party committee of the city, or even of an individual district within a city (Hough 1969, 150–55).

The fact that the Soviet director is generally included within a higher *nomenklatura* than is the enterprise Party secretary is informative as to their relative power positions within the enterprise. But that is not the point of relevance here. Rather, it is that the two individuals are normally within the *nomenklatura* of different Party organizations and that neither of these are sectoral. The particular ministry to which the enterprise belongs contains no Party body that carries out such appointing/confirming functions. The director is responsible both to the sectoral ministry, which seems usually to take the initiative in appointing and transferring him, and to a Party committee that is in no sense parallel to the ministry. The enterprise Party secretary is solely under the formal responsibility of a regional Party committee; the ministry that is responsible for the operations of the enterprise has at most an informal voice in the choice of the Party secretary.

Judging from the data of our sample enterprises in the early to middle 1980s, the Chinese *nomenklatura* system is fundamentally different from the Soviet. The sample characteristics are discussed in the following three categories:

(1) In all thirteen cases for which information was available, the enterprise director and the enterprise Party secretary were within the *nomenklatura* of the same Party committee (or of its "core group"). This was also the case for deputy directors and deputy enterprise Party secretaries.[8]

Only in three instances was any state organization, as such, described as being involved in the appointment or transfer of the enterprise director.[9] But this is not surprising. In general, it seems that Chinese state organizations above the level of the enterprise were at that time expected to function under the leadership of their own Party committees (or, at least, of their Party core groups). Thus, if an enterprise director and Party secretary were appointed by a ministerial Party committee, this meant that they were being appointed by the supreme administrative body of that ministry. As a rule, there was no reason for the management as such of a supervisory body to take formal action in major personnel matters.

(2) Information is available with regard to thirteen enterprises as to the Party organization in whose *nomenklatura* the posts of enter-

prise director and enterprise Party secretary fell. Half of these enterprises were under single-level supervision, while the other half had multiple principals.

For seven enterprises the *nomenklatura* privilege was enjoyed by the Party committee of the principal exercising supervision over the enterprise. In six, the enterprise had only a single principal. Prior to 1984, one of these six enterprises had had its top management within the *nomenklatura* of the Central Committee of the Chinese Communist Party. During that period, profits were given to the municipality along with supervisory rights; both were divorced from the main property rights. The municipality exercised direct supervision over the enterprise and received the profits that it earned, while the national government enjoyed the most important property rights and had provided all of the fixed investment. A reorganization at the beginning of 1984 transferred all supervisory rights to a national corporation (not dissimilar from a ministry), and at the same time the *nomenklatura* was transferred from the Party's Central Committee to this corporation.

For two enterprises the top posts fell within the *nomenklatura* of the Party's Central Committee. One of these enterprises was under the sole control of a national ministry. The other was under the joint control of a province and a national ministry, with the most important property rights belonging to the ministry and all of the fixed investment in it having been provided by the Center. Thus in both cases, the *nomenklatura* privilege was enjoyed by the party enjoying the primary (or all, in one case) property rights. However, the privilege was split away from supervisory authority over the enterprise.

For two enterprises the principal that exercised primary supervision was a higher level body than the one in whose *nomenklatura* these posts fell. Both of these cases were ones of multilevel supervision. And in both of these enterprises, this occurred solely for historical reasons. At the time of the interviews, the Party committees of the supervisory bodies had requested a change in this procedure, and it was expected to be adopted momentarily.

The remaining two of the thirteen enterprises constitute the most significant differences from the dominant *nomenklatura* pattern. In both cases, provincial authorities exercised direct formal supervision over the enterprise, received its profits, and enjoyed the *nomenklatura* privilege. But in one case it was the national government that controlled product distribution, allocated materials, and had provided all of the fixed investment. In the second case, where all three of these functions were split between the national government and the province, it was also the national government that was the dominant actor in all three spheres.

(3) Information is available for eight enterprises as to the Party body that was responsible for the Party activities of the enterprise.

For only four of the eight enterprises was it the same organization in whose *nomenklatura* the appointment of the Party secretary lay. At the time of the interviews, this number was expected to be reduced shortly to two enterprises. (The organization is considered to be the same if it is at the same level: i.e., Party Central Committee, ministry, province, municipality, or county. However, a subunit of a province, municipality, or county is treated as though it were that province, municipality, or county; this definition is used because of a lack of more precise data as to the body supervising Party activities.)

For seven enterprises it was a Party organization at the level of the county or municipality. For two of these enterprises, the municipal Party committee was identical with the provincial one.[10]

For one enterprise the responsible Party organization was a sectoral committee established within a prefecture (the level immediately above the county). This sectoral committee was responsible both to the prefectural Party committee and to a sectoral subcommittee of the provincial Party committee; it was the province that was the supervisory body over the enterprise.

These three categories of data show that invariably in our sample a single Party organization is responsible for the appointment of both the director and the enterprise Party secretary. This unification of authority implies that responsibility for their joint work can also be established. Given such unification at the level of the appointing body, the division of operational authority between the enterprise director and the enterprise Party secretary is potentially much less harmful to the efficiency of the enterprise than it would be in Soviet industry.

Responsibility for the conduct of Party activities within the enterprise is mainly lodged in the hands of a local regional Party body, roughly comparable to the one that would exercise such control in the Soviet Union. This implies a division between authority over the appointment of the enterprise Party secretary and responsibility for supervision over those of his tasks that can be described as "Party activities" as opposed to managerial ones. It is true that this division must frequently be awkward, particularly in the 1980s when the Party secretary's principal functions shifted to greater emphasis on conducting Party activities. However, the gravity with which the difficulties associated with this split authority are regarded must depend upon the import given by Chinese leaders to these Party endeavors. In any case, there are no indications that such difficulties impinge on the relationship between the Party secretary and the enterprise director.

In seven of the thirteen cases, the appointing Party committee is the Party committee of the body exercising primary property and supervisory rights over the enterprise. If we include the changes in *nomenklatura* that had already been formally requested and were expected at the time of the interviews, then 69 per cent of all enterprises for which data were available had such an appointing committee. Of the three cases where the leadership posts fell into the *nomenklatura* of the Central Committee of the Chinese Communist Party, two were instances of joint supervision over the enterprise. In both, a province or municipality was the formal supervisory body, but it was the national government that exercised the most important property rights and had provided all of the fixed investment. In the single one of these cases where such joint supervision was ended, Central Committee *nomenklatura* was abolished at the same time.

Only three (one-fourth) of the cases represent genuine exceptions. One of these had Central Committee *nomenklatura* in an enterprise that was supervised exclusively by a central ministry. The two others are ones in which *nomenklatura* and main formal supervision over the enterprise were united in the hands of a lower level governmental body, although the national ministry was the prime figure both as to property rights and as to investment.

In the Soviet Union, in contrast to our Chinese sample, there has never been unity of supervisory and *nomenklatura* authority except in the case of very small enterprises and for the Khrushchev era. China's difference from the Soviet Union in this respect is as important in reducing in China the damage to efficiency that may occur from dividing authority within the enterprise as is the simple unification of appointment authority over the two key positions of enterprise director and Party secretary. For it means that, in China, all appointment authority, supervisory authority, and property rights over the results of the enterprise activity are consolidated in the same hands. This may explain why a system of split authority within the enterprise was able to function no worse than it did in Chinese industry.

Franz Schurmann (1968) took the position that one-man authority in Chinese enterprises is essential for the successful implementation of central planning; this, he argued, is necessary to ensure that regional Party committees would not override the decisions of branch ministries (259, 278). I have no opinion as to whether Schurmann's view was correct at the time that he was writing, for I do not know where, at that time, the authority was lodged to appoint the enterprise Party secretary. However, by the 1980s, one-man authority seems to have been an irrelevance to the success of central planning. The germane issue was whether regional property rights, with their link to supervisory bodies, were consistent with central planning. So

long as the *nomenklatura* both of director and of enterprise Party secretary was in the keeping of the main supervisory body, the existence of
joint authority within the enterprise was irrelevant to Schurmann's
problem.

A feature in a report by Barry Naughton on interviews in China
during the winter of 1984 is pertinent here. The American Economists'
Study Team, of which he was a member, was particularly interested in
discovering whether the regional Party apparatus is important in solving interenterprise disputes. To put the question another way, did the
analogy of the regional Party secretary and the French prefect work in
China as it did in the USSR? The answer appeared to be negative. Instead, enterprises appealed to their immediate supervisory bodies to
help them with problems. Naughton did not attempt to provide an
explanation of this curious international distinction.[11]

This apparent anomaly is explained neatly by the hypothesis of
property rights. No regional Party committee or Party secretary could
be viewed as an impartial arbiter in such disputes in China. Rather,
unless the committee were the principal of all parties to the dispute, it
would be an interested and thus biased principal.

ONE-MAN AUTHORITY

As pointed out above, it has been widely asserted that most of the
period between the late 1950s and the early 1980s was de facto characterized by one-man authority within the enterprise. In contrast to the
situation in the Soviet Union, however, this one man was the Party
secretary.

Indeed, it was frequently the case that the two posts of Party
secretary and enterprise director were held by a single person. This
was a practice that was introduced during the Cultural Revolution. By
1971, the head of the Revolutionary Committee is said to have commonly combined both roles.[12] As of 1980, such combination of posts
held for three of the nine directors in a sample used by a Western researcher (Laaksonen 1988, 283, 286). It is also known to have applied
to two of our sample enterprises until 1981–82, and for a third until
1983 or 1984; it may have applied to more of them.[13]

The significant issue is whether it makes a difference if the
single person in authority is the Party secretary or the director. Indeed, in one sample enterprise, the two holders of these posts argued
that it would be preferable for a single person to be in charge. They
did not seem to think that it mattered whether this person were the
secretary or the director; unification of authority was their sole concern.[14] If one were to take this view, then one would conclude that
Soviet-style one-man authority has existed in China throughout al-

most all of the history of the People's Republic, except for the later 1950s and the years from about 1981 to 1987.[15]

It seems probable, however, that there has been a significant difference in the backgrounds of the typical Chinese enterprise Party secretary and director—the secretary has been described as being Red as opposed to expert (Schurmann 1968, 283–84). The condition observed in four of our sample enterprises, with only one being a counter case, is exemplified most strongly by the situation existing in one of them as late as 1984. Here, the Party secretary was a veteran pre-Liberation Party cadre, who had come south with the People's Liberation Army in 1949. The director was a 1970 university graduate, whose previous post had been head of the most technically oriented workshop in the same enterprise. Similarly, the Party secretary of another enterprise had earlier been the Party secretary of a rural commune.

One-man authority under the Party secretary was a personification of the slogan made popular during the Cultural Revolution of "politics in command."[16] It was likely to give rise to a system in which final authority within the enterprise was held by a person incompetent in production matters, whose interest and attention was concentrated elsewhere. It is for this reason that the system of one-man leadership by the director—introduced widely in China about 1987—probably involved a significant de facto and not simply de jure difference from the pre-1980 organization.

Furthermore, the role of at least initiating decisions must often have fallen, if only by default, to the director, which is of greatest relevance to the consequence for that period of whether the posts of Party secretary and director were within the same *nomenklatura*. Under such circumstances, the position of director was of significance and thus it would have mattered whether or not the Party committee appointing him was the same one that appointed the Party secretary.

GOVERNANCE BY THE ENTERPRISE PARTY COMMITTEE DURING THE FIRST HALF OF THE 1980s

This is the system that was called "director responsibility under the leadership of the Party committee." Data from the sample enterprises cast light on the functioning of this intra-enterprise managerial system, but they provide little information about the preceding or later systems. What can be said is that it is only in this system that the entire membership of the Party committee (or of its standing subcommittee, presumably the same as the "core group") seem to have been active participants in decision making.

In this director-responsibility system, the post of enterprise director was intended to be separate from that of the Party secretary, and the secretary was expected to concern himself primarily with matters other than production, sales, and finance. The director was responsible both for operational leadership and for making recommendations on policy matters to the enterprise Party committee. Decisions on policy questions—to the degree that these were left within the competence of the enterprise itself—were not in his hands but in those of the Party committee.

Four conclusions about the system can be drawn from the interviews.

1. The membership of the Party committee or its standing committee consisted of only five or six people. Although membership was not completely ex officio, it was a close approximation to this.
2. In most cases, a substantial majority of the members consisted of "political" as opposed to "administrative" cadres. Thus production and economic decisions for the enterprise were being made by a group comprising mainly individuals whose daily activity was directed elsewhere.
3. The powers of the committee were more than nominal. In three of the sample enterprises, there are recorded cases of its reversing the director's recommendations.
4. Under this system, the best documented growth from the later 1970s in the powers of the enterprise director relates to his control over the portion of the managerial line hierarchy that reached into the individual factory. This gain was at the expense of those Party units that functioned at the level of the factory, not of the enterprise. Thus the system can be regarded as representing a major increase in at least the potential for coordination of production activities within the enterprise.

This Party committee is sometimes described as being elected by the members of the Communist Party within the enterprise. In fact, election in the sense of genuine choice seems to apply only rarely to the Party secretary. Not only is this post within the *nomenklatura* of a Party body outside of the enterprise, but the interviews all implicitly present a picture in which this outside body initiates the choice rather than simply approves it. While no information is available with regard to other members of the committee, one would suspect that the same would apply to them, although to a lesser degree.[17]

Data of some sort are available for eight sample enterprises on the composition of the enterprise Party committee or, when the enterprise is a large one, of its executive organ: the standing committee of the Party committee. Complete membership data are available for four enterprises.

In each of the latter four, the Party secretary and the director were members of the Party committee and of the standing committee when this existed. The head of the trade union organization of the enterprise was a member in two of the four. With a total committee membership of five or six persons, the other members were *all* either major, full-time Party functionaries within the enterprise or were deputies to the director. While membership in the Party committee or its standing committee was not completely ex officio, the eligible candidates appear to have been limited to senior officials within the Party apparatus of the enterprise, to the head of the trade union, and to senior managers.

In one enterprise it was noted that the enterprise's higher authorities specified that no more than 30 per cent of the members of the Party committee might be "administrative" as opposed to "political" cadres. In a second sample enterprise, the rules of the supervisory authority allowed only one or two managers to attend any given meeting of the Party committee. Neither of these two enterprises provided full information as to the membership composition, but for the four that did, political cadres (Party and trade union officials) constituted 60–67 per cent of the membership in three enterprises and 33 per cent in the fourth. In a seventh enterprise, all four of the deputy directors were members of the committee, and it seems likely that political leadership was below 30 per cent. It thus seems likely that political cadres constituted some two-thirds of the membership in five of the seven enterprises for which we have information, and one-third in the remaining two.

This appears to be a very heavy predominance of members whose prime responsibility and interest were other than in either production or economic performance. But such a judgment depends on the standard used for comparison. The precisely opposite view was taken by the Party secretary of the supervisory body of one of those enterprises in which the political cadres constituted 60 per cent of committee membership. In commenting on the fact that the current "director-responsibility" system bore the same name as did the 1956–66 one, he stressed that its content was radically different because of the composition of the enterprise committee. In the 1956–66 system, he said, the membership was heavily biased toward model workers; "intellectuals" (i.e., employees with professional knowledge) were not considered to be part of the working class. In contrast, these "intellectuals" were accepted in the 1980s; technically trained managers had become an integral part of the Party committee system.

In one of the sample enterprises, in which 60 per cent of the committee members were political cadres, the committee met weekly during 1983 to discuss issues of personnel and of production. In a second enterprise in the same year, the committee met biweeky, but discussed production and economic matters only once every six weeks. In a third enterprise, where two-thirds of the members were political, the committee itself believed that its members were not competent to make decisions as to production. Thus they regularly held meetings of the committee attended not only by regular members but also by the managers of departments involved in the issues being discussed.

The actual power of the committee is difficult to determine. As one would expect, there appears to have been differences among enterprises, but it seems fairly clear from the sample enterprise data presented below that authority was more than nominal.

In the third enterprise described immediately above, the committee's formal rights included appointment, dismissal, and the setting of bonuses of the middle-level cadres who were under the jurisdiction of the enterprise. The committee determined both long-term and annual plans, and made the more important decisions as to current operations. In cases where the director disagreed with the committee's decision, he was obliged to execute it but could appeal for final arbitration to the supervisory body. (Note that this director's right was similar to the right of the Party committee in a Soviet enterprise when it disagreed with the decision of the director.) This was probably fairly typical of the formal powers of the committees.

In a second enterprise, with 60 per cent political membership, there was a mixed record of support during 1982 for the director. There were rejections of some of his recommendations for appointments to middle-level management posts that were within the *nomenklatura* of the enterprise Party committee, as well as of some of his recommendations for joint ventures with other Chinese enterprises. Indeed, not one but two of these latter strategic recommendations were turned down within a single year by the committee.

In two other enterprises, the Party committee's decisions regarding middle-management personnel were greeted with dismay by the director. In one, the director was described as not being allowed to play any role whatsoever in personnel matters, and thus as being unable to form a managerial team in which he had confidence. In a second, his recommendation for dismissing a workshop head from his post remained under discussion for four months. It was acted upon only when the managerial system was experimentally changed in late 1984 to the system of one-man leadership by the director.

In a fifth enterprise, the only one in which all of the deputy directors were members of the Party committee, each was regarding as holding de facto veto power over production decisions. Since the director was unable to choose his deputies, this situation made for considerable dispersion of authority among executives who were well informed as to operations and for this reason seem to have been willing to use such authority.

Only in one enterprise is there reason to believe that the Party committee played no more than a pro forma role. Here, decisions on all major problems were made at informal meetings of key enterprise personnel, were confirmed by the Workers' Congress, and only at the last stage went to the committee for formal approval.

As indicated above, the growth in the director's powers during the first half of the 1980s is clearest with regard to his control over the part of the managerial line hierarchy that functions at the individual factory or workshop level. Previously, during the Great Leap Forward in the late 1950s and once again during the Cultural Revolution, there appears to have been considerable decentralization of authority within the enterprise to the level of the sizable individual workshop. The Party organization that existed at this level—the General Branch—chose and supervised the workshop management to a large degree; this management was only loosely controlled either by the enterprise director or by the enterprise Party committee.[18] (The parallel is apparent with the situation of the BOALS [Basic Organizations of Associated Labor] in Yugoslav enterprises after the early 1970s.)

This situation was sharply reversed in the early 1980s. Four of our sample enterprises are known to have switched during 1981–83 from control of workshop management by the General Party Branch of the workshop to control by the enterprise director. Prior to that, in the words of one informant, the director's instructions to the superintendent of a workshop could not be executed if the workshop's General Party Branch objected. Only one enterprise is known to have continued operating under the earlier system as late as the end of 1983.

Such control by the director was further strengthened in the system of one-man leadership by the director that was widely introduced about 1987. At this point, the director seems generally to have gained control over the appointment of the deputy directors as well as of the shop superintendents.

Trade Unions, Workers' Congresses, and Democratic Management

Trade unions, workers' congresses within enterprises, and the election of some managerial officials all existed in China prior to the Cultural Revolution. All three were suspended between roughly 1967 and

1978, and were then reinstated. The triad does not, however, seem to play a particularly significant role within Chinese state enterprises.

Trade Unions

On the basis of interviews in Chinese industrial enterprises during the spring of 1966, Barry Richman evaluated Chinese trade unions as being decidedly less important than were those in the Soviet Union (1969, 254). This is also my impression for the 1980s: the situation in China seemed more similar to that of Romania in the early 1970s.[19]

Although the issue of dismissing workers for personal fault was mentioned in several of the sample enterprises, none of the informants suggested that the enterprise trade union was any obstacle to such dismissals. Instead, objections came solely from the local authorities of the area where the worker had his official residence. This is in sharp contrast to the situation in the Soviet Union, where no dismissal is legal unless it wins the prior explicit approval of the enterprise trade union committee.

Only in one sample enterprise was there discussion of the role of the enterprise trade union in handling individual grievances. The two informants, one of whom was the chairman of the union, reported that the union had never handled any directly work-related grievances. No standing committee existed to examine grievances of any type. The only complaints that the union had ever supported were three cases where individual workers did not receive cash subsidies for public transport. The general principle underlying the union's handling of individual grievances was that, when the union considered it appropriate, it would *forward on* the grievance either to the manager or to the Party secretary. The fact that grievance treatment was not discussed at all in any other sample enterprise can probably be taken as an indication of its lack of importance there as well.

This differs radically from the situation in the Soviet Union, where an elaborate trade union system exists at the enterprise level for handling worker grievances. Moreover, this system appears to be widely used. Mary McAuley has estimated from rather extensive sample data that, in Soviet industry of the 1957–65 period, some 3 to 10 per cent of the Soviet industrial labor force was involved each year as plaintiffs in one or another aspect of the grievance procedure (1969, chap. 6).

Chinese enterprise trade unions appear to be involved almost exclusively with matters of worker welfare (e.g., distribution of housing), with running labor competitions and distributing the related bonuses, with cultural and propaganda activities, and with attempting to muster better worker participation in production.

Workers' Congresses (WCs)

The decision to reestablish these bodies in the enterprises was taken in 1978. In the sample enterprises, the WCs appear to have been meeting fairly regularly, two to five times a year, beginning in various years between 1980 and 1982. Their appropriate role was described in a national decree in 1986 as being to examine and discuss the enterprise's major decisions, to supervise administrative leaders, and to safeguard the workers' legal rights and interests; nothing was said as to their constituting a decision-making body. Similarly, Harry Harding in 1987 described them as operating in an advisory or consultative role, without any extensive follow-through on early experiments in which they were the principal source of authority in the state enterprise.[20]

Information from interviews in the sample enterprises is consistent with Harding's description. The normal pattern is probably as reported in one enterprise, in which the WC had the right to discuss problems of prime importance to the enterprise and to decide matters having to do with the allocation of welfare benefits and of special individual awards. In only one enterprise, and that under an experiment of late 1983, did the WC make policy decisions that were binding on the enterprise director, who was regarded as responsible both to the state and to the WC. In a second enterprise as of 1984, the WC also had such formal power with regard to major matters of production and operations; but here the informant said that the WC representatives could do little but agree to the proposals of the director, since the representatives were poorly informed as to the relevant issues.

In six enterprises, the WC has evaluated individual cadres, but in only two is it known to have recommended any appointments or dismissals of cadres at any level. In one of these two enterprises, it seems to have initiated the recommendation of three upper-middle managers who were then appointed. But it had no right to recommend any change in senior management unless the annual production plan was unfulfilled for three years in a row. In the second enterprise immediately above, it had successfully, over a two-year period, recommended the transfer of nine middle-level cadres; no information is available, however, as to whether it initiated these recommendations. In contrast, an informant in a seventh enterprise said that its WC had no right to evaluate cadres in any fashion; for this, it would have to receive special permission from its supervisory body.

The WC is described as being elected by secret ballot. In some cases, but probably not in most, it was also organized in major workshops. It was entirely distinct from the trade union in two enterprises, while in three the union was its working body between sessions.

Elections of Managers

Barry Richman reported that elections of some managers were occurring in about 40 per cent of the enterprises he surveyed in 1966. Most firms engaged in this practice were located in Beijing or Shanghai (1969, 35).

In our sample, five enterprises had engaged in elections at one time or another since 1980, while three had not. Of the five who had, in at least two the practice had been abandoned by the time of the interview, while an informant in a third said that the practice was most unsatisfactory. In one of the five a director had been elected twice on an annual basis; each time the man currently in office was elected, and his continuation required the approval of the Central Committee of the Chinese Communist Party. During the same two years, other managers down through working chargehand were also elected. One other enterprise claimed that its director was elected, with approval required by the supervisory body and by its Party committee. Two others limited their elections to working chargehands. In only one, about which little is known, was it claimed that both middle and upper managers were genuinely elected. It is my impression that, by the mid-1980s, election of managers had ceased to be regarded by supervisory authorities as a worthwhile reform experiment.

Foremen and Political Cadres

The most surprising factual observation made in the course of the interviews is the apparent complete absence of foremen in Chinese industry. I had never previously heard of such a phenomenon in large plants under either socialist or capitalist management.

By foremen, I mean people exercising first-line supervision over workers on a full-time basis and without themselves having obligations of manual labor. All the sample enterprises did have what they called team leaders, but these were working chargehands rather than foremen. Only in one enterprise did an informant express the belief that it would be advantageous to transform the working chargehands into full-time foremen. Nowhere was it reported that foremen currently existed or had existed earlier elsewhere in the country.[21] The first level of full-time line management consists of shop superintendents, and their functions do not appear to include direct supervision of the shop floor.

It is true that there is substantial diversity among countries in the average number of workers supervised per foreman. In a study of factories producing similar products, West German foremen were each in charge of twenty-five workers; this was 50 per cent more than the sixteen workers in the sample French factories (Maurice, Sellier, and Silvestre 1982, 33). But the larger number in West Germany is associated with the prevalence of the apprenticeship system in that country and with the greater discipline and all-around skill of the German manual workers. I would expect the need for foremen in China to be much greater than in France, let alone than in West Germany. This is because of the lower level of Chinese industrial development, with a resulting greater need for timekeeping and other disciplinary forms of supervision over workers, for training, for coping with scheduling problems and with adjustments to shortages of materials and semifinished stocks, for safety supervision, and for handling machine stoppages and other minor repair. Yet the lowest level full-time line manager in our sample Chinese enterprises may be thought of as responsible for at least double the number of manual workers as is the West German foreman.

Upon noting this situation, the first suspicion of the observer is that Chinese factories do have full-time people performing the foreman function but they bear other titles. The most likely candidates for this role would seem to be the political cadres of the enterprise: specifically, the full-time Party, trade union, Young Communist League, and women's association representatives.

This suspicion was explicitly denied in one very large enterprise, where 1.5 per cent of all employees are political cadres. It was stated that not only do they bear no responsibility for production, but that that they are all attached to hierarchical levels which are too elevated to possibly permit them to carry out a shop-floor function.

Three other enterprises, each much smaller (only 2–4 per cent of the size of the first enterprise), also reported quotas of 1.5 per cent political cadres. One of these three enterprises filled its quota, while the number of political cadres in the other two constituted 0.5 and 1 per cent of the work force. These small percentages seem to substantiate the claim that they are not in fact used to fulfill the role of foremen.

The explanation for this state of affairs is totally unknown to me. Foremen appear to have existed during the interwar years, both in the large Shanghai and Tianjin textile factories.[22] They are also reported as existing during the post-Liberation years through 1953.[23] It is possible that foremen existed prior to the Cultural Revolution and were eliminated during that period on political-social grounds. For example, the post of foreman may have been associated by the leadership with the pre-Liberation gang-boss system.[24] But if this were the case, it is surprising that there was no comment in even one sample enterprise that foremen had existed there at an earlier period. Yet no such remarks are recorded in the interview protocols.

Ramon Myers has suggested (pers. com. 1988) that a cultural

phenomenon is at work here. He points to the absence of middle-echelon management in pre-Liberation Chinese firms. Myers remarks that the Chinese have never liked the sort of close supervision that is found in foremanship systems, and that historically—whenever possible—they have strongly preferred contractual relationships, both for gang work within a factory and for transactions between enterprises, to the authority relationships usually found in enterprises.

It would seem reasonable to suggest that this purely organizational pattern may bear some significant part of the responsibility for production inefficiency in Chinese factories.

8

CONCLUSION, INCLUDING EVALUATIONS OF EFFICIENCY

Thematic Summary

The first section of this summary deals with the hypothesis that has linked together the greater part of this book. The summary's remaining portions are organized around disparate themes, each treated quite independently of the study's primary hypothesis. These themes are bound together by the common feature that all deal with some aspect of the uniqueness of the Chinese economy compared to other centrally planned economies.

Property Rights

The main hypothesis of the book is that property rights, held by regional governments, exist and are important in China. Such rights consist primarily of the use of the physical output and the financial cash flow produced by those individual state-owned enterprises which are the agents of such a government. Governments issue directions and provide resources to their agent-enterprises in order to realize their own property rights.

Hypothesis (2.7) stated the critical part of the hypothesis:

> All principals hold property rights in enterprises. These property rights are accompanied by the right to give directions and provide resources so as to realize these rights. A principal other than the national government obtains property rights in a given agent in one of two ways: (1) by historical tradition; or (2) by investment in the fixed capital of the agent.

It contrasts with the alternative hypothesis (2.8) which holds that supervisory rights exercised by individual regional bodies are a consequence of a process of maximization by the Center that is unconstrained by the property rights of other bodies.

The existence of these property rights stands in striking contrast to the situation in the Soviet Union and its East European allies. This distinction has been used throughout this monograph to explain various peculiarities of the Chinese economic system compared with these other centrally planned socialist economies. The property rights hypothesis is tested through its ability to explain what would otherwise be anomalies in four quite disparate aspects of the work of medium-sized and large state-owned enterprises.

The first national peculiarity was treated in chapter 2. This consists of the phenomenon that is labelled by the Chinese as that of "too many mothers-in-law"; that is, there is more than one level of government exercising independent authority over some major aspect of the work of a given enterprise. Nine of the twenty medium-sized and large enterprises in our sample were subject to such joint authority. The phenomenon does not appear at all in the other centrally planned socialist economies.

The property rights hypothesis was used to explain this phenomenon on the basis that different property rights in the same enterprise may belong to varying levels of government, and that authority is exercised by a particular principal in order to protect and enjoy its own property rights. The hypothesis was tested, in accord with (2.7), through examination of the individual histories of the sample enterprises.

Table 2.2 summarized the results. The hypothesized linkage between ownership and control was supported by the experience of thirteen of the twenty sample organizations and was refuted by three; strong support or refutation was provided in twelve and one cases, respectively. For the subset of enterprises under multilevel supervision, three strongly supported the hypothesis while one strongly refuted it.

In chapter 3 I analyzed the second national peculiarity: the ease with which annual enterprise plans can be fulfilled. This was measured by the degree of plan overfulfillment. Taking the enterprise-year as the unit of observation, during 1975–78 the plan for value of output was overfulfilled by more than ten per cent in 33 per cent of the cases (and by more than twenty per cent in 13 per cent of the cases), and the plan for profits by fifty-eight per cent in 21 per cent of the cases. During the reform period of 1979–82, the respective figures rose to 51 (23) per cent and to 74 (55) per cent.[1] What is remarkable about these figures is the fact that occurrences of ten per cent overfulfillment in the Soviet Union and Eastern Europe constitute virtually a null set.

One might suspect that the above phenomenon represents no more than an intercountry difference as to the standard (i.e., the percentage of plan fulfillment) that is taken as the norm. This surmise, however, is refuted by the gauge according to which the performance of Chinese enterprises is theoretically evaluated; as in the case of other socialist countries, this is 100 per cent plan fulfillment. More significantly for purposes of refutation, there appears in practice to be no reward given to enterprises that is linked to the degree of over-fulfillment (see chap. 5), although it is at least claimed that under-fulfillment carries sanctions.

Hypothesis (3.5) presented the empirical link found within our sample between the degree of plan overfulfillment and property rights. Arguments are presented in chapter 3 as to why the observed results should be expected rather than be considered to be ad hoc.

Annual plans of physical output were substantially, but not wildly, overfulfilled by those enterprises for which one or another government level possessed the property right to dispose physically of the product and where it supported the enterprise with substantial allocations of materials and fuels (category A). In contrast, plan over-fulfillment was considerably higher for those enterprises in which property rights were limited primarily to financial returns (category B). During 1975–78, the plan of physical output was overfulfilled in category A enterprises by more than ten per cent in 14 per cent of the cases (and by more than twenty per cent in 5 per cent of the cases), compared with 30 (10) percent for category B. During 1979–82, the comparable figures were 23 (8) and 36 (12) per cent. (See table 3.8.)

Within category A, those enterprises for which value of output and profit plans are set by governmental levels other than those which fix the physical output plans (subcategory A2) show substantially less overfulfillment of the financial plans than do the enterprises for which the same governmental body fixes all the plans (subcategory A1). For value of output, 1975–78 figures were 18 (0) per cent versus 41 (14) per cent; 1979–82 figures were 22 (0) versus 63 (25) per cent. For prof-its, 1975–78 showed 54 (14) per cent versus 82 (42); 1979–82 showed 72 (36) versus 73 (60) per cent. (See table 3.10.) These differences re-flect the separation of the property rights to the physical and financial returns of a given enterprise, as opposed to combining them in the hands of the same principal.

Clearly, property rights do not account for the entire phenome-non of substantial overfulfillment. We see this fact reflected in the fulfillment figures for the type of plan that best serves the same coor-dinating functions as does the Soviet value of output plan: the annual plan for physical production in category A enterprises, where the products are both allocated and substantially supported by alloca-tions of materials and fuels. Here, 14 per cent of the observations dur-ing 1975–78 and 23 per cent during 1979–82 indicated overfulfillment of more than ten per cent. This deviation from the pattern of other planned socialist economies is left unexplained by the property rights hypothesis.

In chapter 4 I discussed the anomaly that two-fifths of all the sample enterprises gave preference during the reform years to financial over production considerations in some incident that was reported in the interviews. This proportion seems particularly high since there was no systematic questioning on this point and the incidents were all volunteered. The situation in the USSR and East European planned economies (even in Hungary) is radically different and can be summed up in Kornai's concept of a "soft budget constraint."

Hypothesis (4.3) and table 4.1 provide an explanation based upon property rights; namely, that under conditions where producer goods are not all allocated, regional governments operate within financial constraints that do not apply to the national government. Thus enterprises differ similarly as to such constraints, depending upon whose agent they are.

Table 4.2 presents the sample results. Only 5 per cent of the total sample reported cases of preference for financial considerations during the pre-reform period when physical allocations dominated. During the 1979–83 years, not a single one of the nontextile enterprises of category A (in which property rights exist as to the distribution of the physical product) showed such consideration. In these later years, one-third (one) of the textile enterprises of subcategory A2 gave such preference; here the principal was a provincial government obliged to deliver a given volume of textile production—but not necessarily from these enterprises—to the national government. In contrast, 57 per cent of the sample enterprises in category B (where no property rights exist as to distribution of physical product) displayed preference for financial over physical results during the years of 1979–83.

Chapter 7 treated the fourth anomaly explained by property rights: the *nomenklatura* of enterprise directors and of Communist Party secretaries. In all of the centrally planned socialist economies, both of these posts are within the powers of appointment (approval) of one or another Party body. The issue is: which Party body?

In the Soviet Union, the *nomenklatura* system is organized on a regional basis. The appointing Party organization may be on any hierarchical level, but it never corresponds to the government body (e.g., ministry) that supervises the enterprise. The final right to appoint an enterprise's chief executive is strictly separated from responsibility for the operations of the enterprise.

In contrast, nine of the thirteen Chinese sample enterprises for which data are available either had *nomenklatura* rights lodged in the

Communist Party committee of the principal organization exercising property rights over the enterprise, or expected that these rights would soon be placed there. In one case, *nomenklatura* rights were lodged in the Central Committee of the Communist Party, despite official direct supervision being exercised at the provincial level; but for this enterprise, the principal property rights were held at the national level. Only three of the thirteen cases should be viewed as amounting to rejections of the principle that the appointing Party committee should be the Party committee of the government body that exercises primary property and supervisory rights over the enterprise. Of these three cases of rejection, two instead followed the principle of uniting *nomenklatura* authority in the hands of the organization which exercised formal supervision over the enterprise.

The hypothesis that property rights are held by different principals in China, in contrast to the Soviet Union where there is only a single principal, explains this difference between the Chinese and the Soviet *nomenklatura* systems. Chinese principals can best be assured of being able to exercise their property rights in an enterprise when they have available to them the instrument of appointing the managers of the agent-enterprise.

THE PROXY PROBLEM

An obvious question in evaluating the above tests of the property rights hypothesis is whether there is some other variable at work for which property rights are only a proxy. I do not intend to raise this query with regard to unobserved variables, but will limit myself to various observed characteristics of the different enterprises. Due to the sample size, I cannot treat this issue in the standard fashion within a regression framework. Instead, I intend to ask how these different characteristics correspond to the property rights that govern the connection between the enterprise and its supervisor(s). (See table 8.1.)

The first characteristic to be considered is the nature of the enterprise's products. On a priori grounds, I would think of this as being the most likely candidate for constituting an underlying variable. Those enterprises for which physical output targets are set by a body that allocates virtually all of the output to users and supports its targets through the provision of planned quantities of inputs (category A), divide into two subcategories. Those for which the value of output plans and profit plans are established by the same regional body that sets the physical output plans (A1) are characterized by the fact that they do not include any producers of consumer goods. On

Table 8.1 Property Rights Relations and Other Characteristics of Enterprises

Property Rights (most to least centralized)	Number in Sample	Type of Product				Size of Labor Force (in thousands)					Size of Urban Area (million nonagricultural population)	
		Con-sumer	Capital Goods	Inter-mediate	Mixed	>53	20–25	6–13	1.5–5	<1.0	>1	<1
Under national con-trol only	3	0	2	1	0	2	0	0	1	0	1	2
Subcategory A1	4	0	2	2	0	2	0	0	2	0	1	3
Subcategory A2	9	3	1	5	0	1	1	4	2	1	6	3
Multiple supervisors	10	2	3	5	0	1	1	2	5	1	5	5
Category B	5	2	1	1	1	0	0	2	1	2	3	2

Note: Two enterprises fall under different regimes of property rights in different years or for different products. They are included in both the A2 and B regimes.

the other hand, there is no particular difference in the frequency with which consumer goods plants fall into subcategory A2 and category B. Thus it is only with regard to the extreme form of concentration or property rights at higher levels that a two-way breakdown of product (combining capital goods and intermediate products) provides information that correlates well with the form of property right. No such information is provided by the three-way breakdown in table 8.1.

Even less correlation with the form of property rights is shown by either of the two variables of size of enterprise and size of urban area in which the enterprise's headquarters is located. So far as can be judged, there is no indication in our sample that property rights is acting as a proxy for some other observed variable.

Tax System

Both Chinese and Soviet budgetary revenues are generated primarily through sales tax on industrial products and by the profits of state-owned industrial enterprises. In China, these two sources account for 88 per cent of total budgetary income. The significant difference between the two systems is that the Soviet sales tax is in practice a value-added tax on consumer goods, while the Chinese tax is levied on both capital goods and intermediate products as well as on industrial consumer items.

In chapter 6 I drew the implication of this distinction. Compared both with the Soviet Union and with the United States, Chinese industrial enterprises have a very low ratio of wage costs to the costs of fuels and intermediate materials (see table 6.6).

This ratio may have been of little significance in the pre-1979 period, when property rights to the financial returns from an agent-enterprise had little value. But it became of major importance during the years of reform, when regional principals operated under hard financial budget constraints. In this period, relative prices of inputs and outputs could influence behavior.

The first result of this is that both profits and cash flow— financial returns that motivate the agent-enterprise's principal who possesses the property right to the first and to the bulk of the second—are high as a proportion of gross output (see table 6.1). It is this that causes the maximizing of profit and cash flow by Chinese enterprises to be virtually indistinguishable from output maximizing behavior. A second result is observed in labor markets and will be examined in the next major section of this chapter.

With the first result, we have one explanation for the apparent anomaly of Chinese economists tending to view Kornai's "soft financial budget" formulation—intended by its author to apply to centrally planned European socialist economies—as being also appropriate to use in describing the Chinese state sector. Despite the radically different terms of tradeoff between financial and production considerations that have existed in these economies after 1978 (see above), enterprises in both usually act as though they are output maximizers.

Incentives

Monetary incentives directed to individual workers in state enterprises have been extremely weak. Increases in wage-grade have not normally accompanied promotions in position, although the situation may have been different for managerial personnel. The evidence (not presented in this book) of our sample suggests that there has been little use of bonuses to differentiate either among individuals or small groups within a given enterprise. However, such weakness of incentive stimulation at the level of the individual would be consistent with the existence of stimulation at the level of the enterprise's work force taken as a whole.

A necessary condition for this latter type of incentive is that relative average rewards between enterprises vary over time. Table 5.3 showed that, although this condition was not met in our sample during the pre-reform years of 1975–78, it was fulfilled during 1979–82. An index of average earnings within each enterprise was obtained by taking absolute average earnings as a ratio of the average earnings of all state employees in Chinese industry in the same year. Of seventeen enterprises for which we have data for the four years of 1978–81, the ratio of the peak-year to the low-year value of the index was greater than 111 per cent for half of the sample. For three of the seventeen enterprises, the ratio was not only higher than 119 per cent, but the enterprise's rank within the sample also changed by six or more places.

I had hoped to be able to correlate changes in relative average rewards given to the workers of individual enterprises during 1979–82 with performance indicators, but all attempts to do so failed (see chap. 5, including the app.). Ordinary least squares regression did not establish any link with profitability ratios, with degree of plan fulfillment of output, with degree of plan fulfillment of profits, or with any combination or lag relation, once control variables were introduced to reduce the strength of spurious coefficients. This phenomenon was tested best for the dependent variables of average total earnings and of bonuses. Furthermore, although the samples were much smaller and the results considerably less reliable, it also appeared to hold for the dependent variable of creation of employment for the family members of current workers, as well as of housing (for which there were only five to seven observations) with respect to all independent variables except that of the degree of overfulfillment of the profit plan.[2] So far as enterprise performance could be measured from the data available, no incentives have been given to the enterprise's work force as a whole. This is a subject to which I shall return in the appendix to this chapter.

I also explored in chapter 5 the issue of whether incentives, distinct from those for the total work force, have existed for upper managerial personnel within the enterprise. Our own sample data allow us to reject such a hypothesis with regard to bonuses, but it is possible that this situation has changed since 1987.[3] Materials from two other sample studies, both carried out during 1985 by Chinese research organizations, strongly suggest the unlikelihood of enterprise performance having had a significant influence on the progress of managerial careers during the reform years.

Coordination Through Plans

Physical coordination of the production and material requirements of medium-sized and large state enterprises is weak by Soviet standards. This is particularly so for national coordination.

Evidence for the first assertion is found in the degree of overfulfillment of annual plans for the physical production of enterprises in cases where the products are allocated and are substantially supported by allocations of materials and fuels. Here, 14 per cent of the observations during 1975–78 and 23 per cent during 1979–82 showed overfulfillment by more than ten per cent. Since in neither period did there appear to be any reward to the enterprise that was linked with the degree to which plans were overfulfilled, plans can have played only a limited role as a binding constraint on the choice of activities by enterprises. It is not surprising that production plans declined in importance as coordinating implements during the reform years. What is more interesting is that, in comparison with the situation in the Soviet Union, their earlier role as well seems to have been quite restricted.

The situation regarding allocation of materials is even more striking, and here both assertions are supported. Data relevant to national coordination are presented in tables 2.1 and 3.1. The first point to be made in this regard is that central allocation has always been carried out at a level of aggregation one to two magnitudes higher in China than in the Soviet Union.

The second significant fact—an anomaly for a centrally planned economy—is that, even in the pre-reform year of 1978, national allocations covered half or less of total usage of coal and cement, and no more than three-quarters of steel, lumber, and trucks. Principals at different regional levels of government exercised considerable authority over the provisioning of their own enterprises. Finally, a fair amount of regional autarchy was built into the system during the prereform years. All this, as such, is relevant only to the assertion as to the weakness of national physical coordination. But its import can be extended to physical coordination in general since, contrary to the situation in the Soviet Union, barter of *outputs* among state enterprises was always a significant source of procurement. During the early 1980s, uncoordinated regional planning and barter were substantially supplemented as mechanisms for distributing materials by the creation of a national marketplace.

The provisioning of factories is treated in detail for our sample enterprises in chapter 4, particularly for the transition period of 1979–83. These sample data strongly support the assertion as to the weakness of physical coordination in general. As conventional wisdom would suggest, allocations by one level of government or another provided the largest share of procurement to those enterprises supervised solely by national ministries, and they offered the least support to the small enterprises under the county organization in our sample. What is startling, however, is the degree of similarity in procurement patterns among enterprises, regardless of the level of their supervising principals. The sample data contradict the view that there either exists or has existed an institutional package consisting of management by central ministries, product allocation, and input allocation. It is not the case that there is a portion of the state industrial sector that lies within the realm of central planning, receiving plans both for outputs and inputs that are reasonably similar to those observed for all enterprises in the Soviet Union. So far as the evidence of our sample goes, this was not so either during the 1970s or in the 1980s.

Yet, at least during the reform years of the first half of the 1980s, the combination of the four forms of coordination—national planning, regional planning, patterns of barter among enterprises, and market forces—worked rather effectively. In chapter 4 I demonstrate this for the sample enterprises on the basis of their not having any serious supply problems other than of electricity. This success in coordination seems first to have been made possible during the 1979–81 period through investment restraint by the national government. In this fashion, buyers' markets were created for various intermediate industrial goods as well as for much machinery. When the effect of this central policy wore off, it was replaced by a major expansion in the scope of multiple prices for the same good at a given moment in time. Thereafter, there presumably existed some legal money price at which virtually unlimited supplies were available to enterprises.

As we shall see below, the system of multiple prices—still another anomaly by the standards of other economies—has probably been considerably more effective in the Chinese state sector than it would have been in an economy such as that of the Soviet Union, which operates with a unified government budget and without property rights for different levels of government.

Allocation of Labor and Determination of Wages

In the introductory chapter I described six aspects of control exercised over urban state-owned enterprises that are unique to China among centrally planned socialist economies, with all six applying to China before the era of economic reforms as well as afterward. The bulk of this book has been devoted to five of the six aspects. The last relates to labor markets and is considered only at this point. The reason for such scanty treatment is that the unique features of the Chinese labor market are explained by the country's status as a less developed socialist country rather than by the existence of regional property rights. Our case studies, however, are rich in data concerning the labor market, and the reader wishing a fuller treatment of the subject is advised to see my forthcoming articles.

The Chinese urban labor market in the state sector is similar to the Soviet and East European in two major respects. The first is that there is the common assumption that governments, rather than enterprises, should have the prime authority in determining the size of an individual factory's work force. The second is that social mores are observed which greatly restrict the ability to dismiss workers on any grounds.

The differences in the treatment of employment are threefold.

(1) The Chinese labor turnover rate is negligible in the state sector, in contrast to the Soviet which has long been at much the same high level as is observed in the West under conditions of low unemployment. The low Chinese labor turnover stems directly from dual labor market conditions in the urban area and is due to the privileged position of regular workers within state-owned enterprises. Such workers would have almost no chance of being employed in another state enterprise if they were to quit the one where they are currently working.

(2) The creation of additional urban jobs has been a major objective both for enterprises and for local authorities in China. Given the existing condition of job shortages, major preference in hiring has

been granted to family members of current workers. Since 1978, such preference has been extended to include the inheritance of jobs as regular state workers. In contrast, neither of these phenomena is observed on a significant scale in the Soviet Union or Eastern Europe; priority in hiring, for example, goes no further there than the informal preference arising from personal recommendations which occurs in all countries.

(3) A multitier system of nonprivate job opportunities within the same industrial sector is a prominent feature of Chinese enterprises, in contrast to the situation in European socialist countries. Engagement as a regular state employee is the preferred employment status in China, and such employment is controlled by national authorities. Membership in a "large collective" (usually, or at least often, affiliated with a state-owned enterprise) is the second choice of workers; this is controlled by provincial authorities. Employment either in "small collectives" or as temporary workers constitutes the least desirable type of urban work. Where the collectives are connected with state-owned enterprises, it is such enterprises and their principals that determine the growth of this employment.

This multitier system is the mechanism used to reconcile the constraints on hirings, imposed by the national authorities, with the job-creation objectives of both enterprises and local (including provincial) governments.

Furthermore, the quantitative significance of the tiers below the most preferred one has grown sharply during the reform years of 1979–84. Moreover, it seems a fair guess that the bulk of the urban expansion in the collective sector has been in employment attached to state-owned enterprises.

When I examined the proportion of net additions to urban employment that occurred outside of state employment, I came up with the estimates shown in table 8.2.[4] Indeed, the degree of expansion of inferior employment is underestimated not only because of the estimation process itself, but also because it excludes temporary workers in state employment.

The result of such growth is considerable weakness in the ability of the Chinese government to restrain that portion of the growth of urban purchasing power which occurs through the expansion of employment. It is true that those levels of government (the national and, to a much lesser degree, the provincial) that have the greatest interest in restraint of hiring are also those that exercise control over the types of net hirings that are most attractive to the workers concerned. But inferior jobs do exist within state enterprises and their dependencies. The expansion of such posts is determined mainly by

Table 8.2 Increases in Nonstate Employment as a Proportion of All Net Additions to Urban Employment (in percentages)

	1966–78	1979–84
For all urban employment	15	56
Of this, in collective units[a]	19	44
For all urban employment in industry	26	46
Of this, in collective units[a,b]	27	42

[a] These probably understate the expansion of the number of urban collective workers, since some are employed directly in state-owned enterprises.
[b] The assumption in these calculations is that industry accounted for the same proportion of total urban private employment both at the end of 1965 and at the end of 1978 as was the case at the end of 1984. Since the figure is only 11 per cent of private employment, our results are quite insensitive to the assumption made in this regard.

local bodies and has increased in reaction to national-level restraint on the hiring of regular state workers.

Such weakness of measures of national restraint applies even more strongly with respect to the average earnings of state-employed workers. Between 1978 and 1984, only one-third of the expansion of the average wage packet was due to increases in base wages, yet this was the only element controlled by the national government (through its ability to set quotas for promotion). The rest was due to the growth of bonuses from a negligible to a major share of earnings, and of a somewhat smaller absolute growth in subsidies.

Within the sample of medium-sized and large enterprises studied, the variation of subsidies among enterprises was even greater than was the variation of bonuses. When I used the average figures for 1979–82 for each enterprise, payments were as follows when the months of base wages was taken as the measure: for an enterprise at the 67th percentile of the sample, subsidies were equal to 160 and bonuses, 126 (enterprise at 20th percentile = 100). Intrafirm variance between years was negligible for subsidies, but substantial for bonuses. Over the period of 1980–82, the average coefficient of variation (standard deviation/mean) was 0.22 for bonuses. The lack of assured permanence of subsidies, and even more so of bonuses, caused them to be regarded by employees as inferior portions of the wage packet. Nevertheless, the inflationary effect of a renminbi increase in such payments is identical to the same absolute increase in that portion of earnings that is under national control.

Within the sample, and perhaps within the entire universe of medium-sized and large state-owned enterprises that it is intended to represent, the interenterprise distribution of bonuses and subsidies during the reform years reduced the relative income inequality ex-

pressed in base wages alone. (Prior to 1979, pure bonuses were virtually nonexistent. As late as 1978, subsidies constituted only half the
proportion of the total wage bill that they reached in 1980.) For an
identical set of eighteen enterprises, the coefficient of variation of
single-year average earnings was reduced from 0.181 in 1975 and
0.163 in 1978 to 0.139 in 1982.[5] Pre-reform income distribution between state enterprises had been influenced primarily by the number
of years of seniority of their work forces, as well as by the individual
enterprise's traditional index value (essentially geographic) as to the
base wage to be paid for a given wage grade. Reduction in interenterprise variation led not only to greater equality of income, but
also to an improvement in equity as evaluated by Chinese authorities,
and quite likely to an improvement in incentives (through bonuses)
for the enterprise work forces. However, national data suggest that
this reduction in interenterprise variation did not apply to state-
owned industry as a whole, when one includes the small enterprises
that are not represented in our sample.

The low ratio of wage costs to the costs of fuels and intermediate products, caused by the tax system as analyzed in chapter 6, plays
an important role in explaining the willingness of lower level regional
bodies to expand employment and earnings in enterprises under their
control. Supervising agencies have considerable authority to regulate
temporary employment and the growth of membership in small collectives that are dependent upon the agent-enterprise, as well as
bonus and subsidy payments made to regular workers within the
state-owned enterprise. The insignificance of total per-unit wage
costs relative to the price of the product causes these supervisory
bodies, whether they be regional governments (and thus principals)
or national ministries (and so agents of the Center), to be much more
tolerant of increased wage costs than would be the case under another system of taxation. This fact significantly reduces the success of
the Center's efforts to restrain inflation in the markets for consumer
goods by restricting urban purchasing power. It explains why the
possession of property rights in the financial returns of the enterprise
does not motivate the principal to exercise the strictness in holding
down wage costs that we might otherwise have expected.

The Pre-Reform and Reform Years: Differences and Continuities

Throughout this monograph, and particularly in the analysis of the
quantitative longitudinal data of the sample enterprises, a distinction
has been made between the reform (post-1978) and the pre-reform
(1975–78) years. This dating is consistent with the fact that, as is uni-

versally agreed, it was at the December 1978 plenum of the Central Committee of the Chinese Communist Party that the critical decisions were taken to embark upon a path of economic reform in the national economy as a whole.

Yet our concern, after all, is not with the entire economy but rather with only a portion of the urban state sector; reform was much slower to catch on there than was the case in the rural economy. Thus it is important to show that the 1975–78 period was really distinct from the 1979–82 years in ways that were relevant to state-owned industry. The second task is to show the continuities between the two periods.

Differences

FINANCE

For the purposes of this monograph, the most important distinction between the two periods is that financial results were of substantially greater significance to the regional principals of agent-enterprises after 1978 than they had been earlier. This was particularly the case for municipalities and counties, to whom legislation in 1979–80 seems to have extended the rights of financial enjoyment of enterprise profits that had been granted to provinces during the early 1970s. Equally important, during 1980–82 extra-budgetary finance expanded sharply and steadily as a source of all nonagricultural investment. Such extra-budgetary finance was controlled predominantly by local authorities.

The economy also began to be monetized after 1978 at the same time that regional principals were increasingly able to keep the cash flow generated by their agent-enterprises. Until then, regional principals had been concerned mainly with producing goods for distribution within their own territories; now their interest turned to goods with high profit margins and sales tax rates. Although considerable regional autarchy was widespread in the earlier period, it had been due to restrictions on the supply side rather than on the side of demand. Now regional protectionism became important, as interior regions attempted to capture the cash flow from their own markets which had earlier gone to Shanghai and to other industrialized areas.

URBAN LABOR MARKETS

The two periods differed radically with regard to the proportion of net additions to urban employment that occurred in collectives. Since no national data are available for the desired years of 1975–78, I shall compare data for the overlapping years of 1971–78 and of 1976–78 with 1979–82. The net additions to all nonprivate urban employment that occurred in the collective sector were 19% (1971–78), 20% (1976–78), and 46% (1979–82). These figures demonstrate that the years 1979–82 saw a substantial growth in the significance of those types of urban job creation that were controlled by regional authorities and by individual state-owned enterprises rather than by the national government. Although the importance of these inferior types of urban jobs was less than it was to become in 1983–84, the differences from earlier years are nevertheless very substantial.

Similarly, the proportion of earnings of state-employed workers that comprised forms controlled by bodies other than the national government became significant only after 1978. Bonuses (including above-quota piece rate payments) and subsidies together constituted 9 per cent of the total national wage bill in 1978 and had been less earlier. By 1979 they were greater than 16 per cent and during 1980–82, the annual figures were 24, 25, and 27 per cent, respectively.

RESULTS FROM THE SAMPLE

The differences in the financial and labor markets between the two periods are known to have existed on a national level. The information sources for such differences lie outside of our sample. However, as seen earlier in this chapter, additional major differences are found within the sample.

The first of these relates to overfulfillment of enterprise plans. During the later period, such overfulfillment increased substantially for all types of plans, presumably indicating that plans were being taken less seriously by the plan-setting principals and that the already-weak coordinating role of plans was further diminishing.

The second difference is that preference for financial over production considerations was reported only once by category B enterprises as having existed during the first period. In the second period, some half of such enterprises reported such preference.

The third difference is that in the 1975–78 period there was almost no intra-enterprise variability of relative average earnings among the sample enterprises; in contrast, such variability was substantial during 1979–82.[6] Monetary incentives for both production and for general economic performance were nil during the first period, while they may have been substantial during the second.

In general, we would not expect to be able to date "reform" as beginning in an individual year. The issue of such dating relates primarily to the classification of 1979. It is both because the critical Central Committee plenum occurred at the end of 1978 and because of the periodization shown by the quantitative data of our sample enterprises that 1979 is treated in our multiyear statistical analyses as having been a year of reform behavior.

Continuities

The principal continuity is the applicability of the hypothesis of property rights enjoyed by regional levels of government. We see this applicability supported in both periods by the national peculiarity of multilevel supervision over individual enterprises, as well as by the distinctions among categories of enterprises in the ease with which annual enterprise plans could be fulfilled. Although we have no direct information for the first period as to the locus of jurisdiction over the *nomenklatura* of enterprise directors and Party secretaries in our sample enterprises, there is nothing either in the general literature or in the interviews to suggest that this national peculiarity changed between the two periods.

Another continuity is the bias toward regional autarchy. The main reason for autarkic behavior by the principals differed sharply over time: the desire in the first period to concentrate on the supply of the physical needs of one's own regions, versus financial motivation in the later years for restricting various kinds of regional exports and imports. The types of products which the principals wished most to develop similarly differed: producers goods in the first period and industrial consumer goods in the second. However, with regard to establishing continuity, what matters is that both motivations led throughout to similar autarkic actions.

In the earlier years as well as in the later, coordination through physical planning was weak if compared with the Soviet Union. Overfulfillment of physical production plans of enterprises was high; allocations were provided in highly aggregated terms; a large proportion of even the most important fuels and materials were obtained outside of the allocation system. Barter by enterprises of their outputs, rather than just of allocated materials and fuels as in the Soviet Union, was permitted and important in both periods.

In neither set of years were incentives provided to individual enterprises for high enterprise performance of *measured* performance indicators. Thus this major ground for suboptimizing behavior by enterprises in the Soviet Union was apparently always absent within medium-sized and large state-owned industrial units of China.

Finally, important continuities as well as differences existed in the urban labor market. During both periods, employment in a state-owned enterprise was generally for life. Furthermore, neither the individual employer nor employee had great authority over the employment decision. In neither period were incentive schemes targeted at the level of the individual worker; piece rate payments, always widely used in the Soviet Union, have played only a negligible role. Although it is true that bonuses had been insignificant during the first period and became important only in the second, what matters here is that neither period saw differentiation of bonuses among individual workers within a single enterprise.

Efficiency Evaluations

Chinese Economic Coordination of Industrial Products

PRE-REFORM

Let us begin with those features of Chinese economic coordination that were prominent in the pre-reform period. It must be admitted, however, that since the interviews in our sample enterprises refer mostly to the reform years, this description is less reliable than is that for the later years. The Soviet central planning system will be taken as the standard of comparison.

(1) There was acceptance of the existence of property rights for different levels of government. This acceptance prohibited the central government from engaging in all-inclusive physical planning of production or physical allocation of materials and fuels. Operating in an environment where money was not a fungible means of exchange, regional principals exercised their property rights by carrying out their own physical planning of the production of their agent-enterprises. Such planning of outputs was supported by regional allocation of inputs.

(2) This system resulted in a fairly autarkic pattern of planning and of economic relations. It was, however, meliorated by:

a. The production that came from those enterprises for which the national ministries possessed the property right to distribute output.
b. The production of other enterprises to which the national government directly distributed some materials and fuels, asserting in return the right to allocate a portion of their output.
c. Claims by the national government upon regional principals for part of their total production of various product aggregates, with counter-deliveries being made of inputs.
d. Barter of products, either directly among principals or by the agent-enterprises themselves.

(3) No great effort was made to fashion a system at any regional level which was internally consistent in an input-output sense. This was due to the fact that there existed various independent sources of supply for individual enterprises of all types, regardless of whether their principal was a national ministry, a provincial government, or a local authority. Perhaps for this reason, enterprises were under less stress than in the Soviet Union to generate intermediate outputs which could relieve strained requirements for inputs of other users. In any case, annual production plans given to enterprises seem to have been less taut than was the case in the Soviet Union.

(4) Elements of multi-pricing for identical products existed. Collectives and even small state enterprises were permitted to sell certain products for higher prices than could be charged by the medium-sized and large state enterprises. Prices for goods allocated by regional authorities were not necessarily identical to those for the same products when allocated by the Center. This pricing policy provided higher monetary earnings directly to high-cost producers, rather than following the Soviet system of subsidizing them in some fashion that did not affect the user directly. Although such pricing caused per-unit input costs to differ by enterprise and period depending upon the source of supply, thus making financial performance more difficult to evaluate, this consequence was fairly innocuous both for larger state enterprises and for their principals. Such harmlessness was due to the unimportance to both of monetary results. Nevertheless, multi-pricing increased the difficulty of meeting the traditional central planning objective of being able to use money as a measure of value and thus of having the rate of profit function as a composite measure of relative efficiency (within some subset of enterprises, or for the same enterprise over some subset of time).

REFORM

The difference between coordination during this period and the earlier one relates primarily to the role of markets. Regional principals below the level of the province were now able to keep a large share of the marginal profits and taxes produced by their agent-enterprises, rather than having to pass them along to higher levels of government. At the same time, the financial retrenchment policies of the central government during 1980 and 1981 caused money increasingly to become the bottleneck constraint in the demand for goods, both by principals and by their agent-enterprises. This result of retrenchment was furthered by the more rapid growth of collective and small-town enterprises than of the state-owned enterprises under the supervision of governmental bodies above the level of the county. Since the enterprises that were expanding most speedily were precisely those permitted to charge higher prices than others, such expansion was a reinforcing factor in bringing effective monetary demand by enterprises closer to the level of existing supply at the differentiated set of fixed prices.

Money was now fungible, at least by earlier standards. Fungibility, combined with what amounted to a sharp reduction in the marginal rates of taxation levied on the monetary revenue of regional principals, caused possession of property rights to the financial returns from enterprises to become of value to principals. In time, the results of the central government's early retrenchment policies wore off, but a national policy of introducing substantially higher prices for nonallocated production was introduced in 1984 and 1985, supplementing the earlier prices that remained relatively frozen. Allocations of fuels and materials could be interpreted as little more than a form of transfer of money income to the recipient.

Throughout the years from at least 1980 on, it would seem from the evidence of our sample that, except for electricity, Chinese state-owned enterprises were free from the plague of shortage of supply that resulted from physical rationing of inputs. To the degree that enterprises could financially afford to pay higher prices for inputs and thus could purchase from collectives and county-supervised state enterprises, they had available to them reasonable approximations to the goods that they wished.

At a bare minimum, our data indicate that this was the case for the years 1980–83. (Such availability of inputs may not have been new with the reform period; the data from our sample do not cast reliable light on earlier years.) This, it is true, is not a long span of time. But there is reason to believe that no such multiyear period existed in the Soviet Union once national central planning had been introduced about 1930.

As I have discussed, the slogan "the socialist economy is a commodity economy" was enunciated by the Central Committee of the Chinese Communist Party only in October 1984. However, despite the rigidity of prices until that time, the central government's retrenchment policy had already brought the reality in China a considerable distance in the desired direction. The roles of annual plans and of physical allocations in coordinating the economy had been reduced considerably during the years since 1978. It is true that these mechanisms continued to be used and that barter of products was not only maintained but was extended to intertemporal barter. Nevertheless, what is most significant is that the marketplace became a significant supplement to these traditional Chinese methods of coordination.

This was possible because, as money became fungible, national policy caused financial constraints to become binding both on regional principals and on their enterprises.

The moderated regional autarchy of the previous period was maintained, although for new reasons. It had existed earlier because of the desire of regional principals to retain their own physical production for use within their borders. Only the mechanism of barter was available to these principals as a means of genuine exchange with other regions, and the transaction costs of such exchange are notoriously high. During the reform years, autarchy continued because the fixed prices and differentiated rates of sales tax set by the central government led to highly variegated returns on investment in different products.[7] Restraints on "exports" of finished products to other regions were replaced by protectionism against "imports" of high-profit items. The aggregate result was similar, although there was a sharp change in the mix of products most affected.

STATIC EFFICIENCY

This evaluation will concentrate upon China in 1980–83, since these are the years for which we have the best interview data. I believe, however, that the evaluation also applies to the earlier and later years. I will leave aside here treatment of X-efficiency, reserving that for the appendix to this chapter.

The main disadvantages of the Chinese system of economic coordination, in contrast with the Soviet, would appear to be the following five factors.

(1) The tendency toward regional autarchy in individual industrial products appears to be much more accentuated in China. The evidence for this is only anecdotal.[8] Nevertheless, it is significant that such regional autarchy is what we would expect to occur due to the presence of property rights for regional governments in China as opposed to the Soviet Union. Furthermore, internal criticisms of regional coordination in the Soviet Union have concentrated far more on the existence of unnecessary crosshauls of products, with resulting strain on the transportation system, than on production in regions with high marginal production costs.

(2) The virtual absence of labor markets in Chinese state-owned enterprises and in large industrial collectives ensures inefficiency in labor utilization in China that goes well beyond what is observed in the Soviet Union.

(3) The considerable extent to which Chinese medium-sized and large enterprises are subject to multiple supervisors, whose interests conflict to at least some degree, makes for difficulties in developing

a coordinated and consistent policy for these individual organizations. Like the first disadvantage, this supervisory difficulty arises from the existence of property rights and multiple principals.

(4) The smaller coverage of national industrial production and of input needs by physical planning, at whatever level such planning may be done, makes coordination of Chinese state industry more dependent than that in the Soviet Union upon the use of nonplanning devices. But under conditions of fixed prices, nonplanning mechanisms are likely to have high transaction costs. This applies most obviously to the barter arrangements of enterprises that were so much a feature of the pre-1979 scene. But it also applies to money transactions, so long as prices are not flexible. (Thus this point has only limited relevance to Chinese industry since 1984.)

(5) The process of evaluating the performance of individual enterprises suffers from the fact that, in China, varying proportions of given inputs are purchased at a variety of price levels. This is the case both among different enterprises of the same industry within any particular year, and across years for the same enterprise. The implication of these differing proportions is that it is more difficult to use a common denominator of performance (i.e., monetary results) to evaluate an individual enterprise, combining what would otherwise be disparate criteria of performance, than is the case in the Soviet Union.

Of these five Chinese disadvantages, at least (1) and (5) have significant offsets and may be much less significant on a net basis than they first appear.

A major counterpart of Chinese regional autarchy is Soviet vertical integration both at the level of the enterprise and of the national ministry. The perennial difficulties of procurement in the Soviet Union cause both enterprises and ministries to strive for the maximum feasible degree of production of their own requirements. In particular, since supply problems are greatest where product-mix considerations are most important, they attempt to concentrate procurement on items that are as homogeneous as possible. Such behavior has led to widespread production of many components and finished products in lot sizes that are uneconomically tiny. All this has been well recognized by Soviet writers and administrators since the middle 1930s, but efforts at change have been successfully resisted.

Although individual Chinese organizations may similarly pursue vertical integration at the enterprise level, the evidence of our sample suggests that such behavior has been much less apparent than in the Soviet Union.

Let us turn to (5): the difficulty in using financial criteria of performance that arises from the payment of differing prices, depending upon the supplier, for an identical input. I do not stress the fact that this Chinese disadvantage has offsets; rather, my emphasis is upon the Soviet situation being already so bad that one wonders if comparisons by supervisors can be made significantly more difficult. The rigidity of Soviet prices makes them so unrepresentative of social opportunity cost that I doubt whether it really matters whether there is minor worsening of the basis for financial comparisons among enterprises and periods.

Counterbalancing the five Chinese disadvantages in efficient economic coordination, there are three advantages.

(1) The first has already been discussed: the lesser degree to which Chinese enterprises suffer from physical bottlenecks in needed supply. The difference arises from the substantially greater independence of Chinese enterprises, not only from allocations of materials and fuels by the Center, but also from allocations set by any other authority.

(2) I would hypothesize that Chinese principals and planners obtain less distorted information from enterprises than do Soviet planners. This is because of the very different role of plan fulfillment in determining rewards for industrial employees in the two countries.

In the Soviet Union, the total average wage packet of managers and of total personnel depends heavily upon the degree of plan fulfillment of their enterprise. Failure to meet plans is not uncommon and is penalized particularly sharply. Thus personnel at the enterprise level are strongly motivated to hide from superiors their actual plant capacity, as well as to understate their productivity in transforming materials and labor into final product. Their interest is best served by providing information that results in as modest a plan as possible.

In our Chinese sample, such motivation seems to have been so reduced as to be of another order of magnitude. Statistical analysis provides no indication that the degree of fulfillment of the two most important plan indicators (value of output and profits) had any consequence for rewards.[9] In theory, only failure to fulfill plans was supposed to have an effect on bonuses, and such effect was intended to be quite minor. In practice, enterprise plans were set sufficiently modestly so that there was little danger of underfulfilling them.

(3) Soviet state industry is ridden with suboptimizing behavior, arising from the effort of enterprises to perform well according to criteria that are measurable in the short run. The targets (plans) for such criteria are set at a level that is difficult to meet; yet for the enterprise, much is riding on such success. Central objectives whose fulfillment cannot be quantifiably measured in the short run do not enter significantly into the reward function. This incentive system has led, over a very long time period, to well-recognized poor performance along

two major dimensions: (1) the introduction of new products and new production technology, and (2) the quality of products. Central authorities have tried to place much greater emphasis upon these success criteria. Despite constant efforts, however, they have been unable to devise schemes which would motivate enterprises to respect such higher relative importance.

I would hypothesize that Chinese state industry suffers much less from such behavior. This is because the plans established for measurable criteria are moderate and easy to meet, and because there is little or no reward for surpassing such targets. Thus there is no particular reason for Chinese enterprises to suboptimize rather than attempt to meet the objectives of their principals.

Of course, the system of multiple principals can lead to behavior (such as regional protectionism) which frustrates maximization of national social welfare. This is a matter that we have discussed above. But it has nothing to do with suboptimization, which relates exclusively to the behavior of an agent vis-à-vis its principal. The key argument of this study is that lower level regional governments in China are not agents of the Center.

DYNAMIC EFFICIENCY

The balance of static efficiency in allocation of factors and products is uncertain, but it was likely to have been to the advantage of the Soviet Union prior to the freeing of Chinese marginal industrial prices in 1984–85. There is, however, a vital facet of dynamic efficiency which favors the Chinese system. This feature is the ability to switch from a system of detailed planning to that of a market economy in which money becomes a fungible means of payment for state enterprises that need not be accompanied by physical allocations in order to be used to purchase inputs. Since the adoption of the new Gorbachev policy of 1987, a substantial change of this nature has been a fundamental objective of the central leadership in both countries.

The Chinese advantage stems precisely from the pattern of multiple principals, which we have seen creates difficulties in the attainment of static efficiency through physical planning. Due to the existence of multiple principals, whatever genuinely national physical coordination of production that may have been present earlier seems to have disappeared before the 1970s. Thus even the first hesitant moves to a market system in China in the early 1980s did not have to combat a living tradition of such coordination. In contrast, efforts to implement national physical planning are still omnipresent in the Soviet Union.

Furthermore, regional principals in China have had a strong

material interest in proceeding to a system of market coordination. Prior to this, the only mechanism available to them to reduce the costs of regional autarchy was barter. The creation of a national market system provided a supplementary means with substantially lower transaction costs. Local governments could gain significantly from the use of this additional mechanism, and this would resound to the credit and power position of the upper officials of such governments (these officials should be regarded as middle level from the standpoint of China as a whole).

Thus, one would think that monetization of the state sector must have had substantial support among middle-level state and Party bureaucrats throughout China. This constituency was presumably a powerful force for marketization during the 1980s. In contrast, discussions of the monetizing reform process in the Soviet Union have placed emphasis upon the personal interest of the counterpart of these personnel in retaining the status quo. This, it has been argued, is due to the high psychological costs to Soviet middle-level bureaucrats of learning to operate in a new environment, combined with the absence of benefits specifically directed toward them. Psychological costs must have been lower for Chinese bureaucrats because planning had never been so omnipresent and thus they were accustomed to unplanned trade, although of an inefficient form; moreover, and of greater importance, there were personal benefits that were potentially significant.

The System of Multiple Prices

The system of multiple prices has served since late 1984 as a major instrument of marketization in the Chinese state sector. Although this period transcends that for which substantial information is available from our sample enterprises, it would seem that virtually all state enterprises must have bought their marginal material inputs other than electricity and water at market prices and sold their marginal output similarly. Relevant differences among medium-sized and large enterprises of any single sector have probably related only to the proportion of the quantities of inputs and outputs for which prices were subject to these marginal conditions, rather than to the pertinence of such market prices to the individual enterprise.

Chinese reformers have been divided as to the value in attempting to bring decentralization down from the level of regional governments to that of the individual state enterprise. The most vigorous marketeers have wished to create a system in which state enterprises would themselves be independent principals, maximizing their own profits or at least the difference between their gross monetary revenues and their nonwage costs. To these reformers, the main economic problem in the middle 1980s was diffusion of the power to manage the enterprise; they viewed "ownership reform" as being the priority task.[10]

This group supported the system of multiple prices on the ground that it would permit the market system to perform its function. At least as of 1986, they felt that there was no immediate need for any further change in the pricing system. In contrast, the main opposing camp of reformers seems to have been much less interested in changing the ownership system of state enterprises, and they also rejected the existing system of multiple prices.[11]

The contrasting attitudes of these two wings of the reform movement toward the expropriation of the property rights of regional principals over state enterprises appears to be in contradiction to their approaches with regard to the multi-price system. I would expect the multi-price system to become much less effective in realizing allocative efficiency if investment decisions were made by enterprises rather than by principals. At least this should be the case when objectives are financial, as all reformers have wished them to be. The same expectation, phrased differently, is that the multi-price system can be effective in reaching allocative efficiency only so long as investment decisions are made by regional principals rather than by the enterprises.

ANALYSIS

The ceteris paribus of the following analysis is threefold:

1. There is the continuation of the existing system of deliveries of a portion of the production of enterprises to one or another state organ, with counterpart allocation of part of the input requirements for materials and fuels. A system of multiple prices, with the lower prices applying to such planned outputs and inputs, requires such continuation. For symmetry, so as to concentrate our attention on the effect of the price system, we should make the same assumption in examining the working of a single-price system.
2. The rates and form of taxation are the same under both systems. Such taxation, however, need not be that currently predominant in the Chinese state sector.
3. The degree of monopoly power exercised in individual regional markets is the same under both systems. This amounts to assuming that, even if regional principals lose their powers to control enterprises, they will continue the same degree of protectionism which they would otherwise provide. This

might occur because of the allocation of a portion of taxes to the region in which the goods are produced and because of the favorable direct effects of such protectionism on regional state employment (which has relatively high average income).

When we limit our attention to noninvestment decisions, the multiple-pricing system should be a reasonable substitute for a single-price system in which the price is set on the marketplace. This is so regardless of the degree of enterprise autonomy in decision making. The reason is that, in both systems of decision making, marginal revenue and marginal cost are functions only of the market-determined price, provided that there is no binding cash (borrowing) constraint. Enterprises can legally barter or sell inputs that they are allocated at less than the market price. Thus an optimizing management, under standard assumptions, will set its relative use of inputs at the point where the isoquant for a given product is tangent to that price vector whose elements are exclusively market prices. Similarly, its choice of the quantity of output is based on the same price vector. Fixed prices affect input-combination and output decisions only to the degree that a cash constraint is binding. Since allocation decisions relate to exchange at fixed prices, they can be interpreted as constituting lump-sum transfers; they affect only corner solutions. (See eq. [4.2] and the accompanying discussion.)

The situation, however, is different with respect to investment decisions. Here the enterprise's optimizing choice, even for a problem that has an internal solution, will depend upon its estimate of the effect of the proposed investment upon future administrative decisions to be made by planning authorities. This is because such future administrative decisions, interpreted as lump-sum transfers, may have a major effect upon the profitability of the investment. For example, if an enterprise's management were to believe that an expansion in its capacity would lead to a growth in the absolute volume of its products that are allocated, and that the negative financial effect of such increased allocation would not be fully offset by an increase in the input allocations that it receives, then it might choose not to make the necessary investment at all.[12] With the enterprise determining investment, even without any binding constraint as to the availability of funds, the decision would include among its arguments those fixed prices that are relevant for allocations of both products and inputs. Quite aside from its effect upon the uncertainty of the enterprise decision maker, a multiple-price system will generate nonoptimal investment choices.

This conclusion, however, does not apply when the investment decision is made by the principal of the enterprise. Here there are two distinct cases. The first is the one in which the principal exercises only financial property rights, but not those of allocation, and in which it itself, together with the agent-enterprise, provides the needed investment funds. In this situation, our sample data indicate that it is reasonable to assume that there will be no future reaction to new investment by the other principal that exercises the right to physical allocation. Thus the financial principal's interior optimizing solution is a function only of the prices set on the marketplace and not of the fixed prices as well.

The second case is where there is a single principal exercising control over the agent-enterprise. If this principal chooses to expand product allocation as a result of increased capacity, then the financial returns on its investment will be a function of the fixed price as well as of the market-determined price of the product. But since the principal is not constrained to make this allocation choice, its investment decision should be founded on a calculation that is based only on the higher, market-determined prices for both inputs and output. Once the additional capacity is in place, the principal can determine the appropriate increase in allocation by equating its own marginal utility from such supplementary product allocation to the opportunity cost to it of foregone financial revenue.

I had considered that the waters might be muddied by the fact that bank loans finance a significant portion of the investments of state enterprises. Such muddying could follow from the assumption that, in evaluating a loan request, banks are concerned with the security of the proposed loan and thus with the expected statistical distribution of the purely financial return from the investment being financed.

However, it is frequent (although far from universal) that both the interest and repayment of principal on bank loans are financed from a variety of sources. Incremental income earned as a result of the investment is only one of these; in the case of the two enterprises for which we have such a division, it constituted no more than one-third to one-half. Repayment from amortization allowances for the new investment was the second source, despite the fact that only about half of such amortization would have been kept by the enterprise. The third major source is the sales tax paid on the products produced from the new investment; this constituted one-half and one-third, respectively, for the two enterprises. The determination as to whether amortization allowances will be available for repayment seems to be made by the principal of the borrowing enterprise, but it is possible that the decision with regard to sales tax is frequently or even generally made by national authorities.

Curiously, there was no mention in the interviews that the flow of total profits earned by the enterprise, let alone the enterprise's assets, could have constituted security for the payment of interest and principal if all else failed. Indeed one enterprise, for whom the repayment schedule of one investment loan had had to be renegotiated, was shortly afterward readily granted substantial new bank loans for investment purposes, one of these loans being from the same bank that had made the loan that was still overdue. It was specifically noted in the interviews that both of the lending banks involved considered only the investment in question, ignoring the total financial capability of the enterprise.

The significance of the above facts is that a bank loan for investment purposes is granted, de facto, to the principal of the enterprise concerned. For it is this principal that will determine what funds will be made available for repayment and interest. It can refuse to permit the use of sales tax or amortization revenues. On the other hand, if total funds generated by the investment are insufficient, it can make available "special funds." When renegotiation of one loan agreement in our sample occurred, it was not because of the financial position of the investment or of the enterprise; rather, it was because the principal was encountering declining revenue and believed that it should not sacrifice the combination of profit revenue, sales tax revenue, and amortization revenue that was called for by the agreement. Of greatest interest was the process of negotiation in this matter between the bank, the enterprise, and the principal. In at least this city, it was the principal (the municipality itself) that was empowered to give the final verdict. Indeed, the interviews convey the impression that none of the lending banks were really major players in the decisions as to bank financing of specific investments. It is this above all that allows us to ignore the position of banks in making loans under a multiple-price system.

We can conclude that, given the current Chinese environment in which a state enterprise is an agent (whether it be of one or of several principals), a multiple-price system should have all the favorable allocation effects that pertain to a market-determined single price. However, if state enterprises should be transformed into profit-maximizing principals, a multi-price system would be much less satisfactory.[13]

THE ISSUE OF SECOND BEST

In the evaluation of multiple prices, it has been assumed that market pricing of products and of material inputs improves allocative efficiency. This assumption immediately raises the welfare problem of what happens when one source of inefficiency is removed but others remain; will the overall situation improve? In general, there is no reason to believe that it will.[14]

I have nothing particular to say as to the effect of monopoly conditions on the markets either for products or for material inputs, fed as they both are by regional protectionism and by lack of economic development. The same is true with regard to externalities. All of these involve market failures that are not improved by a switch to the system of multiple prices. Such failures are similar in kind to those observed in capitalist economies.

On the other hand, something can be said as to factor markets. One should consider the joint effect of the requirement that enterprises employ a designated number of persons as permanent state workers, and of the fact that nonprofit-maximizing incentives exist for regional authorities and for the enterprises themselves to expand the number of other workers directly and indirectly employed. It seems safe to hold that this effect is that the marginal value of the product of labor typically falls below the wage. Yet this very situation makes it likely that the size of the labor force does not normally change in response to marginal changes in projected output. Thus both marginal wage costs and marginal value of the product of labor are quite low. I would consider a model in which both are equal to zero in the medium-size and large state enterprise as being exaggerated, but as nevertheless capturing the essence of the situation in the labor market. To the extent that this is true, imperfections in the labor market can be treated as constituting lump-sum transfers to the employed workers; they do not interfere with optimality in the marginal conditions.

Is capital seriously underpriced at the margin? There is no question that it has been for the enterprise, even well before the major increase in inflation that began in 1985. This was partly due to the low rates of interest charged on loans, but even more to the fact that the sum borrowed could to a considerable degree be repaid out of depreciation allowances, profits, and even sales tax which would otherwise have been paid to one or another level of government. But if we view investment decisions as being made by the enterprise's principal and consider that this principal had to invest its own funds, then the marginal opportunity cost of capital to the party making the investment decisions may have been fairly appropriate to the situation. This is particularly the case if we posit, as seems reasonable, that individual principals have normally functioned with access to a fairly fixed volume of total bank loans.[15] Given the property rights of principals, one might then consider the marginal conditions to be reasonably satisfied in the capital market.

What can be said as to the market for land, often required for expansion of the enterprise and of its housing? In terms solely of the financial payment, generally made to rural communities, land is very cheap.[16] But, at least in our sample, the bulk of the real cost to the purchaser consists of a guarantee of jobs in the state-owned enterprise. Given the limits imposed on hirings, together with the demand for these jobs, the opportunity cost of such land is substantial, both to the principal and to the enterprise itself.

In short, if we measure the price of factor inputs in terms of money costs, they depart sharply from the optimum marginal conditions. However, when the measurement is in terms of all aspects of marginal opportunity cost to the principal, it is not at all clear that the deviations are substantial.

I conclude from the above that, while the quantitative dimensions of the second-best problem must be greater in China than is generally the case in developed capitalist market economies, this is due more to a combination of regional protectionism and of shortage of transport, leading to monopoly pricing of products, than because of the situation that exists in the factor markets. The probability that static efficiency is improved by an expansion of the degree to which prices, on the margin, represent market conditions seems to be within the same broad range in China as in capitalist economies. This is not to deny that the expected value of this probability is lower in China than in capitalist economies.

Regional Property Rights

The system of multiple principals, with property rights belonging to regional levels of government, is a fundamental characteristic of contemporary Chinese society but not of the Soviet or East European centrally planned economies. What can be said as to the appropriateness of this system?

The economic advantages and disadvantages have already been discussed in this chapter. To summarize, the economic advantages are twofold:

1. Greater dynamic efficiency in the sense of making it easier to shift to a market economy for the state sector. This is due to the creation of a substantial constituency for such a shift among middle-level state and Party bureaucrats.
2. Greater static allocative efficiency than would occur under conditions of a multiple-price system in which investment decisions were taken by the enterprise. At the same time, much greater decentralization is attained than if the state sector had only a single principal.

The existence of multiple principals has permitted China effectively to engage in a form of partial price reform that has not been used in the other socialist countries and that has the advantage of not requiring introduction on an all-or-nothing basis. Both of these are advantages of transition, rather than of a steady state.

The economic disadvantages, in contrast, relate solely to static efficiency; they occur regardless of the degree of marketization. The main two are:

1. The promotion of regional autarchy, due to different products having differential profitability (at allocation prices) and being subject to varying sales tax rates.
2. The lack of coordination that arises from the existence of multiple supervising principals for a single enterprise.

A potential major political gain from this system is pluralism. The division of economic power among regions may lead to division of political power as well. Individuals might be offered greater choice as a result of differences in the behavior of individual regional principals, both from one another and from that of the central government. Political stability would be promoted through the unlikelihood that a switch in central policy alone could determine fundamental and drastic national political change.

It seems to be taken as an article of faith by some political scientists that pluralism in political power follows from pluralism in the economy. If this assumption is correct, then certainly this potential political improvement is the most important product of the system of multiple principals. Unfortunately, China as yet gives no evidence of political pluralism. (This sentence was written prior to the events of June 1989. These events provide considerable corroboration.) In saying this, however, we should remember that the system of multiple principals may have a history that is no longer than two decades. This, it might be argued, is too short a time to overcome the lags between economic and resulting political change.

Appendix: The Chinese Incentive System in State Industry

This brief theoretic appendix, which continues the efficiency evaluations of the text of the chapter, is directed exclusively to economists.

The Chinese and Soviet incentive systems for personnel in state-owned enterprises appear to be similar in that there are significant monetary rewards attached to the success of the individual enterprise as a whole, but little incentive for superior performance by the individual or small group.[17] Where the two systems differ is in the procedure by which enterprise success is measured. Evaluation in the Soviet Union is according to the degree of fulfillment of annual plans, using for this purpose only standards that are quantifiable. Enterprise personnel know beforehand the criteria that will be used, the base level for each of them, and usually their relative weights. In China, on the other hand, evaluation (judging particularly by the evidence of the sample) appears to be subjective and ex post.

Using a principal-agent model for both countries, with the principal determining the incentive system that applies to the personnel of the enterprise-agent, one can model the difference between the two systems as follows:

(8A.1) The Soviet incentive system for enterprise n:
Maximize: $U_{n,t}([\tau_n \div \bar{\tau}_n]_t)$

Subject to: $[\zeta_n \ \phi_n]_t$ leads, with low probabilities ε_ζ and ε_ϕ, to a penalty when any element of either ζ_n or $\phi_n <$ the corresponding element of γ. (γ constitutes a vector of values resulting from standardizing the mean.) ζ and ϕ are nonquantifiable variables, but are subject to being observed with regard to whether their individual elements lie in the set of $(<\gamma)$ or of $(\geq\gamma)$, which together constitute the domain of all possible values.

The Chinese incentive system for enterprise n:
Maximize: $U_{n,t}(\tau_n, [\tau_n \div \bar{\tau}_n], \zeta_n, \phi_n)$, where ζ, ϕ are nonquantifiable and often nonobservable variables, and where the weights of the different arguments are not specified.

Subject to: each element of $(\tau_n \div \bar{\tau}_n) \geq 1$.

$U_{n,t}$ is a function of the direct arguments of various types of reward, which in turn are functions of the diverse criteria of success set forth by the principal. Thus these success criteria are indirect arguments in $U_{n,t}$.

Vector $(\tau_n \div \bar{\tau}_n)$ is composed of the elements, for enterprise n, of performance divided by plan with respect to each of the criteria that are quantifiable and subject to continuous rather than discrete measurement, and are also evaluated as being of particular importance as aspects of success. The elements of vector $(\tau_n \div \bar{\tau}_n)$ are $([\tau \div \bar{\tau}]_{n,1}, [\tau \div \bar{\tau}]_{n,2}, [\tau \div \bar{\tau}]_{n,\ldots})$.

Vector $(\boldsymbol{\tau}_n \div \tilde{\boldsymbol{\tau}}_n) = (I\tilde{\tau}_n')^{-1}\tau_n I$, where I = the identity matrix.

Vector $\boldsymbol{\tau}_n$ is composed of the elements of performance for those criteria that are quantifiable and subject to continuous measurement.

Vector $[\boldsymbol{\zeta}_n, \boldsymbol{\phi}_n]$ is similarly composed of criteria evaluated as important elements of success. Its elements, however, are nonquantifiable variables which may also be nonobservable.

In the case of Soviet industry, the two most important of the constraint variables $(\boldsymbol{\zeta}, \boldsymbol{\phi})$ have been the success of the enterprise in introducing new products and new technology into production in a timely fashion and the achievement of high-quality products. Notwithstanding efforts at quantifying measures of quality and of meeting, out of the state budget, the opportunity costs to the enterprise of introducing new products, it has so far proven impossible for the Soviet principal (the state) to deal successfully in these ways with these variables. Because of this failure, it has not been possible to introduce them into the vector $(\boldsymbol{\tau}_n \div \tilde{\boldsymbol{\tau}}_n)$, which is to be maximized. Nor has it seemed desirable to eliminate them entirely as indirect arguments in the combined utility function and constraint of the enterprise, where such arguments consist of all those aspects of performance that have a direct effect upon reward.

The Soviet principal has clearly regarded these tasks, for which degree of fulfillment cannot be continuously measured, as of considerable consequence. Despite this, there has been reluctance to weight them heavily in the determination of rewards given to the enterprise. This reluctance is due to the measurement problem. The question of whether performance by the agent has been satisfactory in period (t) must rest upon a subjective evaluation in ($t + i$) by the principal. The entire philosophy of Soviet incentives has been opposed to the use of such variables.

Yet it is essential that these tasks be incorporated in some fashion into the agent's utility function. The very uneasy Soviet compromise is to treat them as constraints for which there exist finite but low probabilities of negative action being taken by the principal if they are violated. Unfortunately, this form of inclusion has not been sufficient to cause agents to pay much attention to these tasks, and agents have instead concentrated upon maximizing the measurable $(\boldsymbol{\tau}_n \div \tilde{\boldsymbol{\tau}}_n)$ vector.

Apparently, Chinese principals have been more fearful than has the Soviet state of the ill effects of enterprises concentrating upon $(\boldsymbol{\tau}_n, [\boldsymbol{\tau}_n \div \tilde{\boldsymbol{\tau}}_n])$. Either that, or in choosing their system of evaluation they

have given considerable weight to the issue of "fairness" among enterprises. On these grounds, they appear to have been willing to sacrifice the incentive advantages of having personnel know ahead of
time the weighted combination of criteria by which their enterprise
will be judged.

I would expect enterprise personnel to respond with less effort to the Chinese than to the Soviet type of incentive system. On
the other hand, the Soviet system induces behavior on the part of the
enterprise that is seriously suboptimal from the standpoint of the
principal. Compared with the Soviet system, the Chinese sacrifices
X-efficiency in return for greater allocative efficiency. Unfortunately, I
have no basis for estimating the terms of the tradeoff and thus for
offering a view as to whether the Chinese system is the more appropriate for Chinese conditions.

NOTES

Some of the works frequently cited in the notes and references have been identified by the following abbreviations:

B.B.I.	Berichte des Bundesinstituts für ostwissenschaftliche und internationale Studien, Köln
B.R.	Beijing Review
C.D.S.P.	Current Digest of the Soviet Press
C.Q.	China Quarterly
J.C.E.	Journal of Comparative Economics
JEC	U.S. Congress. Joint Economic Committee
JPRS-CEA	U.S. Government. Joint Publication Research Service. China Report. Economic Affairs
Narkhoz SSSR	TSSU pri Sovete Ministrov SSSR, Narodnoe khoziaistvo v . . .
TSSU SSSR	Tsentral'noe Statisticheskoe Upravlenie SSSR

Chapter 1

1. Back in 1976, Ben Ward wrote the following: "I know of no substantial evidence with which to refute the claim that the Chinese planning system works, at both national and provincial levels, in ways essentially similar to socialist counterparts elsewhere. But I am aware of very little evidence of any kind on this topic. . . . This gap in the argument renders the conclusion more speculative than even the student of other Soviet-type economies feels comfortable with" ("The Chinese Approach to Economic Development," in Dernberger [1980], 94–95).

2. JEC (1986), 123, 532–35. Wu Jinglian and Zhao Renwei, "The Dual Pricing System in China's Industry," J.C.E. 11, no. 3 (September 1987):312.

3. By the end of 1986, three-quarters of all small state-owned commercial enterprises had been converted in one or the other of these ways (State Statistical Bureau, in B.R. 30, no. 9 [2 March 1987]:24). For a discussion of such leasing practice in state-owned industrial enterprises, where the extent of such conversion has been considerably less, see Yue Haitao, in B.R. 30, no. 27 (6 July 1987):24–27.

4. Yue Haitao, in B.R. 30, no. 27 (6 July 1987):27.

5. Lu Dong, minister in charge of the State Economic Council, is responsible for the first figure (B.R. 30, no. 30 [27 July 1987]:8). The second

figure is cited in an article by Zhang Zeyu, in *B.R.* 30, no. 34 (24 August 1987):4.

6. Shareholding is a major form of this, but has apparently had only very limited success in achieving such separation. See the article by the Investigation and Research Group of the State Commission for Economic Reconstruction, in *B.R.* 30, no. 40 (5 October 1987):22–24.

7. See Ta-kuang Chang, "The Making of the Chinese Bankruptcy Law," *Harvard International Law* 28, no. 2 (Spring 1987):333–72, and especially 356–57 and 369. It should be noted that contract workers still constituted only 5 per cent of all workers in Chinese state-owned enterprises as of the end of 1986, although this represented an increase from 4 per cent at the end of 1985 (State Statistical Bureau, *B.R.* 30, no. 9 [2 March 1987]:26, and *Renmin Ribao* [21 January 1987], as reported by Yun-Wing Sung and Thomas M. H. Chan, "China's Economic Reforms: The Debates in China," *Australian Journal of Chinese Affairs* 17 [January 1987]:49).

8. The great expansion of bonus payments, with substantial inflationary effects, occurred in 1984 prior to the introduction of the new regulations. One Western expert has described the Chinese situation in 1986 as being that in which all but the most poorly run state enterprises usually pay the full four-month bonus that is exempt from taxation, while virtually none pay bonuses above this level (Andrew G. Walder, "Wage Reform and the Web of Factory Interests," *C.Q.* 109 [March 1987]:355).

Hungarian control over bonus payments shifted to formal dependence on taxation around 1970 in the same fashion that the Chinese control shifted in 1984. The effect of this Hungarian change seems to have been miniscule.

9. Furthermore, it was announced in early 1986 that slowing the economy and consolidating past reforms, rather than moving onward, would be the key goals for the year. In 1987, political disagreement among the Party leaders, if nothing else, effectively prevented further reform. The keynote address by Zhao Ziyang to the national Party Congress in October 1987 emphasized both the importance of continuing economic reforms and the gradualness of the process (see his speech in *B.R.* 30, No. 45 [15 November 1987]: i–xxvii).

10. Rock Creek Research, Inc., *1987 China Statistical Handbook* (Washington, D.C.:1987), 1. Comparison is of net material product measured in current prices and in constant 1980 prices.

11. A particularly interesting one is a description of the Beijing No. 1 Machine Tool Plant in 1961. The case study was sponsored by the vice premier responsible for economic work within the Communist Party's Central Committee, and the materials were made available at the time only to high officials. It was published in 1980. (Ma Hong and others, in Xiaoyu [1980]).

12. The most appropriate data source to use as a base of comparison is that described in Granick (1976). Other useful case studies have been done on Yugoslav, Hungarian, and Polish enterprises.

13. *Statistical Yearbook of China 1983*, 220, 238. Each industry's size classification is defined differently in the Chinese statistics; not unreasonably, it

seems intended to serve as a relative classification only. For some classifications, see Christine Wong, "Ownership and Control in Chinese Industry," in
JEC (1986), 601. A detailed breakdown of the size of the category in 1984,
treating each industrial subsector separately, is presented in *Statistical Yearbook of China 1986*, 275–82; see also 744–45.

The only uniform classification system of which I am aware was intended to classify state-owned industrial enterprises for applicability of the
law shifting from profit sharing to taxation; for this purpose, "small" enterprises were defined as those with both fixed assets of less than 1.5 million
renminbi and annual profits of less than 0.2 million renminbi (Statement of
the Finance Minister in U.S., *Foreign Broadcasting Information Services* 1,
no. 086 [3 May 1983]: K11).

14. *Zhongguo Gongye Jingji Tongji Ziliao 1987* (1987, 142).

15. Calculated from *Statistical Yearbook of China 1986*, 142–43, and
from *Zhongguo Gongye 1987* (1987, 142–43).

16. Taking the ratio of large to medium industrial enterprises in 1986
to be 100, the ratio in 1982 for the number of enterprises was 96, while the
ratios for output, fixed assets, and (profits + taxes) were between 89 and 92
(*Zhongguo Gongye 1987* 1987, 37).

17. Ibid., 142. For the sample enterprises, only those personnel are
counted who were considered state employees or collective employees filling
positions within the state enterprise proper. A number of these enterprises
would be much larger if employees of collective enterprises which were fully
dependent on the state enterprise were also included. I presume that the
same definition is used in the description of the population, but no explicit
statement in this regard is made in the source.

18. Of the twenty organizations in the sample, 2 had over 55,000 employees each in 1982; 2 had 20,000–55,000; 3 were between 9,500 and 13,000
in size; and 3 were 6,000–7,000. But 6 employed between 2,300 and 5,000 personnel; 2 employed 1,500 to 2,000; and 2 employed between 400 and 700.

19. Here, and throughout the book, the province-level municipalities
of Beijing, Shanghai, and Tianjin will be classified as provinces rather than as
municipalities.

20. Temporary workers are included. For national date, see *Statistical
Yearbook of China 1983*, 490.

21. The years of transition were 1979 and 1980.

22. *Zhongguo Gongye 1987* (1987, 142–43); *Zhongguo Tongji Nianjian
1988* (1988, 194).

23. It is much better to use the median figure for the sample rather
than the mean (unweighted) because the latter is heavily affected by a single
enterprise which, as of 1978, had undergone fairly recent major expansion of
both capital and labor that had not yet been reflected in output expansion.

It would be preferable to measure capital productivity in terms of productive capital alone, particularly since investment by enterprises in housing
has been substantial during these years. High capital productivity in year (t)
may lead to substantial housing construction in ($t+1$). This might well lead to
capital productivity in 1982 being no better than in 1978, despite the fact that

the situation would look very different without such an investment pattern. Indeed, if we measure capital productivity by gross output in 1970 prices divided by the original value of fixed capital in production facilities alone, the median annual rate of change for our sample enterprises is +1.5 per cent, as opposed to the −0.1 per cent calculated when using the definition in table 1.3.

Unfortunately, no data are available for all Chinese state industry that would permit calculation of the preferred measure of capital. The estimates of Kuan Chen et al., "New Estimates of Fixed Investment and Capital Stock for Chinese State Industry," *C.Q.* 114 [June 1988], combine the reevaluation of stock figures with the elimination of housing. The resulting stock data are not comparable with the data available for the sample enterprises.

24. However, an unstated number of the seventeen enterprises within the county organization in the sample did suffer losses.

25. Yan Kalin, in *B.R.* 28, no. 10 (11 March 1985), 25; *JPRS-CEA-85-048* (23 May 1985), 103 (the original source is Gong Zongwen, in *Caizheng* 3 [8 March 1985]:7–8); and *JPRS-CEA-85-048,* 128–33 (circular of the State Economic Commission and the Ministry of Finance, from *Jingji Ribao* [22 April 1985]:2). Profits earned are from *Statistical Yearbook of China 1984,* 262. The *Beijing Review* article seems the least reliable, but its figures of losses for 1983 are the same as those given in the better source.

26. However, a substantial portion of losses was due to the interaction of state pricing policy and the product specialization of the enterprise. This was officially described as accounting for 40 per cent of all losses by state-owned industrial and commercial enterprises in 1983 and for 60 per cent in 1984 (*JPRS-CEA-85-048* [23 May 1985], 129). It is difficult to judge whether this product-mix effect bore particularly heavily on the smaller enterprises.

27. *Zhongguo Gongye 1987* (1987, 144). State-owned enterprises constituted 94 per cent of the total. It is true that the ratio of enterprises either suffering losses or earning profits of less than ¥10,000 in 1986 was 63 per cent as high among large and medium industrial enterprises as among all industrial enterprises in China (141–42). However, four-fifths of all Chinese industrial enterprises were collectively rather than state owned, so this ratio may not be representative of the ratio to state-owned industrial enterprises alone.

28. The criterion used by the Chinese in choosing "key enterprises" is unclear. One such enterprise in our sample is one of the two smallest of the nineteen enterprises.

29. However, informants in a fourth small enterprise in the sample said that theirs was also a winner and that there were twelve winners nationally.

30. The enterprises were selected by the Chinese, although I do not know which Chinese organizational body made the decision. The criterion of reform was used because the Chinese researchers hoped to learn something from the study as to the advantages and disadvantages of different variations of reform.

It should be noted that the terms "reform" and "experimental" have been given a broad definition in Chinese usage. As of early to mid-1980, there were already 6,600 experimental industrial enterprises. Although they constituted only 16 per cent of all state enterprises, they produced 60 per cent of gross output and earned 70 per cent of the profits of the state industrial sector (Remyga 1982, 103, 163; Barry Naughton, "False Starts and Second Wind," in Perry and Wong [1985], 230). From these figures, one can see that they must have constituted a large proportion of the enterprises within the large and medium-sized subsector of state industry.

31. But note that the inverse relation may be caused by a misspecification of the relevant implicit regression equation. The standard against which relative success was judged (in order to derive the null-hypothesis prediction of the number of sample successes) assumed that the percentage of national quality awards won by the sample enterprises depended only on their share of the national labor force working in all large and medium state-owned industrial enterprises. One might argue that the sample's share of the total number of such enterprises should be included as a second independent variable in the implicit regression equation. Thirty-seven per cent of the sample enterprises did win these quality awards.

32. This conclusion is supported by a comparison of data for nine of the sample enterprises with the subpopulation of all medium and large industrial enterprises, both in 1986. Using various performance ratios, only 2 to 3 of the 9 sample enterprises did worse than the average of the population, and between 1 and 5 did twice as well. A further test is made for the subindustry of textiles (excluding dyeing, silk, and knitting). Here, data in 1986 are available for 3 sample enterprises, and these have been compared with a sample of 181 enterprises from the total population. Two out of the 3 textile enterprises did better in terms of a profit ration, 1 of these 3 having a ratio three times as high as the average (*Zhongguo Gongye 1987* 1987, 142–43, 166–81; *Zhongguo Tongji 1988* 1988, 412; *Zhongguo Gangtie & Gongye Nianjian 1987* 1987, 533–34).

33. William Byrd et al., "Recent Chinese Economic Reforms: Studies of Two Industrial Enterprises," *World Bank Staff Working Paper* no. 652 (1984), App. A and B, and W. A. Byrd, "The Shenyang Smelter: A Case Study of Problems and Reforms in China's Nonferrous Metals Industry," *World Bank Staff Working Paper* no. 766 (1985), stat. app.

Chapter 2

1. If decisions are instead viewed as arising out of a process of negotiation, then they cannot in general be treated as stemming from some "composite" social welfare function. This is Arrow's impossibility theorem (see Arrow 1951).

2. Normally, the principal-agent analytic model is used to handle problems of the possession by the agent of private information which the principal can obtain only at prohibitively high transaction costs. The existence of such private information is not, however, an intrinsic part of the model, and it is not relevant to my use of it here.

3. For a powerful argument in favor of such pluralism, see Hough (1977), chapters 4, 8, and 10.

4. For an example of such a model, see David Granick, "Institutional Innovation and Economic Management: The Soviet Incentive System, 1921 to the Present," in Guroff and Carstensen (1983), 223–57.

5. It is, in fact, the distribution of the expected responses that matter.

6. A central government principal has a number of central ministries under its hierarchical control as agents. The same applies to an individual regional principal, which makes hierarchical use of industrial bureaus and corporations. Since individuals also have ownership rights (to their jobs), they will not be treated as agents. They are, of course, also not to be considered as principals, since my usage is to restrict this term to organizations.

7. The tax analogy in capitalist systems would be the changing of the combination of tax rates and exemptions to a package that was regarded by the public as being confiscatory at a fairly low level of wealth. One might, for example, think of a combined gift/inheritance tax with only a very low lifetime exemption and, more importantly, with avoidance procedures being successfully outlawed. In the United States, the federal inheritance tax is commonly described as being voluntary. If it were to become both "compulsory" and substantially higher in rates, it would represent such a revolution.

8. I am indebted to my colleague, Peter Streufert, for this game theory interpretation.

9. See A. M. Honoré, "Ownership," in Guest (1961), 107–47, for a breakdown of ownership into its various attributes, for the idea that different attributes may be held by distinct parties, and for the concept that several parties may simultaneously exercise a particular attribute of ownership over the same good. I am indebted to my colleague, Michael R. Carter, for calling my attention to this source.

10. See Gilbert Rozman, "Social Integration," In Rozman (1981), 161–63, for a comparison of national levels of administrative centralization based on the paucity of small cities in China in the first half of the nineteenth century. Rozman describes the China of the eighteenth and nineteenth centuries as a country in which the central government acted to create and preserve a society that was held together by ideology far more than by formal organization (171).

G. William Skinner dates decentralization in Chinese government at a point earlier than that proposed by Rozman. He writes of a steady secular decline in the effectiveness of government from about the tenth century on. This, he asserts, is evidenced by a steady reduction in the coverage of the administrative governmental functions exercised at the basic level of the society. Skinner believes that this reduction almost certainly occurred because of the problem of control within the government apparatus. See his "Introduction," in Skinner (1977), 19–20.

11. Not entirely, because the ministry itself may receive aggregate profit figures from the Ministry of Finance which are inconsistent with the aggregate output figures that it receives from the State Planning Commission. Such inconsistency will then have to be passed down to the individual enterprise. But this necessity would hold irrespective of whether these restrictions applied to different functional bodies within the ministry, as they do in our

example in the text, or to a single body. The inconsistency between the sets of planning figures that the ministry itself receives can be viewed as resulting from time pressures that constrain the higher bodies.

12. The enterprises were a cement plant and a machine tool producer. The bodies in charge of top management appointments were, respectively, the province and the county where the enterprise was located.

13. Remember, as was noted in chapter 1, that Beijing, Shanghai, and Tianjin are all classified throughout this book as provinces rather than as municipalities.

14. The province or municipality was not acting as an agent of the Center, since the production quota assigned to it was less than the total capacity of its enterprises. Rather, it was an independent principal able to lay claim to the production of its agent enterprises, but one that was obliged to make specified deliveries to another principal (the Center).

15. In 1985, 38 per cent of all gross industrial output in the Soviet Union was in this category, being produced by enterprises under joint national and republic control through Union-Republic ministries (*Narkhoz SSSR* 1985, 95). However, since such output is heavily concentrated in the food industry, the proportion of value added would be substantially less.

16. Tsimerman (1984, 5–6, 36, 53–54, 61–62, 146–47). K. Kiss, "Domestic Integration of the Soviet Economy," in Hungarian Scientific Council for World Economy, *Trends in World Economy*, no. 56 (1987), 77, takes a similar position to that which I take here. After discussing the regulation both of production and of personal consumption, he writes that "The elbow room of the republic authorities is confined more or less to pricing."

17. The formal budgetary relations between the Center and the provinces during the period 1950–83 are described by Michel Oksenberg and James Tong in "The Evolution of Central-Provincial Fiscal Relations in China, 1950–1983: The Formal System" (typescript, 1987). Unfortunately, as the authors declare, the treatment is weakest for much of the 1960s and 1970s because of the paucity of textual and statistical sources for these years.

18. Kiss, "Domestic Integration," 37, 78–80. An interesting treatment (referred to by Kiss) of finance at the level of government units below the republic level is that of M. V. Vasil'eva in *Finansy SSSR*, 1984, no. 7:46–51. Among other things, she shows the stability in local budget receipts of profit payments from subordinate enterprises: 19.3 per cent in 1968 and 20.1 per cent in 1982. A very mild improvement in incentives at this level, if it exists at all, seems to date from a law passed in 1981. See also Davies (1958, 297–98, 302–4); Gallik, Jesina, and Rapawy (1968, 55); and Garvey (1977, 85–86).

19. These proportions refer to the plans as they existed at the end of the period. Samples for such data are 40 to 50 per cent larger in the number of enterprise-years covered than are those that relate output to the plan as it was originally given, and the former data are also doubtless more reliable. Furthermore, it is such data on plan fulfillment which correspond to those reported for European socialist countries and for the Soviet Union. If we took fulfillment as a ratio of the original output plans, then the figures would be 26, 18, 53, and 33 per cent, respectively.

20. Wong, "Material Allocation and Decentralization," in Perry and Wong (1985), 261. Nevertheless, one would guess that industry was somewhat less centralized then than in either 1957 or 1963 (see 260–61).

21. *JPRS-CEA-85-054* (18 June 1985), 32. The article summarized is by the Research Institute on the Work of China's Factory Directors, in *Jingji Guanli*, no. 3 (March 1985).

22. A municipality had been accustomed to call upon one of our sample enterprises to lend it technical personnel. After this enterprise was shifted from municipal to provincial supervision, it responded to such a request by loaning only "average quality" rather than "good" technicians.

23. Thomas P. Lyons (1987) writes of ownership rights of regional bodies over industrial enterprises throughout the 1958–78 period and extending beyond (236). However, while his explanation does not address the issue of the conflicting predictions of hypothesis (2.7) and alternative hypothesis (2.8), and is not completely inconsistent with (2.7), it seems to be essentially an application of (2.8). He views the underlying decision as that of the central authorities on how best to compartmentalize the planning process (chap. 7). Although he treats phenomena such as those of different regional units sacrificing potential economies of scale by investing in similar facilities in the same locality so as to satisfy their own needs for the product, he considers these examples as abuses that represent only the temporary loss of control by the central authorities (259–61).

Lyons regards the regional compartmentalization of planning as having in fact been harmful in the long run for efficiency; but, the explanation that he offers for this compartmentalization is that of poor analysis by central authorities (273–78), rather than the presence of other considerations.

A Soviet author, V. N. Remyga, supports alternative hypothesis (2.8) with two arguments. The first is that of the efficiency case in which regional compartmentalization is seen as intended to free central authorities from as much of the burden of planning as feasible. The second is based on the political reasoning that it was aimed at making local authorities responsible for raising living standards, thus diverting popular dissatisfaction from the central government (1982, 119–22, 164).

24. Eckstein (1977, 132) and Wang Haibo, "Greater Power for the Enterprises," in Wei and Chao (1982), 72.

25. Wang Haibo, in Wei and Chao (1982), 72–73. The author, at the time of publication, was a staff member of the Institute of Industrial Economics under the Chinese Academy of Social Sciences. For the transfers of enterprises at this time, see also Harding (1981, 175–82), Lardy (1978, 32–46, 90–136), and Schurmann (1968, 205–8). Schurmann is explicit that the regional authorities kept a share of above-plan production, but he was writing at a time when Chinese sources were much less explicit and reliable than they were by the 1980s.

26. This is, indeed, suggested by Wang Haibo in Wei and Chao (1982), 72. But the writing is insufficiently clear to allow one to be certain as to the author's meaning. Schurmann (1968, 207) suggests the same thing. Lee (1987, 58) points out that local authorities received substantial amounts of extra-

budgetary income in 1958. He quotes the estimate of Parris Chang, *Power and Policy in China* (1975, 58) to the effect that their extra-budgetary revenues at the beginning of the year were 20 to 30 per cent of their budgetary income. Certainly the local authorities must have had a significant degree of control over the use of these funds.

27. Wang Haibo, in Wei and Chao (1982), 74–75. In early 1962, Liu Shaoqi asserted that the central government should possess the authority to appropriate the products and profits of local enterprises, even if those enterprises were built by local government investment. Although Mao Zedong softened this statement, Liu seemed in practice to proceed along his preferred lines (Lee 1987, 82, 84).

28. Lee (1987, 75) and Cyril C. Lin, "The Reinstatement of Economics in China Today," *C.Q.* 85 (March 1981):46.

29. There were 10,533 such industrial enterprises, 13 per cent more than in 1958 (*Dangdai Zhongguo de Jingji Tizhi Gaige* 1984, 137).

30. Wong, in Perry and Wong (1985), 260. Michael Carter has pointed out to me that this slogan is very Lockian in the basis that it provides for property rights; it is a clear counterpart to John Locke's justification through the transformation of nature. It is the opposite of the usual treatment of the right to manage as an attribute of ownership (A. M. Honoré, in Guest [1961], 116–17); here, instead, ownership becomes an attribute of management.

31. For the decentralization of 1970–73, see Wang Haibo, in Wei and Chao (1982), 75–76, and Riskin (1987, 197–98). For a view that 1973 represented a critical moment for the shift in ownership rights from the Center to lower bodies, see Naughton (1986, 188–99). Naughton, "Finance and Planning Reforms in Industry," in JEC (1986), 607, points out that, beginning in 1972, counties were allowed to keep 60 per cent of the profits from newly built factories.

32. *Dangdai* (1984, 137). Xing Hua, "Changes of the Financial System during the Turbulent Decade from 1966 to 1976," in *Caizheng*, 1983, 8:22–24 and 9:8–10, gives a somewhat higher figure for the number of industrial enterprises left to the Center: 700 civilian enterprises plus military enterprises, as opposed to the "a little over five hundred" that is reported in *Dangdai*.

33. *Dangdai* (1984, 141–42). In fact, however, the Center continued to directly provision many of the regionally controlled enterprises.

34. The percentage for the mid-1970s is consistent with the application of the "4-3-3 system" that was officially introduced in 1974; namely, 40 per cent of investment was to be financed and arranged solely by the Center, 30 per cent by regional governmental bodies, and 30 per cent jointly (*Dangdai* 1984, 143).

35. *Dangdai* (1984, 138–41), and Xing Hua, "Changes of the Financial System." I am indebted to William A. Byrd, in "The Shenyang Smelter: A Case Study of Problems and Reforms in China's Nonferrous Metals Industry," *World Bank Staff Working Paper* no. 766 (1985), for the references to these two sources.

36. See also Chen Jiyuan, "Technological Renovation and the Restructuring of the Economy," *Social Sciences in China* 6, no. 2 (1985):32–33.

37. A 1967 regulation provided that enterprises under the control of local authorities were to keep their own amortization funds rather than turn them over to central authorities (see Naughton, in Perry and Wong [1985], 227, and Byrd 1983, 79). In fact, this meant that the local authorities gained control of such funds. It would seem that, sometime prior to late 1978, enterprises lost this formal right, for it was given to some experimental enterprises as part of the beginning of the reform movement (Wang Haibo, in Wei and Chao [1982], 83–84).

38. Barry Naughton, "The Decline of Central Control over Investment in Post-Mao China," in Lampton (1987), 51–79, and in Perry and Wong (1985), 223–52; William A. Byrd, "The Shenyang Smelter," 31, fn.18. See also Riskin (1987, 343).

After the passing of a law in 1979 modifying relations among different regional levels of government, a Chinese author wrote that, up until that time, administrative units of local government operated essentially under the direction of corresponding organs (whether branch or functional) at higher levels, rather than under the control of their own levels of government (Xu Chongde, in B.R. 22, no. 51 [21 December 1979], 19). To the extent that this was indeed the case, it would suggest that any financial decentralization to the subprovincial level that may have occurred in 1970 was probably more de jure than de facto.

39. Naugton, in Perry and Wong (1985), 227–28; Wong, in ibid., 256; Naughton, in Lampton (1987), 57, fn.11, and 72–73; Wang Haibo, in Wei and Chao (1982), 76; JPRS-CEA-85-048 (23 May 1985), 121 (original article is by Fu Jiaji, in Jingji Guanli, 1985, Nr. 2 [5 February], 22–26).

40. Almanac of China's Economy in 1981 (1982, 223–25, 387, 543–54); Donnithorne (1981, 4–5). Nevertheless, it should be recognized that the assurances that were given of five-year stability in the financial relations between the provinces and the Center were, de facto, seriously compromised by the requirement placed on the provinces both to buy treasury bonds and to make a special large loan in 1981 (see Audrey Donnithorne, "New Light on Central-Provincial Relations," The Australian Journal of Chinese Affairs, no. 10 [July 1983]:99–100). These requirements can be explained by the inflationary problems of the period linked to budgetary deficits of the national Treasury; the latter in turn may have been partly due to the fact that, when the financial arrangements between the provinces and the Treasury were originally made, they were intended to allot leadership over certain large enterprises to the Center so as to improve the finances of the Center through absorption of their profits and amortization allowances. As pointed out earlier, this intended recentralization did not occur (see JPRS-CEA-83-339 [16 May 1983], 48, from the article by Zhu Fulin, in Caizheng, 1983, Nr. 2 [8 February]:16–17).

This decentralization of property rights followed a political decentralization to the local level that had occurred in 1979 (see Xu Chongde, in B.R. 22, no. 51 [21 December 1979]:17–20, for a description of this Local Organic Law).

41. JPRS-CEA-84-063 (1 August 1984), 53–61. (The original article is by He Zhenji, in Jingji Yanjiu, 1985, Nr. 5 [20 May].)

42. Naughton, in Lampton (1987), 55–56, 80; and Byrd (1983, 27–28,

99). Such finance as a proportion of all fixed-capital investment in total state-owned facilities (not just industrial) rose annually, from 35 per cent in 1979 to 63 per cent by 1982. Lower percentages are presented for the capital construction portion of total fixed-capital investment, but the trend is similar (Oksenberg and Tong, "Evolution of Central-Provincial Fiscal Relations").

The same sharp increase in the share of nonbudgetary investment occurred in agriculture, but this is irrelevant for our purposes here and, furthermore, expenditures in agriculture had always represented a surprisingly small proportion of budgetary investment (Lardy 1983, 130–31, 134; Perry and Wong, in Perry and Wong [1985], 22).

43. Naughton, in Lampton (1987), 71. There are also some indications that in the middle 1980s there were transfers of enterprises from both national and provincial supervision to municipal control (Jonathan Unger, "The Struggle to Dictate China's Administration: The Conflict of Branches vs. Areas vs. Reform," *Australian Journal of Chinese Studies* 18 [July 1987]: 37, fn.33).

44. Naughton, in Lampton (1987), 52.

45. This, however, was only within the bounds of a total allocation to nonferrous metallurgy in the province. The latter was determined by the national State Planning Commission.

46. Donnithorne (1981, 4–5, 11–12, 14); Byrd (1983, 54); Wong, "Ownership and Control in Chinese Industry," in JEC (1986), 586; Wang Haibo, in Wei and Chao (1982), 75–76; and Riskin (1987, 197–98).

It should be noted that profits, regardless of whether they went to the central or local government, were part of budgetary receipts. In contrast, amortization funds were extra-budgetary. Thus, during the pre-1980 period, control of amortization funds was presumably much more significant in the eyes of local government, particularly of governments below the level of the province, than was control over profits.

47. In the case of a locomotive repair plant, the city received 30 per cent of the amortization generated, the ministry received 20 per cent, and half was retained by the enterprise itself. With regard to the enterprise in the petroleum field, the Ministry of Petroleum originally gave all of the amortization to the province. This was changed for 1979 and 1980 to 10 per cent, with 30 per cent going to the Ministry of Finance and 60 per cent retained by the enterprise. Between 1981 and 1984, the provincial receipt of amortization was reduced to zero, the Ministry of Finance continued to get 30 per cent, the Ministry of Petroleum, 20 per cent, and the enterprise was reduced to 50 per cent. These frequently changing proportions are fully consistent with the concept that the provincial share represented either a side payment or a gift.

48. Even this change is not certain. The petrochemical plants that were merged into the eighth enterprise, to be discussed in the appendix to this chapter, provided at least the bulk of their profits to the Center at a time when they had a municipality or province as their "leading body."

49. Roemer (1982) relates such exploitation particularly to endowments of human capital in addition to ownership over means of production. But the spirit of Roemer's treatment permits extension to the geographic region in which one lives, age cohort, and position within the family.

50. Farmers on state farms have always been numerically insignificant in China, although not in the Soviet Union. In 1978, which was probably a high point, Chinese state farms had a total labor force of only 5.1 million (*Statistical Yearbook of China 1985*, 287; Lardy 1983, 4).

51. The first two mechanisms are the prime ones used in developed capitalist economies; it is the latter two which are relied upon in the Soviet Union.

52. The foregone opportunity from such deliveries may be the opportunity to sell such products in private markets or to the state itself at higher than quota prices, or for the farmers to consume the products themselves. In the Soviet Union in most periods—even today when there are substantial budgetary subsidies for agriculture—all three alternative opportunities have existed. In China, sales in private markets were essentially illegal and, apparently, small from 1966 through 1978, as well as earlier during 1955–56 and from 1958 extending to either 1959 or 1961; but prices paid by the state that can be differentiated as between quota and above-quota deliveries have existed since circa 1970. In the light of the restricted level of per capita consumption of agricultural products by farm families, the last alternative of consumption in kind has always been attractive. See Perkins (1966, 14, 17, 158, 226) for private grain sales during the pre-1966 period, and Lardy (1983, 51, 91–92), both for later years and for differential state delivery prices.

53. There is, however, no extraction by the state of differential rent from land that collective farmers use for private plots. One Soviet author uses this as a major explanation for regional differences in the proportion of peasant income that comes from such plots (Afanas'evskii 1976, 119).

54. Such other natural conditions should include closeness to urban markets and land/labor ratios existing on the farms.

55. See Gray (1976, 63–72, 105–6, 294). The potential ability of Soviet planners to utilize differences between quota and above-quota prices in order to extract differential rent is indisputable. However, there are no studies to my knowledge that indicate whether such pricing is in fact so used.

Despite the absence of such positive support for the argument in the text, it should be noted that the opportunity cost to the Soviet government of failing to use the above mechanism for this purpose would have been very high. Let us first follow a traditional analysis of national policy making under Stalin, viewing it as that of trying to extract the maximum feasible surplus from agriculture for purposes of nonagricultural investment and of defense. Under these circumstances, the government should be thought of as attempting to keep all farmers at a minimum subsistence level plus any additions needed for incentive purposes. Both of these considerations are likely to have been best served through the absorption of differential rent by the state, although the analysis must depend upon assumptions as to the form of relevant incentive effects.

In the post-Stalin era, concern with equity as such should have entered with greater weight into the Soviet leaders' social welfare function. This concern should result in similar usage of the dual pricing system. The only major consideration pointing in the opposite direction might be the existence of rural outmigration under conditions where the shadow price of farm labor is significant. Soviet planners might be led by efficiency considerations to attempt to distribute voluntary outmigration among farms in such a way as to lead to improved equating of the marginal product per worker among different collective farmers. For this purpose, one would presumably wish lower average earnings to be received by farms whose marginal product per worker was lower. If we think of effort as being the same per farmer, this would entail leaving higher earnings per farmer to farms with better natural conditions (at least when we consider the labor/land ratio as constituting part of these "better conditions").

I should note that in China, throughout the history of the P.R.C., labor conditions in rural areas have been such as to render the use of differential income distribution in compensation for identical effort totally unnecessary as a means of handling the problem of undesirable rural outmigration. Although such rural outmigration has existed and been combated by the government, the objection to it has had nothing to do with its negative effects on agricultural production. Rather, it has been the negative effects on the cities which were of concern. Thus the caveat relevant to the Soviet Union does not apply to China.

56. For both, data requirements force us to concentrate upon grain crops. In view of the dominance of grain in Chinese agriculture, this is not as serious a limitation as one might at first think.

57. Walker (1984, 182) is consistent with Lardy, showing the annual average of 1977–80 as 72 per cent of that of 1953–57.

58. Louis Putterman, "The Restoration of the Peasant Household as Farm Production Unit in China," in Perry and Wong (1985), 79.

59. *Statistical Yearbook of China 1985*, 238, 255. The figure for total output is in constant prices, found by chain linking. Industrial output in rural areas is included in the output figures.

60. The tax take was estimated as constituting, in the early 1950s, some two-thirds of the former land rent in areas where cultivation had been by tenants (Eckstein 1977, 68, 323). Eckstein's supporting data suggest that, for China as a whole, the land tax in the early 1950s took some 80 per cent of the proportion of agricultural net income that had gone to rent plus tax in 1933.

61. Compare Lardy (1983, 104) with *Statistical Yearbook of China 1985*, 417.

62. Irene Wegner, "Chinas neue Agrarpolitik: Gespräche im chinesischen Wirtschaftsministerium," *B.B.I.*, 1981, Nr. 29:12. This report was based upon interviews during August 1980 in the Ministry of Agriculture.

63. The regional variation that one might expect is indicated by the rapid progress of the Green Revolution in China. By 1977, new varieties of fertilizer-responsive rice were cultivated on 80 per cent of China's rice area, as compared with 25 per cent in the rest of Asia (Lardy 1983, ix). The economic gains to be reaped from these new varieties must have differed substantially among geographic areas.

64. Calculated from Lardy (1983, 34, 104). The calculation assumes

that all state procurement consisted of quota deliveries. Since premia for above-quota deliveries to the state were not introduced nationally until 1970, this assumption is probably not too bad.

65. Terry Sicular, "Rural Marketing and Exchange in the Wake of Recent Reforms," in Perry and Wong (1985), 89, 291, calculates a statistic for 1978 which implies the stated decline if one uses the tax figures of Lardy (1983, 104) and the assumption in n.64 above for 1957. The increase in quota tonnage is based on the same assumption for 1957, and upon my own calculations for 1978, relying on the data provided in Lardy (1983, 34, 104, 108, 236).

66. Sicular, in Perry and Wong (1985), 89, 291, estimates a decline in the total of taxes plus quota deliveries of 24 per cent between 1978 and 1981. Since, as previously indicated, taxes are said to have risen between 1978 and 1984, it seems reasonable to assume that they did not fall between 1978 and 1981.

67. See Statistical Yearbook of China 1985, 254, showing a 6 per cent decline (from 85 to 80 per cent) between 1957 and 1978 in the proportion of crop area that was sown to grain. Less surprisingly, in view of the emphasis that had been placed on grain output during the period of the Cultural Revolution, the decline continued between 1978 and 1984.

68. Comparisons are made for the 1981–85 period between chemical fertilizers and chemical pesticides and the chemical industry as a whole, and for agricultural machinery in contrast to the machinery industry as a whole. All three industrial inputs into agriculture are also compared with heavy industry as a whole. All sectors relate to state industry alone (Statistical Yearbook of China, various issues). The two measures employed for the comparison are profit + sales tax as a percentage of: (1) the original value of all fixed assets, and (2) the gross value of output.

69. Roll (1974, 5–7); Perkins and Yusuf (1984, 110); Irma Adelman and David Sunding, "Economic Policy and Income Distribution in China," J.C.E. 11, no. 3 (September 1987):453, table 6; and World Bank (1985, 29).

Mark Selden, "Income Inequality and the State," in Parish (1985), 209–18, is more pessimistic about the Gini coefficient for 1979 than are the above authors about the one for 1978. He estimates a coefficient of 0.37 and, if I understand his calculations on pp. 212–13, this is an underestimate from his data because of an algebraic error. For the purposes of the conclusion in the text, however, Selden's results are not too different from those of others. Implicitly, his data raise a question as to whether the late 1970s represented any improvement in rural equality compared to 1934; certainly, this must be an exaggerated result.

70. Lardy (1983, 171, 174–75), and Statistical Yearbook of China 1981, 441. The all-China data are for 1979, taken from a sample survey of peasants in 1981.

Keith Griffin points out, quite correctly, that the standard of half the average income (50 yuan) should not be used to indicate malnutrition, since these receipts include only a portion of rural family income (1984, 17–19).

71. These three products have been the standby of Chinese consumption, the items rationed in urban areas throughout most of the history of the P.R.C.

72. Since the shift in national policy to that of regional self-sufficiency forced grain production upon micro-regions that were ill adapted for it and thus sharply depressed income levels in these areas, one might question whether it is correct to state that property rights in land were respected. I ignore this issue here on the ground that governmental respect for property rights is not usually defined as including immunity from nontax public policy changes that affect the value of these rights.

73. F. W. Mote, "Political Structure," in Rozman (1981), 74–75, and Wang (1973, 7, 61).

74. Walder (1981, 51, 182, 209–10); Andrew G. Walder, "Some Ironies of the Maoist Legacy in Industry," in Selden and Lippit (1982), 224–25.

75. It would appear that urban-rural income differentials narrowed somewhat between 1957 and 1979 when judged on a per worker basis, but widened when measured on a per capita basis (Perkins and Yusuf 1984, 125–27).

76. See Kraus (1981) and the articles by Kuhn, Schram, and Watson, in Watson (1984). These authors treat various criteria of social classification and stratification discussed and used at different times in the P.R.C. None of the criteria seems to have had a regional dimension.

77. Harding (1981, 72–73); Kraus (1981, 145); and Martin King Whyte, "Who Hates Bureaucracy? A Chinese Puzzle," in Nee and Stark (1989), 246.

78. Teh-Wei Hu, "Health Care Services in China's Economic Development," in Dernberger (1980), 241–42, and Whyte and Parish (1984, 65–66). The system was introduced in 1951 and revised in 1953.

79. At the end of 1985, females constituted 32 per cent of the labor force of all state-owned (essentially urban) units in all sectors, as compared with 47 per cent in collectively owned units (*Statistical Yearbook of China 1986*, 98, 100, 103).

For the 1970s, interviews with urbanites who had emigrated to Hong Kong between 1972 and 1978 provided information on 1,865 individuals. These interviews yielded sample results in which employment in state enterprises was 45 per cent female, while employment in neighborhood collective enterprises was 59 per cent female (Martin King Whyte, "Sexual Inequality Under Socialism," in Watson [1984], 217).

80. See Stacey (1983) for an interesting treatment of Chinese Communist Party policies toward women. Despite actions taken in the P.R.C., particularly in the 1950s, to combat sexual discrimination and social inequality, sexual relations were never assimilated to class relations.

81. Between 1969 and 1976, the only academic requirement for a candidate for higher education was to show that his education was the equivalent of that received from a lower middle school (Jürgen Henze, "Die Reform des Schul- und Hochschulwesens in der Volksrepublik China seit 1976," *B.B.I.*, 1982, Nr. 11:27).

82. The complicating feature here is the uncertainty both as to the probable length of the period of rustication, ranging from a year or two to life, and as to the location of such rustication. I know of no evidence correlating social category or education of youth with these critical attributes of rustication. Whyte and Parish (1984, 39–41) discusses rustication. The authors es-

timate that, in the early 1970s, over half of urban Chinese youth were sent to the countryside. But in their sample, almost half of the males sent to the countryside appear de facto to have been spending more than six months each year back in the city. While rustication was originally intended to be for life, it was eventually softened to allow many to return legally to their urban home after a two-to-three-year stint. See Bernstein (1977) for the most extensive treatment of rustication. He quotes one "not implausible" estimate to the effect that one-fourth of youth rusticated between 1968 and late 1973 had returned to urban residences by 1975 (247).

83. The exception here is that the average standard of rural education appeared to improve at the same time that urban education was deteriorating (Suzanne Pepper, "Chinese Education after Mao," *C.Q.* 81 [March 1980], 26–44).

84. In the late Imperial period, migration from rural to urban areas may have been much easier. The population of the cities is said to have been heavily male, a phenomenon due to many males leaving the countryside in their teens to work in the cities and then returning to rural life when they were in their forties (Whyte and Parish, 1984, 11). F. W. Mote claims that, judging by European standards, traditional China through the late Imperial period showed a lack of differentiation between urban and rural areas (Frederick W. Mote, "The City in Traditional Chinese Civilization," in Liu and Tu [1970], 42–49). Cyril E. Black and Marion J. Levy, Jr., "Conclusions: China's Modernization in Historical Perspective," in Rozman (1981), 502, quote the Mote article in support of their view that China may have been unique internationally in its lack of urban-rural differentiation.

85. One source estimates that nearly half of the urbanites who began work in the early 1950s were migrants. But strict laws passed in 1958 ended this. (Schurmann 1968, 382; Whyte and Parish 1984, 17–20.)

There have been several Chinese reports since 1982 that some 13 to 14 million peasants were recruited to work in the cities between 1966 and 1976, presumably as temporary workers (see, e.g., Thomas Scharping, "Comments," and Kam Wing Chan, "Reply," *C.Q.* 109 [March 1987]:103, 108–9). Nevertheless, particularly since the urban dismissals of the early 1960s were repeated in 1973–74 (Chan, "Reply," 108), presumably at the expense of such rural temporary workers, one would seem justified in accepting the prevailing view that rural migration during the 1960s and 1970s was successfully blocked (see, e.g., Perkins and Yusuf 1984, 124).

86. See, for example, Schurmann (1968, 400–401), and John P. Emerson, "Manpower Training and Utilization of Specialized Cadres, 1949–68," in Lewis (1971), 192.

87. This was less true for women than for men, in view of the Chinese tradition of exogamy in rural marriages.

88. In Eastern Europe especially, such extension of the private sector has occurred most prominently in the service sector, including particularly restaurants and other forms of catering, and in the sector for maintenance of consumer goods.

89. The earliest case of which I know is in one of our sample enter-

prises located in Shanghai. Shares with a fixed return of 0.024 of 1 per cent were "made available" in 1980 to employees, one-third of whom bought them. This was to help finance a joint venture with collective enterprises and communes. The experiment ended in 1981, with the shares being redeemed.

90. *JPRS-CEA-85-097* (1 November 1985), 21–30 (the original article is by Cao Wenlian, in *Jingji Yanjiu*, 1985, Nr. 8 [20 August]:41–46); Xu Jinq'an (deputy director of the Institute of Economic Structural Reform), "Stock System: A New Exploration of China's Economic Reform," *J.C.E.* 11, no. 3 (September 1987):509–10; and *The Economist*, 18 April 1987, 77–78. *B.R.* 29, no. 33 (18 August 1986):6–7, cites Shenyang as the second city with a stock market.

91. The Investigation and Research Group of the State Commission for Economic Restructuring, in *B.R.* 30, no. 40 (5 October 1987):22–24.

92. Individuals holding posts at particular levels may, indeed, have such property rights; an example is that of personal contracts with golden-parachute clauses. Such rights act as constraints upon higher levels in the organization, but they are not owned by any managerial body or position as such, and are not received automatically by the successors to the current tenants of these posts.

93. A. M. Honoré, in a legal essay, discusses the general power of the state to expropriate, as opposed to the limitation of its power to expropriate to restricted classes of things and for certain restricted purposes. He holds that such general power, even when accompanied by the duty to provide adequate compensation, would imply the destruction of the institution of ownership as we know it. Only a fungible claim (i.e., money) would be owned (Guest 1961, 119–20). "General power" in this context seems equivalent to the notion used here of the absence of self-restraint by government.

94. An interesting treatment of such continuity in an area of the economy reasonably remote from the subject matter of this study is that of David M. Lampton, "Water: Challenge to a Fragmented Political System," in Lampton (1987), 157–89. It is an example of the apparent virtual unanimity of observers in finding such self-restraint to be present in quite disparate activities.

95. Ma Hong (1983, 44, 94), writing in May 1982, agrees that this assumption was an appropriate description of current reality at that time. He strongly urged an end to such treatment of state-owned enterprises.

96. See, for example, William Byrd, "The Atrophy of Central Planning in Chinese Industry," *J.C.E.* 11, no. 3 (September 1987):295–308.

97. County authorities claim that the county's target is set in a fashion which makes it at best only loosely related to the sum of the sectoral plans established by higher authorities. Municipal authorities held that the plan was intended only as a measure of economic development of the county. They argued that placing great emphasis upon it would have the harmful effect of causing the enterprise to try to produce expensive products, even if they were nonmarketable and could only be accumulated in inventory.

98. William Byrd et al., "Recent Chinese Economic Reforms: Studies of Two Industrial Enterprises," *World Bank Staff Working Paper* no. 652 (1984), 76. They write that the plant's supervisory body has changed eleven times since 1949, and that no other enterprise among the forty-two subordinate to

the Municipal Machine-building Bureau has such a complex supervisory structure.

99. For example, the county is responsible for allocating electricity.

100. See, for example, Riskin (1987, 198). The smelter also fitted this pattern during the period through 1983.

101. There was disagreement among the informants as to whether or not the province received any portion of the enterprise's production for its own allocation system. In any case, the share was negligible.

102. As with other enterprises, there is always some quid pro quo. In this case, the supervising ministry pointed out that localities handle such inputs as electricity, and that they would have "less enthusiasm" for meeting enterprise needs if the enterprise's results had no effect on local budgets. Thus a side-payments argument could be made.

103. It is true that provincial and municipal authorities dictated a profit plan for the enterprise which implied higher output than was required by the national output plan. But failure to meet this profit plan had no implications for the enterprise's receipts of bonuses, and profit retention by the enterprise was also fixed by national rather than by local authorities.

104. It is true that its supply is allocated by the ministry to a provincial organ above the enterprise level, but that is only because the enterprise is a small plant which is administered together with a number of other small state plants by this organ. Since the central allocation is to this specific organ rather than to the province in general, I treat it as being comparable to central allocations to larger enterprises.

105. But both together were relatively small, constituting only 21 per cent of total investments made during this period. Seventy-five per cent of all net investments came from the enterprise's own funds. In this calculation, no account is taken of investment from the enterprise's major repair fund. See Naughton, in JEC (1986), 607, for the distinction between this fund and the enterprise's basic amortization fund; the latter was used for financing 95 per cent of the enterprise's investments.

The view taken above as to amortization funds follows the Chinese formal treatment of the matter. A strong case could, however, be made for considering the governmental unit responsible for financial control over the enterprise as having made the investments coming from the enterprise's depreciation fund (see Naughton, in Lampton [1987], 54). If this approach were taken, then the province would have to be considered as having supplied almost five times as much investment resources during 1975–82 as had the central government.

106. One could argue whether either of these types of control represented multilevel leadership; the issue would seem to be to a considerable degree a semantic one. The enterprise itself did not make this complaint.

107. It is true that the provincial Commerce Department had the right to insist on purchasing whatever share it wished of the enterprise's products. But, as a general rule, it was the enterprise that was pushing the Commerce Department to increase rather than to decrease its purchases.

108. It is quite possible that this decentralization was restricted to this particular province. I have not run into it elsewhere.

109. It is perhaps indicative that, in an interview during December 1983 in which the director of the mill participated, it was stated that the mill was then under the dual leadership of the municipality and the province. Certainly this statement reflected the reality of the situation.

110. *Statistical Yearbook of China 1985*, 344.

111. Cotton textiles, tobacco, iron and steel, and armaments are said to be the only fields thus prohibited. The prohibition did not apply to the occasional state-owned firm which might exist in rural areas under county auspices (John Enos, "Commune- and Brigade-Run Industries in Rural China," in Griffin [1984], 241). Presumably, this prohibition was due to the fact that cotton textile sales were rationed, and it was believed convenient for the enforcement of such rationing to limit production to state-owned enterprises. Sale of homespun yarn and handwoven cotton cloth was also forbidden (Lardy 1983, 123).

112. Exports were also under national control. See Zhang Pu, "Structure of the Textile Industry," in *JPRS-CEA-84-061* 212 (the translation constitutes selections from Ma Hong and Sun Shangqing, eds., *Studies in the Problems of China's Economic Structure* [Beijing 1981]).

Chapter 3

1. There is an extensive literature dealing with the advantages and disadvantages of "taut planning" as a motivating device. The seminal article is that of Holland Hunter, "Optimum Tautness in Developmental Planning," *Economic Development and Cultural Change*, July 1961, pt. 1:561–72.

2. Perkins, "The Central Features of China's Economic Development," in Dernberger (1980), 120–50.

3. The number of items for which production is planned centrally in the Soviet Union (whether by producing central ministries, by other central bodies, or by the Councils of Ministers of Union Republics) is described for the early 1980s as being 45,000 to 47,000 (Ukrainskii and Kiperman 1984, 71). This figure is roughly the same as the number of products centrally allocated in 1973 (see table 3.1). Particular central organs, of course, may plan the output of a larger or smaller number of products than they allocate. In the middle 1970s, for example, the Soviet State Planning Commission planned the production of more individual products than it itself allocated (Smirnov 1975, 62).

4. The period of 1972–78 is anomalous with regard to the small number of products that were allocated by the Planning Commission and State Supply Bureau. This is said to have been linked to the fall from power of Liu Shao-Chi, Mao's chosen successor during the mid-1960s, who was expelled from the Chinese Communist Party in October 1968 and was posthumously rehabilitated only in February 1980. Liu had helped to create and staff the State Supply Bureau; it was known as a Liu Shao-Chi agency and was one of the central bodies most devastated during the years of the Cultural Revolution (Michel Oksenberg, "Economic Policy-Making in China: Summer 1981," C.Q. 90 [June 1982]:183–84).

What is of greater importance, however, is that the total number of products allocated centrally had by 1973 recovered to their level of the mid-

1960s. A shift had occurred with regard to which agencies did the allocation, but it is not clear that any more was involved than the rise and fall of individual organizations.

As of the end of 1984, it was predicted within the State Planning Commission that the number of products allocated by the Commission together with the Supply Bureau would once again be reduced almost to the 1972–78 level. A figure of 65 products was predicted (*JPRS-CEA-84-105* [21 December 1984], 31–32, citing a Beijing radio broadcast). But there was no indication as to whether it was believed that this would have any effect on the total number centrally allocated.

5. The first of these factors is the more highly developed nature of the Soviet economy and thus the larger mix of its products. There is also evidence that many of the ministerially allocated items may be used primarily by enterprises within the allocating ministry. Of the 40,000+ such items in the Soviet Union in 1973, over 12,000 of them were chemical reagents (Kurotchenko 1975, 85). Thirty per cent of the total number of centrally allocated items in China in 1982 were chemical products (Naughton 1986, 127). Finally, the actual number of items allocated may be different from the theoretic numbers listed. In China in 1984, 256 commodities were theoretically being allocated by nonministerial central bodies, i.e., they were under "unified allocation." The actual number, however, was said by Chinese sources to be only slightly over 100 (Naughton 1986, 127). We have no similar information with regard to the Soviet Union.

6. See Thomas P. Lyons, "China's Cellular Economy: A Test of the Fragmentation Hypothesis," *J.C.E.* 9, no. 3 (September 1985):125–44.

7. William Byrd, "The Atrophy of Central Planning in Chinese Industry," *J.C.E.* 11, no. 3 (September 1987):299, table 1. Diao Xinshen, "The Role of the Two-Tier Price System," in Reynolds (1987), 36–37, presents somewhat different figures, but this is because of errors in this rendering of the Diao Xinshen article into English from its original Chinese source.

8. For historical analysis of this question with regard to the Soviet Union, see Zaleski (1980, pt. 2).

9. For the period through early 1966, see the interviews in Richman (1969, 465).

10. V. P. Shaikin, in *Ekonomika i Matematicheskie Metody* 10, no. 1 (1974):98–109.

11. The final 1982 physical output plan for clocks for one of our sample enterprises was established only in mid-December 1982. However, the enterprise had requested in midyear a 50 per cent reduction from its initial plan target because of sales difficulties. In September, it requested a further reduction to the level that was finally approved in December. One might surmise that planning authorities were guided, for at least the second half of the year, more by what was eventually formalized as the final plan than by the initial one.

12. Shaikin, in *Ekonomika i Matematicheskie Melody* 10, no. 1 (1974): 98–109. A summary treatment of Shaikin's data is presented in D. Granick, "The Ministry was the Maximizing Unit in Soviet Industry," *J.C.E.* 4, no. 3 (September 1980):259–60.

13. It is unclear whether these data refer only to industry or to a larger segment of the economy, and there is no indication which types of final plans are involved (P. Krylov, in *Planovoe Khoziaistvo* 6 [1980]:22).

14. Alice C. Gorlin and David P. Doane, "Plan Fulfillment and Growth in Soviet Ministries," *J.C.E.* 7, no. 4 (December 1983):418.

15. Granick, "Ministry as the Maximizing Unit," 262.

16. *Pravda,* 10 August 1955, p. 1.

17. See, respectively, A. N. Kosygin, in *C.D.S.P.* (7 April 1976):9; A. Triain, in *Planovoe Khoziaistvo* 3 (1978):97; A. Dadashev, in *Voprosy Ekonomiki* 8 (1979):45; and A. Duginov, in *Planovoe Khoziaistvo* 8 (1979):97.

18. Shaikin, in *Ekonomika i Matematicheskie Metody* 10, no. 1 (1974): 98–109.

19. Granick (1976, 227) discusses this. National figures were 95 per cent of firms fulfilling final sales plan in 1972, 98 per cent in 1973, and "over 90 per cent" in 1975. In 1980, 99 per cent of industrial *Kombinate* and VVBs fulfilled their plans, but these are much larger units than enterprises and thus the data for them are not comparable.

20. Ibid., 192–94, 227.

21. Ibid., 95. The data are for "units," which are mostly enterprises but sometimes are grouping of enterprises in *centrale.* For output, only 2 per cent of the units are *centrale.*

22. Ibid., 96–99.

23. A sixteenth enterprise also provided such data, but it was discarded on the basis of inconsistencies in the reporting.

24. Data for fulfillment of value of output, of output of the single main product, and of profit were combined, and each observation was treated as a vector consisting of two columns of fulfillment of initial plan and of final plan. An F test was then run, comparing the sum of the variances for each observation with the variance of the entire sample of plan fulfillment. This test requires the assumption that, in the underlying population from which the sample is drawn, the items in each column of the observation vector are distributed normally around the observation mean. Differences were highly significant in both the pre-reform and reform period between the fulfillment of initial plan and fulfillment of final plan. A less rigorous test, the comparison of the means of fulfillment of initial and final plans, showed similarly high significance of differences.

25. Commenting on the situation in the mid-1960s on the basis of a sample of Chinese enterprises, Barry Richman (1969, 474) hazarded the guess that formal revisions in aggregate targets of enterprise plans appear to be more common than in Soviet industry. I would not feel comfortable in hazarding a guess on the subject for any period.

26. At least, there are no changes which show up in our groupings of observations.

27. When all observations are combined, it is the fulfillment of the plans for the secondary products that come closer to being exactly fulfilled than do those for the main product: 102 versus 118 per cent. The statistically significant test for fulfillment of the initial plan of the reform years shows a similar result: 99 versus 111 per cent. The only subtests that indicate greater

departure of output from plan for secondary products are the three that fail to show significance even at the 50 per cent level. There is no indication in these data of carelessness in the planning of the secondary products. Similarly, there is no indication that the enterprises were cavalier with regard to meeting their targets for secondary products. Only in one statistically significant case did plan fulfillment average less than 100 per cent (as well as in the non-significant case of the final plan for pre-reform years), and in both instances it fell short by less than 1 per cent.

28. As one might expect, it is extremely difficult to test the ratchet effect hypothesis, not only because of problems in obtaining the information specified above but also because of the difficulties in setting ceteris paribus constraints. Testing the hypothesis with regard to output plans established for Soviet ministries (but not for Soviet enterprises), I have concluded that the hypothesis is unsupported by the data both of the 1950s and of the 1970s (Granick, "Ministry as the Maximizing Unit," 255–73). This conclusion was rebutted by Michael Keren in "The Ministry, Plan Changes, and the Ratchet in Planning," *J.C.E.* 6, no. 4 (December 1982):327–42, and the controversy was continued by the two authors in *J.C.E.* 7, no. 4 (December 1983):432–48.

29. Let K be the unobserved variable (in using data relating to other enterprises) of capacity; P is the observed dependent variable of plan; A is the observed independent variable of performance. K is dated as of the end of the period. If we assume that, in fact, planners do not use the ratchet principle of planning, but that they do have independent information as to changes in the capacity of firm (i), and that enterprises do not restrain their performance because of a belief in the existence of the ratchet effect, then we would expect the following:

Covariance($[A_{i,t} - A_{i,t-1}], [K_{i,t-1} - K_{i,t-2}]$) > 0 and approaches 1;
Covariance($[P_{i,t} - P_{i,t-1}], [K_{i,t-1} - K_{i,t-2}]$) > 0 and approaches 1; and therefore,
Covariance($[A_{i,t} - A_{i,t-1}], [P_{i,t} - P_{i,t-1}]$) > 0 and approaches 1.

30. Since the mid-1960s, Soviet leaders have espoused the notion of setting at the beginning of each five-year-plan period the next five annual plans for enterprises. The argument is that, if this can be done, enterprise management will cease to believe that the ratchet effect operates within the five-year-plan period, and thus its reactions to its perception of the ratchet effect will be attenuated.

31. It does not matter whether or not the expected value of plan fulfillment is 100 per cent since, if it should be higher or lower, this can easily be taken into account into the calculation of expected resources available for allocation.

32. This is the sort of situation described as having originally followed the 1970 decentralization of authority over enterprises, in which central ministries kept the right to assign mandatory output plans but the supervising localities could add a supplementary output plan (Christine Wong, "Material Allocation and Decentralization," in Perry and Wong [1985], 260–61).

33. Despite the fact that hypothesis (3.1) is formulated in terms of variance, the analysis below will not use σ^2 but will instead rely upon the grouping of observations with respect to the level of plan fulfillment. The reasons for not using σ^2 are twofold.

First, the degree of plan fulfillment is highly asymmetric and reaches some extremely large numbers for initial and especially for final plans. It seems unlikely that the difference between substantial numbers such as 130 and 1,100 per cent of plan fulfillment has any particular consequences; thus I am reluctant to give much meaning either to a mean of plan fulfillment or to raw deviations from it. (This is part of the reason why, when I later discuss the size of the respective tails of the distributions of plan fulfillment, I do this with respect to 100 per cent fulfillment, regardless of the fact that 100 per cent is well below the mean value.)

The second reason is that we could not properly use a χ^2 test of the significance of the difference between the variations in two categories of enterprises, since the variations themselves have a distribution very far from normal. Given the absence of a ready test of significance, it seems preferable to rely on a less summary measure of the distributions. This measure is presented in tables 3.8 and 3.10.

34. The category A enterprises include three textile plants. These three do not receive physical output plans or materials allocations directly from the Center, but each enterprise's superior (the province) receives such plans, as well as allocations on an aggregative basis for all textile enterprises. Two of the seventeen enterprises are counted in both categories, either for different products or for different years.

35. All nine are for underfulfillment of the final plan; neither of the two enterprises provided any data as to initial plan.

36. Although this form of protectionism is frowned upon by the Center, it appears extensively even in the 1980s both in the sample and in reports from other sources as to economic behavior in China.

37. There is some confirmation of the hypothesis with regard to the final profit plan for 1975–78.

38. I put together the data for both categories and both subcategories, after eliminating the 1975–77 data from two category A enterprises which were explained above as a happenstance. The percentage of all observations, within each category being compared, in which plan fulfillment was less than 90 per cent were as follows:

0% of observations (for each category): 6 final plans and 4 initial plans;
1–6% (for the highest category only): 3 final plans and 1 initial plan;
10% (for the highest category only): 1 initial plan;
Over 10% (for the highest category only): 1 initial plan supports hypotheses, and 1 final plan and 1 initial plan refutes hypotheses.

Note that "highest" means that category of enterprises that has the largest percentage of observations for which plan fulfillment is <90 per cent.

The above situation, where 55 per cent of the comparisons show zero per cent for each category, contrasts with the case of 90–99 per cent fulfillment, where only 30 per cent of the comparisons are of this sort. The percentage of observations, within each category being compared, of plan fulfillment of 90–99 per cent were:

0% for each category: 2 final plans and 1 initial plan;
0% for subcategory A1 and nonzero for subcategory A2: 1 final plan
    and 1 initial plan;
Nonzero for both categories: 3 final plans and 2 initial plans.

Thus it would appear that the reason that underfulfillment is un-affected by the category into which the enterprise-year falls is that, with the exception of what occurred for two enterprises over a period of three years, all planning organizations have set final plans which have been almost uniformly fulfilled by at least 90 per cent. This, as we would expect, is less true for initial plans, but it is still a fairly good approximation.

39. If they were believed to be maximizers, there would have been no need for the supervisory bodies of enterprises in subcategory A2 to have given plans higher than those set by higher planning levels. Indeed no planner would have had to set a production plan higher than epsilon.

40. An alternative explanation seems more satisfactory in explaining the similarity of underfulfillment results in subcategories A1 and A2, but it has two disadvantages: (1) it encounters difficulties with the facts of over-fulfillment, and (2) it does not apply to the similarity as to underfulfillment between categories A and B. This explanation leans upon the fact that fulfillment figures for value of output and for profit depend heavily upon the product mix produced by the enterprise, where this mix is a function of the degree of concentration by the enterprise in those goods that are more highly priced relative to their opportunity cost to the producer. Such variation is most possible in the case of aggregates of items that are allocated to users, for which there is normally greater demand than supply at the prices set. Physical output plans are less aggregative than are plans expressed in monetary terms; therefore, they permit less manipulation by enterprises.

High profit and/or high value-of-output plans might be set by regional planners not simply to influence the level of aggregative physical output by the enterprise, but also to direct the enterprise's choice of product mix to higher value items. This latter objective is feasible where the physical output targets can be fulfilled. But if the physical output targets cannot be fulfilled even by concentrating on those items which yield the best results in terms of these targets, the enterprise may be totally uninfluenced by the profit or value-of-output plans. Indeed, the regional authorities might not even wish to influence the enterprise to choose a product mix which would further worsen its performance as measured along the dimension of physical output. This would explain why regional planners treat subcategory A2 enterprises asymmetrically, depending upon whether they are likely to under-fulfill their physical output plans set by higher authorities.

This interpretation explains the similarity of proportions for under-fulfillment between subcategory A1 and A2 enterprise-years, but it eliminates the explanation offered earlier for the difference in proportions of substantial overfulfillment. Why should a single authority, planning physical output as well as the value-of-output and/or profit targets, not use the latter two to affect product mix? The explanation offered might be that it is the regional authorities that are much more concerned with profitability, since they are the main recipients of enterprise profits, while the central authorities take a broader perspective. (Remember that, in the production of those goods that are sold at state-set prices, there is no reason to believe that a product mix that maximizes profits is a socially optimal mix.) This explanation leads to the prediction that the difference in planning procedures between regional and central authorities should be greater during the reform years than earlier, and thus that the ratio of subcategory A2/subcategory A1 in substantial plan over-fulfillment should be smaller in the later period. But this prediction is not borne out; it is wrong in two of the three cases that we can analyze (see table 3.10).

41. Tidrick, "Planning and Supply," in Tidrick and Chen (1987), 182, points to the existence of such complaints in three of the sample enterprises. He accepts for the year 1982 the statements made in two of these enterprises, in interviews held at the end of 1983, that regional superiors did not want plan overfulfillment. Tidrick describes this latter as a "pattern (which) appears to be a recent development, limited to Shanghai." One of the seven enterprises listed did not make such complaints. But it held back shipments during each December so that it could boast each year of greater production than in the previous year. I take this to represent a belief in at least an implicit ratchet method of judgment by superiors.

42. These six are the auto enterprise in subcategory A1, the smelter, steel, cement, and textile plants in subcategory A2, and the textile mill in category B.

43. The three are the auto and steel enterprises and the textile mill in category B.

44. The four enterprises are the auto, steel, and two textile plants. Others, not analyzed here, also shifted away from central allocation. This is clear at a minimum for the machine tool and the pump factories. In both of these latter cases, it is probable that changing market conditions were the main cause.

The two enterprises are the smelter and cement plants. One might also categorize the auto plant there for the years 1983–85, but I believe that this case is better classified as representing reform in the sense of allocation to individual provincial governments of steel (as a type of money, or "cigarette currency") rather than trucks.

45. Since the mandatory plan and total physical output plan are identical for two of the smelter's main products, we might have placed this plant in the first set of two cases, but that would have been overly formalistic.

46. The balancing of freight transport availability and needs is the principal reason for wanting low variance at an enterprise, and not simply a

branch, level. Differences in capacity among enterprises with regard to features of detailed product mix is a second reason.

47. Gene Tidrick, in discussing our same sample of enterprises, describes plans as being "neither taut nor firm" (Tidrick and Chen 1987, 198). Although he is certainly correct as to the first characterization, the data in tables 3.3a and 3.3b that show the relation between the fulfillment of original and final plans indicate that he is wrong by any reasonable standard with regard to the second.

The relative firmness of Chinese enterprise plans by the standards of European socialist countries casts doubt, in my view, on Tidrick's opinion (ibid., 198–99) that "everything is negotiable" in the Chinese economy. Much of what Tidrick treats as bargaining would, I believe, be better considered in terms of the property rights of different regional organizations. I do not interpret the sample data as showing any unusual degree of bargaining by the enterprises themselves when judged according to the standards of other socialist countries.

48. In fact, however, it provided in 1982 only 70 per cent of the steel required for total output.

49. William Byrd, "The Shenyang Smelter: A Case Study of Problems and Reforms in China's Nonferrous Metals Industry," *World Bank Staff Working Paper*, no. 766 (1985), table 1.2, gives estimates of national production of four nonferrous metals.

50. Intriguingly, the enterprise is allowed to sell on its own 12 per cent of its output of one of these products so that it can negotiate tied-sales of a byproduct that would otherwise have insufficient customers. The State Materials Bureau regulates the proportions of the two products called for in the individual tied-sale contracts. Moreover, while these sales are made directly by the enterprise, they are to users designated by central authorities.

51. This is not certain. One respondent claimed that the enterprise had received oral authority to sell to other customers metal refined from its own scrap purchases. But no one suggested either that this was important quantitatively or that such sales were made at higher prices than those charged to the State Materials Bureau.

52. There is no reason to believe that the foreign exchange needed for the imports was provided by anyone other than the central government.

53. Presumably, these barter deals constituted sales by both parties at official prices. Informants in all plants, however, describe such sales as "exchanges."

54. Cement supplied to the central ministry for allocation purposes was 102.2 per cent of plan in 1981, but thereafter stayed between 100 and 100.4 per cent.

Chapter 4

1. See Granick (1967, chap. 5) for an historical treatment of the Soviet experience under planning. S. A. Kheinman has been the leading Soviet author in this field.

2. Gene Tidrick, "Planning and Supply," in Tidrick and Chen (1987), 189, especially table 8-1.

3. This implicit prohibition took the form both of the requirement that individual regions be self-sufficient in grain and of the movement away from the tendency during the 1950s of permitting the agricultural tax to be paid either in cash or in crops other than grain. Between 1953–57 and 1978, interprovincial grain transfers other than for national export are estimated to have declined from 5.0 per cent of all grain production to 0.8 per cent, with an intermediate figure of 2.8 per cent in 1965 (N. R. Lardy, "China's Interprovincial Grain Marketing and Import Demand," [typescript, 1988], table 1.) Although the agricultural labor force grew by almost 70 per cent between 1957 and 1978/79, grain sold to peasants increased by only one-third; this was from a base where something like half of all peasant households in China were, during a given year, purchasers (gross, not net) of grain (see Lardy 1983, especially pp. 32 and 52).

4. See Wong (1979). These enterprises were intended to meet rural requirements for industrial inputs, and they were run primarily at the county level. During the 1980s as well, there was major expansion of rural industrial production. But this latter surge occurred for reasons of profit seeking in a market economy, rather than being directed toward filling local needs that would otherwise have gone unsupplied.

5. See Christine Wong, "Ownership and Control in Chinese Industry," in JEC (1986), 575, for a discussion of the importance of such barter trade.

6. Provincial agreements of this sort between Shanghai on the one hand, and Shanxi, Shandong, and Hebei provinces on the other, were signed near the end of 1982 (China Daily, 6 January 1983, p. 1).

7. The fact that prices were obviously not market clearing is irrelevant to this issue. In an interview in one of the sample enterprises, it was specifically stated that exchange ratios between physical quantities of goods need bear no relation to their monetary prices; net cash payments are made to take care of the difference between the two sets of ratios.

8. In interviews with Soviet emigrés of the late 1970s who had been managers or professional staff in the Soviet economy, twenty-two respondents were asked whether plan fulfillment required their enterprise to work at "full capacity" (undefined). Only two answered negatively (Susan J. Linz, "Managerial Autonomy in Soviet Firms," Soviet Studies 40, no. 2 [April 1988]: 180–82).

9. Soviet enterprises are obliged to deliver to the state all of the output counted toward plan fulfillment. (In integrated plants, there is sometimes some modification in that a shop may use as an input a product produced and already counted in the enterprise's plan.) In contrast, our Chinese sample contains at least one clear case (the cement factory) in which a portion of the nationally planned output was left to the plant explicitly for barter purposes during this first procurement stage as well as during the latter two.

To the degree that plants are allowed to retain a portion of their planned output for purposes of barter, the issue of taut plans is irrelevant to the exchange of output between enterprises. However, it may be doubted that taut central planning would in practice be consistent with such permission.

10. A third difference is that Soviet barter is not accompanied by money payments and leaves no paper trail through the respective enterprises' bank accounts.

11. Reported by Christine Wong, "Material Allocation and Decentralization," in Perry and Wong (1985), 265–66.

12. This referred to coke supplied to one factory. Producers were said to have sold their above-plan output at a price 14 per cent higher than was allowed for their planned output.

13. See Thomas M. H. Chan, "China's Price Reform in the Period of Economic Reform," *The Australian Journal of Chinese Affairs* 18 (July 1987): 93. Chan believes that these price differentials date particularly from the middle 1970s.

14. Between 1978 and 1983, grain tonnage increased by an annual compound figure of 4.9 per cent, while gross agricultural output value in constant prices (excluding industrial production and other "sideline" activities that increased even more rapidly) grew by 6.6 per cent (*Statistical Yearbook of China 1985*, 239, 255).

15. N. R. Lardy, "China's Interprovincial Grain Marketing," table 1.

16. Barry Naughton, "False Starts and Second Wind," in Perry and Wong (1985), 249. See also Christine Wong, in Perry and Wong (1985), 265.

17. Barry Naughton, "The Decline of Central Control over Investment in Post-Mao China," in Lampton (1987), 67.

18. Ibid., 51–80, goes so far as to equate completely the two categories of central and budgetary investments. However, the data presented by Christine Wong, in JEC (1986), 583–85, and by Vivienne Shue, "Beyond the Budget," in *Modern China* 10, no. 2 (April 1984): 147–86, make me believe that Naughton's interpretation is too strong to be supported by the known facts.

19. Naughton, "Finance and Planning Reforms in Industry," in JEC (1986), 628–29.

20. Naughton, in Lampton (1987), 63.

21. This difference is offset only to a slight degree by differences in inflation. The general retail price index rose by 3.4 per cent compounded annually during the three years of 1980–82 compared with 1.2 per cent during 1976–79 (*Statistical Yearbook of China 1985*, 530).

22. For the 1950s, see Lardy (1978, 54–55). For the latter period, extrabudgetary revenues come from Zhao Ziyang, "Report on the Seventh Five-Year Plan," *B.R.* 29, no. 16 (21 April 1986): II, and from *JPRS-CEA-85-053* (17 June 1985), 114, translating materials from *Caizheng*, 1985, no. 2 (8 February): 5–7. Budgetary revenues are from *Statistical Yearbook of China 1985*, 523. M. Oksenberg and J. Tong, "The Evolution of Central-Provincial Fiscal Relations in China, 1950–1983: The Formal System," (typescript, 1987), cite fairly similar figures.

23. G. K. Shekovtsov in *Finansy SSSR*, 1984, no. 8 (August): 22–25. This represented an increase from 22 per cent during 1961–65, but otherwise showed no trend. It includes the budget of the state social insurance system,

property and personal insurance, bank credit and cash revenue, and financial plans of individual state organizations, collective farms, and other cooperatives. Of these four subdivisions of extra-budgetary revenue, only the last is considered by Shekovtsov to be "decentralized."

24. Chen Yizi, Wang Xiaoqiang, and colleagues, "Reform: Results and Lessons from the 1985 CESRRI Survey," *J.C.E.* 11, no. 3 (September 1987):474.

25. This is exemplified by the fact that the First Ministry of Machine-building, in agreement with the State Pricing Committee, permitted enterprises to reduce prices for sixteen types of products by up to 20 per cent. This permission applied to various sorts of machine tools, tooling, compressors, and to spare parts for trucks (Remyga 1982, 103).

26. This information comes from a purchasing manager in one of the sample enterprises, who said that this was the only year for which this was the case. According to this informant, no allocations were made either to enterprises or to regions. It is possible, however, that he was wrong and that there were central allocations to provinces but that this enterprise's province received more steel than it could use.

27. During 1980, 11 per cent of the national supply of rolled steel was sold without allocations by the producing enterprises. In the same year, 46 per cent of the production of the First Ministry of Machine-building (presumably, representative of civilian engineering equipment) was distributed in this fashion (*Almanac of China's Economy in 1981* 1982, 336, 616).

28. See Dorothy J. Solinger, "The 1980 Inflation and the Politics of Price Control in the PRC," in Lampton (1987), 81–118. She writes, for example, that "Anhui [province] was one of the last to hold onto the reform policies until nearly the end of November [1980], directing its localities to 'go on with reform,' even on the eve of the official shutdown of this policy" (95). For a Chinese view that is fundamentally similar, see Wu Jinglian and Zhao Renwei, "The Dual Pricing System in China's Industry," *J.C.E.* 11, no. 3 (September 1987):311–12.

29. Wu Jinglian and Zhao Renwei, "The Dual Pricing System," 312.

Data for 31 January 1986 for Canton show that the free market prices for particular specifications of thread-rolled steel, cement, cold-rolled sheet steel, and copper were only 5 to 12 per cent higher than the plan prices for these products. In contrast, free market prices were 99 to 133 per cent higher for hot-rolled sheet steel, aluminum ingot, and steel rod (Thomas M. H. Chan, "China's Price Reform," 100). Floating prices for industrial products, which could exceed the planned prices by as much as 20 per cent, appear to have dated from 1981–82. But the 1984 demarcation between prices for planned quotas and for above-plan production does not seem to have existed earlier (94–95).

30. For a description of varying views, as expressed in the first national symposium (6–13 November 1984) after the October 1984 decision of the Central Committee of the Communist Party, see Hans Zhiguo, "Symposium on Restructuring China's Economy," in *Social Sciences in China* 6, no. 3 (1985):16–17. A normative model of such dual pricing, with market-based

pricing applying to above-plan output, is presented by the Soviet author V. M. Polterovich, "Optimal'noe raspredelenie resursov po stabil'nym i dogovornym tsenam (model' sinteza mekhanizmov)," in *Ekonomika i Matematicheskie Metody* 22, no. 5 (1986):871–85.

31. E.g., Wu Jinglian and Zhao Renwei, "The Dual Pricing System," 312.

32. Naughton, in JEC (1986), 628–29.

33. Only the quality of paint is complained about.

34. These are actual receipts from allocations. During 1983 and 1984, the enterprise received only 85 and 63 per cent, respectively, of the allocations that had been made by the Center. I assume that in earlier years there probably was better delivery of allocations.

35. This refers to predecessor mills that were later merged into the enterprise where the interviewing was conducted.

36. When purchasing within an allocation quota, "standard" freight costs are included. These are much less than the actual transport costs when long distances are involved.

37. In China generally, permission was not granted until 1984 for enterprises to charge higher prices for above-plan production. In this province, however, such permission was given at least for state-owned coal and coke producers even before the beginning of the reform period. As we have seen, coal producers were treated much more generously than were producers of coke.

38. It is not known, however, whether money payments were made that compensated for the different barter terms.

39. This may have been particularly so because the enterprise was considered experimental with regard to financial arrangements. As the municipal authorities described the situation, "if the enterprise doesn't receive sufficient materials, the experiment will stop." This was the only enterprise in the sample for which such an explicit statement was made.

40. These coupons were issued by the plant itself. The phenomenon resulted from the fact that, since 1980, it had been given the right to sell on its own some portion of its production. Coupons were useful, however, only for a few types of watches which were temporarily in short supply. By 1983 such shortage items had disappeared from the enterprise's repertoire.

41. The one-half refers to the situation in one enterprise prior to 1978.

42. Min Zhu, "Decentralization in the Chinese Foreign Trade Sector," in Chinese Young Economists (1987), 242-3.

43. Bruce L. Reynolds, "Trade, Employment and Inequality in Postreform China," in *J.C.E.* 11, no. 3 (September 1987):483.

44. Min Zhu, in Chinese Young Economists 1987, 242-10. The author writes that his information is drawn primarily from firsthand observations during various assignments from Fudan University and from the Shanghai Economic Reform Commission.

45. Information as to the prices received for exports is available for only two enterprises. These are in separate provinces and in very distinct industries. One enterprise was made financially responsible for its exports in

1981. Thereafter, through at least 1983, it received a lower price in domestic currency for its exports than for its sales within China. (This was despite the fact that a subsidy over and above the official exchange rate was paid by the national corporation of the industry. This subsidy is included in the price calculated as being received for exports by the enterprise.) In compensation, the enterprise was allowed to retain one-fifth of its foreign exchange earnings, and its province kept at least as much. The second enterprise suffered a price cut of 15 per cent on export sales in 1983, when the national subsidy for the exports of its industry was reduced. In this year (if not before), the export price in domestic currency for the industry was divorced from the domestic price.

It is interesting that two provinces are known to have taken different approaches as a response to the reduction of the national subsidy on the relevant product. The province supervising the sample enterprise forced the enterprise itself to take the price cut, in this fashion reducing the enterprise's total profits. In the second province, the exporting enterprises were completely shielded; the provincial financial department compensated with its own subsidy. Since enterprise profits in both cases mainly went to the supervising province, the net effect on provincial finance differed little between the two provincial approaches.

Partial information is available for a third enterprise which, since the early 1970s, paid a reduced price for a share of a major input where this share was linked to its exports. However, we do not know the nominal price that the enterprise received for its exports, and thus cannot judge whether on balance it received a higher price for exports than it did for production directed at the domestic market.

46. Zhao Ziyang, Report of 27 March 1985 to the Third Session of the Sixth National People's Congress, in B.R. 28, no. 16 (22 April 1985), viii. Zhao writes that, "In a sense, in the last few years it was . . . the large enterprises that aided the reforms in small enterprises."

47. Shen Liren, a senior economist at the Chinese Academy of Social Sciences, reported the same thing in 1984. "Those [enterprises] with relatively greater plan assignments feel 'burdened,' while extraplan enterprises are reaping all the profits." Christine Wong, an American specialist on the Chinese economy, seems to agree (see Wong, in JEC [1986], 596–97).

48. It is certainly conceivable that the automotive enterprise may have reasoned that, if it were to sell scrap on the open market rather than use it for barter, its quota for deliveries of scrap to the state would be increased in the following year. Thus this may be an artificial example. But there was no indication in the interviews that this possibility was a consideration.

49. However, at the time of the interviews the enterprise was building its own thermal electric power station, intended to come on line in 1985.

50. Municipal authorities, on the other hand, claimed that it was due instead to the fear of overstretching managerial capacity by undertaking the project.

51. It is true that during the second stage some open market prices, particularly those for products of nonstate enterprises, seem to have been es-

sentially free. But this, at least in spirit, was a violation of the official pricing system rather than an application of it. It was stressed by several informants that only the selling enterprise, and not the buyer, was subject to penalties for transactions that occurred at illegal prices.

52. Robert J. Barro and Herschel I. Grossman, "A General Disequilibrium Model of Income and Employment," *American Economic Review* 61, no. 1 (1971):82–93, and "Suppressed Inflation and the Supply Multiplier," *Review of Economic Studies* 41, no. 1 (1974):87–104.

53. Richard Portes and David Winter, "Disequilibrium Estimates for Consumption Goods Markets in Centrally Planned Economies," *Review of Economic Studies* 47 (1980):137–59. Richard Portes, "Central Planning and Monetarism: Fellow Travellers?," Birkbeck College Discussion Paper no. 80 (July 1980), 4.

54. The identical supply and demand conditions could have been generated by administrative decisions that took the form of lump-sum transfers (see Terry Sicular, "Plan and Market in China's Agricultural Commerce," *Journal of Political Economy* 96, no. 2 [1988]:283–307).

55. Kornai (1980, 61–63, 191–95, 556, 569).

Nicholas Lardy, "Economic Relations between China and the United States," in JEC (1987), 306–7, describes current managers of Chinese enterprises as "asset maximizers." This description, of course, comes to the same thing as Kornai's assumption. But Lardy's reason for it is quite different; his is specific to the current Chinese financial and planning system and does not, for instance, apply to the period prior to 1967.

56. Hungary is explicitly included in this class—the existence of physical planning is not a requirement for membership—but Yugoslavia is excluded. Kornai specifically describes the class as characterized by an idealized description of historically developed and existing East European systems. He writes that he is not dealing with "what the socialist economy would be like if it functioned otherwise than as it does" (1980, 3). His descriptive term for the class is socialist, but it seems to be better labelled as centrally planned socialist.

57. For example, one might envision an economy in which money is used only as a unit of account. Enterprise managers receive without compensation all the resources that they request. However, if their average output-input ratio should fall below a certain level for a specified time period, the future lifetime income of these managers would be reduced to a minimum subsistence level. Both the ratio and the time period are uniform for all enterprises, and thus are not subject to individual bargaining, which would make them "soft" in Kornai's terminology. Given both concavity of the production function and a proper choice of the ratio and time period by higher authorities, one might expect that there would be no "shortages" of resources. (Compare the treatment by Trevor W. Buck in "Soft Budgets and Administration," *Comparative Economic Studies* 30, no. 3 (Fall 1988):55, 58.)

58. Indeed, Kornai writes that "the explanation of chronic shortage is to be found *not in the financial sphere* . . . but at a deeper level, in institutional relationships and in behavioral regularities which these institutional relations foster in decision-makers" (Kornai's emphasis; 1980, 559).

59. Elsewhere, Kornai stresses that the degree of softness of the en
terprise's budget constraint is a part of the *expectation* by the decision-making
enterprise manager. What matters is his perceived subjective probability of
receiving external assistance from the state in the event of financial difficulties
(Kornai, "Gomulka on the Soft Budget Constraint: A Reply," *Economics of
Planning* 19, no. 2 (1985):49–50).

60. Kornai (1980, 204–6, 532, 556, 559, and chap. 22). Since Kornai
discusses the role of institutional relations in only a very sketchy fashion, it is
difficult to be sure whether he regards them as sufficient to obtain his results.
I prefer to believe that he also implicitly holds to the informational assumption presented in the text.

61. Kornai writes that, in his opinion, a socialist firm that is offered
bank credit to be repaid with interest would never reject it on the grounds
that "we are afraid that the investment might not be a success financially, and
we would get into trouble in the repayment of the credit." Private conversa-
tions, he adds, revealed that several Hungarian economists could not even
imagine a situation where the supply of credits to finance investment exceeds
the demand for them (ibid., 208, 520–21).

62. See, for example, the Chinese Academy of Social Science Group
for Studying the Experience of the Sixth FYP, "Economic Construction and
Reform during the Sixth Five-Year Plan Period," *Social Sciences in China* 7, no.
2 (June 1986):41. In writing of the problems of controlling investment during
the inflationary period of 1984–85, the authors point to the fact that the enterprises were not responsible for profit and loss.

In general, Kornai's analysis of East European centrally planned economies appears to have had considerable influence on the way that many Chinese
economists interpret the situation facing Chinese state-owned enterprises.

63. There is, however, the important difference that, in the second
and especially in the third procurement stages, the Chinese regional governmental bodies find that the (n) specific resource constraints applicable to each
are fungible. (Such fungibility can also be achieved in the first procurement
stage through interregional barter, which from the point of view of the regions is similar to international trade.) This is because resources from other
regions are available to them in exchange for money.

In contrast, both the Soviet and the Chinese national governments are
subject to (n) distinct resource constraints. Their fungibility can occur only
through international trade.

64. This is in contrast with what might be commanded from the peas-
antry of the same region through market transactions.

65. A countervailing historical phenomenon, present during both the
second and third stages, is that it is the national government which was most
concerned with fighting inflation and thus felt most financially constrained,
and the regional governments which were in the better financial situation.
The strength of support for hypothesis (4.3) is indicated by the evidence in
table 4.2, which shows the weakness of the net effect of this countervailing
phenomenon.

Chapter 5

1. This refers to the treatment in the latter part of chapter 4, where I dealt with the degree of enterprise concern for financial results.

2. The issue does not arise in the analysis of state industry in the East European planned economies. It is a maintained assumption that, in each of these economies, there is only a single principal.

3. Granick, "Institutional Innovation and Economic Management: The Soviet Incentive System, 1921 to the Present," in Guroff and Carstensen (1983), 223–57.

4. Blue collar workers whose earnings are lower than those with comparable skills in other enterprises may be expected to quit and find work elsewhere, and the quality of the enterprise's work force may rapidly deteriorate. This will have serious implications in the following period for the evaluation of management by its supervisory body, and thus for the lifetime earnings of the enterprise managers.

5. See, especially, Granick, "Soviet Research and Development Implementation in Products: A Comparison with the G.D.R.," in Levcik (1978), 37–56, and Granick, in Guroff and Carstensen (1983), 223–57.

6. The 50 per cent figure refers to all enterprises that were supervised by the Russian Republic office of the State Bank. Sources are those cited in Granick (1972, 278); N. Fedorenko and P. Bunich, *Mekhanizm ekonomicheskogo stimulirovaniia pri sotsializme* (Moscow, 1973), 249, as quoted in J. Adam, "The Present Soviet Incentive System," *Soviet Studies* 32, no. 3 (July 1980):360; Iu. Artemov in *Voprosy Ekonomiki*, 1975, no. 8:40–42; and *Sotsialisticheskii Trud*, 1980, no. 6:45, and 1982, no. 11:44.

7. The 1934 sample covered 747 top managers. A broader coverage reported in the same original Soviet study for the same month, that included all managers and professionals who were working at the level of plant administration, had a sample size of 21,092 and showed similar results.

8. Explicit weighting began only in 1965. It existed in the most uniform fashion (and for this reason was most clearly described in the Soviet literature) during the period from 1965 through the early 1970s, but such weighting has continued thereafter.

9. In the GDR, the entire labor force of an enterprise shares in the bonus fund. The percentage is calculated from Granick (1976, 218–19) and from average monthly earnings in industry in 1972 (*Statistisches Jahrbuch 1974*, 73).

10. This estimate is made on the basis of full coverage of all top managers in six industrial ministries during 1969 and part of 1970 (Granick 1976, 105–8).

11. See Granick (1976, 88–89, 100–109).

12. A 1985 circular of provincial authorities in Shaanxi defined the "leading body" of a factory as consisting of eight persons who included, in addition to five in standard management posts, the secretary and associate secretary of the Party unit and the trade union president (*JPRS-CEA-86-007* (21 January 1986), 30, referring to a report in *Shaanxi Ribao* (9 August 1985), 1).

Our sample provides information for five enterprises as to whether the trade union president was included in this group. He was included in two and not included in three.

13. The issue of this group's relative income will be pursued further in the following section. Interviews in Hong Kong during 1979–80 with seventy Chinese emigrants revealed an insistence on their part that leading executives have never received bonuses or incentive pay (Walder 1981, 113, fn.6). What is of interest in this result is not the question of the accuracy of the data, but rather the apparent absence at that time of popular belief in "abuses" of the bonus system in favor of upper echelon personnel.

14. In general, it is said that none were paid in China. However, four of our twenty sample enterprises did make such payments during each year of 1975–77. For two of these enterprises, the peak payment was 0.3 per cent of the average annual earnings paid in all state-owned industrial enterprises in China in that year; it was substantially less for the other two.

15. Thirteen of the twenty sample enterprises describe themselves as having given bonuses in 1978. However, only two of the thirteen paid an average bonus that was at least 0.56 per cent of the average earnings paid in all state-owned industrial enterprises in China during that year, and none provided a bonus greater than 0.66 per cent. Since most enterprises in China are said to have issued year-end bonuses for 1978, it is likely that this accounts for the bulk of the bonuses of these thirteen (see *B.R.* 22, no. 16 [20 April 1979]:5–6). It is possible that some of the remaining seven also issued such bonuses, but included them in their 1979 accounts.

16. This is likely to be a fairly good assumption in most cases. However, although we have no data that bear on this issue, it is quite possible that in some enterprises a portion of special incentive pay provided to top managers was hidden in the form of "subsidies" to the job. Although such subsidies would have come mainly or entirely from the enterprise's bonus pot, they would probably not have been counted in the statistics compiled by our sample enterprises as to bonuses received by top managers.

17. In four of the five cases where the proportion was above 100 per cent, top-management income never totalled more than 121 per cent of that of the average employee. The fifth case occurred in 1978. In the following year, the bonus/income ratio for top management compared to all employees in this enterprise fell from 130 to 72 per cent.

18. For the period after 1982, but only for this period, there were two cases in which bonus awards for top management of enterprises were intended to be unusually high if the enterprise earned large profits. One of these plants was supervised by a municipality and the other by a province.

The first case (1984) was intended to apply for only one year. It is not known either whether the enterprise met the necessary standard or whether such bonuses were paid. In the second case (for 1985 and 1986), the enterprise did meet the standard but no bonus was paid. The director, commenting on the fact that he had not been offered the money, said that he would not have dared to accept it if offered; this, he said, was because of the egalitarian mindset that existed in his enterprise.

19. In a larger sample of eleven enterprises and forty-one enterprise-years, the absolute bonus received by upper management was less than that of the average employee in just half the cases. In nine of the eleven enterprises, there was at least one year in which the bonus was less; in ten, there was at least one year in which it was greater.

20. The six indicators, each for the same year as the dependent variable, are: profits as a percentage of sales; profits as a percentage of the original value of fixed capital used in production; value of output as a percentage both of the original and of the final planned figure; profits as a percentage both of the original and of the final planned figure. The sample covers eleven enterprises and forty-one enterprise-years; ten additional enterprise-years (with only partial data) were also used to extend the analysis.

21. Yuan Zhen, in *Renmin Ribao* (4 May 1984), 5, as translated in *Chinese Economic Studies* 18, no. 4 (1985):80.

22. This was the view of one of my Western colleagues who participated in the conducting of the interviews.

23. I have raised this question with a number of Western experts more familiar than I am with contemporary Chinese mores. All agreed that dismissal from a major post solely on such grounds was unlikely. One well-informed Chinese in Beijing expressed privately the same opinion.

24. Sample A is discussed by Song Shiqi and Wu Xuelin, in *Renmin Ribao* (12 September 1985), 1, as reported in *JPRS-CEA-86-001* (2 January 1986), 49–50.

25. Yang Guansan, Lin Bin, Wang Hansheng, and Wu Qahui, "Enterprise Cadres and Reform," in Reynolds (1987), 74–85. This English translation has been supplemented by references to the original in China Economic System Reform Research Institute (1986). I am grateful to Professor Mou Ying of Beijing Normal University for the translations.

26. The conclusion as to the levels of management included in the two samples is based on the number of personnel per enterprise in the respective samples. Sample A averages thirty-one people per enterprise, compared with one and one-half in sample B.

27. Analogous materials for Hungary indicate that age sixty has consistently been a comparable retirement date for senior line management in that country. In census figures for 1960, 1970, and 1980, and in special statistical surveys conducted for the Council of Ministers during 1981 and 1983, 3 to 4 per cent of such managers have been over the age of sixty while the proportion aged fifty-six to sixty has been substantial (Judit Székely, "Some Data to the Analysis of the Educational Level of Top Managers in Economy," table 8, and János Bernáth, "Recruitment and Mobility of State and Cooperative Leaders," figure 1, in *Education, Mobility and Network of Leaders in a Planned Economy*, ed. György Lengyel, Working Paper no. 3 [April 1987], Karl Marx University of Economic Sciences, Department of Sociology, Budapest).

28. Although we do not have age data for enterprise directors compared to deputy directors in Eastern Europe, we do know the number of previous posts they had held as either deputy director or director. Directors had held about twice as many such posts (ranging between 0.9 and 1.8, depend-

ing on the country) as had their deputies (whose range was between 0.4 and 0.9). Promotion through the ranks of management seems to have been much more important in these countries. (Data are from a 1981 survey of enterprise directors and their deputies in the electronic, energy, chemical, food, and light industries [Pál Bóday, "Careers of Top Enterprise Leaders in International Comparison," in Lengyel, *Education, Mobility*, 84–86].)

29. This compares with 68 per cent in Hungary as of 1981 who had been appointed to their current post more than three years earlier. This sample has a broader sectoral coverage than industry alone, and it seems probable that the industrial subsector has an even higher percentage (Bernáth, "Recruitment," 59).

30. Of the post-1980 appointments in sample B, 72 per cent had been of people whose positions in 1980 were below the hierarchical level of deputy director; a minimum of 80 per cent of all post-1980 appointments were given to those who had already worked in that same enterprise for at least four years. This last figure of 80 per cent is based on the assumption that the same proportion of post-1980 appointments as of 1976–79 appointments were from people working in the enterprise prior to 1977. This biases the figure upward. On the other hand, there is a much sharper downward bias that arises from the implicit assumption made in the calculation that all post-1980 appointments were actually made in 1981; in fact, about half were made during 1984–85.

31. In neither sample, however, do the sources state whether the figures refer to completion of higher education.

32. Richman (1969, 145). This relatively low level of education among top managers was not so much due to the rarity of higher education in the thirty-eight industrial enterprises in which Richman interviewed—5,569 people or 3.7 per cent of the labor force in these enterprises had such education. Rather it was because neither the job of director nor that of Party secretary was then viewed as requiring technical expertise (145, 154–56). Just as is the case for the 1980s samples, Richman fails to state whether the figures refer to graduations or simply to participation in higher educational programs; one would assume the former, but it is unclear.

33. In the United States, even in 1964 and for a group restricted to the top two officers, the figure had not passed 74 per cent (Granick 1972, 168). In Eastern Europe, a 1981 survey of enterprise directors and their deputies in the electronic, energy, chemical, food, and light industries showed the following percentages as having higher education: Bulgaria, 98.8; Poland, 98.5; Hungary, 87.7; and Czechoslovakia, 60.5 (Pál Bóday, "Careers," 84–86). For Hungary, a 1983 survey with a much larger sample is probably more reliable: for all of industry, the figure for a comparable population was 70.2 per cent (Judit Székely, "Some Data," 35–37). It is probable that the Romanian figure, like the Bulgarian and Polish, was in the top decile, while the East German was similar to the Czechoslovak (see Granick 1976, table 14.3).

34. Although we have no data permitting direct comparison with the industrial labor force, the proportion of the total Chinese population age twenty-five or older who had received higher education or its equivalent was

1.3 per cent at the time of the 1982 population census. (I cannot tell whether these include only those with the equivalent of university degrees.) Excluding servicemen from the enumeration by type of education but including them in the population, the census showed that 0.6 per cent of all ages had "university or equivalent" education (*Statistical Yearbook of China 1985,* 191). Including servicemen in the enumeration by education, 0.5 per cent of the population were university graduates or the equivalent, and another 0.2 per cent had had some university training (*Statistical Yearbook of China 1986,* 79). It is the 0.6 per cent figure that is used in my calculations.

If we make two upward-biasing assumptions—that all those with higher education were living in urban areas and that the proportion of the population over age twenty-four was the same in urban as in rural areas—the comparable urban adult population ratio with higher education was 6.5 per cent. This is an upperbound estimate, which can be taken as generally consistent with the 1966 figure of 3.7 per cent that was given by Richman for the industrial work force of 150,000 in enterprises in which he interviewed (1969, 156).

If this 6.5 per cent figure is considered as at all approximating reality, it is amazingly high in comparison with some developed countries. (The same is true if we take 4.6 per cent, or five-sevenths of the 6.5 per cent, on the basis that the higher figure may represent all those with the equivalent of some university education.) In France in 1962 (census data), for example, only 2.6 per cent of the male population over age twenty-two had completed higher education, despite the fact that the higher educational proportion for males was higher than that for females.

No further analysis of the dimensions of the stock of Chinese graduates of higher education will be attempted, since the issue has only the most peripheral relevance for this study.

35. The requirement of Party membership, at least for the vast bulk of appointees, appears to have remained in force. At least minimal work experience must also have been demanded.

36. Data for 1966 are from Richman's interviews in industrial enterprises. Of the twenty-one directors whose previous position is known, eight were promoted from within the enterprise, four came directly from the armed forces, and five had been Party secretaries elsewhere (1969, 302).

Relevant data from our own sample enterprises are extremely scanty; all relate to 1983–84. In one of these enterprises, three of the top eight managers had been in the post for the past ten years, with two having been promoted from within the enterprise and one brought in from the outside. Finally, the two top executives of this enterprise were on temporary duty from the supervising municipal body. A discussion of the situation pertaining to the total domain of the supervisory body of a second enterprise stressed substantial movement of managerial personnel in both directions between the supervisory body and the enterprises it controlled. In a third enterprise, the two top executives (Party secretary and enterprise director) had each held the same function at least since 1979. In a fourth organization (the county administration in charge of seventeen state enterprises), forty-nine Party secretaries and factory directors had been replaced since 1979, representing a rate of change of 144 per cent over a little more than four years. It is difficult to sum up this material with other than a single word: diversity.

Walder (1986, 72) claims that the career pattern of top executives and political cadres of an enterprise typically spans a number of enterprises and even overlaps the jurisdiction of any single supervisory body. However, Walder (1981, 47) also wrote that such careers were conducted in more than one enterprise. Thus his data presumably refer to information dating from 1980 and earlier. In neither source does he document his claim. I presume that it rests upon his interviews in 1979–80 in Hong Kong with emigrants.

37. Given the low likelihood that they will be promoted to a more important enterprise, this type of career advancement would have to be to an organization above the level of the enterprise. In view of the limited number of such organizations in industry, there would be a very low probability of attaining such a post sufficiently senior for it to be attractive.

38. We have no information as to the proportion of top managers who were members of the Chinese Communist Party, but one would expect it to be very high. For a similar population in Eastern Europe covered by a 1981 survey, the percentage of enterprise directors and their deputies who were Party members was 100 for directors and 93–94 for deputies in Poland and Czechoslovakia, but only 82–88 for directors and 75–78 for deputies in Hungary and Bulgaria (Pál Bóday, "Careers," 84–86).

39. There were seventy-one enterprise-years of information, which divided as follows: <100%, 9; 100–150%, 12; 151–75%, 24; 176–200%, 21; 201–15%, 4; and 232%, 1. The data as to total income of upper managers are based on the assumption that the subsidies they received were identical to the average subsidies of the total work force of their enterprise.

40. The East European countries are Hungary, the GDR, Romania, and the Slovenian portion of Yugoslavia (Granick 1976, 459–62).

41. Data regarding the absolute level of average income of top management in 1980 are available for eleven of the twenty enterprises. The two organizations with the highest income averaged, respectively, renminbi 154 and 160 monthly. In contrast, three staff members in a hospital with a total work force of 830 people earned salaries in the same year of renminbi 200 monthly, which was about 300 per cent of the average salary in that hospital (Henderson 1982, 32, 131). These three staff members constituted 0.4 per cent of the hospital's work force, a proportion higher (thus displaying lower selectivity in choosing the group) than that in 60 per cent of the enterprises in our sample for which we have top management income data. The percentage was higher than that of six of the seven enterprises for which we have data as to both numbers and total earnings of top managers.

42. A set of regulations issued jointly in September 1986 by the Party's Central Committee and the State Council suggested that the factory director should earn two to four times as much as an ordinary worker. This ratio was to hold in the developing "director responsibility system" which, as of mid-1987, covered one-third of all state-owned enterprises (*B.R.* 30, no. 32 [10 August 1987], 4, 14).

43. Due to the erratic timing of wage increases during the history of the post-1949 regime, the advantaged group has been composed particularly of those already working by the mid-1950s. It seems likely that top management personnel constituted an older group in the mid-1970s than it did in the early 1980s. This probably explains why, out of the eight enterprises for which we have data covering five or more years, five display a secular decline in the multiple of average income of top management compared to that of all employees.

44. Indeed, in certain respects industrial managers should feel even more solidarity with their work force in China than in Japan. This is because Japanese managerial careers in large firms, although normally limited to a single enterprise, commonly involve frequent geographic moves among the enterprise's units located within Japan. In contrast, Chinese managers—even top managers—have grave difficulties in moving from one location to another within the enterprise because of restrictions on registration of residence. Our sample provides information as to only one enterprise which, due to merger, saw many of its managers move from the locality of the original enterprise to another urban area. None of these managers were able to take their families with them, despite the fact that these had mostly urban registration. Presumably as a result, half of all workers and managers who had moved from the original site and who were still there two years after the merger, returned within the following year to their home location. Even three years after the merger, no manager had been able to change his own official urban registration to the new location.

See, however, Walder (1986) who places emphasis upon the discord in relationships within the blue collar labor force of a factory between activists and all others. Nevertheless, this type of conflict need not spill over into discord between managers and the remainder of the work force. In Walder's account, it even neutralizes to some degree the inherent conflict between managerial and blue collar personnel within an enterprise.

45. Walder, describing particularly the years 1973–76, stresses the decline in work discipline in factories because of managers' reluctance to antagonize the blue collar work force (1986, 205–10).

46. William Byrd and Gene Tidrick, in their treatment of the sample Chinese enterprises, suggest instead the concept of a hierarchy of motives that drive enterprises, with the satisfaction of each motive having to reach a threshold level before the others come into play. Two of the motives that they list are expansion and improvement of technology ("Factor Allocation and Enterprise Incentives," in Tidrick and Chen [1987], 62–67).

A Maslowian (Maslow 1954) hierarchical structure of motives would be an extremely complex concept to use in the analysis of enterprises. To make it operational, one would have to specify the hierarchical order, a series of threshold levels for each motive, and a vector of marginal rates of substitution in the satisfaction of different motives after the crossing of thresholds. The resultant matrix would have to be estimable, given characteristics of the enterprise itself and/or of its environment. Such estimation would be a formidable undertaking; Byrd and Tidrick make no attempt at it.

47. The average for the enterprise applies to its state-employed labor force as a whole, and includes temporary workers. Members of collective enterprises who work within the state enterprise are excluded. Separate data as to average earnings of temporary and permanent manual workers are available for seven enterprises. The ratio of the two within a given year in the same enterprise varies from 62 to 133 per cent; four of the seven enterprises provide data for at least one year in which the ratio is 96 per cent or higher. But 72 per cent is the peak ratio for one enterprise, and 80–82 per cent for two others. Thus there is enormous disparity, both between enterprises and, to a lesser degree, between years for the same enterprise, in the earnings of temporary as compared with permanent manual workers.

48. We also have 1986 data for nine of the sample enterprises. Comparing only end-years for these nine, changes in the peak-year index of average earnings between 1982 and 1986 seems to have been fairly similar to what they were during the reform years treated in table 5.3. The same is true with respect to changes in rank between the two years.

Peak-Year Index of Average Earnings as Proportion of Index of Low Year (comparison of first and last year)

	Number of Enterprises		
Proportion	1982–86	1978–82	1978–86
≤111 per cent	4	5	2
112–19 per cent	0	1	0
≥120 per cent	5	3	7

Changes in Rank Among the Nine Enterprises (between end-years)

	Number of Enterprises		
Rank Changes	1982–86	1978–82	1978–81
0–1	4	3	2
2–3	1	5	4
4–5	3	0	3
6–7	1	1	0

49. The peak bonus of the period was paid in 1978; in only one enterprise did it then reach even 0.7 per cent of the annual total earnings.

50. $\bar{R}^2$ in the above regression, with 9 degrees of freedom, is extremely high: 0.824. However, when the same regression is run without PROVST, it falls to 0.378. This decline seems to be due primarily to two enterprises which had the highest values in the sample both for the dependent variable and for PROVST, and were in the smallest POP category.

51. Of the enterprises excluded, three had improved their relative earnings substantially during 1978–81. But the fourth had only bounced around, and the fifth had actually deteriorated.

52. It is conceivable, although it seems unlikely, that this situation of volatility changed after 1984. At that time, there was the introduction of taxation of those bonuses that averaged above one-third of base wages in the individual enterprise. One Western scholar describes the situation in mid-1986 as having been one in which virtually all state enterprises paid bonuses up to the untaxed limit, and none paid more than this (A. G. Walder, "Wage Reform and the Web of Factory Interests," in *C.Q.*, no. 109 [March 1987]:355). However, the data of note 48 above with respect to nine of our sample enterprises suggests that volatility did not decline. For these enterprises, it was at least as great between 1982 and 1986 as it had been through 1982.

53. A lag of two years rather than one is chosen partly with an eye to dampening the autocorrelation between successive observations for a single enterprise. Each of the four reform years analyzed is necessarily correlated with only one other year, rather than having two of them necessarily being correlated with two other years, as would be the case with a one-year lag. For the two enterprises in which merger was known to be the dominant cause of labor force growth, the years of rapid growth were treated as though the rate of expansion had been the same as the average in all state-owned industry. This was done in an attempt to eliminate increases that should not be expected to affect age, and thus average wage grade, of the work force.

54. Both coefficients are highly significant. The t-values are -3.1 for β and 4.1 for α.

55. An unsuccessful attempt was made to incorporate retirements into the regression. This was done to take account of the fact that the ratio of pensioners to state-employed workers has become significant, and that this is a recent phenomenon. All, or essentially all, of these pensioners formerly worked in the state-owned sector.

Such significance is shown by the following data. The State Statistical Bureau gives the "number of people retired or resigned from jobs" as of the end of 1985 as 8.6 per cent of the total nonagricultural population in all 150 cities with a population over 200,000, and as 18.6 per cent in Shanghai (*China Urban Statistics 1986* 1987, 468–69, 218–19). For China in 1985, it has been estimated that the number of pensioners equaled some 15 per cent of the labor force of all state-owned units in all sectors of the economy (Huang Xiaojing and Yang Xiao, "From Iron Rice Bowls to Labor Markets," in Reynolds [1987], 148). A Chinese study intended to represent the total labor force of Shanghai yielded (in preliminary results) a value of 25.3 per cent for the proportion of pensioners to the total labor force at the end of 1983. Most significantly, two-thirds of these Shanghai pensioners had retired after 1977 (*JPRS-CEA-85-027* (19 March 1985), 108–13, reproducing Chen Huili and Gu Renzhang's study in *Shehui Kexue*, no. 11 [15 November 1984], 30–32).

For eight enterprises, we have data on the number of pensioners as of 1982. The stylized assumption was made that these individuals all retired during the reform years. This is not too great an exaggeration because of the strong retirement incentives that existed in this period due to children being able to inherit the family's jobs. On this basis, the variable Z was created, where $Z = $ (number of pensioners in 1982)/(total work force in 1978). This variable was added as an independent variable to the regression in which the left-hand side is (EARNAVCHIIND$_t$ − EARNAVCHIIND$_{t-2}$). The resulting signs of the coefficients were correct (i.e., negative), but the coefficients themselves were not significant. Moreover, the coefficient of Z was very close to zero. Nevertheless, the issue is extremely troublesome. Of the nine enterprises for which we have data, Z takes a value of <4 per cent for three, and of >20 per cent for three others. As one might expect, it is in the older plants that we observe the high values.

56. Unfortunately, it also serves as a proxy for some portion of any secular change in the enterprise's relative average earnings due to multicollinearity of (EARNAVCHIIND$_{i,t}$ − EARNAVCHIIND$_{i,t-2}$) and (TOQST$_{i,t}$/ TOQST$_{i,t-2}$).

57. While the above describes the official pattern, most enterprises in our sample in fact received fewer targets than these eight for most of the period studied. In cases of less than 100 per cent plan fulfillment, at least two of the enterprises were theoretically subject to reduction of retained profits rather than of bonuses. There are no known instances in which any of our sample enterprises had their bonuses reduced; none were affected by the provisions that formally govern with regard to reductions in bonuses. One enterprise was, however, affected in 1982 with regard to retained profits.

One of our sample enterprises operated in 1983 under a scheme where bonus was to be increased in steps depending on the achievement of varying levels of above-plan physical production. This is the only case, and that only for one year, in which our sample showed violation of the general rule that bonuses would remain unchanged with above-plan performance.

58. Of the twenty sample enterprises during 1979–82, one-half financed bonuses entirely, or almost entirely, out of retained profits, and another one-quarter financed about 80 per cent of bonus expenditures from such profits. Only one-fourth of the sample used this source for 50 per cent or less of the financing.

59. These special bonuses were often, although not always, excluded from the limits that existed through most of 1984 on the maximum permissible ratio between bonuses and the enterprise's base wages. Thus in 1979, national regulations were issued which exempted from these limits all bonuses awarded for the saving of ten specified types of fuels, raw materials, and intermediate products. Such bonuses were never paid from retained profits; instead, they were included in production costs (*Almanac of China's Economy in 1981* 1982, 200).

60. This discontinuity assumption was tested by running the same regressions as are reported in the appendix to this chapter, but treating all "performance as per cent of plan" figures that fall below 100 per cent as though they were only one-third of their actual value. There are only four such cases.

61. This "cash flow" is differentiated from the term cash flow as used in chapter 6 by the fact that here profits include those used to fund bonuses.

62. We could instead take the amortized value of all fixed capital, plus working capital invested in inventories, as the proxy for capital. But this would have the disadvantage of not distinguishing between fixed capital

used for production purposes and that used for nonproduction objectives (primarily housing).

63. Statistically significant dependence refers to the t-statistics for individual regression coefficients, rather than to an F-test for the equation specification as a whole. Even equations that restricted the independent variables solely to Control variables were highly significant when judged by the F-test.

64. The regression of EARNAVCHIIND on Profits/Personnel and Profits as Percentage of Final Plan, but without any Control variables, yielded t-ratios of 2.1 and 2.9, respectively. However, when the same regression was run adding YRSEC as a Control variable (this reduced the degrees of freedom from 13 to 4), both of these t-ratios became less than 0.3.

65. B.R. 25, no. 41 (11 October 1982), 27–28. The information came from a "responsible official" of the Bureau of City Housing under the Ministry of Urban and Rural Construction and Environmental Protection. If these figures are at all correct, the share of individual ownership in the total urban housing stock must be a fairly large multiple of the 18 per cent figure. Although such ownership dates primarily from pre-1949 property rights and from inheritance, 2 to 3 per cent of all urban housing construction during 1979–80 was by private individuals (*China Official Annual Report 1981* 1981, 753–54, and *Almanac of China's Economy in 1981* 1982, 129). Beginning in 1983, existing urban apartments began to be sold by government bodies; total sales during 1983 and 1984 seem to have been about the same as the volume of private urban building during 1979–80 (*B.R.* 28, no. 25 [24 June 1985], 6–7).

Although in principle organizations rent only to their own labor force, this maxim is abused by former members of the organization and even by their heirs. For an example of de facto inheritance, see Suzanne Pepper, "China's Universities," in *Modern China* 8, no. 2 (April 1982):160, 188.

66. In 1981, enterprises were said to be responsible for two-thirds of housing construction in Shanghai. I have not heard of a similar institutional situation existing in other Chinese cities except for Tianjin; it applied there only to that portion of enterprise housing which, as part of the process of expansion of capacity and labor force, was financed either by the state or through bank loans.

67. *JPRS-CEA-86-035* (1 April 1986), 15–16, presents data for five of the cities on per capita living space in 1982, 1983, and 1984. Comparisons of these figures with those for 1984 from *Statistical Yearbook of China 1985*, 53–184, can be made for four relevant cities. The former figures range between 118 and 194 per cent of the latter, and average 150 per cent. This suggests that the former figures refer to official residents only, while the latter (used for two enterprises) divides total living space by all inhabitants. This comparison indicates that our figures for most of the cities are overstated estimates of per capita living space, and thus that the advantage of living in enterprise-owned housing is understated in the text.

68. The figure of 4.0 persons per household is taken from 1983 data for sample households in cities of the relevant size (*Statistical Yearbook of China 1984*, 470). Census data for 1982 gave 4.2 persons in all larger cities (Thomas Scharping, *Chinas Bevölkerung 1953–1982*, pt. 3 [*B.B.I.*, 43-1985], 10), and 3.95

for all urban households ("A Report on the International Seminar on China's 1982 Census," in *Social Sciences in China* 6, no. 1 [1985]:49).

For living space as a percentage of total space, the official Chinese figure used is 58 per cent, while 66 per cent was shown in a survey of 323 cities that was conducted during 1985–86 (see note 91, in this chap.). Two of our sample enterprises are characterized by a ratio of 60.8 per cent.

69. These ratios are bottom estimates, since they probably overestimate the per capita living space for most of the cities (see note 67 above).

70. See, for example, Zhang Shaojie, Cui Heming, Xu Gang, and Ji Xiaoming, "Investment: Initial Changes in the Mechanism and Preliminary Ideas about Reform," in Reynolds (1987), 118. They argue to the effect that state enterprises have a bias against investment in productive facilities and toward investment in housing. It is true that one sample enterprise (not included in the seven noted above in the text) reported that any of its workers who wished could receive enterprise housing but that municipal housing was both of superior quality and more spacious. This is the only such case that has come to my attention. Further, a statement about averages does not mean that those workers who choose to live in this enterprise's housing do not profit from the opportunity.

71. See the Chinese source quoted by Barry Naughton, "The Decline of Central Control over Investment in Post-Mao China," in Lampton (1987), 67.

72. The financing in the case that is better documented occurred between 1978 and 1980. In early 1984, the workers of the same enterprise were enthusiastic about the likelihood of further expansion on the basis that it would again lead to new housing paid for by the national government. In the second case, this practice similarly seemed to continue into early 1984.

73. In all urban areas of China from 1978 through 1983, the number of new hires within the state sector as a proportion of all new hires (including self-employed) plus unemployed ranged annually between 36.5 and 46.3 per cent (calculated from Jeffrey R. Taylor, "Labor Force Developments in the People's Republic of China, 1952–83," in JEC [1986], v. 1, 255).

74. One author talks of thirty-five as the maximum age of eligibility for inheriting a job in an urban state enterprise. The statement is based on anthropological work conducted during 1979 and 1980 in one brigade in Guangdong province. This is the only reference I have seen to an age above thirty (Sulamith Heins Potter, "The Position of Peasants in Modern China's Social Order," *Modern China* 9, no. 4 [October 1983]:483).

75. B. Naughton, "False Starts and Second Wind," in Perry and Wong (1985), 225.

76. Clearly, the test is a very weak one. Among other things, it is meaningful only to the degree that the size of the enterprise's profits are closely correlated with the size of profits per employee, or with some other profit ratio that is taken seriously by supervisory bodies. Nevertheless, the 3 per cent figure is low enough so that the result is worth reporting. I calculated this figure through path analysis. What is reported is that $\bar{R}^2 = 0.325$ between change in gross profits and retained profits, and 0.084 between change in retained profits and per capita bonuses.

The study was conducted by the China Economic System Reform Institute. The coefficients of determination are reported as pertaining to 1984 in *JPRS-CEA-86-027* (17 March 1986), 2, and in Chen Yizi, Wang Xiaoqiang, and colleagues, "Reform: Results and Lessons from the 1985 CESRRI Survey," *J.C.E.* 11, no. 3 (September 1987):464. However, Xia Xiaoxun and Li Jun, "Consumption Expansion: A Grave Challenge to Reform and Development," in Reynolds (1987), 89–90, report them as pertaining to change during the first half of 1985. All authors are from the same institute and appear to have taken part in the study.

77. It should be noted that the October 1984 plenum of the Party Central Committee voiced the view that enterprises should be put to the test of the marketplace "so that only the best survive" ("Decision," in *B.R.* 28, no. 35 [2 September 1985], x). This reads as if it were the acceptance of financial results as a proxy for efficiency.

78. To overcome the difficulty that, given the current pricing system, one cannot link bonuses to profits, "the Party Committee and the People's Government of Anhui province . . . fix bonuses according to the concrete situation, exercise discretion, and try to be reasonable." (Yuan Zhen, "On the Question of Understanding the Improvement in the Method of Bonus Distribution," in *Chinese Economic Studies* 18, no. 4 [Summer 1985]:78–80. The article first appeared in *Renmin Ribao* [4 May 1984], 5.)

79. We have direct data for five cases concerning bonuses paid per enterprise employee for such national awards. As a proportion of average annual earnings in the enterprise, they were the following: (1) 0 per cent; (2)–(4) 1.8 to 2.5 per cent; and (5) 5.1 per cent.

Three enterprises are included in the above four cases in which bonuses were paid. In one, the bonus paid for the award was not included within the limit on bonuses allowed to be paid that year within that enterprise. In a second (for two years), these bonuses were included; however, it seems likely that the retained profits of the enterprise would have been insufficient to have permitted reaching the limit except for the bonus paid as a result of the award. We have no data on this matter with regard to the third enterprise.

80. Of the four bonus payments made in connection with the award, one was to an enterprise whose total earnings per capita were extremely low; two others were to an enterprise in the unusual position of having insufficient retained earnings to pay out the permitted level of bonus without receiving this special source of bonus funds.

81. Here we measure capital by the original value of fixed assets in productive facilities alone. Both the measures of labor and of capital productivity take gross output as their numerator, rather than the conceptually preferable but much less reliable data for value added.

82. The most frequent Western calculations of both capital productivity and of total factor productivity show no improvement for Chinese industry as a whole over the period of 1953 through the early 1980s. This result would be consistent with our expectations from the incentive results of the sample.

However, a calculation that explicitly attempts both to deflate figures of capital stock and to remove housing from the capital stock—and in this sense is methodologically sounder—shows an improvement in total factor productivity that is much more respectable. But this calculation may in fact be engaged in double deflation for price changes.

Over the years 1953–82, productivity in this calculation is estimated to have grown at a compound annual rate of 1.1 per cent when evaluated with a Cobb-Douglas function, and of 1.7 per cent with a translog function. If one begins after the end of the early spurt of growth and restricts oneself to 1957–82, the figures are still 0.4 and 1.2 per cent. (K. Chen, G. H. Jefferson, T. G. Rawski, H. C. Wang, and Y. X. Zheng, "New Estimates of Fixed Investment and Capital Stock for Chinese State Industry" and "Productivity Change in Chinese Industry: 1953–1985," Working Papers, Department of Economics, University of Pittsburgh [August and October 1987]. See especially table 4 of the latter paper, which is reproduced in an article with the same title in *J.C.E.* 12, no. 4 [December 1988] : 583. For the suggestion as to possible double deflation, see Nicholas Lardy, "Technical Change and Economic Reform" (typescript, 1987).

83. Ramon Myers, "Economic Structure and Growth," in Rozman (1981), 121; Gilbert Rozman, "Social Integration," in ibid., 159–61. The British and French comparative data relate to the eighteenth century, and the Japanese and Russian to the latter part of the nineteenth century. Rozman used his data to make an entirely different point than the one in the text, but the two points are in no way contradictory.

Loren Brandt (forthcoming). Thomas G. Rawski has painted an analogous picture.

84. Rozman, in Rozman (1981), 179.

85. There was also experimentation with redefining the POP variable. Separate treatment of cities with an urban population over three million has the disadvantage that most such centers in our sample are treated in Chinese law as constituting independent provinces. There is a high correlation between the value of PROVST and the dummy value of those localities with a population of more than three million. In order to reduce the multicollinearity problem, all centers with an urban population over one million were combined. This specification, however, considerably reduced the $\bar{R}^2$ and was discarded.

86. For bonuses, the data set is restricted to 1980–82, with the earliest $(t-1)$ year thus being 1979. This was done because many enterprises showed no bonus distributions at all in 1978 and, in any case, distributions in 1978 were governed by different rules than those applying to later years.

87. One enterprise claimed a growth of 159 per cent between 1980 and 1982, but the reported data appear to be in error.

88. In this calculation, I assume that all of those lodged in the dormitories were employed by the enterprise. More arbitrarily, I assume that each family in family housing contained an average of 1.5 workers in that enterprise. Assumptions of this sort (although not these numbers) are necessary to combine dormitories with family housing.

89. Comparison is made between the situation in 1978 and 1982. Examination of intermediate years, as well as of the pre-1978 period, suggests that the results are reasonably robust with regard to the choice of end-years.

90. The independent variable of Output as Percentage of Final Plan could not be used here, as we would have lost two of our seven observations.

91. The official Chinese ratio is 58 per cent. Presumably, this comes from sample studies. (Yuh-Jiun Lin, "The Supply of and Demand for Urban Housing in Mainland China" [in Chinese], Chung-Hua Institution for Economic Research, *Economic Papers*, no. 100 [October 1986], 7. I am grateful to my colleague Kang Chao for supplying me with this source.)

The 1985–86 survey of 323 cities, described as the first general survey of urban housing but, in fact, limited to cities, showed a ratio of 66.2 per cent between "living space" and "usable floor space" (calculated from State Statistical Bureau, *B.R.* 30, no. 19 [11 May 1987], 25).

92. These data are modified for two enterprises in which growth was due primarily to mergers.

93. Such failure of relation is not because of a lack of dispersion. With regard to the dependent variable, four of the nineteen enterprises had either a decline in labor force or an increase of less than 10 per cent; four others had an increase of more than 40 per cent.

94. Here, as well, there was no lack of dispersion in the dependent variable. Three out of fourteen enterprises had no cooperative employment, while the ratio for four others was 10 per cent or less of the number of state employees. In contrast, four firms had ratios of 70 to 120 per cent.

Chapter 6

1. That sales tax receipts as well as profits are important to localities is shown by the fact that, in 1980, eight of twelve provinces described kept between 42 and 88 per cent of all sales tax generated in their region (World Bank, *China: Socialist Economic Development,* Annex A [1 June 1981], 121, and Audrey Donnithorne, "New Light on Central-Provincial Relations," *The Australian Journal of Chinese Affairs* 10 [July 1983]: 97–99). In one county that provided net revenue to higher authorities, state sales tax constituted 27 per cent of the county's budgetary revenue in 1966 and ranged annually between 44 and 51 per cent during 1976–81 (Vivienne Shue, "Beyond the Budget: Finance Organization and Reform in a Chinese County," *Modern China* 10, no. 2 [April 1984]: 150–51).

2. Sales tax, as applied to the Soviet Union, is usually translated literally as "turnover tax." There seems to be no good reason to use such a translation, particularly since it leads to confusion by suggesting that the tax cascades as taxed items become purchases of other production enterprises. This is not generally the case in the Soviet Union, although it is in China.

3. I have included virtually all taxes paid by Soviet state firms and assumed that the portion other than sales tax was distributed between the industrial sector and all others in accord with their respective total profits. If we exclude payments made on capital and as rent (in Soviet accounting, these are charges paid from profits), the Soviet figure falls to 54 per cent.

4. *Statistical Yearbook of China 1984,* 419, and *Narkhoz SSSR 1922–82,* 549–50, 561. To achieve comparability, social security premiums (paid by enterprises) have been excluded from Soviet government income. Government revenue coming from all sources other than sales tax and levies of any type on state-owned enterprises cannot have been very far from 9 per cent of the total Soviet government income.

Chinese financial statistics treat financial losses due to overvaluation of the renminbi in foreign trade and to subsidization of grain sales by the government as reductions of total income from profits of nonindustrial organizations, rather than as budgetary expenditures. This is why profits from state industrial enterprises appear to be no smaller than profits from all state enterprises in 1980. Such statistical treatment presumably contributes to the fact that Chinese budgetary revenue is less diversified between industrial and other state sectors than is the Soviet.

5. The single major exception is oil refining, presumably existing there as a means of taking account of depletion. See John Pitzer, "Gross National Product of the USSR, 1950–80," in JEC (1982), 35.

6. Table 6.1 shows a ratio of tax plus profits to industrial output in China in 1984 similar to that in the Soviet Union in 1972. I would suppose that this comparison must be faulty, but I am unable to discover why.

7. The justification for treating profits similarly to indirect taxes is that both serve essentially the same purposes: they are primarily either sources of government finance or are used to finance expenditures that would otherwise be paid directly by the government.

Official data for both countries show industrial production to have constituted 43 per cent of net material product in China in 1972 versus 52 per cent in the Soviet Union in the same year (*Statistical Yearbook of China 1986,* 40, and *Narkhoz SSSR v 1972 g.,* 532). The figures did not change greatly in later years. One would think, however, that this relatively small difference is to a large degree explained by the fact that the sales tax plus profits (both of which are included in net material product) constitute a higher proportion of industrial output in China than in the Soviet Union. The latter would be the case for the reason that is treated at length above.

8. National Chinese data in all columns of table 6.1 that take output as their denominator are for 1984 because that is the only year for which output data are published in current prices.

9. Working capital data are available for the Chinese sample but not for the Soviet branches.

10. Chinese national branch data for all state enterprises yield results similar to those of the sample. The national branch data are for a slightly overlapping, but generally later, period: 1981–85. In fact, interbranch differences are less among the eight industries that can be compared using the national data than is shown by the sample data (*Statistical Yearbook of China,* various years). The national branch data have the disadvantage, in comparison with the sample data, of including nonproduction assets (of which housing is the largest item) as part of the fixed-capital denominator of the ratio.

11. Since only a very minor branch of the food industry is represented, it is possible that this conclusion is an artifact of the Chinese sample.

12. The term must be distinguished from "cash flow" as used in chapter 5, which included the profits used to pay bonuses.

13. Fairly similar results are shown in the Chinese national branch data for state enterprises (*Statistical Yearbook of China*, various years). The differences in profit margins for the same branches do not seem to be any greater when one uses the national data and in fact are probably somewhat less.

14. When data were missing, this was almost always during 1975–78.

15. A test of the significance of the difference between means of all observations during the years 1975–78 compared with 1979–82 showed that the increase in the ratio of profit to output measured in current prices was significant at the 5 per cent level. (The increase would have been considerably greater if we had not made a deduction of profits used for bonuses, since such use was quite exceptional prior to 1978.) This increase was counteracted by a small and nonsignificant decline in the rate of tax to output. The decline was sufficient, however, so that the increase in the ratios of neither profit + tax nor of cash flow were significant at the 5 per cent level.

16. The branch data are from He Jianzhang, Kuang Ri'an, and Zhang Zhuoyuan, "Reform of the Economic Structure Requires Industrial Pricing Based on Production Price," in *Social Sciences in China* 2, no. 1 (March 1981): 121. The identical figures were repeated in 1986 by Liu Guogang, in *B.R.* 33 (18 August 1986): 14. Such repetition many years later adds somewhat to the credence of the figures, but it also confirms what is observed in the translated Chinese literature; namely, the paucity of data as to profitability in open Chinese sources.

Capital includes both total fixed assets, valued here at original cost minus depreciation, and working capital inventories. Not included are accounts payable, cash balances, and financing of goods in transport. Note that housing is included in this expression of total capital.

17. *Statistical Yearbook of China 1984*, 262–63. The Statistical Bureau points out that its figures differ from those of the Ministry of Finance.

18. N. R. Lardy, "Economic Relations Between China and the United States," in JEC (1987), 299–300.

19. Jonathan Unger, "The Conflict of Branches vs. Areas vs. Reform," *Australian Journal of Chinese Studies* 18 (July 1987): 31.

20. Group for Studying the Experience of the Sixth Five-year Plan, "Economic Construction and Reform During the Sixth Five-Year Plan Period," *Social Sciences in China* 7, no. 2 (June 1986): 44–45.

21. Xu Yi, Chen Baosen, and Liang Wuxia, *Socialist Price Problems* (in Chinese; Beijing: Chinese Finance and Economic Press, 1982), as translated in *JPRS-CEA-85-019* (10 February 1985), 72.

22. Lin Zili, "Initial Reform in China's Economic Structure—The Experiments in Giving Greater Autonomy to Enterprises in Sichuan, Anhui, and Zhejiang Provinces," in *Social Sciences in China* 1, no. 3 (September 1980): 185.

23. This is the case provided that

$$\gamma > \delta\rho \text{ where } \gamma = a_{l_i x}/a_{lx}, \ \delta = c_i/c, \text{ and } \rho = a_{l_i c_i}/a_{lc}.$$

Assuming that, as is in fact the case in China, agricultural labor and consumer goods constitute a substantial portion of the respective totals, γ is much greater than one, while δ is much less than one. ρ can be greater than, equal to, or less than one; it seems unlikely that it will deviate from one by as much as does either γ or δ.

24. I reject the level of economic development as a causal factor on the basis of historical American data, using benchmark years for the period 1904–77. If one compares the 1939 and 1977 proportions for the United States as shown in table 6.5, the proportions in 1977 are lower, and thus more similar to the Chinese, in eleven cases. Only in two cases are they more similar in 1939. If we were to believe the temporal direction indicated by these differences, then taking account of the level of development would only leave more to explain in the intercountry differences.

For manufacturing as a whole in the United States, the cost of materials fell as a proportion of gross value of production between 1904 and 1967, but only from 57 to 54 per cent (C. D. Romer, "Is the Stabilization of the Postwar Economy a Figment of the Data?," *American Economic Review* 76, no. 3 [June 1986]:328; this result is based upon U.S. Census of Manufactures data, as are the American figures in tables 6.5 and 6.6).

25. It is assumed in this discussion that differences are not a response to price variations between labor and materials, but that they instead represent differences in the slopes of the rays from the origin that connect the vertices in national Leontief isoquants. The effect of substitution due to price differences should make the ratios in the two countries more, rather than less, similar.

26. This is so as long as the price elasticity in the use of labor and materials is less than one.

27. One definitional difficulty drives in the other direction. Chinese state enterprises use not only the labor of direct employees, but also that of members of collectives who work primarily or exclusively for them. The payment of such collective workers is not, however, counted in wages, but rather is lumped with other purchases. However, such statistical treatment does not apply to at least two of the three enterprises in our sample where there is a significant use of collective workers who are integrated into normal operations. For the other cases, it is parallel to the use of subcontractors in the United States when these are fully dependent on the contracting enterprise. Thus it is not too serious a problem for our current statistical analysis.

28. Bonuses are excluded from profits for both countries, and output is measured in current rather than in constant prices.

It is true that these results are not confirmed by the ratio of profits + sales tax to fixed capital. The Chinese ratio is higher in only four of the ten subbranches and is no more than two-thirds as high for state-owned industry as a whole. As discussed earlier, however, Chinese data on fixed capital constitute a highly unreliable indicator of replacement costs.

29. W. Byrd, "The Shanghai Market for the Means of Production," *Comparative Economic Studies* 27, no. 4 (Winter 1985):1–29, and *Shanghai gongye jingji bao* (22 July 1985), 4. For steel rod, dimensions are slightly wider

(0.8–1.5 mm) in the July 1985 source than in the source presenting data for 1979–81. For cement, the July 1985 source fails to specify the grade. I am grateful to Loren Brandt for calling my attention to the 1985 source, as well as for translating it.

Chapter 7

1. As one would expect, both state and Party control are also exercised through functional bodies.

2. For discussions of one-man control in the enterprise, see Granick (1954, 16–28, 224–31), and Hough (1969, 80–100).

3. See, for example, Hough (1969, 94).

4. It appears never to have been implemented universally. In fact, there was even a statement by Mao Zedong that he was not aware of those management decisions that were taken both by the Center and by the localities prior to 1956 (Lee 1987, 30).

5. During the later 1960s and continuing into the early 1970s, it was the Revolutionary Committee rather than the Party committee that really governed.

6. For a fine historical treatment of Chinese intra-enterprise management through 1986, see Heath B. Chamberlain, "Party-Management Relations in Chinese Industries: Some Political Dimensions of Economic Reform," *C.Q.* 112 (1987):631–61. See also Pang Song and Han Gang, "The Party and State Leadership Structure: Historical Investigation and Prospects for Reform," *Social Sciences in China* 8, no. 4 (December 1987):29–56.

7. For an excellent discussion of the Chinese *nomenklatura* system, based heavily on published Chinese sources, see John P. Burns, "China's Nomenklatura System," *Problems of Communism* (September-October 1987): 36–51.

8. In all the interviews, the relevant Party body was always referred to as the Party committee. Ibid., 37–38, 48–50, refers to the body as the "Party core group" (*dangzu*) and describes it as existing (at least in 1980) independently of the Party committee of the same organization. Song and Gang, "The Party and State Leadership Structure," 31, 35, 42, provide a similar treatment to that of Burns. Melanie Manion, "The Cadre Management System, Post-Mao," *C.Q.* 102 (June 1985):209 writes that the Party core group is superior to the comparable Party committee.

The Party core group of bodies with ministerial status is described as consisting of three to five persons, with the minister or a deputy minister normally acting as its leader (Burns, "China's Nomenklatura System," 37). Such composition is fairly similar to that described in the interviews for the standing committee of the enterprise Party committee, with the enterprise director not being singled out but always being a member. (I presume that the term standing committee that was used in the interviews is simply a different translation than Party core group for *dangzu*, although the standing committee is implicitly portrayed somewhat differently.)

9. One organization was the State Council, the highest governmental

body. The second and third were provincial bodies. In one case, but not in the other, the provincial body also confirmed the Party secretary of that particular enterprise.

10. This was for two of the three municipalities in China that have provincial status.

11. Barry Naughton, "Contribution to a Trip Report," (4 February 1985), 31. Typescript.

12. Andrew Walder, "Some Ironies of the Maoist Legacy in Industry," in Selden and Lippit (1982), 237, fn. 12.

13. Among the East European socialist countries and the Soviet Union, Romania is the only nation where Party and governmental jobs are combined (although, as of mid-1988, the USSR also seemed to be moving toward such a system). This has been done in Romania at all levels since 1967 (Edith Lhomel and Madeleine Balussou, "L'économie roumaine à l'heure de la rigueur," *Le Courrier des Pays de l'Est* 275 [July-August 1983], 7). However, the post of director of an enterprise or *centrala* seems never to have been merged with that of Party secretary in Romania; certainly they were not as of 1970.

14. In a second enterprise, a former director seemed to feel the same way. But this is not certain, since the reporting of the interview is confusing.

15. In September 1986, national regulations were issued requiring the introduction of the new system of full leadership by the director in all state-owned enterprises. As of the end of June 1987, it was present, at least in form, in one-third of all state-owned industrial enterprises in China (*B.R.* 30, no. 32 [10 August 1987]:4).

16. This was pointed out to me by Warren Palmer.

17. In one sample enterprise, the Party committee was elected in 1979 by secret ballot of the Party members of the enterprise, with fourteen or fifteen candidates for eleven posts. In theory, it is this Party committee which elects the Party secretary. However, in this enterprise it is the five-person standing committee of the Party committee that really exercises authority. This standing committee was elected by the Party committee and its membership may have been little affected by the results of the election for the three or four contested seats in the Party committee.

18. See Schurmann (1968, 294–303), and Walder, in Selden and Lippit (1982), 233.

19. See Granick (1976, 118–120).

20. *B.R.* 30, no. 32 (10 August 1987):4, and Harding (1987, 181).

21. The presence of foremen has been occasionally reported in Western writing such as that of O. Laaksonen in two articles in 1984. However, my correspondence (1986) with Laaksonen revealed, after he had had an opportunity to check with his interpreter, that his "foremen" were all engaged in manual work and were thus really working chargehands. I am very obliged to Professor Laaksonen for having gone to the trouble to check on this matter.

22. For Shanghai, see Honig (1986, 45, 85, and 256, fn.4). However, Japanese and British factories employed about half of the workers of this industry in Shanghai (30–31), and the author does not make clear whether foremanship was introduced under their influence.

For Tianjin, see Hershatter (1986, 142, 150, 159, 164). The author implies that foremen were not only used under the Japanese, but earlier as well when the factories were under native Chinese ownership (28, 49, 142).

23. Brugger (1976, 187, 211–12). Remyga (1982, 15) also reports their existence, quoting a document issued in March 1953 by the Ministry of Heavy Industry.

24. The prime function of these gang bosses had been to recruit labor; they were often linked to criminal gangs. But it is claimed that at least sometimes they also exercised a supervisory function on the job. See Brugger (1976, 43–44, 92–93, 211).

Chapter 8

1. These figures refer to overfulfillment of the plan as it stood at the end of the period concerned. The figures with regard to overfulfillment of the initial plan are surprisingly similar.

2. The paucity of observations caused me to restrict the number of control variables in the housing regressions to between zero and two. It is quite possible that it is only this limitation on the use of control variables that led to any positive results whatsoever in the three relevant housing regressions.

3. This has been suggested to me in private correspondence (1989) by Professor Gary H. Jefferson, based upon an analysis of eleven responsibility contracts for medium and large state enterprises in force in 1989. Of these eleven, the managers in four enterprises received bonuses related in a specified fashion to the degree to which planned profits were exceeded. However, it is unclear what proportion of managerial bonuses in these four enterprises were covered by these provisions. Furthermore, such contracts may be renegotiated or even ignored. In the case of one of our sample enterprises, such a contract existed for 1985 and 1986 but was not respected; indeed, in commenting on the situation, the director stated that he would not have dared to accept the special incentive, even if it had been offered, because of the egalitarian spirit that existed among the labor force in his enterprise.

4. These estimates understate the proportion of expansion in urban employment as a whole, although not in industry.

5. See table 5.3 for further comparison of the 1975–78 period with that of 1979–82.

6. During 1978–81, none of the enterprises had a peak-year index of average earnings which was more that 11 per cent greater than the low-year index. During the second period, eight of seventeen enterprises showed more than an 11 per cent difference and four showed more than a 20 per cent difference. (The index of average earnings consists of the average earnings in the individual enterprise as a percentage of those of all state employees in Chinese industry during the same year.)

7. Our information in this regard ceases before the development of major gaps between the marginal and average prices paid to state-owned enterprises.

8. Thomas P. Lyons, in "Explaining Economic Fragmentation in

China: A Systems Approach," *J.C.E.* 10, no. 3 (September 1986):210, refers to more systematic results of his own, which show growing autarchy in the industrial sector of China during 1958–78.

9. As noted above, analysis on the basis of five to seven observations suggests that this statement may not apply to the reward of improved housing.

10. See Jinglian Wu and Bruce L. Reynolds, "Choosing a Strategy for China's Economic Reform," *American Economic Review* 78, no. 2 (May 1988): 461–66. According to these authors, this branch of the reform movement became dominant in Chinese economic policy making during the last quarter of 1986.

11. Ibid., 464–66.

12. If, under conditions of decreasing returns to scale, the enterprise did choose to invest, its expansion of capacity would be less than would have been the case under the assumption that the volume of allocations would be unaffected.

13. A leading Chinese economist, in private correspondence, expressed scepticism as to my evaluation of the multiple-pricing system: "Due to the peculiarities of the Chinese economic system, the performance of the multiple price system might not be as successful as the author evaluated." Presumably, he is referring to limitations on the degree to which Chinese state-owned enterprises are motivated by profits. The case studies of this book provide no basis for evaluating the multiple-pricing system. If the issue is lack of profit motivation, however, a system in which a single price was established on the marketplace could not resolve the problem.

14. R. Lipsey and K. Lancaster, "The General Theory of Second Best," *Review of Economic Studies* 24(1), no. 63 (1956–57):11–32.

15. Clearly, this has not been the case during the inflationary years after 1984, but I believe that these years should be treated as an aberration, representing the loss of control over bank credit by the national government.

16. This financial payment is defined to include the evaluation of land as a contribution to joint ventures between the original owner of the land and the "purchasing" enterprise.

17. In principle, there are supposed to be rewards for small groups and even for individuals in both countries. But the granting of such payments appears to be thwarted in practice, even when the system of piecework payment is used. For a discussion of this question with regard to the Soviet Union, see Granick (1987, chap. 8).

REFERENCES

Afanas'evskii, E. A. 1976. *Legkaia promyshlennost': ekonomicheskie problemy raz-meshcheniia.* Moscow: Mysl'.

Almanac of China's Ecomomy in 1981. 1982. Compiled by the Economic Research Centre, the State Council of the People's Republic of China, and the State Statistical Bureau, under the general editorship of Xue Muqiao. New York and Hong Kong: Modern Cultural Company, Ltd. and Eurasia Press.

Arrow, Kenneth J. 1951. *Social Choice and Individual Values.* New York: Wiley.

Bergson, Abram, and Herbert S. Levine. 1983. *The Soviet Economy: Toward the Year 2000.* London: George Allen & Unwin.

Berliner, Joseph. 1957. *Factory and Manager in the USSR.* Cambridge, Mass.: Harvard University Press.

———. 1976. *The Innovation Decision in Soviet Industry.* Cambridge, Mass.: The MIT Press.

Bernstein, Thomas P. 1977. *Up to the Mountains and Down to the Villages.* New Haven: Yale University Press.

Brandt, Loren. Forthcoming. *Commercialization and Agricultural Development: Central and Eastern China, 1870–1913.* Cambridge, England: Cambridge University Press.

Brugger, William. 1976. *Democracy & organization in the Chinese industrial enterprise (1948–1953).* Cambridge, England. Cambridge University Press.

Byrd, William. 1983. *China's Financial System: The Changing Role of Banks.* Boulder: Westview Press.

Cambridge Encyclopedia of Russia and the Soviet Union. 1982. Cambridge, England: Cambridge University Press.

China Economic System Reform Research Institute, Comprehensive Investigation Group, eds. 1986. *Gaige: Women Mianlin de Tiaozhan yu Xuanze (Reform: The Challenges and Choices We Face).* Beijing: Zhongguo Jingji Chubanshe.

China Official Annual Report 1981. 1981. Hong Kong: Kingsway International Publications, Ltd.

China Urban Statistics 1986. 1987. Compiled by the State Statistical Bureau, People's Republic of China. Longman Group, Ltd. and China Statistical Information & Consulting Service Center.

Chinese Young Economists, Inc. 1987. *The Third Economics Symposium.* Papers from a symposium held at the University of Michigan, Ann Arbor, June. Mimeo.

335

Dangdai Zhongguo de Jingji Tizhi Gaige (*Reform of the Economic System in Modern China*). 1984. Zhou Taihe, chief editor. Beijing: Zhongguo Shehui Kxue Chubanshe.

Davies, Robert W. 1958. *The Development of the Soviet Budgetary System*. Cambridge, England: Cambridge University Press.

Dernberger, Robert F., ed. 1980. *China's Development Experience in Comparative Perspective*. Cambridge, Mass.: Harvard University Press.

Donnithorne, Audrey. 1981. Centre-Provincial Economic Relations in China. *Contemporary China Papers*, no. 16. Canberra: Australian National University.

Eckstein, Alexander. 1977. *China's Economic Revolution*. Cambridge, England: Cambridge University Press.

Gallik, David, C. Jesina, and S. Rapawy. 1968. *The Soviet Financial System: Structure, Operation and Statistics*. U.S. Bureau of the Census. Washington, D.C.: Government Printing Office.

Gallik, Dimitri M., B. L. Kostinsky, and V. G. Treml. 1983. *Input-Output Structure of the Soviet Economy: 1972*. U.S. Bureau of the Census, Foreign Economic Report no. 18. Washington, D.C.: Government Printing Office.

Garvey, George. 1977. *Money, Financial Flows, and Credit in the Soviet Union*. Cambridge, Mass.: Ballinger.

Granick, David. 1954. *Management of the Industrial Firm*. New York: Columbia University Press.

———. 1967. *Soviet Metal-Fabricating and Economic Development*. Madison: University of Wisconsin Press.

———. 1972. *Managerial Comparisons of Four Developed Countries: France, Britain, United States and Russia*. Cambridge, Mass.: The MIT Press.

———. 1976. *Enterprise Guidance in Eastern Europe*. Princeton: Princeton University Press.

———. 1987. *Job Rights in the Soviet Union: Their Consequences*. Cambridge, England: Cambridge University Press.

Gray, Kenneth Royal. 1976. The Efficient Location and Specialization of Soviet Agricultural Procurement. Ph.D. diss., University of Wisconsin. Ann Arbor, Mich.: University Microfilms International.

Griffin, Keith, ed. 1984. *Institutional Reform and Economic Development in the Chinese Countryside*. London and Basingstoke: Macmillan & Co.

Guest, A. G., ed. 1961. *Oxford Essays in Jurisprudence*. Oxford: Clarendon Press.

Guroff, Gregory, and Fred V. Carstensen, eds. 1983. *Entrepreneurship in Imperial Russia and the Soviet Union*. Princeton: Princeton University Press.

Harding, Harry. 1981. *Organizing China: The Problem of Bureaucracy 1949–1976*. Stanford: Stanford University Press.

———. 1987. *China's Second Revolution*. Washington, D.C.: The Brookings Institution.

Henderson, Gail. 1982. Danwei, The Chinese Work Unit: A Participant Observation Study of a Hospital. Ph.D. diss., University of Michigan. Ann Arbor, Mich.: University Microfilms International.

Hershatter, Gail. 1986. *The Workers of Tianjin, 1900–1949.* Stanford: Stanford University Press.

Honig, Emily. 1986. *Sisters and Strangers: Women in the Shanghai Cotton Mills, 1919–1949.* Stanford: Stanford University Press.

Hough, Jerry F. 1969. *The Soviet Prefects.* Cambridge, Mass.: Harvard University Press.

———. 1977. *The Soviet Union and Social Science Theory.* Cambridge, Mass.: Harvard University Press.

Ivanov, N. V., E. Iu. Lokshin, and G. M. Demichev. 1969. *Ekonomika i planirovanie material'no-tekhnicheskogo snabzheniia promyshlennosti.* Moscow: Ekonomika.

Kornai, János. 1980. *Economics of Shortage.* Amsterdam: North-Holland.

Kraus, Richard Curt. 1981. *Class Conflict in Chinese Socialism.* New York: Columbia University Press.

Kurotchenko, V. S. 1975. *Material'no tekhnicheskoe snabzhenie v novykh usloviiakh khoziaistvovaniia.* Moscow: Ekonomika.

Laaksonen, Oiva. 1988. *Management in China during and after Mao.* Berlin: Walter de Gruyter.

Lampton, David M., ed. 1987. *Policy Implementation in Post-Mao China.* Berkeley: University of California Press.

Lardy, Nicholas R. 1978. *Economic Growth and Distribution in China.* Cambridge, England: Cambridge University Press.

———. 1983. *Agriculture in China's Modern Economic Development.* Cambridge, England: Cambridge University Press.

Lee, Peter N. S. 1987. *Industrial Management and Economic Reform in China, 1949–1984.* Hong Kong and Oxford: Oxford University Press.

Levcik, Friedrich. 1978. *International Economics—Comparisons and Interdependencies.* Vienna: Springer-Verlag.

Lewis, John Wilson, ed. 1971. *The City in Communist China.* Stanford: Stanford University Press.

Liberthal, Kenneth, and Michel Oksenberg. 1988. *Policy Making in China: Leaders, Structures, and Processes.* Princeton: Princeton University Press.

Liu, James T. C., and Wei-Ming Tu, eds. 1970. *Traditional China.* Englewood Cliffs, N.J.: Prentice-Hall.

Lyons, Thomas P. 1987. *Economic Integration and Planning in Maoist China.* New York: Columbia University Press.

Ma Hong. 1983. *New Strategy for China's Economy.* Beijing: New World Press.

McAuley, Mary. 1969. *Labour Disputes in Soviet Russia 1957–1965.* Oxford: Clarendon Press.

Maslow, A. H. 1954. *Motivation and Personality.* New York: Harper.

Maurice, Marc, François Sellier, and Jean-Jacques Silvestre. 1982. *Politique d'éducation et organisation industrielle en France et en Allemagne.* Paris: Presses Universitaires de France.

Naughton, Barry John. 1986. Saving and Investment in China: A Macroeconomic Analysis. Ph.D. diss., Yale University. Ann Arbor, Mich.: University Microfilms International.

Nee, Victor, and David Stark, eds. 1989. *Remaking the Economic Institutions of Socialism: China and Eastern Europe.* Stanford: Stanford University Press.

Parish, William L., ed. 1985. *Chinese Rural Development: The Great Transformation.* Armonk, N.Y.: M. E. Sharpe.

Perkins, Dwight H. 1966. *Market Control and Planning in Communist China.* Cambridge, Mass.: Harvard University Press.

Perkins, Dwight, and Shahid Yusuf. 1984. *Rural Development in China.* Baltimore: Johns Hopkins University Press, for the World Bank.

Perry, Elizabeth J., and Christine Wong, eds. 1985. *The Political Economy of Reform in Post-Mao China.* Cambridge, Mass. and London: Harvard University Press.

Prime, Penelope B. 1987. The Impact of Self-Sufficiency on Regional Industrial Growth and Productivity in post-1949 China: The Case of Jiansu Province. Ph.D. diss., University of Michigan. Ann Arbor, Mich.: University Microfilms International.

Remyga, V. N. 1982. *Sistema upravleniia promyshlennost'iu KNR (1949–1980).* Institute of the Far East of the Academy of Science of the USSR. Moscow: Nauka.

Reynolds, Bruce L., ed. 1987. *Reform in China: Challenges & Choices.* Prepared by the staff of the Chinese Economic System Reform Research Institute. Armonk, N.Y.: M. E. Sharpe.

Richman, Barry M. 1965. *Soviet Management.* Englewood Cliffs: Prentice-Hall.
———. 1969. *Industrial Society in Communist China.* New York: Random House.

Riskin, Carl. 1987. *China's Political Economy: The Quest for Development since 1949.* Oxford: Oxford University Press.

Roemer, John E. 1982. *A General Theory of Exploitation and Class.* Cambridge, Mass.: Harvard University Press.

Roll, Charles Robert, Jr. 1974. The Distribution of Rural Incomes in China: A Comparison of the 1930s and the 1950s. Ph.D. diss., Harvard University.

Rozman, Gilbert, ed. 1981. *Modernization of China.* New York: Free Press.

Schurmann, Franz. 1968. *Ideology and Organization in Communist China.* 2d ed. Cambridge, England: University Press.

Selden, Mark, and Victor Lippit, eds. 1982. *The Transition to Socialism in China.* Armonk, N.Y.: M. E. Sharpe.

Skinner, G. William, ed. 1977. *The City in Late Imperial China.* Stanford: Stanford University Press.

Smirnov, P. V. 1975. *Organizatsiia i planirovanie sbyta promyshlennoi produktsii v SSSR.* Moscow: Ekonomika.

Stacey, Judith. 1983. *Patriarchy and Socialist Revolution in China.* Berkeley: University of California Press.

Statistical Yearbook of China. Various years. Compiled by the State Statistical Bureau, People's Republic of China. Hong Kong: Economic Information & Agency.

Statistisches Jahrbuch 1974 der Deutschen Demokratischen Republik. 1974. Staatliche Zentralverwaltung für Statistik. Berlin: Staatsverlag der DDR.

Tidrick, Gene, and Chen Jiyuan, eds. 1987. *China's Industrial Reform.* New York and Oxford: Oxford University Press, for the World Bank.

Tsentral'noe Statisticheskoi Upravlenie SSSR (TSSU SSSR). 1982. *Narodnoe khoziaistvo SSSR 1922–1982.* Moscow: Finansy i Statistika.

Tsimerman, Iu. S. 1984. *Deiatel'nost' khoziaistvennykh organov ugol'noi promy-shlennosti*. Moscow: Nedra.

Ukrainskii, D. V., and G. Ia. Kiperman. 1984. *Planirovanie i otsenka raboty promyshlennogo predpriiatiia*. Moscow: Ekonomika.

U.S. Congress. Joint Economic Committee. 1982. *USSR: Measures of Economic Growth and Development, 1950–80*. 97 Cong. 2 sess. Washington, D.C.: Government Printing Office.

———. 1986. *China's Economy Looks Toward the Year 2000*. 99 Cong. 2 sess. Vol. 1. Washington, D.C.: Government Printing Office.

———. 1987. *Symposium on U.S.-Pacific Rim Relations*. Hearings. 99 Cong. 2 sess. Washington, D.C.: Government Printing Office.

Walder, Andrew George. 1981. Work and Authority in Chinese Industry. Ph.D. diss., University of Michigan. Ann Arbor, Mich.: University Microfilms International.

———. 1986. *Communist Neo-Traditionalism: Work and Authority in Chinese Industry*. Berkeley: University of California Press.

Walker, Kenneth R. 1984. *Food Grain Procurement and Consumption in China*. Cambridge, England: Cambridge University Press.

Wang, Yeh-chien. 1973. *Land Taxation in Imperial China, 1750–1911*. Cambridge, Mass.: Harvard University Press.

Watson, James L., ed. 1984. *Class and Social Stratification in Post-Revolution China*. Cambridge, England: Cambridge University Press.

Wei, Lin, and Arnold Chao, eds. 1982. *China's Economic Reforms*. Philadelphia: University of Pennsylvania Press.

Whyte, Martin King, and William L. Parish. 1984. *Urban Life in Contemporary China*. Chicago: University of Chicago Press.

Wong, Christine Pui. 1979. Rural Industrialization in China: Development of the "Five Small Industries." Ph.D. diss., University of California, Berkeley.

World Bank. 1985. *China: Long-Term Issues and Options*. Baltimore: Johns Hopkins University Press.

Xiaoyu, Cai, ed. 1980. *Beijing Diyi Jichuang Chang*. Beijing: China Social Sciences.

Zaleski, Eugène. 1980. *Stalinist Planning for Economic Growth, 1933–1952*. Chapel Hill: University of North Carolina Press.

Zhongguo Gongye Jingji Tongji Ziliao 1987 (*Statistical Material on China's Industrial Economy, 1987*). 1987. Compiled by the State Statistical Bureau, People's Republic of China. Beijing: State Statistical Bureau Publishing House.

Zhongguo Tongji Nianjian 1988 (*Statistical Yearbook for 1988*). 1988. Beijing: State Statistical Bureau Publishing House.

Zongguo Gangtie & Gongye Nianjian 1987 (*China Iron and Steel Yearbook 1987*). 1987. Beijing: Metallurgy Industry Publishing House.

INDEX

Agents: definition of, 32; in Soviet Union, 21–22; state-owned enterprises and governments as, 22

Agriculture: innovations in, 1, 4; land tax on, 50–54; profit-seeking behavior in, 118

Allocation: problems of efficiency of, 150; of products by central administration, 29–31, 72–74, 251–52; rejection of, 142–43; shift from central administration of, 98; support to enterprises through central administration, 138

Amortization funds, 42

Autarchy, regional, 252, 259, 263–64

Auto enterprise: division of allocation and distribution in, 103–4; insufficient central allocation for, 98; materials allocation and procurement for, 125–26

Bank loans, 270–71

Bankruptcy legislation, 5

Barro-Grossman disequilibrium analysis, 149

Barter, 252; decline with development of markets, 120; exchange ratios for, 115; as means to reduce monetary purchasing costs, 125–26; as procurement mechanism between regions, 115–16, 139

Bonus system: before and after reform, 258, 313; increase in supplement to earnings, 255;

interenterprise distribution of, 255–56; regression analysis of, 181–84, 191–95; in Soviet Union, German Democratic Republic, and Romania, 163–65; for top management in state enterprises, China, 165–67, 250

Budget, central state, 45

Career development: Eastern Europe and U.S., 314–15, 317; of top plant managers, 167–73. *See also* Incentives

Case studies of state enterprises, 2–6; sample properties, 7–14

Cash flow as property right, 32, 257

Cement factory: insufficient central allocation for, 98; materials allocation and procurement for, 128; multilevel supervision and financing of, 63–64; plan fulfillment for, 108; plan linked to property rights, 88

Center: constraints on actions of, 22; definition and role of, 21; maximizing process of, 22

Centralization of industrial enterprises, 41

Central ministries as agents, 32

CMEA. *See* Council of Mutual Economic Assistance

Collectives, 254

Communist Party: state enterprise Party committee management, 233–37; structure of enterprise